ReFocus: The Films of Rachid Bouchareb

ReFocus: The International Directors Series

Series Editors: Robert Singer, Stefanie Van de Peer, and Gary D. Rhodes

Board of Advisors:
Lizelle Bisschoff (University of Glasgow)
Stephanie Hemelryck Donald (University of Lincoln)
Anna Misiak (Falmouth University)
Des O'Rawe (Queen's University Belfast)

ReFocus is a series of contemporary methodological and theoretical approaches to the interdisciplinary analyses and interpretations of international film directors, from the celebrated to the ignored, in direct relationship to their respective culture—its myths, values, and historical precepts—and the broader parameters of international film history and theory. The series provides a forum for introducing a broad spectrum of directors, working in and establishing movements, trends, cycles, and genres including those historical, currently popular, or emergent, and in need of critical assessment or reassessment. It ignores no director who created a historical space—either in or outside of the studio system—beginning with the origins of cinema and up to the present. *ReFocus* brings these film directors to a new audience of scholars and general readers of Film Studies.

Titles in the series include:

ReFocus: The Films of Susanne Bier
Edited by Missy Molloy, Mimi Nielsen, and Meryl Shriver-Rice

ReFocus: The Films of Francis Veber
Keith Corson

ReFocus: The Films of Jia Zhangke
Maureen Turim and Ying Xiao

ReFocus: The Films of Xavier Dolan
Edited by Andrée Lafontaine

ReFocus: The Films of Pedro Costa: Producing and Consuming Contemporary Art Cinema
Nuno Barradas Jorge

ReFocus: The Films of Sohrab Shahid Saless: Exile, Displacement and the Stateless Moving Image
Edited by Azadeh Fatehrad

ReFocus: The Films of Pablo Larraín
Edited by Laura Hatry

ReFocus: The Films of Michel Gondry
Edited by Marcelline Block and Jennifer Kirby

ReFocus: The Films of Rachid Bouchareb
Edited by Michael Gott and Leslie Kealhofer-Kemp

ReFocus: The Films of Teuvo Tulio
Henry Bacon, Kimmo Laine, and Jaakko Seppälä

edinburghuniversitypress.com/series/refocint

ReFocus:
The Films of Rachid Bouchareb

Edited by Michael Gott and
Leslie Kealhofer-Kemp

Edinburgh University Press is one of the leading university presses in the UK. We publish academic books and journals in our selected subject areas across the humanities and social sciences, combining cutting-edge scholarship with high editorial and production values to produce academic works of lasting importance. For more information visit our website: edinburghuniversitypress.com

© editorial matter and organization Michael Gott and Leslie Kealhofer-Kemp, 2020
© the chapters their several authors, 2020

Edinburgh University Press Ltd
The Tun—Holyrood Road
12 (2f) Jackson's Entry
Edinburgh EH8 8PJ

Typeset in 11/13 Ehrhardt MT by
IDSUK (DataConnection) Ltd

A CIP record for this book is available from the British Library

ISBN 978 1 4744 6651 6 (hardback)
ISBN 978 1 4744 6653 0 (webready PDF)
ISBN 978 1 4744 6654 7 (epub)

The right of the contributors to be identified as authors of this work has been asserted in accordance with the Copyright, Designs and Patents Act 1988 and the Copyright and Related Rights Regulations 2003 (SI No. 2498).

Contents

Figures   vii
Note on Translations   viii
Notes on Contributors   ix
Acknowledgments   xiii

    Introduction: Rachid Bouchareb—A Global French Filmmaker   1
    Michael Gott and Leslie Kealhofer-Kemp

Part I   A Multidimensional Oeuvre

1. Rachid Bouchareb's Cinema as a "Vehicle for Encounters":
   Cultural Mixings and the Pre-production Process   25
   Leslie Kealhofer-Kemp
2. The Road from *Baton Rouge*: Mapping Rachid Bouchareb's
   Transnational Mobile Movies   40
   Michael Gott
3. Questions of Gender and Embodiment in the *Intimiste* Films
   of Rachid Bouchareb   64
   Kaya Davies Hayon
4. Genre and Universalism in the Films of Rachid Bouchareb   82
   David Pettersen
5. The American Dimensions of Rachid Bouchareb's Cinema   99
   Nabil Boudraa and Ahmed Bedjaoui
6. We Could Be Heroes: "Arabs" Becoming Brave in Rachid
   Bouchareb's Cinema   117
   Julien Gaertner
7. Globalization, Cinema, and Terrorism in Rachid Bouchareb's
   Films: *London River*, *Baton Rouge*, and *Little Senegal*   131
   Mireille Rosello

Part II Case Studies

8 Aesthetics of Confinement: Space, *Memento Mori*, and the
   Recording of History in Rachid Bouchareb's *Poussières
   de vie/Dust of Life* 151
   Michael O'Riley

9 The Door of No Return: A Cinema of (Up)rooting and
   Decentering in Rachid Bouchareb's *Little Senegal* 166
   Gemma King

10 Rachid Bouchareb's *Hors la loi/Outside the Law*:
   A Lesson in History, Reception, and Artistic License 181
   Jennifer Howell

11 Postcolonial Feminism, Gender, and Genre in
   Rachid Bouchareb's *Just like a Woman* 197
   Anne Donadey

12 Relations of Disjuncture in a "World-in-motion": Rachid
   Bouchareb's *La Voie de l'ennemi/Two Men in Town* 215
   Valérie K. Orlando

Appendix: Filmography of Rachid Bouchareb 235
Index 238

Figures

2.1	The French travelers enjoy a moment of solidarity and song on the road aboard a touring gospel choir's bus	47
2.2	The dreary roadside on the outskirts of Baton Rouge	48
2.3	Soldiers inspect Elisabeth's passport at the closed border between Turkey and Syria in *Road to Istanbul*	56
2.4	A large world map looms in the background at the moment when the trio from *Baton Rouge* finds a way to get to the United States	59
3.1	A close-up of Malika's tearful face as Merwan cuts her hair in *Cheb*	68
3.2	Nora at Karole's bedside in *My Family's Honor*	73
3.3	Marilyn and Mona belly dance on stage together for the first time in *Just Like a Woman*	76
5.1	Forest Whitaker and Dolores Heredia in *Two Men in Town*	104
5.2	The three brothers in *Outside the Law*	108
5.3	Golshifteh Farahani and Sienna Miller in *Just Like a Woman*	113
7.1	Ousmane and Elisabeth on a public bench in a park in London	138
7.2	Ousmane praying under olive trees in the south of France	141
8.1	Son records the history of the internment camps	161
9.1	Alloune at antebellum cemetery, South Carolina	174
9.2	Modern cemetery containing Robinson family grave, New York	174
9.3	Alloune at Hassan's grave by the sea, Gorée	175
12.1	*Two Men in Town*, Garnett facing the desert	225
12.2	*Two Men in Town*, Garnett and Agati in the town diner	227

Note on Translations

Unless otherwise indicated, all translations from French to English were done by the author(s) of the individual chapters. For reasons of space, we have opted to include only the English translations. In a few instances, however, when the original French citation is not easily accessible (for example, quotes from television or radio interviews that are not available online or those from the film *Cheb*, which is not available on DVD), we have included the French in the notes.

Notes on Contributors

Ahmed Bedjaoui graduated from the Paris Institute of Cinematographic Studies. He also holds a PhD in American Studies (on Scott Fitzgerald in Hollywood). He is currently Professor of Audiovisual Communication and Cinema Studies at Algiers University 3. He also serves as the Artistic Manager of the Algiers International Film Festival. His publications include the following books: *Images et visages* (2012), *Cinéma et guerre de libération, des batailles d'images* (2014), *Littérature et cinémas arabes* (2016), *La Guerre d'Algérie dans le cinéma mondial* (2016), and *Le Cinéma à son âge d'or* (2018), all published by Chihab Algiers. *The Role of Images During the Algerian War for Independence* is forthcoming with Palgrave Macmillan. He has also published two articles for *NHK Review*. He has been curator for many film weeks and exhibitions, among them *The Saga of the Algerian Cinematheque* and *The Algerian Films on Posters* (2018). In 2015, Ahmed Bedjaoui received the UNESCO Federico Fellini Medal for his contribution to the world of film culture. He was appointed as the feature films Jury President of the FESPACO (Ouagadougou, Burkina Faso, 2019).

Nabil Boudraa is Professor of French and Francophone Studies at Oregon State University. Nabil has received several grants and awards, including a Fulbright Scholar Award (2011) and three NEH Summer Institute Grants (2017, 2014, and 2007). His publications include the following books: *Algeria on Screen: The Films of Merzak Allouache* (forthcoming), *Francophone Cultures through Film* (2013, coauthored with Cécile Accilien), *Hommage à Kateb Yacine* (2006), and *North African Mosaic: A Cultural Re-appraisal of Ethnic and Religious Minorities* (2007, coedited with Joseph Krause). Nabil is also the coeditor of two special issues of the *Journal of North African Studies*, devoted to cinema, literature, and the arts in the Maghreb. Nabil has also published articles in refereed journals on various topics, including French cinema, landscape in Édouard Glissant's work, Albert Camus and Algeria, the language issue in the Maghreb, Berber oral tradition, the use of history in Maghrebian literature, and William Faulkner and the Francophone world.

Anne Donadey is Professor of French and Women's Studies at San Diego State University. A specialist of francophone literature and film, she is the author of *Recasting Postcolonialism: Women Writing between Worlds* (2001), coeditor of *Postcolonial Theory and Francophone Literary Studies* (2005), and editor of *Approaches to Teaching the Works of Assia Djebar* (2017). She has also published articles on Rachid Bouchareb's *Hors la loi* in *L'Esprit Créateur* (2014), *Studies in French Cinema* (2016), and *Contemporary French and Francophone Studies* (2018). Other articles have appeared in journals such as *PMLA: Publications of the Modern Language Association of America*, *Signs: Journal of Women in Culture and Society*, *Research in African Literatures*, *College Literature*, *World Literature Today*, *French Cultural Studies*, and the *International Journal of Francophone Studies*.

Julien Gaertner, a historian, teaches cinema history and screenwriting at the Université Côte d'Azur and the Paris Political Sciences Institute. After the adaptation of his PhD thesis, *Arabs in French Cinema*, as a TV documentary, he became the screenwriter and director of several documentary films.

Michael Gott is Associate Professor of French and program director for the Film & Media Studies BA at the University of Cincinnati. He is author of *French-Language Road Cinema: Borders, Diasporas, Migration and "New Europe"* (Edinburgh University Press, 2016) and coedited *Open Roads, Closed Borders: The Contemporary French-Language Road Movie* (2013), *East, West and Centre: Reframing European Cinema since 1989* (Edinburgh University Press, 2014), and *Cinéma-monde: Decentred Perspectives on Global Filmmaking in French* (Edinburgh University Press, 2018).

Kaya Davies Hayon is a post-doctoral researcher in the College of Arts at the University of Lincoln. Her research focuses on the intersections of gender, sexuality, and ethnicity in contemporary Maghrebi films. Her first monograph, *Sensuous Cinema: The Body in Contemporary Maghrebi Film*, was recently published as part of the *Thinking Cinema* series.

Jennifer Howell is an Associate Professor of French and Francophone Studies at Illinois State University, where she teaches postcolonial francophone literatures and cultures, with a focus on North African comics, photography, and crime fiction. Her scholarly work has appeared in journals such as

Contemporary French and Francophone Studies, the *Journal of North African Studies*, *Modern & Contemporary France*, *European Comic Art*, and the *French Review*. She is the author of *The Algerian War in French-Language Comics: Postcolonial Memory, History, and Subjectivity* (2015).

Leslie Kealhofer-Kemp is Associate Professor of French and Film at the University of Rhode Island and the author of *Muslim Women in French Cinema: Voices of Maghrebi Migrants in France* (2015). Her research focuses on representations of minority-ethnic characters in French cinema and on television, as well as on the films and careers of actors and actresses of North and West African descent in France. Her work has appeared in journals such as the *French Review*, *Modern & Contemporary France*, *Studies in French Cinema*, and *Contemporary French Civilization*.

Gemma King is Senior Lecturer in French Studies at the Australian National University. Her research focuses on contemporary French and francophone cinemas and museums, specializing in the representation of immigration, colonialism, violence, and multilingualism. Her writing has been published in *French Cultural Studies*, *Contemporary French Civilization*, *L'Esprit Créateur*, the *Australian Journal of French Studies*, *Francosphères*, *Linguistica Antverpiensia*, and numerous edited volumes. Her first book, *Decentring France: Multilingualism and Power in Contemporary French Cinema* was published in 2017, and she is currently working on the contracted monograph *Jacques Audiard* for the *French Film Directors* series.

Michael O'Riley is Professor of French and Italian at the Colorado College. He has published three books and numerous articles on postcolonial theory, French and francophone cinema and culture, and terrorism. His most recent book, *Cinema in an Age of Terror: North Africa, Victimization, and Colonial History* (2010), explores the relationship between cinema, terrorism, and colonial history. He is currently working on two books, one treating new immigration in France and another on the relationship between immigration and the mafia in Italy.

Valérie K. Orlando is Professor of French & Francophone Literatures at the University of Maryland, College Park, Fulbright-Tocqueville Distinguished Chair Award recipient (Université de Lyon-Lumière II, Lyon, France, fall 2019), and Research Fellow at Le Collegium de Lyon (L'Institut d'études avancées de l'université de Lyon, spring 2020). She is the author of six books, the most recent of which include *The Algerian New Novel: The Poetics of a Modern Nation, 1950–1979* (2017), *New African Cinema* (2017), and *Screening Morocco: Contemporary Film in a Changing Society* (2011). She has published with Pamela Pears *Paris and the Marginalized Author: Treachery, Alienation, Queerness, and Exile* (2018) and with Sandra M. Cypess *Reimaging the Caribbean: Conversations among the Creole, English, French, and Spanish Caribbean* (2014). She is also series editor for *After the Empire: The Francophone World and Postcolonial France*.

David Pettersen is Associate Professor of French and Film and Media Studies at the University of Pittsburgh. His first book, *Americanism, Media and the Politics of Culture in 1930s France*, was published in 2016. He coedited a special journal issue of *Écrans*, entitled *Politique des auteurs/Auteur theory: Lectures contemporaines* (published in fall 2017). He is currently finishing a second book, *French B-Movies: Suburban Spaces, Universalism and the Challenge of Hollywood*, about the use of Hollywood genre traditions in contemporary French suburban and postcolonial cinema. His articles have appeared in *Cinema Journal, Modern & Contemporary France, Romance Studies*, and *Studies in French Cinema*. In 2017, he was inducted into the French Order of Academic Palms as a Knight.

Mireille Rosello teaches at the University of Amsterdam in the Department of Literary and Cultural Analysis and the Amsterdam School for Cultural Analysis. She focuses on globalized mobility and queer thinking. Her latest works are a special issue of the journal *Culture, Theory and Critique* (on "disorientation," coedited with Niall Martin, 2016), an anthology on queer Europe, *What's Queer about Europe? Productive Encounters and Re-Enchanting Paradigms* (coedited with Sudeep Dasgupta, 2014), and a collection of articles on multilingualism in Europe (*Multilingual Europe, Multilingual Europeans*, coedited with László Marácz, 2012). She is currently working on rudimentariness.

Acknowledgements

We would like to begin by thanking all of the authors who contributed to this volume. Thank you to the *ReFocus* series editors, Gary D. Rhodes, Robert Singer, and Stefanie Van de Peer, for their enthusiastic support from the moment we proposed the idea and the guidance that they have offered along the way. Likewise, Gillian Leslie and Richard Strachan at Edinburgh University Press have been immensely supportive and helpful. Many of the ideas that inspired and that are found in the volume are the results of ongoing intellectual conversations. Alec Hargreaves provided invaluable advice, guidance, and encouragement from the beginning of the project. Bill Marshall and the organizers of the Cinéma-monde conference in May 2018, at the University of Stirling in Scotland, helped facilitate important dialogue on Rachid Bouchareb's work and on this project in particular. Mireille Rosello granted us permission to reprint her chapter on Bouchareb's work from the 2018 book *Cinéma-monde: Decentred Perspectives on Global Filmmaking in French* (also published by Edinburgh University Press). That essay was clearly influential to several contributors, and we thought that it would be fruitful to bring it back into dialogue with the latest work on Bouchareb by including it under the same cover. Lastly, Gemma King, who also contributed a chapter to this volume, kindly allowed us to include the table that she created on Bouchareb's filmography in the Appendix. We would also like to thank the Center for the Humanities at the University of Rhode Island, which awarded the project a subvention grant that enabled us to have the volume professionally indexed.

Michael Gott would like to thank the Taft Research Center and the Center for Film and Media Studies at the University of Cincinnati for research funding. Leslie Kealhofer-Kemp would like to thank Thibaut Schilt for encouraging her to pursue this project and for offering valuable feedback. She is also grateful to the College of Arts and Sciences, the Office of the Provost, the Department of Modern and Classical Languages and Literatures, and the Harrington School of Communication and Media at the University of Rhode Island for research and travel support. Last but not least, she would like to thank her family for their unwavering support and encouragement.

Introduction: Rachid Bouchareb— A Global French Filmmaker

Michael Gott and Leslie Kealhofer-Kemp

Born in Paris in 1953 to Algerian parents, Rachid Bouchareb became one of France's first directors of North African descent. With a career that now spans over forty years, he is an internationally recognized filmmaker and producer. His works are remarkably varied in their themes, formal elements, languages, budgets, production contexts, and narrative settings, ranging from Senegal, England, Vietnam, and Algeria, to France, Belgium, Turkey, and the United States. Yet they are also connected by key concerns, such as the meetings and mixings of cultures, engagement with contemporary political issues and debates, immigration, movement and mobility, borders, and identity. His life and career in the cinema and television industries have also paralleled— and been shaped by—periods of significant change in France, as well as internationally. This includes the aftermath of the French colonial empire, which ended officially in 1962 following the bloody Algerian War of Independence and led to the emigration to mainland France of over a million *pieds-noirs* (settlers of European descent); the rise of the far-right Front National political party and its anti-immigrant agenda, beginning in the early 1980s; the coming of age and increased visibility and cultural output of the children of Maghrebi migrants (sometimes referred to as "*beurs*" or "second-generation Maghrebis");[1] ongoing debates as well as new legislation in France relating to national identity, integration, and immigration; and the rise of Islamophobia and Islamic terrorist attacks, including 9/11 in the US, the 7/7 London bombings, and the 15 November 2015 attacks in Paris.

Since his feature-length debut *Bâton Rouge/Baton Rouge* (1985), Bouchareb's films have engaged with and reflected on a variety of crucial social and historical issues, from the role of colonial conscripts in the French army during the liberation of Europe in World War II, to terrorism in contemporary Europe and the Middle East. As will be discussed further in this introduction, Bouchareb's work has drawn a cinematic map of the world that is best described as an archetype of what some scholars have now labeled as cinéma-monde, and in many ways, his profile complicates the very idea of what defines French cinema.[2] France and the French film industry are often present and perhaps even central in historical, cultural, or production senses even while the centrality of France is repeatedly questioned or the French language used only minimally. Bouchareb's cinema has examined the relationship between France and its former colonies in the Maghreb and, most recently, it has brought him back to North America (a setting of five of his eleven feature films) to make several features that have still been (co)produced and funded by France. Bouchareb's fascination for the landscapes and people of the American South and West places him in a lineage with other global filmmakers whose works have traced routes through Hollywood's terrain, including Michelangelo Antonioni, Wim Wenders, Aki Kaurismäki, Walter Salles and, most recently, Andrea Arnold. His geographically and linguistically diverse oeuvre has in particular explored a variety of locales and routes linked to the francophone world, from Vietnam to Senegal and Belgium to Baton Rouge, Louisiana, while emphasizing the cultural mixings that occur in these spaces. Throughout his career, the director has been influenced by American culture and cinema, from Spike Lee to Hollywood blockbusters, and this has impacted his cinema in key ways.

Although Bouchareb's films have garnered both mainstream and critical success, including three Oscar nominations and many other national and international awards, there currently exists no book-length study—in French or English—on the director's body of work. *ReFocus: The Films of Rachid Bouchareb* seeks to fill this gap, examining Bouchareb's work from an interdisciplinary perspective, exploring key influences on his output, and considering new theoretical approaches to his filmmaking. In what follows, we will provide an introduction to Rachid Bouchareb's films and career trajectory, taking as points of departure two understudied elements that serve as a useful prism through which to consider his career: his 1983 short film *Peut-être la mer/Perhaps the Sea*, and his work as a film producer. We will then theorize Bouchareb's cinema through a broader lens in relation to discursive and critical categories such as cinéma-monde, francophone cinema, French national cinema, "*beur*" and *banlieue* cinema, and transnational cinemas. Ultimately, we suggest that Bouchareb does not quite fit any of these categories, and we propose that he is best defined as a "Global French Filmmaker." Finally, we will conclude with an overview of the chapters that make up the volume, many of which situate Bouchareb and his work in relation to the aforementioned categories.

LAYING THE FOUNDATIONS: RACHID BOUCHAREB'S EARLY CAREER

After completing a two-year degree in mechanics, Bouchareb decided to embark on a different path and attend film school. From there, he worked in the French television industry from the late 1970s into the early 1980s, during which time he also began to make short films. His fourth short, *Perhaps the Sea*, was selected for competition at the 1983 Cannes Film Festival in the category "French Cinema Perspectives."[3] This was the first of what would become many festival selections and major awards and nominations for his films, both in France and abroad. These include three Oscar nominations in the category of Best Foreign Language Film (*Poussières de vie/Dust of Life*, 1995, *Indigènes/Days of Glory*, 2006, and *Hors la loi/Outside the Law*, 2010), a César award for Best Screenplay for *Days of Glory*, and films selected for competition at Cannes and the Berlin International Film Festival, among many others. He has also been nominated and awarded several prizes for his work as a producer, as will be discussed in more detail below.

The fifteen-minute-long *Perhaps the Sea* is an apt starting point to discuss Bouchareb's filmmaking because it foreshadows many of the themes and subjects that have become cornerstones of his work. This includes immigration, identity, cultural mixings, borders, and the place of Maghrebi migrants and their children in France. It also brings to the fore the social, historical, and political contexts in France that shaped the first part of Bouchareb's career (and beyond), notably the legacy of France's colonial empire and the Algerian War of Independence, and the impact of these on the lives of the descendants of Maghrebi migrants in post-colonial France. The protagonists of *Perhaps the Sea* are two boys of Algerian descent—one of whom is named Rachid—who decide to leave their working-class Parisian suburb of Bobigny (also Bouchareb's hometown) and head to Algeria. Rachid's friend persuades him to accompany him there with the promise of sunny weather and warm water for swimming at the beach. Although Rachid has never been to Algeria, or to the sea for that matter, his friend has spent time there with his family, and he is eager to go back. The first sequence of the film is set in a port authority office in Le Havre, where the two boys are held and being questioned by officers. From there, the narrative cuts back and forth between scenes in this enclosed space and others that will eventually piece together how the boys ended up in this port city in northern France. The boys scrape together meager travel funds by washing car windshields at stoplights as they talk about what they will do upon their arrival in Algeria. Although they lack the exact address of an uncle with whom they plan to stay, this does not deter them. After acquiring some supplies—namely sunglasses, towels, and T-shirts for the beach—they set off, unbeknownst to their families. Unable to afford plane tickets to Algeria or even train tickets to Marseille, the typical point of departure for travelers taking ferries across the Mediterranean, they decide to hop on a train for Le Havre, the closest large port. They plan to stow away on a ship to Algeria and manage to gain entry to a large vessel flying under an Algerian flag. Their plans are foiled, however, when the ship enters a dry dock instead of heading out to sea. In the final sequence, the boys' optimism and excitement turns to disappointment and disbelief. After the ship stops moving, they run up on deck only to realize that it is no longer in the water and that they will therefore remain on dry land, in France.

Underpinning the film's light-hearted narrative is the exploration of questions of cultural mixings and complex identities with reference to children of Algerian migrants in France. This is framed by reminders of the colonial and post-colonial connections that exist between France and the Maghreb (and Algeria in particular). The film's thirty-second title sequence introduces these themes in a subtle manner. It begins with a postcard of Paris that depicts iconic images of the city: the Eiffel Tower, Notre-Dame Cathedral, Sacré-Coeur Basilica, and the Arc de Triomphe. Accompanying this visual is Arabic instrumental music, which continues to play as the frame cuts to the reverse of the postcard, where there are handwritten words. These do not form a message or recipient's address, as one might expect, but rather, they provide information relating to the film. The French production company (L'Oeil en boîte) and film title appear in the message box on the left, and on the address lines on the right are the words "A film by Rachid Bouchareb." These are surrounded by images, words, and symbols of France, resulting in a layout that underscores that both film and filmmaker are French and part of the French film industry. In the upper left corner is a small map of France; on the bottom left is the word "Paris," along with the names of the sites found on the front of the card; in the middle, running vertically, is the name and address (in Paris) of the company that made the postcard, along with the words "Made in France." Finally, in the top right corner are two French stamps depicting the image of Marianne, a symbol of the French Republic.

At the same time, the pairing of Arabic music with these quintessentially "French" markers contributes additional layers of meaning to the words and symbols relating to France and perceptions of "Frenchness" that are presented in a seemingly uncomplicated way on the postcard. This combination posits at the very beginning of the film the idea of French-Maghrebi identity, or what Bouchareb would later call a kind of double culture ("*bi-culture*"), as the child of Algerian migrants born and raised in France.[4] The idea of a double culture, as well as the connections between France and Algeria, both past and present, are evoked by the two Marianne stamps. One is green, the other is red—respectively the colors of Algerian and French passport covers—and they are connected by a postal marking that resembles a crescent moon (as the ink of the marking did not fully transfer to the postcard to complete a full circle). The overall image is therefore reminiscent of the Algerian flag, but one in which French and Algerian national symbols intertwine to evoke the dual identity of Bouchareb (who has both French and Algerian nationality) as well as that of the protagonists of *Perhaps the Sea*. In addition, the flag of Algeria, which was also used during the struggle for independence, serves as a reminder that the end of colonial rule in Algeria—which as an overseas *département* was considered part of France until 1962—occurred just over twenty years prior to the film's release.[5]

The Arabic music continues on the soundtrack as the film cuts to the front of a second postcard, this time of Oran, Algeria. It contains four images that highlight the beauty of the city: beaches, sunset, coastline, and mountains. On the back, a handwritten text presents the names of the actors who appear in the film. The beautiful images of the postcard align with how the film's young protagonists envisage Algeria and foreshadow what will motivate their attempted voyage. This perception of Algeria is complicated, however, by the postcard images of Paris and Algeria that follow and form the rest of the title sequence. They situate the film within a larger context: the history of French expansionism and colonialism in Africa dating back to the nineteenth century. The first is an image of the Grande Poste (main post office) in Algiers, a white, neo-Moorish style building—and a striking example of Orientalism in architecture—built by the French colonial government in 1911. Following this is an image of the obelisk situated at the Place de la Concorde in Paris. Originally from the Temple of Luxor in Egypt, it arrived in 1836 (as a gift) after several years of planning, via the port of Le Havre—where the narrative of *Perhaps the Sea* begins. The historical timeframe evoked by this image also connects to the early years of French colonization of Algeria, which began in 1830. The final images of the title sequence present an exotic vision of Algeria, complete with camels, sand, and palm trees.

The subtleties and deeper meanings at work here come into clearer focus as the film progresses. *Perhaps the Sea* suggests that the questions of identity and belonging with regard to the children of Maghrebi migrants are not clear-cut. Rather, they are part of a large and complex historical framework that links colonial and post-colonial France and the Maghreb and has shaped perceptions of the Maghrebi population in France by the majority-ethnic population—as well as self-perceptions.[6] These issues are highlighted with particular clarity in the first scene of the film when the principal investigator at the port authority asks his colleague if they have any information on the two boys in custody. His colleague responds that they have nothing, other than a legal text relating to the question of nationality, which informs them (and reminds viewers) that children born in French territories after 1 January 1963 hold French nationality.[7] Yet when the investigator asks the children:

"So you are French?" Rachid answers: "No, we're Algerian!" The irony, of course, is that Rachid has never been to Algeria, has been raised in France, and speaks French with ease—unlike his father, who came to France as a migrant worker and, as Rachid explains to his friend, does not understand French well.

With the benefit of hindsight, we can identify several aspects of *Perhaps the Sea* that would become recurrent through Bouchareb's film corpus (to varying degrees) and are touched upon throughout this volume. In addition to the themes of immigration, identity, and cultural mixings, there is the interest in contemporary issues, debates, or events that underpin his work and are often political in nature. This includes unemployment in France in the early 1980s (*Baton Rouge*), the rise of Islamic fundamentalism in Algeria (*Cheb*, 1991) and in Europe (*La Route d'Istanbul/Road to Istanbul*, 2016), terrorism (*London River*, 2009), and the international drug trade (*Le Flic de Belleville/Belleville Cop*, 2018). Other films have adopted an approach that connects contemporary concerns (sometimes indirectly) to a larger framework of past injustices and/or human rights abuses. This includes slavery (*Little Senegal*, 2001), re-education camps in the aftermath of the Vietnam War (*Dust of Life*), the forgotten role of colonial troops in World War II, discrimination in the ranks, unequal pensions (*Days of Glory* and the short film *L'Ami y'a bon/The Colonial Friend*, 2004), and colonialism and the Algerian War of Independence (*Outside the Law*). We can also note Bouchareb's interest in telling stories from the perspective of children or youth (*Baton Rouge, Cheb, Dust of Life, L'Honneur de ma famille/My Family's Honor*, 1998), especially during the first half of his career. Protagonists who are in movement, on a voyage, and/or crossing or seeking to cross various kinds of borders have also formed a key current throughout his filmography, connecting *Baton Rouge, Cheb, Little Senegal, Days of Glory, London River, Just Like a Woman* (2012), and *Belleville Cop*. Finally, *Perhaps the Sea* even provides a nod to Bouchareb's longstanding interest in the United States, American culture, and Hollywood cinema. It comes in the form of an R2D2 toy from the Star Wars franchise that the two boys have brought with them for their trip. It provides a moment of comic relief when the customs officer confiscates the toy and then sets off the sounds as he plays with it in his office.

Perhaps the Sea is also a useful point of departure to consider how Bouchareb's filmmaking has diverged, evolved, and gone in new directions since the start of his career. The director's corpus now includes small- and big-budget films, made-for-television films, and most recently, a commercially oriented film, *Belleville Cop*. In addition, the meetings and mixings of cultures evoked in *Perhaps the Sea* have extended well beyond the France/Maghreb dynamic. As Alec Hargreaves has observed:

Far from being preoccupied with the fates of narrowly defined Maghrebi-French characters or situations, Bouchareb's vision is much more global in scope, blending the specificities of a wide range of social and ethnic milieus with an underlying concern for universal principles of individual freedom and equality.[8]

Writing about Bouchareb's 2010 film *Outside the Law*, Will Higbee notes how far the director—and the French film industry itself—have come since the beginning of his career:

Made for a budget of €20m, released on more than 400 prints and starring Jamel Debbouze—a French-born actor of Moroccan immigrant parents and one of French cinema's biggest stars—*Hors-la-loi* enjoyed the kind of distribution and marketing conditions reserved for only the most high-profile French mainstream productions.[9]

As Hargreaves convincingly argues, the existence of established and bankable Maghrebi-French stars, including Debbouze, had also been crucial to the creation, financing, and success of Bouchareb's blockbuster *Days of Glory* and was not something that existed in the early 1980s.[10]

Indeed, the French film industry was a decidedly different place at the start of Bouchareb's career. There were few filmmakers of North African origin in France, and the French cinematic landscape provided very limited opportunities for minority-ethnic directors and actors. According to Higbee, in the 1970s there were "a handful of militant, low-budget films by immigrant directors located on the margins of the French film industry," and in the 1980s he cites "the small but influential number of films made by French directors of North African immigrant origin," including Bouchareb.[11] In a 1991 televised interview, the director reflected on some of the specific challenges that he faced during the first part of his career in the French film industry, in particular obtaining financial backing for the kinds of films that he wanted to make. He explained that he wanted to tell stories relating to his own experiences and cultural make-up ("*coloration culturelle*"), immigration, and his parents' experiences in particular, yet he encountered roadblocks. In his words:

In the economic landscape of French cinema, it isn't easy—or at least back then it wasn't, even if things have evolved a little—to make films whose main characters are named Ali or Mohamed. While it's true that it's changing, it's been difficult. It's changing because there are more and more of us making films. There are more and more. There are more of us in music, painting, and fashion now. So for the past few years, that has been taken into account somewhat, but around 1977, when I started making my short films, there was no openness at all. So I did these films myself because I wanted to do them. From an economic standpoint, it was difficult.[12]

Bouchareb was able to secure financial support for his first feature film, *Baton Rouge*, a collaboration between French producers Lyric International and TF1 Films Production. Funding came notably in the form of an *avance sur recettes* (an advance against earnings designed to support first films) from the National Cinema Center (Centre national du cinéma et de l'image animée or CNC).[13] In order to receive funding from this source, "a proposal must either show evidence of 'quality' (a sound script, a star cast) or potential as a self-expressive *auteur* film."[14] Although *Baton Rouge* received some media attention and was reviewed in major French print media outlets upon its release (*Le Monde*, *Libération*, *L'Express*, *Le Point*, and *L'Humanité*, among others, as well as the industry publication *Cahiers du Cinéma*), the film was not successful at the box office, selling only 72,222 tickets.[15] Thus in order to make his second feature film, *Cheb* (1991), Bouchareb decided that it was necessary to create a production company. He founded 3B Productions, with Jean Bréhat—with whom he continues to collaborate—and Jean Bigot, his coscreenwriter for *Perhaps the Sea*. According to Bouchareb:

> After my first film I realized pretty rapidly that it was going to be difficult to get my projects off the ground through more traditional routes and that it was also unlikely that I, a young second generation North African, was going to get a directing gig at one of the French broadcasters any time soon. It seemed to make the most sense to go into production. It was almost an obligation.[16]

Bréhat summed up their decision to go into production in the following terms: "You have to give yourself the means to do what you want."[17] They began working out of the studio apartment of Bouchareb's sister due to limited financial means, and 3B Productions produced their first film, *Cheb*, in partnership with Algeria's state-funded National Audiovisual Production Company.[18] Since then, Bouchareb and Bréhat have (co)produced all of Bouchareb's films—and numerous others—either via 3B or the second company that they founded, Tessalit Productions.[19]

Although Bouchareb's career as a producer stemmed from necessity and a desire for artistic liberty, it has by no means been limited to producing his own films. In total, 3B or Tessalit Productions have (co)produced over fifty films. A particularly noteworthy part of Bouchareb's efforts has been to support the work of other Maghrebi-French filmmakers. These films also feature Maghrebi-French actors in the lead roles and focus on the lives of Maghrebi and Maghrebi-French protagonists, thus contributing to increasing the representation of people of North African origin in France on the big screen. Films in this category include Bourlem Guerdjou's *Vivre au paradis/Living in Paradise* (1998), starring Roschdy Zem (who has also acted in six of Bouchareb's feature films, dating back to *My Family's Honor* in 1998); Zem's *Omar m'a tuer/Omar Killed Me* (2011), starring Sami Bouajila, another frequent collaborator of Bouchareb; and Karim Dridi's *Chouf* (2016).

It is also worth citing Bouchareb's collaborations with historian Pascal Blanchard, which have resulted in two series of short films made for broadcast on French television (produced and directed by Bouchareb): *Frères d'armes/Brothers in Arms* (fifty 2-minute films, broadcast in 2014–15) and *Champions de France/France's Champions* (forty-five 2-minute films, broadcast in 2015–16). These projects aim to make known and celebrate the contributions of people of diverse backgrounds and origins to France and French history, in both colonial and post-colonial contexts. As such, they clearly connect to Bouchareb's *Days of Glory*, as the tag lines for each project underscore: "They have fought for France for over a century" and "They have won for France for more than a century." The short films also serve to remind viewers of the diversity of contemporary France and of the French population. Each forgotten hero or sporting champion featured in a short is presented by a well-known artist or public figure of a diverse background. These include Roschdy Zem, actor and comedian Jamel Debbouze, actress Rachida Brakni, journalist Audrey Pulvard, and author Dany Laferrière, among many others. Writing about this choice with regard to *Brothers in Arms*, Bouchareb and Blanchard stated:

> Short films are the best medium by which to reach a large public and raise awareness about veterans who came from around the world to defend the values of the Republic and the ideals of Liberty. Calling upon today's well-known public figures to talk about yesterday's heroes creates a strong sense of citizenship. It serves to make them into great French heroes and to make the history of France.[20]

The timeframe within which each series was broadcast on French television was also strategic, serving to connect past and present: *Brothers in Arms* was broadcast during centennial commemorations of World War I and the seventieth anniversary of the liberation of France during World War II. *France's Champions* was broadcast in the months leading up to two major sporting events held in the summer of 2016: the men's European football championship, hosted by France, and the Olympics in Rio de Janeiro.

Bouchareb has also made his mark in the realm of production in other ways. 3B and Tessalit have gained national and international notoriety thanks to the nomination of their films at prestigious festivals in France and abroad. In a

2006 interview, Jean Bréhat cited festival recognition as having been crucial to 3B's ability to make films outside of mainstream commercial channels.[21] The year 2006 was particularly significant for Bréhat and Bouchareb in terms of their production careers: both 3B and Tessalit had films nominated for the Palme d'Or at Cannes—and thus they were in the rare position of having films competing against each other. The films were Bruno Dumont's *Flandres/Flanders* and Bouchareb's big-budget war film *Days of Glory*. 3B or Tessalit have produced all of Dumont's films, and the director has had considerable success at Cannes: *La Vie de Jésus/The Life of Jesus* won the Caméra d'Or in 1996, *L'Humanité/Humanity* and *Flanders* each won the Grand Prix (in 1999 and 2006, respectively), and *Jeanne/Joan of Arc* earned the Jury's Special Mention in the category "Un Certain Regard" in 2019. Dumont's other films selected for competition at Cannes include *Ma Loute/Slack Bay* (2016) and *Hors Satan/Outside Satan* (2011). Bouchareb and Bréhat have also produced films by Lebanese director Ziad Doueiri, including *L'Insulte/The Insult*, which earned a 2018 Oscar nomination for Best Foreign Language Film.

An interview in which Bouchareb discusses the production side of filmmaking vis-à-vis his film *Dust of Life* underscores the transnational connections that epitomize nearly all of the films that he has directed, and many of those that he has had a hand in producing. In many ways, this sums up the crossings and mixings that have shaped his career, not to mention his persistence. In the words of the director:

> Convincing Chinese and Algerians, along with Europeans, to produce a film shot in Malaysia about Amerasians born out of the Vietnam War was not exactly a walk in the park. The undertaking was more than a little risky (faraway countries, shooting in the jungle, climate) but we had a good story and experience in this kind of film shoot; these two arguments, among others, convinced the investors.[22]

Although Bouchareb's filmmaking has evolved considerably since *Dust of Life*, he has retained an approach that involves the constant mixing of cultures and languages within the narratives and in the production. His most recent feature, *Belleville Cop*, is set in a transcultural milieu in Paris and in Miami and stars Omar Sy alongside Hollywood actor Luis Guzmán (whom Bouchareb had cast in his 2014 film *La Voie de l'ennemi/Two Men in Town*). The narrative features significant amounts of dialogue in French, English, Spanish, and Mandarin.[23] According to Sy, the set was equally polyglot. As he describes it: "It felt like we were in the Tower of Babel: on the set, we were speaking English, French, Spanish, Chinese . . ."[24]

Another notable—and equally polyglot—aspect of Bouchareb's filmmaking process is his casting. Several actors have collaborated with Bouchareb on multiple films. In addition to Luis Guzmán, mentioned above, Roschdy Zem, Sami Bouajila, Chafia Boudraa, Brenda Blethyn, and Sotigui Kouyaté have all acted in more than one project (and sometimes several, as in the case of Zem) helmed by Bouchareb. Their appearances represent a wide variety of roles, contexts, and geographical settings. One potential point of comparison to this practice is the work of Robert Guédiguian, another French director known for working with the same actors repeatedly. Guédiguian leans on the same circles of actors (Gérard Meylan, Arianne Ascaride, and Jean-Pierre Daroussin, now frequently joined by Anaïs Demoustier, Robinson Stévenin, and Grégoire Leprince-Ringuet) to forge a sense of tightly knit solidarity and friendship based on proximity and community links.[25] The associative networks that keen viewers of Bouchareb's films might perceive through the director's repeated casting choices are more wide-ranging. To take perhaps the best example, Roschdy Zem (a French actor and director of Moroccan descent) is sometimes cast as Algerian (*Days of Glory*, *Outside the Law*) or Maghrebi-French (*My Family's Honor*), plays an immigrant in the US with unspecified Arab/Muslim origins in *Little Senegal* and *Just Like a Woman*, respectively, and in *London River*, he is part of a network of French-speaking characters that connects to the mosque (Bouajila's character is the French- and Arabic-speaking imam of unspecified national origins). Meanwhile, Bouajila, a French actor of Tunisian descent, plays the Algerian brother in arms of Zem's character in *Days of Glory* and his actual brother in *Outside the Law*, in addition to the role in *London River*.

Bouchareb's desire to work with specific actors or actresses has also shaped his film projects. For example, when asked why he chose to set the narrative of *London River* in London as opposed to Madrid or Bali (both of which had also been affected by terrorist attacks), Bouchareb said: "It was purely because of Brenda [Blethyn]. For years, I wanted to do a film with Brenda but I didn't have the framework for it. I also wanted to make a film again with Sotigui Kouyaté" (who had the lead role in the 2001 film *Little Senegal*).[26] Bouchareb told Blethyn that he wanted to work with her again after *London River* and envisaged a very different role for her. According to the director:

> At the end of shooting *London River*, I told Brenda that we'd make another film together, and I imagined her wearing a gun on her belt. She was very surprised! When she read the script of *Two Men in Town*, she wasn't sure if she would be able to play this probation officer. But look at the result on screen! She's perfect.[27]

The fact that Blethyn did not speak French before she was cast in *London River* (where her character communicates in French) did not deter Bouchareb from giving her the role. Similarly, Samy Naceri, who plays a Moroccan colonial soldier serving under the French flag in *Days of Glory*, did not speak Arabic but learned some in order to play the role. Bouchareb's films can also incorporate the native and/or second languages of the various actors (sometimes with variations in accents). To cite a few examples: Blethyn speaks English with a British accent in *London River* and an American accent in *Two Men in Town*; Guzmán, born in Puerto Rico, speaks both English and Spanish in *Belleville Cop* and *Two Men in Town*; Forest Whitaker uses English, Spanish, and Arabic in *Two Men in Town* (and he studied Arabic extensively for this role, as Valérie Orlando discusses in Chapter 12); Bouajila, Zem, and Debbouze communicate in French and Arabic in their various roles; and Omar Sy uses French, English, and (more rudimentary) Mandarin, as well as a little Spanish, for his role in *Belleville Cop*.

A GLOBAL FRENCH FILMMAKER

Bouchareb's filmmaking practice and films are always on a border: between national and transnational, between languages, between geographic contexts. It is therefore difficult to settle on one label or theoretical framework to apply universally to his work. Nonetheless, some terms and concepts provide useful—and often overlapping—lenses through which we can consider his diverse oeuvre and the multitude of links among the films, their themes, their sociopolitical contexts, and the production processes behind them.

To begin, Bouchareb should be identified as a French filmmaker. This appellation, however, does not sufficiently describe his work, which includes a number of films which, as Valérie Orlando puts it in Chapter 12, have credits rolling in French but dialogue in English or a mix of languages. Bouchareb's unusual relationship to French national cinema is one of the more interesting elements of his career. This dates back to *Baton Rouge*, his unconventional take on what would later be called the *banlieue* film category, which was the point of entry for many Maghrebi-French or "*beur*" directors in the 1980s and 1990s.[28] His work is not delimited by France or directly French concerns yet cannot be disassociated from the French industry. Bouchareb's trajectory provides a fascinating case study on the evolution of French cinema as a national category: first increasingly diverse (with *Perhaps the Sea* and *Baton Rouge* associated with the emergence of "*beur*" cinema and cultural consciousness), then connected with the post-colonial world of French influence and interest, and finally more geographically and linguistically disparate. All of his features, although often international coproductions, have been at least funded in part by France. Bouchareb's status as a French director therefore requires some qualification. In Chapter 7, Mireille Rosello proposes that Bouchareb's work is best understood as "rearranged national" cinema. Drawing on Hamid Naficy's concept of "accented cinema," she proposes that "his relationship to the idea of the national—and specifically to France and Frenchness—has never been straightforward... Bouchareb's French films all have an 'accent.'"[29]

Bouchareb's parents were born in Algeria, and he holds dual French and Algerian citizenship. His Algerian roots and connections are frequently highlighted, and he is often described as a French-Algerian director. Indeed, links to Algeria have a key place in his work and are reflected in thematic interests in that nation (notably in *Cheb*, *Days of Glory*, and *Outside the Law*) and his collaboration with Algerian author Yasmina Khadra on the screenplay for *Two Men in Town*. In addition, several of his films are Algerian coproductions, and his three Oscar nominations have all been Algerian submissions. However, as Leslie Kealhofer-Kemp demonstrates in Chapter 1, the network of personal connections that informs his body of work is certainly not exclusively delimited by his Algerian origins. *Two Men in Town*, for example, is set in the American Southwest and has no evident link to Algeria despite the writing collaboration with Khadra. Moreover, the transnational issues and settings that define Bouchareb's work often do not directly involve or implicate either France or Algeria at all. The example of *Two Men in Town* demonstrates that "francophone," another categorization (or qualifying adjective that sometimes implies that the work is not quite French) that is commonly applied to French artists with post-colonial backgrounds, is again not entirely adequate in Bouchareb's case. Although many of his films are set at least partly in places that are connected to France through their colonial past (Louisiana, Senegal, Vietnam, Algeria), the scope of his oeuvre extends far beyond the boundaries of the francophone world. Bouchareb's films also do not always neatly fit the "francophone cinema" label. *Two Men in Town* and *Just Like a Woman* contain no French dialogue while *Dust of Life*, *London River*, and *Belleville Cop* feature French in varying degrees within a multilingual context. Even if we accept that the "francophone" classification "belies the polyglot nature of dialogue in many films, whether voyage narratives or stories set in linguistically diverse places, borderlands, or spaces of transit"[30] and that linguistic boundaries are often "fuzzy,"[31] the prevalence of primarily English-language or multilingual films in Bouchareb's catalog renders it impossible to understand his body of work as solely francophone.

Indeed, the very concept of what is French and francophone, both within and beyond the film and media industry, has evolved.[32] Leslie Barnes and Dominic Thomas observe that "both the noun—France—and the adjective—French... continue to travel" beyond the national boundaries of France and of francophone spaces as typically conceived.[33] On one level, this development, as reflected in Bouchareb's films, is consistent with global trends in transnational filmmaking. As Elizabeth Ezra and Terry Rowden observe:

> The global circulation of money, commodities, information and human beings is giving rise to films whose aesthetic and narrative dynamics, and even the modes of emotional identification they elicit, reflect the impact of advanced capitalism and new media technologies as components of an increasingly interconnected world system.[34]

Yet Bouchareb's constantly evolving work does not entirely fit into some of the parameters of transnational cinema. First, as *Just Like a Woman* and his recent comedy *Belleville Cop* make clear, the "sense of loss" at the center of transnational cinema's "narrative dynamic" is not always present in the director's work.[35] Secondly, the transnational framework often brings to the fore the question of inherently "uneven economic conditions that affect funding and distribution of film projects between center and periphery."[36] Despite the difficulties he faced at the start of his career, and in part because of his decision to launch his own production company, Bouchareb has been able to secure French funding for all of his projects and has made several films with very large budgets by European standards (notably *Days of Glory*, *Outside the Law*, and *Belleville Cop*). He has enjoyed a degree of artistic freedom that many transnational filmmakers often find elusive.

Bouchareb's career tests the limits of common categories and analytical frameworks in a number of ways. He has made five features set primarily or entirely in the United States and his work often engages with or intersects with Hollywood in his casting choices—actors such as Sienna Miller, Forest Whitaker, and Luis Guzmán feature in Bouchareb's last three American-set films—and generic inspiration (most notably *Belleville Cop*, which is clearly situated in the lineage of 1980s Hollywood cop comedies). There are several complicating factors that must also be taken into account. First, Bouchareb's American work—even in ostensibly more popular genre films such as *Belleville Cop*—is decidedly more focused on the spatial, cultural, and ethnic margins of America than Hollywood cinema is. Secondly, his films all rely on French funding. Bouchareb has made fourteen features and made-for-television productions and runs an influential production company, and therefore he should be considered an industry insider in France. This distinguishes his recent work from many transnational film auteurs, particularly the interstitially positioned filmmakers explored by Hamid Naficy in his work on "accented cinema."[37] Bouchareb's profile within French and global cinema is therefore that of a filmmaker positioned somewhere between inside and outside. From both positions, he has taken a critical approach to questions of identity, politics, and racial and economic justice, sometimes leading to controversy. This was the case with the reception of *Outside the Law*, as we see in Chapter 10 by Jennifer Howell. In this sense, Bouchareb's French-funded global productions do not fit the common pattern of French—or more broadly, European—production support coming with ideological strings attached. As Randall Halle argues, the "neo-Orientalism" of transnational European film funding involves hierarchical economic relations that often affect cinematic storytelling.[38] With reference to a specifically French context, Florence Martin has argued that institutional initiatives such as the plural appellation *Les Cinémas du monde* ("Cinemas of the World," cosponsored by the Institut français and the CNC) that are represented annually at the Cannes Film Festival and disseminated by French networks with global reaches, are fundamentally political instruments. As an extension of the French state, the Cinemas of the World initiative aims to promote the use of the French language and the ideals of the French Republic.[39] Bouchareb has used his unique vantage points to make French-funded films that are often highly critical of France or have no clear narrative relation to France or French Republican ideology.

One classification that appears particularly applicable to Bouchareb's work is the intentionally broad and inclusive cinéma-monde label, which a number of the contributors have drawn on in their engagements with Bouchareb's filmography or approach to filmmaking. As a critical framework or optic through which to approach films that are made in, tell stories about, or receive funding from parts of the world that could be considered as part of the "francosphere"[40] but which do not neatly correspond to national labels or classifications like "francophone," cinéma-monde is particularly applicable to Bouchareb's geographically and linguistically diverse body of films. His work always contains a "narrative, cultural, symbolic, practical, or financial" link to the francosphere.[41] When compared to the world cinema and transnational cinema categories, cinéma-monde is slightly less broad in scope: it is "transnational, and it is of the world or greatly concerned with the world and its others."[42] However, as the French term *monde* suggests, it is more limited by design to include linguistic and cultural connections that belong to the francosphere.[43] Bouchareb is closely linked to French cinema and the French cinema industry's institutional framework, but his work is also part of a wider conversation on global cinema. His films, whether individually or collectively, could therefore be productively explored in dialogue with global directors such as Oliver Laxe, who has made French-funded films in Arabic or Galician, or Asghar Farhadi, whose productions with dialogue in Persian, Persian/German/Spanish, and English/Catalan have all been financed by France. Ultimately while cinéma-monde appears to be a useful optic through which to approach parts of Bouchareb's filmography, Bouchareb himself is perhaps best classified as a Global French filmmaker, since his films are part of the French cinematic funding, production, and distribution apparatus but also forge an ever diversifying map of the globe.

In the chapters that follow, the contributors to this volume draw on cinéma-monde and a variety of other theoretical frameworks. They also propose some new concepts to apply to Bouchareb's body of work or to individual films. The chapters are divided into two sections: Part I: A Multidimensional Oeuvre, and Part II: Case Studies. Part I includes seven chapters that take a wider perspective on Bouchareb's work by considering at least two films by the director. Each of the five chapters in Part II focuses on one film, and this section is organized in chronological order. Collectively, the chapters cover (to varying degrees) all of Bouchareb's feature films released as of 2019, including a number that have received scant scholarly attention thus far. Some of the films addressed within the context of broader discussions in Part I are the focus of more detailed analysis in Part II. The contributions from scholars in the US, the UK, Australia, France, and Algeria cover a wide range of approaches and vantage points.

To different degrees, all of the chapters in Part I take broad approaches to Bouchareb's work and could be used as introductions to his cinema. Chapters 1 and 2 in particular were conceived as extensions of sorts of this Introduction, each focusing on a key component of the director's oeuvre and approach to filmmaking. In Chapter 1, Leslie Kealhofer-Kemp draws on an extensive range of interviews with Bouchareb in order to explore how he conceives of and makes films. Kealhofer-Kemp suggests that Bouchareb's pre-production process is often overlooked but is a unique feature of his work. Throughout his career, the director has actively promoted different kinds of meetings and encounters, particularly during the pre-production phase, as a means of informing his creative process. Often involving people from different cultures, languages, and religions, and in transnational contexts, these willed encounters have led to some unexpected outcomes and have had an impact—sometimes major—on the projects in question. The chapter proposes the concept of an archipelago (drawing on Édouard Glissant's theorization of the term), or a constantly expanding sphere of creation, as a way of conceptualizing Bouchareb's work, and it argues that the pre-production process forms a key part of this.

In Chapter 2, Michael Gott considers Bouchareb's debut feature, *Baton Rouge* (1985), in comparison with three later productions: *Little Senegal* (2001), *London River* (2009), and *Road to Istanbul* (2016). When examined together, Gott argues, these films can be understood as what he defines as transnational mobile movies, a category that is inclusive of but broader than road movies. Linking the key themes, tropes, and images from *Baton Rouge* to the director's later work, Gott suggests that Bouchareb is always situated on a border, whether physical or sociocultural. He argues that the director uses mobile movies to question a Francocentric outlook on belonging and citizenship and posit a potentially more pliable transnational and mobile concept of identity that breaks free of the constraints of the *"beur"* and *banlieue* cinematic categories that his first feature was lumped into.

Chapter 3, by Kaya Davies Hayon, takes a similar approach by following one theme as it appears throughout some twenty years of Bouchareb's career. She examines the representation of Arab women and their bodies in three of Bouchareb's more introspective, *intimiste* films: *Cheb* (1991), *My Family's Honor* (1998), and *Just like a Woman* (2012). Davies Hayon argues that the director's work clearly reveals a keen interest in gender politics in Arab Muslim cultures but questions the extent to which the representation of women and their bodies in the three films reinforces the Western feminist perspectives that position the West as more liberated than the supposedly oppressed and patriarchal cultures of North Africa and the Middle East.

In Chapter 4, David Pettersen looks at Bouchareb's oeuvre from a wider angle, focusing on the impact of genre filmmaking in general, and references to American genre films in particular, on the director's work. The topic of genre has been a neglected angle in scholarship on Bouchareb, with the exception of the blockbuster *Days of Glory* and highly controversial *Outside the Law*, and Pettersen therefore opts to focus on lesser-known or less widely discussed examples: *Cheb*, *Dust of Life*, *Two Men in Town*, and *Belleville Cop*. Drawing on Bouchareb's deployment of the cinematic language of three genres—the war film, the Western, and the interracial buddy comedy—Pettersen considers how the director uses genre conventions to reframe questions of migration, immigration, diaspora, and colonial history for mainstream audiences.

Chapter 5 expands on the examination of Bouchareb's interest in American genre films. In this chapter, Nabil Boudraa and Ahmed Bedjaoui draw on their 2018 and 2019 interviews with the director to examine and explain what they call the American dimensions of Bouchareb's cinema. Bouchareb's persistent interest in America and American cinema, they suggest, originally derived from his childhood in an immigrant family in France and his desire to escape to new places. They proceed to trace the director's fascination with American culture and cinematic genres from *Baton Rouge* through his most recent film, the 2018 *Belleville Cop*.

In Chapter 6, Julien Gaertner considers Bouchareb's deployment of what he calls "Arab heroes," a problematic term that the author opts to use to represent prevalent cultural and cinematic discourses. Gaertner argues that a comparison of these figures in *Days of Glory* and *Outside the Law* demonstrates the extent to which collective memories are still raw when the colonial past resurfaces in contemporary social and political debates. Gaertner suggests that by highlighting the decisive role of colonial soldiers and subjects in the liberation of France in 1945, the massacres of Sétif, and the Algerian War of Independence, Bouchareb presents heroic cinematic figures that challenge the collective French imagination of what those perceived in French culture, and often on cinema screens, as "Arabs" can become.

In Chapter 7, Mireille Rosello examines Bouchareb's critique of the traditional Western view on terrorism while arguing that cinemas participate in a cultural struggle about how to understand and represent terror. In her analysis of *London River* within the wider context of Bouchareb's career and *Baton Rouge* and *Little Senegal* in particular, Rosello contends that cinema, globalization, and terrorism are inextricably linked in Bouchareb's cinematic interpretation of the world.[44]

Chapter 8 opens Part II, in which each of the contributions focuses on one film from Bouchareb's corpus. Michael O'Riley examines Bouchareb's 1995 Oscar-nominated film *Dust of Life*, which has been the subject of very little scholarly attention. The film reveals the forgotten and buried stories of the so-called "dust of life," street children and orphans who were confined in re-education camps after the North Vietnamese conquest of South Vietnam. He interprets the film as a *memento mori*, "a tribute to death and to the death of memory itself," which by remembering these children also engages with repressed traumas and histories of imperialism in Vietnam.

Gemma King's Chapter 9 uses Bouchareb's 2001 film *Little Senegal* as a starting point for a wider exploration of what she describes as the importance of "transnational movement, translingual dialogue, and the decentered relationship with the anglo- and francospheres" within Bouchareb's corpus. King engages with recent scholarship on cinéma-monde to suggest that *Little Senegal* exemplifies the transnational trajectory of Rachid Bouchareb's filmmaking career, revealing a linguistic, cultural, and geographic hybridity central to his filmmaking endeavors.

In Chapter 10, Jennifer Howell examines the controversy surrounding the release of *Outside the Law* within the context of the significant political and social impact that *Days of Glory* had previously had in France. She argues that *Outside the Law* belongs to a new "moment of memory" that corresponds to the election of Nicolas Sarkozy in 2007 and his subsequent "Debate on National Identity," which included efforts to roll back the process of national repentance for colonialism. Howell suggests that the dramatically different receptions of *Outside the Law*—a film about the Algerian quest for independence from France—and *Days of Glory*, which memorializes the contribution of colonial soldiers to the liberation of Europe in World War II, offer some important lessons about the role of politics and political pressure in on-screen representations of France's colonial past.

Chapter 11, by Anne Donadey, considers Bouchareb's 2012 female-centered road movie *Just Like a Woman*. Donadey assesses the film's status as a "post-colonial feminist film" and suggests that Bouchareb's mastery of the "*intimiste* tone" allows him to depict intercultural and female relationships in a compelling fashion. Bouchareb, she contends, "is one of too few male filmmakers who pays regular attention to women's issues and recurrently features prominent migrant or multicultural female characters."

Finally, in Chapter 12, Valérie K. Orlando uses *Two Men in Town*, set in the American Southwest, to demonstrate how Bouchareb's oeuvre approaches local and global perspectives. Using the work of theorist Arjun Appadurai as a framework, Orlando offers a detailed analysis of how the film's portrayal of African American protagonist William Garnett (Forest Whitaker) and his attempts to rebuild his life in a small community near the US–Mexico border after many years in prison reveals the stresses of globalization in the twenty-first century.

Together, the chapters in this volume offer an interdisciplinary approach to Rachid Bouchareb's work, highlighting connections between his diverse films while also engaging in a broader exploration of the arc of the director's career. They point to Bouchareb as a Global French filmmaker whose work is rooted in, yet extends well beyond, the French national context.

NOTES

1. We have opted to include quotation marks around terms that we find problematic for various reasons but that are difficult to avoid because they were or still are commonly used in French public or political discourse or in academic parlance. "*Beur*" is one example of this. The term was also commonly used at the start of Bouchareb's career.
2. See Bill Marshall, "*Cinéma-monde?* Towards a Concept of Francophone Cinema," *Francosphères* 1, no. 1 (2012): 35–51; Michael Gott and Thibaut Schilt, ed., *Cinéma-monde: Decentred Perspectives on Global Filmmaking in French* (Edinburgh: Edinburgh University Press, 2018).
3. Bouchareb wrote the film with Jean Bigot.
4. "Entretien avec Rachid Bouchareb," 28 January 1991, *dossier de presse*, *Cheb*.
5. Morocco and Tunisia were protectorates and gained independence in 1956.
6. While the film does not broach directly the subject of discrimination or racism faced by populations of Maghrebi origin in France, it certainly reminds viewers of France's colonial history and that this is tied to the presence and perceptions of the Maghrebi population in France.
7. The remainder of the text, which he also reads, informs them that youth can choose to renounce this nationality six months prior to the legal age of adulthood (eighteen years old).
8. Alec G. Hargreaves, "From 'Ghettoes' to Globalization: Situating Maghrebi-French Filmmakers," in *Screening Integration: Recasting Maghrebi Immigration in Contemporary France*, ed. Sylvie Durmelat and Vinay Swamy (Lincoln: University of Nebraska Press, 2011), 35.
9. Will Higbee, *Post-Beur Cinema: North African Émigré and Maghrebi-French Filmmaking in France since 2000* (Edinburgh: Edinburgh University Press, 2013), 1.
10. Alec G. Hargreaves, "*Indigènes:* A Sign of the Times," *Research in African Literatures* 38, no. 4 (2007): 204–16.
11. Higbee, *Post-Beur Cinema*, 2.

12. "Dans le champ économique du cinéma français, c'est pas évident que tu puisses faire des films—en tout cas à l'époque, même si les choses ont un peu évolué aujourd'hui—dont le héros principal s'appelle Ali ou Mohamed. Ça change, c'est vrai, mais ça change difficilement. Ça change parce qu'on est de plus en plus à faire des films, on est de plus en plus. Ça existe aussi dans la musique, ça existe dans la peinture, ça existe dans la mode maintenant. Donc depuis quelques années, on a pris un peu ça en compte, mais à l'époque dans les années 1977, quand j'ai commencé à faire mes court-métrages et tout, il n'y avait pas d'ouverture du tout. Donc je les ai faits quand même, ces films, parce que j'ai envie de les faire. D'un point de vue économique, c'était difficile." *Rencontres*, episode "Cinéma et immigration," aired 26 January 1991, on France 3.
13. For further information about the *avance sur recettes*, see "Avance sur recettes avant réalisation," CNC website, accessed 17 March 2020, https://www.cnc.fr/professionnels/aides-et-financements/cinema/production/avance-sur-recettes-avant-realisation_191260.
14. Carrie Tarr, *Reframing Difference:* Beur *and* Banlieue *Filmmaking in France* (Manchester: Manchester University Press, 2005), 26.
15. Ibid., 214.
16. Melanie Goodfellow, "Rachid Bouchareb Receives Abu Dhabi Film Festival Honour, Talks Career," *Screen Daily*, 25 October 2014.
17. Ange-Dominique Bouzet, "Le coup double cannois de 3B," *Libération*, 17 May 2006, https://next.liberation.fr/cinema/2006/05/17/le-coup-double-cannois-de-3b_39538.
18. Ibid.
19. The companies are distinct in a legal sense but are headed by Bouchareb and Bréhat and share the same website, http://3b-productions.com. A frequent collaborator is Muriel Merlin, who is also a producer for 3B and Tessalit. In addition, in 1996, Bouchareb, Bréhat, and Merlin founded Tadrart Films to distribute the films produced by 3B.
20. *Dossier de presse*, *Frères d'armes*, accessed 25 March 2020, https://www.thuram.org/wp-content/uploads/2017/10/Freresdarmes_dossier-presse.pdf. A very similar statement accompanied the second project: *Dossier de presse*, *Champions de France*, accessed 25 March 2020, https://www.lesbdm.com/files/bdm/images-contenu/3_references/3-8_France-televisions/dossier-de-presse-champoin-de-france.pdf.
21. Bouzet, "Le coup double cannois de 3B."
22. "Entretien avec Rachid Bouchareb," *dossier de presse*, *Poussières de vie*, accessed 17 March 2020, http://www.3b-productions.com/tessalit/films/poussieres_vie/entretien.html.
23. The dialogue of this film is an example of "translanguaging," a dynamic and multidirectional process, which involves moving among language and using language in diverse ways. Language choices can underline "the complex interplay between language, culture and power the practices of code-switching and translanguaging can entail." Gemma King, *Decentring France: Multilingualism and Power in Contemporary French Cinema* (Manchester: Manchester University Press, 2017), 9.
24. "Entretien avec Omar Sy," *dossier de presse*, *Le Flic de Belleville*, accessed 17 March 2020, http://www.3b-productions.com/tessalit/leflicdebelleville/download/dp-flicdebelleville.pdf.
25. For an analysis of how proximity connects to a reading of Guédiguian's cinema through the lens of friendship, see Joseph Mai, "The Ideal of Ararat: Friendship, Politics and National Origins in Robert Guédiguian's *Le Voyage en Arménie*," in *East, West and Centre: Reframing Post-1989 European Cinema*, ed. Michael Gott and Todd Herzog (Edinburgh: Edinburgh University Press, 2015), 279–92.
26. Rob Carnevale, "London River—Rachid Bouchareb Interview," indieLondon, accessed 17 March 2020, http://www.indielondon.co.uk/Film-Review/london-river-rachid-bouchareb-interview.

27. "Entretien avec Rachid Bouchareb," *dossier de presse*, *La Voie de l'ennemi*, accessed 17 March 2020, http://www.3b-productions.com/tessalit/lavoiedelennemi/download/la-voie-de-l-ennemi-dp.pdf.
28. The "*beur*" and *banlieue* contexts in Bouchareb's early work are discussed in more detail in Chapter 2 and Chapter 5. See also Alison J. Murray Levine, "Mapping Beur Cinema in the New Millennium," *Journal of Film and Video* 60, no. 3/4 (2008): 42–59; Will Higbee, "Re-Presenting the Urban Periphery: Maghrebi-French Filmmaking and the 'Banlieue' Film," *Cineaste* 33, no. 1 (2007): 38–43; and Michael Gott, "'Bouger pour voir les immeubles': *Jeunesse dorée* (2001), *L'année suivante* (2006) and the Creative Mobility of Women's *Banlieue* Cinema," *Modern & Contemporary France* 21, no. 4 (2013): 453–72.
29. See Hamid Naficy, *An Accented Cinema: Exilic and Diasporic Filmmaking* (Princeton: Princeton University Press, 2001).
30. Michael Gott and Leslie-Kealhofer Kemp, "Introduction: World Cinema and Television 'in French,'" *Contemporary French Civilization* 43, no. 1 (2018): 5.
31. Charles Forsdick, "Global France, Global French: Beyond the Monolingual," *Contemporary French Civilization* 42, no. 1 (2017): 17.
32. There has been a clear shift toward promoting "French" as an economic and cine-industrial label as much as a cultural or linguistic one on the part of UniFrance Films, the organization charged with promoting French cinema around the world, and by official entities that program and promote cinema, such as the Tournées Film Festival and the virtual "festival" MyFrenchFilmFestival.com. The latter has a title in English, even on the French site, and is sponsored by the Institut français and the CNC (Centre national du cinéma et de l'image animée). See Gott and Kealhofer-Kemp, "Introduction," 1–16.
33. Leslie Barnes and Dominic Thomas, "Introduction: Global France, Global French," *Contemporary French Civilization* 42, no. 1 (2017): 1–11.
34. Elizabeth Ezra and Terry Rowden, "General Introduction: What Is Transnational Cinema?" in *Transnational Cinema: The Film Reader*, ed. Elizabeth Ezra and Terry Rowden (Abingdon: Routledge, 2006), 1.
35. Ibid., 7.
36. Kathleen Newman, "Notes on Transnational Film Theory," in *World Cinemas, Transnational Perspectives*, ed. Nataša Ďurovičová and Kathleen Newman (New York: Routledge, 2010), 3–11.
37. Naficy, *An Accented Cinema*. Although Naficy cites Bouchareb in his 2001 book and mentions *Cheb* briefly, Bouchareb's more recent films do not fit squarely into this framework.
38. Randall Halle, "Offering Tales They Want to Hear: Transnational European Film Funding as Neo-Orientalism," in *Global Art Cinema: New Theories and Histories*, ed. Rosalind Galt and Karl Schoonover (Oxford: Oxford University Press, 2010), 303–19.
39. Florence Martin, "*Cinéma-monde*: De-orbiting Maghrebi Cinema," *Contemporary French Civilization* 41, no. 3–4 (2016): 463.
40. By "francosphere," we are referring to a sphere of influence or interaction of the French language, France, and other (at least partially) French-speaking nations. This includes, among other things, former colonies and possessions of France and Belgium, Quebec, and other Canadian provinces with French-speaking communities.
41. Michael Gott and Thibaut Schilt, "Introduction: The Kaleidoscope of Cinéma-Monde," in *Cinéma-Monde: Decentred Perspectives on Global Filmmaking in French*, ed. Michael Gott and Thibaut Schilt (Edinburgh: Edinburgh University Press, 2018), 2.
42. Ibid., 9.
43. Ibid., 9.

44. This chapter was originally published in the 2018 collection *Cinéma-Monde: Decentred Perspectives on Global Filmmaking in French*, edited by Michael Gott and Thibaut Schilt. We opted to include it here because it covers terrorism, an important and recurring theme in Bouchareb's work, within a discussion of the director's positioning along a local–national–global axis. The pertinence of Rosello's chapter to the topic of Bouchareb's work is demonstrated by the fact that the initial manifestation of her chapter is cited by a number of contributors. We hope that including her insightful work here will help further the dialogue between her writing on Bouchareb and that of the other contributors.

PART I

A Multidimensional Oeuvre

CHAPTER I

Rachid Bouchareb's Cinema as a "Vehicle for Encounters": Cultural Mixings and the Pre-production Process

Leslie Kealhofer-Kemp

As the chapters in this collection reflect, the films that make up Rachid Bouchareb's body of work are extremely diverse and can be approached from multiple analytical angles. With narratives set in many different places and time periods, the films embody a level of diversity that also extends to genres, aesthetics, languages, filming locations, and funding sources. The director's filmmaking and artistic approaches are continually in movement, shifting and reacting to previous projects, new ideas, and current events.[1] All of these factors, among many others, are what make Bouchareb's films so engaging and worthy of attention. Yet, at the same time, this also results in a body of work that does not lend itself readily to a single overarching analytical framework, categorization, or classification. This chapter proposes to engage with the cinema of Rachid Bouchareb by taking a step back from the films themselves and considering instead what we can learn about Bouchareb's filmmaking by examining the projects as they develop in the pre-production phase.

In order to conceptualize Bouchareb's pre-production process and to consider the ways in which it fits in with and informs his filmmaking more broadly, I have found it useful to draw on recent discussions relating to the concept of cinéma-monde. I take as a starting point Bill Marshall, David Murphy, Elizabeth Ezra, and Cristina Johnston's characterization that

> in terms employed by Caribbean theorist Édouard Glissant, Francophone cinema as *cinéma-monde* is an archipelago, devoid of an "organic authority" associated with a "continent," and fit for "a non-systematic inductive thought, exploring what is unexpected in the world-totality" (*Introduction à une poétique du divers*, 1996).[2]

I propose that the concept of archipelago is a useful lens through which to consider the body of work of Rachid Bouchareb. Here, the archipelago is a sphere of creation. It continues to expand, as each island, or film, is produced through a volcanic, changing, and ever-evolving creative process, leading to outcomes that are sometimes unexpected. In what follows, I focus on one part of this creative process, the pre-production phase. Drawing on print media, television, and radio interviews given by the director since 1985 in which he discusses this aspect of his work, I map out and analyze various interworkings of this process, during which projects are molded, take shape, and, as we shall see, are sometimes even significantly reshaped. For the purposes of this chapter, I define "pre-production" in very broad terms as everything that occurs before filming. It thus encompasses moments of inspiration, conceptualization, ideas, research, interviews, writing, and other preparations and considerations. In the case of some of Bouchareb's films, this time period may span as many as fifteen or twenty years.

This chapter is divided into two parts. In the first, I adopt the metaphor of the archipelago as a means of conceptualizing Bouchareb's work through the lens of pre-production. Specifically, I seek to answer the following question: What links together such diverse films—or metaphorically, islands—other than the fact that they have the same director? In analyzing Bouchareb's discourse about this part of his creative process, I identify two key phases that can shape his projects at this early stage. The first is a conceptual moment (or period), and in particular, an important motivation, catalyst, and/or inspiration. This involves a personal connection between the director and the subject or characters. In particular, it relates to immigration, the Maghrebi-French population in France, and/or the feeling of belonging to more than one culture—a cultural mixing he identifies with as the son of Algerian migrants, born in France. In the words of Bouchareb:

> The subjects that I choose to address enable me to find myself. It's tough to make a film. You need infinite amounts of passion, energy, love, hope ... I don't think that I'd be capable of liberating these things if I didn't identify with the subjects.[3]

Another source of inspiration for Bouchareb's projects are current events or situations, notably with a strong political dimension, such as the 7 July 2005 bombings in London (*London River*, 2009) or the stories of young people from Europe who become radicalized and travel to Syria to join Islamic State (*La Route d'Istanbul/Road to Istanbul*, 2016). The second pre-production phase comprises a more active, on-the-ground process that is driven by the director (and can be more involved and in-depth for some films than for others). Here,

Bouchareb (aided by cowriters and associates) writes, conducts research, and interviews people who often offer different and sometimes conflicting perspectives from each other as well as the director. Throughout his career, Bouchareb has actively promoted different kinds of *rencontres* (meetings/encounters), particularly, but not exclusively, during pre-production, as a means of informing his creative process. Often involving people from different cultures, languages, and religions, these willed encounters have led to some unexpected outcomes and had an impact—sometimes major—on the projects in question. I argue that this active on-the-ground approach is reflective of Bouchareb's philosophy that "cinema is a vehicle for encounters, for emotions, which, above all, pushes us to feel, even if it also pushes us to discover."[4]

I conclude the chapter with a case study of the film *Little Senegal* (2001), the seeds of which were planted in the early 1980s while Bouchareb was researching and filming his first feature, *Bâton Rouge/Baton Rouge* (1985), in the United States. *Little Senegal* is a useful lens through which to assess the impact on Bouchareb's work of the cultural mixings and encounters that the director actively sought to cultivate, as the film brought together both of the phases of pre-production just described and involved especially revealing and impactful encounters. It also serves as one example of how Bouchareb incorporates new ideas and realizations into his films as his own assumptions and perspectives are reformulated, refined, and challenged. Finally, while my objective is to shed light on some recurrent elements that come to the fore when we consider the pre-production stage of Bouchareb's projects over the course of his career, with special consideration given to *Little Senegal*, my intention is not to suggest that the director has a set process or fixed method that he follows for each film. Although there are guiding principles, it remains a process that changes and develops.

CINÉMA-MONDE: BOUCHAREB'S CINEMA VIEWED AS AN ARCHIPELAGO

Other than having the same director, what is it that binds these very diverse films together as an archipelago, within a shared body of water, so to speak, as opposed to simply being single, scattered, islands? In this section, I discuss in detail the two recurrent elements that I have identified, one or both of which tie his films to the others: a personal connection or affinity between Bouchareb and the themes or characters in his films, notably relating to cultural mixing; and/or a link with a current event, which served as a starting point or catalyst for a specific project.[5] I will consider each in turn, connecting them with specific films.

In a televised interview about his second feature film, *Cheb* (1991), Bouchareb stated:

> When I came to cinema [in the 1970s], the first thing I wanted to do was to talk a little about my experiences and my cultural make-up . . . and, if you like, the experience of immigration in France through my parents, what I personally experienced, and also my Algerian origins.[6]

This attention to Maghrebis and their descendants in France and North Africa dominated the first part of his career (1980s and 1990s) in feature films like *Baton Rouge*, *Cheb*, and the téléfilm *L'Honneur de ma famille/My Family's Honor* (1998). It is also a key component of later films, most notably *Indigènes/ Days of Glory* (2006) and *Hors la loi/Outside the Law* (2010). In addition, Maghrebi and/or Muslim characters have supporting roles in other films, including *Little Senegal, London River, Just Like a Woman* (2012), *La Voie de l'ennemi/Two Men in Town* (2014), *Road to Istanbul*, and *Le Flic de Belleville/ Belleville Cop* (2018).

The affinity or personal connection that informs his body of work is not strictly defined by or limited to his Algerian origins, however. There is also the sentiment, for Bouchareb, that he belongs to more than one culture. The idea of cultural mixing is recurrent in his interviews and omnipresent in his films. It is reflected in his cinema through diverse contexts and populations, often in transnational settings. When speaking about *Poussières de vie/Dust of Life* (1995), for example, the director stated that "making this film was, for me, a continuation of the subject that I had already introduced in *Cheb*, my previous film, on the intermixing of races and cultures."[7] In a different interview, he expanded on this idea and attested to having a shared affinity with the characters in *Dust of Life*—the children of Vietnamese mothers and American fathers who are confined to "re-education camps" after the fall of Saigon in 1975—precisely because they embody a cultural mixing. The director noted that some members of his family had fought in Indochina,

> because Algeria, at that time, was French, and I felt close to these children who found themselves like that, in a situation . . . They had been completely abandoned by the American army in Saigon . . . It linked up with my preoccupations. I don't belong to the same group as those children, but we share a cultural mixing.[8]

This aligns with Alec G. Hargreaves's observation that "far from being preoccupied with the fates of narrowly defined Maghrebi-French characters or situations, Bouchareb's vision is much more global in scope, blending the specificities of a wide range of social and ethnic milieus with an underlying concern for universal principles of individual freedom and equality."[9]

Rachid Bouchareb's work thus stems from the creation of productive points of contact between the personal and the universal, which are anchored in various kinds of cultural mixings. A prime example of this dynamic can be seen in the process of writing *Dust of Life*. Along with Bernard Gesbert, Bouchareb adapted Duyên Anh's autobiographical novel *La Colline de Fanta/Fanta Hill* (1989) into the screenplay of *Dust of Life*, and in doing so he deliberately added an additional layer of cultural mixing.[10] Whereas the protagonist in Anh's book is the son of a white American serviceman and a Vietnamese woman, the (unseen) father of the main character in Bouchareb's film is African American. Speaking about the ethnic and cultural background of his protagonist, Bouchareb explained:

> His ethnic mixing was important. It provided me with a personal connection that enabled me to become submerged in a completely Vietnamese environment without feeling as if I was a total stranger to it. Through the problems of this minority of kids who are caught between two races, I interweave the difficulties of cultural mixing that I am familiar with as a child of Algerians in France. Exclusion. The dream of returning, or leaving, toward an inaccessible elsewhere. This is also what inspires the escape that I make the heroes of *Dust of Life* experience, which was not part of the book. In fact, all of my films deal with that.[11]

These underlying motivations and connections, personal yet situated within a broader framework, are also evident in other films, including *Days of Glory* and *Outside the Law*. In interviews, Bouchareb has discussed the involvement of his family members in World War I and World War II, as well as Indochina and the Algerian War of Independence.[12] During the 2006 Cannes Film festival, where *Days of Glory* was in competition, Bouchareb said that he had wanted to make the film for ten years and referred to a personal motivation: to better understand himself and his place in French society. He explained that he had

> nothing to prove, just this desire. I was born in France, I live in France, but I wanted to know more so that I could better understand myself, my place in French society, my future. So I took an interest in this chapter of France's history.[13]

In a 2007 interview about *Days of Glory*, Bouchareb again referenced a personal connection while emphasizing his desire to make known the role of North African soldiers in the French armed forces: "This personal connection is only one reason among others. The history of these North African soldiers had never been examined through cinema, or only very marginally. I felt that it was necessary to remedy this."[14]

In addition to these kinds of connections that inform Rachid Bouchareb's creative process in this conceptual phase, there is a second recurrent link (which can sometimes overlap with the first) between many of the films in his diverse corpus. It is a connection to contemporary events or situations, and specifically those of a political nature. Speaking about the political dimension of his work, Bouchareb has explained: "I am mindful of the political dimension of things because it directly affects people and their daily lives."[15] In the films that have such a connection, the director examines larger, and often contemporary, questions and concerns through the individual experiences of the protagonists. In order to illustrate this, I will provide a few brief examples. *Baton Rouge* (1985) is set against the background of unemployment in France in the early 1980s, which affected many young people, and especially youth of Maghrebi origin. The three male protagonists, Mozart, Karim, and Abdenour, seek out new job opportunities in the United States, but only one of them, the majority-ethnic character Mozart, remains there (thanks to a love interest, not a job opportunity).[16] Through the theme of unemployment, the film also connects to contemporaneous debates about immigration and the place of children of Maghrebi migrants in France, many of whom—like Bouchareb—were coming of age around this time and facing roadblocks in French society because of their ethnic origins.[17] The question of identity and the place of youth of Maghrebi origin in France during the specific context of the late 1980s are also explored in *Cheb* (1991). It brings to the fore the consequences of the *double peine* (double punishment) law in France and the rise of Islamism in Algeria at the end of the 1980s.[18] Both of these affect the film's main character, Merwan Kechida, a young man raised in France from a young age (but with Algerian nationality) who is expelled to his parents' country of origin, Algeria, after he committed a crime and served prison time in France. In a 1991 interview, when Bouchareb was asked where his idea for the film came from, he explained that he had been on vacation in Algeria visiting family when he came across an article about an expulsion. In the words of the director:

> That was when everything clicked. It all came together. I thought, I was in Algeria, on vacation, and everything was fine. But what if, from one day to the next, I was kicked out of France and had to live in Algeria for the rest of my life? How would I react to that? It would be brutal, difficult to bear. My idea for the film stemmed directly from these feelings and raw emotions.[19]

Contemporary debates on immigration in transnational contexts—and especially in the United States (*Little Senegal*, *Just Like a Woman*, and *Two Men in Town*)—also inform films released later in Bouchareb's career.

Political events or situations can also manifest themselves in Bouchareb's films in more indirect ways. For example, the director felt that there were connections between the human rights abuses in Vietnam—which he chose to portray through the trials of mixed children in re-education camps in *Dust of Life* (1995)—and those that were occurring in the 1990s in Yugoslavia and Rwanda, which were fueled by ethnic differences and tensions. For Bouchareb, "these are not lessons that we remember."[20] Similarly, the point of origin of *London River* (2009) was the 7 July 2005 bombings in London, yet the film does not take place during the bombings themselves and is not overtly political. Rather, it takes place during the chaotic aftermath of the events and brings together two very different people who have come to London in search of their missing children (who, unbeknownst to either of them, were dating and living together). For Bouchareb, this film

> is less about the bombings themselves than the relationship between these characters that develops as a result of them. That's what is important for me, that these two characters who meet are united by the same problem, their desire to find their respective children.[21]

A final example encapsulates these personal, political, and contemporary strands that can lead to a film project. *Road to Istanbul* (2016) directly engages with contemporary political situations and societal preoccupations in a way similar to *Cheb*, and also connects with *London River* through the theme of a parent searching for a missing child in a transnational context. It follows a Belgian mother, Elisabeth, in search of her daughter, Élodie, who has left Belgium for Syria to join Islamic State. Bouchareb framed the origins of the project in the following terms:

> Like for all of my films, I started from one particular event for the simple reason that it touched me: a woman I saw on television one evening who had tried to cross the border to Syria to find her daughter . . . I tell nothing but these "small stories," even if sometimes, like in *Days of Glory*, they intersect with big stories like war or colonization.[22]

There, the idea of "small stories" as forming a larger picture echoes the metaphor of the archipelago as a way to conceptualize Bouchareb's cinema.

As these examples have highlighted, creative sparks in the conceptual period of Bouchareb's projects can stem from a personal connection or an issue that the director seeks to explore, which ties to a contemporary event or social preoccupation, most often of a political nature. I will now consider a second recurring element of Bouchareb's pre-production phase, an active on-the-ground process that involves research and encounters with people and places. It should be noted that these two components are not necessarily features of all of his projects, nor do they necessarily occur successively; they might take place concurrently or even in a back-and-forth process of ideas and encounters.

RENCONTRES FORMING AND INFORMING BOUCHAREB'S FILMMAKING

Analysis of media, television, and radio interviews given by the director since 1985 reveals the significance of the idea of *rencontres* and cultural mixings in his work—before, during, and after the filmmaking process—and underscore his philosophy that cinema is, itself, a "vehicle for encounters."[23] Bouchareb has expanded upon this notion elsewhere, stating:

> All of my films talk about encounters between different people from different countries and different worlds. This theme is always at the heart of my films, because the characters are always on a journey. And this phenomenon goes beyond the characters on the screen. It even extends to the actors.[24]

We can again situate Bouchareb's work within a cinéma-monde framework as set out by Michael Gott and Thibaut Schilt, who observe that

> much like David Damrosch's (2003) definition of "World Literature" ... cinéma-monde is fundamentally about "encounters" between different cultures and perspectives (2003: 5) ... To different degrees—or different "scales," to use Hjort's term (2010: 13)—these encounters and connections are all transnational.[25]

Indeed, throughout his career, Rachid Bouchareb has actively promoted different kinds of transnational meetings and encounters, particularly during the pre-production phase, as a means of informing his creative process. As we shall see, Bouchareb's orchestration of *rencontres* can lead to creatively productive, and sometimes unexpected, outcomes. To return to Glissantian terms, we can view these encounters as fostering a kind of *créolisation*, or "(ethnic) mixing that produces the unforeseeable."[26] Consideration of *rencontres* in Bouchareb's filmmaking raises the following questions, among others: What kinds of encounters does the director seek out? To what extent do these meetings have an impact on the projects in question? What from these *rencontres*, if anything, does Bouchareb eventually incorporate into his films? In the remainder of this chapter, I will explore these questions through consideration of *Little Senegal*, released in 2001.

Little Senegal follows a West African man, Alloune, on his journey from Senegal to Harlem via the American South (notably South Carolina). Through his travels, he traces the history of his ancestors who were sold into the slave trade. Eventually, he meets Ida, an American descendant of his family tree who lives in New York. When Bouchareb was asked in an interview to explain the origin of this film, he said that it actually stemmed back to the making of his very first feature, *Baton Rouge* (released in 1985):

> In *Baton Rouge* . . . a Frenchman of Maghrebi origin was on a road trip from New York to Florida, by way of Louisiana. This gave me the chance to mix with the African American community and make African friends. The moment came when I wanted to bring these two communities together. I was curious to put them into physical contact with each other.[27]

Bouchareb's visits to specific sites, and especially plantations, where he met descendants of slave owners and saw slave quarters first-hand, also fueled a desire to examine slavery through film.[28]

These meetings and encounters in the United States thus planted the seeds for a future film, and it was an idea that the director would return to well over a decade later, after making three others (*Cheb*, *Dust of Life*, and *My Family's Honor*). As Bouchareb explored what this kind of encounter—the bringing together of African Americans and Africans in the context of the United States—might entail, he began a long process of research and interviews, primarily in the United States but also in Senegal. He explained: "My coscriptwriter, Olivier Lorelle, and I made several trips to meet these two communities in order to interview them and get their reactions to their cohabitation."[29]

In total, the director spent fifteen months in the United States.[30] What he learned during these visits surprised him and even led to unanticipated changes to his original vision for the film. In a 2001 television interview, he framed his original perceptions and ideas, as well as the unanticipated evolution of the project, in the following terms:

> After my numerous visits to the United States and Africa, I wanted to make this encounter happen in cinema, and I thought, it's clear that the reunions are going to be terrific. And then, after long months of research and inquiries, then interviews with the African American community and the African community, [I found that] it wasn't the case at all. It's a conflictual and very difficult relationship. And the relationships . . . and cohabitation don't work well.[31]

This reality ran counter to Bouchareb's assumption (and also one of the principles that guides much of his work) that cultural mixing is something positive, or at least productive. Furthermore, this and other findings that came out of his research and interviews influenced not only how he had originally envisaged the role of the film's main character, but also the entire message of hope and reconciliation that he had originally intended to convey through the film: "I started with the idea that Alloune would reunite these two communities in order to bring a message of hope and to say that these encounters are possible. It's clear that the reality is far more complex."[32] Bouchareb's real and imagined encounters are in line with Gott and Schilt's observation about transnational encounters in films that fall under the purview of cinéma-monde. Despite the positive potentials of encounters engendered in cinéma-monde, they provide a reminder that "even when potentially meaningful encounters result, the transnational is not *a priori* positive, liberating, celebratory, or virtuous (Ezra and Rowden 2006: 9; Hjort 2010)."[33]

Bouchareb's separate on-the-ground encounters with members of the two populations—whom he had originally conceived of as "cousins"—dispelled another preconceived notion that he had regarding the potential for creating a positive encounter and outcome between Alloune and Ida, the main characters of his film. He explained: "What surprised us was discovering the racism and violence in what these two 'cousins' said. One might have thought that the encounter would be harmonious and natural due to their common root, Africa."[34] As Delphine Letort's analysis of *Little Senegal* reflects, Bouchareb's own realizations were incorporated into the film's narrative and are transmitted in particular via the ever-evolving perspective of Alloune, as he traces his family tree from South Carolina to Harlem. She writes:

> As Alloune's investigation progresses and takes him further to the north, the film moves from an essentialist understanding of the diaspora to the recognition of its heterogeneity and diversity. Through portraying the difficulties encountered by the post-colonial subject in *Little Senegal*, Bouchareb calls attention to a fractured diaspora and interrogates the Afro-centric myth.[35]

Bouchareb's experiences on the ground in the United States also dispelled for him any potential for a kind of Pan-Islamism that might be a way to bind together the diverse African and African American populations. He expressed his surprise at learning that not even a shared religion, Islam, was enough to bring members of the two communities together; he discovered that there were separate mosques for the different populations, all located in the same area.[36] According to Bouchareb:

There's been an African American mosque in Harlem for years. One might have expected religion to serve as a possible bond. But the African community preferred to have its own mosques. So there really are no harmonious relationships or direct connections. The African community made its own African Chinatown in the heart of Harlem, its "Little Senegal."[37]

These *rencontres* on American soil shaped more than the film's characters and its narrative arc; they were also an important source for the film's dialogues. As Bouchareb has explained, he decided to incorporate directly into the script some phrases of the people that he interviewed: "All of the dialogues in the film were given to me by the two communities, African American and African. I didn't invent any of it."[38] This suggests that, for the director, this practice was intended to lend authenticity to the film and its characters, especially since he was telling the story as an outsider.

The discoveries that Bouchareb made during pre-production, and the ways in which he chose to incorporate them into the script, also impacted casting in two distinct ways. First, some of the real people that Bouchareb met during his research, as well as where they lived and/or worked, eventually became part of *Little Senegal*.[39] This included employees in museums and libraries in Senegal and the American South, as well as descendants of slave-owning families who still lived on the family plantations. Here, the film blends fiction with reality, as the non-professional actors "play" themselves during interactions with Alloune as he pursues his journey of discovery.[40] A second factor that impacted casting was Bouchareb's decision to portray conflict, and sometimes racism, between the two communities in Harlem. Because of this, some actors declined parts in the project. According to the director:

> Some actors . . . refused to be in the film because they found it to be too violent, too racist, casting the confrontation between the two black communities in far too negative a light: it's "between blacks," whereas popular belief is that blacks are victims of racism by whites.[41]

This case study illustrates the extent to which willed encounters led to significant changes to the overall vision for *Little Senegal*, and it highlights various facets of Bouchareb's creative approach and process during pre-production. Encounters have continued to shape Bouchareb's projects and inform his creative process since the release of *Little Senegal* (which from a contemporary vantage point represents the middle of Bouchareb's career). After *Little Senegal*, Bouchareb went on to make *Days of Glory*, which necessitated a research phase that lasted over a year. During this time, Bouchareb (along with coscriptwriter Olivier Lorelle) interviewed numerous veterans from North and West Africa who served under the French flag during World War II.[42] These meetings served as a creative spark for *Outside the Law*. As Bouchareb later explained: "The people that I interviewed for *Days of Glory* told me their entire story: World War II, their return home, Sétif, the expectations regarding decolonization, disappointment, resistance, and so on. *Outside the Law* emerged directly from these accounts."[43] In the case of *London River*, the crucial encounters that occurred during pre-production did not involve interviews with people who were affected by the London bombings (as Bouchareb felt that there had already been sufficient news coverage documenting this).[44] Rather, he focused on the meeting and relationship between the film's two lead actors, Sotigui Kouyaté and Brenda Blethyn, as he felt that this was crucial for the film: "I wanted to take these two actors, live with them, see how they were going to approach their characters and what relationship would develop between them: their encounter. That's what gives the film its universality."[45] Finally, interviews and research conducted on the ground would again be a significant part of Bouchareb's pre-production process for *Two Men in Town*, set along the New Mexico–Mexico border, and a source of inspiration for the script. The diversity of the interviewees is particularly striking in this case and included members of the Tea Party, various sheriffs, and so-called Minutemen (unregulated militia groups that patrol the border).[46]

As I have endeavored to show in this chapter, each of Bouchareb's films—or each island in the archipelago of his oeuvre—takes shape in its own way through a process that is volcanic, changing, evolving, and leads to outcomes that are sometimes unexpected. These individual projects form part of a larger archipelago that continues to expand, and whose contours are shaped by personal connections and affinities, contemporary and often political events or moments, and key *rencontres* with people and places.

NOTES

1. For example, Bouchareb said that after completing *Indigènes/Days of Glory*, he was motivated to make *London River* because unlike the former, it was a project that allowed for flexibility and freedom. "Interview avec Rachid Bouchareb," *dossier de presse, London River*, accessed 18 March 2020, http://3b-productions.com/wp-content/uploads/2015/11/Dossier-Presse-18-juin-2009.pdf.
2. "*Cinéma-monde:* Film, Borders, Translation," unpublished conference rationale, University of Stirling, Scotland, 2017, quoting Édouard Glissant, *Introduction à une poétique du divers* (Paris: Gallimard, 1996). The term "francophone cinema" is not entirely apt here and is problematic when considered as a conceptual category, as Marshall underscores in "*Cinéma-monde?* Towards a Concept of Francophone Cinema," *Francosphères* 1, no. 1 (2012): 35–51.
3. Yves Alion, "Entretien avec Rachid Bouchareb," *Avant-scène cinéma* 564 (2007): 3.

4. "Entretien avec Rachid Bouchareb," *dossier de presse*, *Indigènes*, accessed 18 March 2020, http://3b-productions.com/wp-content/uploads/2015/11/INDIGE%CC%80NES_DP-planches.pdf.
5. As is highlighted throughout this chapter, Bouchareb has used a variety of words and expressions more or less interchangeably to express the idea of belonging to more than one culture. This includes *mixité culturelle* (cultural mixing), *coloration culturelle* (cultural makeup), *métissage culturel* (a cultural melting pot or cultural mixing) and *brassage des races et des cultures* (intermixing of races and cultures).
6. "Quand je suis arrivé au cinéma [dans les années 1970], les premières choses dont j'ai eu envie c'était de raconter un peu mon vécu et un peu ma coloration culturelle . . . et le vécu, si tu veux, de l'immigration en France à travers mes parents, ce que j'ai vécu moi, et puis mes origines algériennes quand même." *Rencontres*, episode "Cinéma et immigration," aired 26 January 1991, on France 3.
7. He goes on to explain that he did this despite the fact that it was a challenge to make a film in the French cinema industry in which the protagonist's name was Ali or Mohamed, and he had to overcome financial difficulties to do so. "Entretien avec Rachid Bouchareb," *dossier de presse*, *Poussières de vie*, accessed 17 March 2020, http://www.3b-productions.com/tessalit/films/poussieres_vie/entretien.html.
8. "parce que l'Algérie à l'époque était française, et je me suis senti proche à ces enfants qui se retrouvaient comme ça . . . Ils ont été complètement abandonnés par l'armée américaine à Saigon . . . Ça rejoignait mes préoccupations. Je ne suis pas du même peuple que ces enfants-là, mais dans cette mixité culturelle." *JA2 Dernière*, aired 18 January 1995, on France 2.
9. Alec G. Hargreaves, "From 'Ghettoes' to Globalization: Situating Maghrebi-French Filmmakers," in *Screening Integration: Recasting Maghrebi Immigration in Contemporary France*, ed. Sylvie Durmelat and Vinay Swamy (Lincoln: University of Nebraska Press, 2011), 35.
10. Duyên Anh, *La Colline de Fanta*, trans. Pierre Tran Van Nghiêm and Ghislain Ripault (Paris: P. Belfond, 1989).
11. Ange-Dominique Bouzet, "Rachid Bouchareb. 'Recouper les difficultés du métissage culturel.' *Poussières de vie*," *Libération*, 19 January 1995, https://next.liberation.fr/culture/1995/01/19/rachid-bouchareb-recouper-les-difficultes-du-metissage-culturelpoussiere-de-vie_119377
12. See, for example, his interview in the *dossier de presse* of *Days of Glory*.
13. "rien à prouver, seulement cette envie. Je suis né en France, je vis en France, j'avais envie d'avoir plus d'éléments, un peu pour me comprendre moi-même, comprendre mon présent dans la société française, mon futur, et donc je me suis intéressé à ce chapitre de l'histoire de France." *19/20: Édition nationale*, aired 25 May 2006, on France 3.
14. Alion, "Entretien avec Rachid Bouchareb," 3.
15. Ibid., 4.
16. The film ends on a positive note, however, with regard to employment. As Carrie Tarr has observed, "they form a collective to set up a burger bar, together with the people from the queue outside the Employment Agency . . . It is authenticated by a final credit which reminds the audience that the 'California Burg' in Argenteuil was set up in 1981." *Reframing Difference:* Beur *and* Banlieue *Filmmaking in France* (Manchester: Manchester University Press, 2005), 35–6.
17. Within the same context also grew the 1983 March for Equality and against Racism, a march across France in which many (though not exclusively) Maghrebi-French youth participated. Colloquially, it came to be known as "*La Marche des beurs*."
18. *La double peine* refers to the double punishment that residents of France who do not have French nationality can suffer after committing a crime: first, a prison sentence, and second, deportation.

19. "Entretien avec Rachid Bouchareb," 28 January 1991, *dossier de presse, Cheb*. It should be noted that Bouchareb was speaking in hypothetical terms. He was born in France, and given his French citizenship, he could not actually have been deported.
20. "Ce ne sont pas les leçons qu'on retient." *JA2 Dernière*, aired 18 January 1995, on France 2.
21. "Interview avec Rachid Bouchareb," *dossier de presse, London River*.
22. Irène Berelowitch, "La Guerre en arrière plan," *dossier de presse, La Route d'Istanbul*, accessed 18 March 2020, http://download.pro.arte.tv/uploads/La-route-distanbul-ARTE-Fiction.pdf.
23. "Entretien avec Rachid Bouchareb," *dossier de presse, Indigènes*.
24. "Interview avec Rachid Bouchareb," *dossier de presse, London River*.
25. Michael Gott and Thibaut Schilt, "Introduction: The Kaleidoscope of Cinéma-Monde," in *Cinéma-Monde: Decentred Perspectives on Global Filmmaking in French*, ed. Michael Gott and Thibaut Schilt (Edinburgh: Edinburgh University Press, 2018), 10, quoting David Damrosch, *What is World Literature?* (Princeton: Princeton University Press, 2003); Mette Hjort, "On the Plurality of Cinematic Transnationalism," in *World Cinemas, Transnational Perspectives*, ed. Nataša Ďurovičová and Kathleen Newman (New York: Routledge, 2010), 12–33.
26. "Édouard Glissant définit la 'créolisation,'" video interview, 2002, www.edouardglissant.fr/creolisation.html.
27. "Dans *Bâton Rouge* . . . un Français d'origine maghrébine faisait un road movie de New-York à la Floride, en passant par la Louisiane. Cela m'a donné l'occasion de côtoyer la communauté afro-américaine, de me faire des amis africains. A un moment, j'ai eu envie de faire se rencontrer ces deux communautés. J'étais curieux de les mettre en contact physiquement." "Entretien avec Rachid Bouchareb," 3B Productions, accessed 23 January 2015. The production company's website has undergone a redesign since I accessed this interview, and unfortunately it is no longer available. The original link was http://www.3b-productions.com/fr/films/little_senegal/entretienrachid.html.
28. "Festival 24: master class de Rachid Bouchareb," UnivJeanMoulin Lyon3/YouTube, 12 March 2019, https://www.youtu.be/x5KjTAAmll4.
29. "Avec mon co-scénariste Olivier Lorelle, nous avons fait plusieurs voyages à la rencontre de ces deux communautés pour les interviewer et avoir leurs réactions sur leur cohabitation." "Note d'intention du réalisateur," 3B Productions, accessed 23 January 2015. The production company's website has undergone a redesign since I accessed this interview, and unfortunately it is no longer available. The original link was http://www.3b-productions.com/fr/films/little_senegal/noteintention/html.
30. Noël Tinazzi, "Africains et Afro-Américains, un mauvais feeling," *La Tribune*, 18 April 2001, 1.
31. "Après mes nombreux voyages aux États-Unis et en Afrique, j'avais envie de provoquer cette rencontre au cinéma, et je me suis dit, c'est évident que les retrouvailles vont être formidables. Et puis après des longs mois de recherches et d'enquêtes et puis d'interviews de la communauté afro-américaine et de la communauté africaine, c'est pas du tout ça. C'est plutôt une relation conflictuelle et très difficile. Et les relations . . . et la cohabitation ne fonctionnent pas bien." *Des Mots de minuit*, aired 11 April 2001, on France 2.
32. "J'étais parti de l'idée qu'Alloune réunissait ces deux communautés pour apporter un message d'espoir et dire que les retrouvailles sont possibles. Il est évident que la réalité est bien plus complexe." "Note d'intention du réalisateur," 3B Productions.
33. Gott and Schilt, "Introduction," 10, citing Elizabeth Ezra and Terry Rowdon, "General Introduction: What Is Transnational Cinema?" in *Transnational Cinema: The Film Reader*, ed. Elizabeth Ezra and Terry Rowdon (Abingdon: Routledge, 2006), 1–12; Hjort, "Cinematic Transnationalism."

34. "Ce qui nous a étonné, c'est de découvrir le racisme et la violence des propos entre ces deux 'cousins.' On aurait pu penser que la rencontre serait harmonieuse et naturelle du fait de leur racine commune, l'Afrique." "Note d'intention du réalisateur," 3B Productions.
35. Delphine Letort, "Rethinking the Diaspora through the Legacy of Slavery in Rachid Bouchareb's *Little Senegal*," *Black Camera* 6, no. 1 (2014): 143.
36. "Entretien avec Rachid Bouchareb," 3B Productions. It is worth mentioning that the mosque in *London River* is portrayed very differently, as a multilingual and multicultural space.
37. "A Harlem, il y a une mosquée afro-américaine depuis des années. On aurait effectivement pu penser que la religion allait être un ciment possible. Mais la communauté africaine a préféré créer ses propres mosquées. Il n'y a donc pas vraiment de relations sereines, de liens directes. La communauté africaine s'est fait son Chinatown africain au cœur d'Harlem, son 'Little Senegal.'" Ibid.
38. "Tous les dialogues qui sont dans le film m'ont été donnés par les deux communautés, afro-américaines et africaines. Je n'ai rien inventé." *Des Mots de minuit*.
39. "Entretien avec Rachid Bouchareb," 3B Productions.
40. This technique is not limited to *Little Senegal* or even to the pre-production phase. As a 1985 article in *Le Matin* reveals, the impact of on-the-ground encounters dates back to Bouchareb's first feature, *Baton Rouge*: "To capture the discord between imagination and reality, Rachid drew on the reactions of the film crew who, in the vast majority of cases, didn't know America. Over the course of filming, dialogue and situations changed as a result of these meetings and the connections that were forged between the actors and Louisiana residents. In some scenes, local farmers and cops make brief appearances." Frédéric Dupré, "Le cinéma d'un melting-pote," *Le Matin*, 11 December 1985.
41. "Certains acteurs ont . . . refusé de jouer dans le film parce qu'ils le trouvaient trop violent, trop raciste, donnant une image trop négative de la confrontation des deux communautés noires: on est 'entre Blacks,' alors que le lieu commun voudrait que ce soit des Noirs victimes du racisme des Blancs." "Entretien avec Rachid Bouchareb," 3B Productions.
42. "Entretien avec Rachid Bouchareb," *dossier de presse*, *Indigènes*.
43. Éric Libiot, "Rachid Bouchareb: '*Hors-la-loi* est un film sur l'injustice,'" *L'Express*, 23 September 2010.
44. "Interview avec Rachid Bouchareb," *dossier de presse*, *London River*.
45. Ibid.
46. "Entretien avec Rachid Bouchareb," *dossier de presse*, *La Voie de l'ennemi*, accessed 17 March 2020, http://www.3b-productions.com/tessalit/lavoiedelennemi/download/la-voie-de-l-ennemi-dp.pdf.

CHAPTER 2

The Road from *Baton Rouge*: Mapping Rachid Bouchareb's Transnational Mobile Movies

Michael Gott

Rachid Bouchareb's work has typically been approached by scholars and critics through the optic of French identity debates and the place of colonial and post-colonial subjects who find themselves on the margins of French society.[1] Due to his Algerian background and occasional cinematic interest in and connection to Algeria, Bouchareb's filmography is often assessed by scholars through the prism of a "double culture."[2] When he speaks to the press about his films, the topic often turns to questions of integration, even when it is not immediately present in the narrative in question.[3] While he did emerge on the scene in the era of French "*beur*" cinema in the 1980s and gained fame and a much wider audience for historical genre films about key moments in French history in the 2000s, Bouchareb's corpus is particularly remarkable for the way that it transcends and complicates national boundaries and typical *métropole*-colony binaries. By extension, it also functions beyond or altogether outside of the well-trodden parameters of French and French post-colonial identity debates. This chapter considers how one current of Bouchareb's oeuvre travels through the world, charting new maps and relationships within, and also beyond, what might be considered the francosphere.[4] Although he is a French filmmaker by most definitions of the term, in a significant number of his films, France is not central and is not—or scarcely—seen or evoked. And although his work does frequently address issues of Maghrebi-French belonging in France and often connects to Algeria in narrative and production senses, the idea of double affiliation fails to capture the complexity of Bouchareb's trajectory and the variety of his work. Bouchareb's oeuvre has regularly engaged with identity and difference, making him "the most cosmopolitan of Maghrebi-French directors."[5] His "kaleidoscopic" vantage point on the world and his films have long been aligned with what scholars have recently theorized as cinéma-monde, an approach and an ethic that involve floating across fluid margins and facilitating lateral encounters.[6]

In this chapter, I will sketch out a cartographic overview of Bouchareb's decentered world and his cinematic routes through it. I focus on *Bâton Rouge/Baton Rouge* (1985), his debut feature, but frame my analysis through a retrospective look at how the tropes, themes, ideas, and techniques featured in the film reappear in subsequent works. Starting with *Baton Rouge*, Bouchareb has demonstrated an affinity for road movies and has to date made four features that clearly fit into this cinematic category: *Baton Rouge*, *Just Like a Woman* (2012), *Poussières de vie/Dust of Life* (1995), and *La Route d'Istanbul/Road to Istanbul* (2016). In this chapter, I consider two of these—*Baton Rouge* and *Road to Istanbul*—and expand the frame of discussion to two others that involve and are fundamentally about movement and mobility but which are not, strictly speaking, road movies: *Little Senegal* (2001) and *London River* (2009). In this way, I aim to delineate a key strand of Bouchareb's oeuvre that has developed over the three decades following his debut feature by focusing specifically on how Bouchareb "maps" the world and the places and movements of people that he focuses on. The places shown and visited in these films are Belgium, Paris, the border between Turkey and Syria, London, New York (specifically Harlem), South Carolina, Louisiana and elsewhere in the American South, and Gorée Island, Senegal. What particularly interests me in the following discussion is how these places are linked and how the passage between them or among numerous locations is portrayed in narratives, in technical terms, and symbolically throughout Bouchareb's oeuvre. I will suggest that when examined together these films can be understood as what I will term transnational mobile movies, a category that is inclusive of but broader than road movies. The contemporary world's state of constant movement and its inherent potential for interconnectivity, intrinsic socioeconomic unevenness, and sense of unease are embedded into the very DNA of transnational mobile movies and evident in their narrative spaces and production contexts. In this sense, they exhibit the characteristics of transnational cinema as identified by Elizabeth Ezra and Terry Rowden:

> The global circulation of money, commodities, information and human beings is giving rise to films whose aesthetic and narrative dynamics, and even the modes of emotional identification they elicit, reflect the impact of advanced capitalism and new media technologies as components of an increasingly interconnected world system.[7]

By decentering narratives and situating the quests (in search of opportunities, enlightenment, or ancestors, or to escape imprisonment) outside of France, Bouchareb uses mobile movies to question a Francocentric outlook on belonging and citizenship and posits a transnational and mobile concept of identity that is potentially more pliable—if often fraught with difficulty and cast in the shadow of historical travails and suffering.

These four films share a common "mobile vision," as theorized by Dimitris Eleftheriotis, that is both a political stance and articulated through the technical approach to filming the movement of characters through space.[8] I offer a close reading of the ways in which Bouchareb has deployed travel as a narrative device and a trope in these films. In particular I will pay close attention to two aspects that are integral to road narratives. First is use of "traveling shots" (a tracking shot at hyperhuman speed, as David Laderman theorizes it),[9] a technique Bouchareb deploys to shift the parameters of his filmmaking and to look aslant at binary identity formulations and view the world in a complex, kaleidoscopic fashion. If not all of these films can be interpreted as road movies *per se*, the shared focus on and interest in the process of movement and the infrastructures of mobility links these films and blurs the boundaries of what is commonly theorized as road cinema. The second ubiquitous element of road cinema that all of Bouchareb's transnational mobile movies engage with are borders. Borders, whether physical-geographical or symbolic, are particularly central to contemporary European road cinema. In her study of diasporic films, Daniela Berghahn perceptively notes the link between European road movies' critique of "hegemonic and territorialized conceptions of identity and belonging" and their "emphasis on borders and border crossings—political, cultural, social and linguistic" which draws "attention to the barriers that a territorialized understanding of nation and national belonging entails."[10] The idea of borders brings us back to the aforementioned notion of cinéma-monde, a concept that Bill Marshall argues directs critical attention to four elements: borders, movement, language, and lateral connections.[11] Each of these elements has an important function in the four films that I will discuss below. It should be emphasized that in Marshall's formulation and in the four films by Bouchareb, a border is not simply (or always) something to be crossed or a positive conduit that facilitates connections. At times protagonists confront borders (linguistic, cultural, geographic) as barriers that, while not entirely impermeable, are nonetheless obstacles. I start with a discussion of the spatio-cultural context of *Baton Rouge*, followed by an analysis of how this road movie depicts traveling shots and the spaces of travel and how its travelers grapple with borders. I will then explore how these crucial elements reappear in the three later films.

BATON ROUGE: MOBILE PERSPECTIVES AND TRAVELING SHOTS

The social and cultural context of the spatial dynamics of *Baton Rouge* is an essential starting point to the discussion of mobility in Bouchareb's oeuvre. Bouchareb made his cinematic debut at a time when the nascent Maghrebi-French filmmaking scene ("*beur*" cinema, as it was generally known then) was inextricably associated not only with identity issues but also particularly, and often problematically, with specific spaces. "*Beur*" filmmakers and their work were generally inextricably associated with the *banlieue* category of films (whether made by Maghrebi-French or other filmmakers) that portrayed life in the suburban outskirts of Paris that were home to many immigrants, or with often involuntary "return" voyages to North Africa.[12] *Le Thé au harem d'Archimède/Tea in the Harem* (Mehdi Charef, 1985) and *Baton Rouge* were the feature films "that put what came to be known at the time as 'Beur cinema' on the collective radar" in the mid-1980s.[13] As Murray Levine argues, *Tea in the Harem*

> defined a space, a narrative form, and an aesthetic that has since become familiar, if not banal, to contemporary French audiences: a group of unemployed, disaffected youths circulate among the grim concrete high-rises of a low-income French housing estate, experiencing various kinds of misadventures but eventually going nowhere.[14]

The above description of Charef's film outlines the broader contours of what would crystallize in popular and critical imaginations as *cinéma de banlieue*. The immobility of *banlieue* protagonists is a crucial component. Perceived spatial isolation from the center of Paris is perhaps the single most important and ubiquitous element of the *banlieue* stereotype (cinematic or otherwise).[15] As James Austin contends, it is "'out there' that the cars burn, that the riots recur, that police stations, schools, and libraries are destroyed and degraded."[16] Likewise, the corpus of *banlieue* cinema "appears as immobile in nature as the state response to the *banlieues* themselves," often repeating and perpetuating representational stereotypes associated with the suburbs' spatial otherness.[17] Indeed the *banlieue* film would seem inevitably constrained in its spatial possibilities. As Will Higbee observes, *banlieue* cinema is the first category of film since the Western to be primarily defined by its geographical location.[18] Likewise within this context, Bouchareb's intent to complicate—but certainly not avoid—these associations of Maghrebi-French identity with specific spaces is particularly striking. Bouchareb's first feature opens and closes in a *banlieue*, but it nonetheless exhibits a clear contrast with Charef's film. For one thing, the suburbs are represented differently, with the protagonists' unnamed *cité* (housing project) presented in what Higbee labels a more "stylized" fashion[19] that entirely avoids many of the typical representational clichés that would come to predominate in films set in the disadvantaged suburbs of Paris: drugs, racist and violent police, rap music, and graffiti-covered concrete expanses.[20] Bouchareb has affirmed that he wanted to avoid highlighting the well-known and documented drudgery of life in the suburbs and focus on moments of fun and friendship.[21] Even more importantly for my argument, the protagonists in *Baton Rouge* diverge from what would become the early "*beur*" and *banlieue* templates in their interest in—and success at reaching—other horizons. To adapt Austin's assessment of the *banlieue* as immobile, *Baton Rouge* is uncompromisingly mobile in its outlook.

Baton Rouge recounts the story of three young Frenchmen—the blond-haired Mozart (Jacques Penot) and the Maghrebi-French Abdenour (Pierre-Loup Rajot) and Karim (Hammou Graïa)—who are each dissatisfied with their lives in the (unnamed) suburbs of Paris for different reasons. They also share a common desire to escape the cycle of dead-end temporary jobs, symbolized by recurring scenes of the trio lining up outside an employment office. One temporary posting on a plane-cleaning crew at Orly inspires a far-fetched scheme to stow away in a USA-bound flight. That plan does not get off the ground, but they benefit from an almost equally improbable happenstance that makes their Atlantic crossing possible. While working as cleaners for a multinational enterprise, Mozart answers a phone call from a travel agent requesting clarification of some the details of a requested ticket purchase. Mozart plays along, pretending to have the role of a decision maker at the organization, and addresses the requests. Just as he is about to hang up, he is inspired to request three tickets to New York for him and his two friends. They pick them up the next day, pretending to be the association's courier, and soon are flying away on an American Airlines plane like those that they once prepped for others to depart in. The results of the ensuing voyage are decidedly mixed. On the positive side, Mozart falls in love with an African American jazz singer, the group discovers an affinity for black musical culture and enjoys the hospitality of a bus packed with cheerful gospel singers, and despite their financial limitations they even manage to purchase a used car and achieve their intended destination of Baton Rouge, Louisiana. However, in order to fund their onward progress, they are compelled to find a series of jobs that are just as menial, unpleasant, and sometimes unhealthy as those that they fled in France, if at times more exotic (for instance, when they work on an alligator farm).

The narrative and aesthetics of *Baton Rouge* clearly align it within the typical road movie template. As Jason Wood posits: "In archetypal terms, road movies commonly entail the undertaking of a journey by one or more protagonists as they seek out adventures, redemption or escape from the constricting norms of society and its laws."[22] When Bouchareb made the film, the cinematic road was still primarily the purview of men.[23] Male road protagonists were often on the road to escape the perceived constraints of domestic space associated with females or perhaps to meet, seduce, and (frequently) ultimately cast aside women encountered en route.[24] Focused on three male protagonists, *Baton Rouge*, as Carrie Tarr argues, "fails to find a place for the representation of *beur* women."[25] It also conforms loosely to the masculine road movie model, given that one of the primary motivations behind the trip to the United States was Abdenour's plan to visit a young tourist from the

American South whom he met in Paris. The voyage also becomes a quest for romance on the part of Mozart, who meets touring singer Victoria Paine after being drawn to the sounds of her voice singing Billie Holiday while he is out on a drive. Road narratives are frequently propelled by "road events," seemingly unexpected happenings that slow down and/or change the course of the journey,[26] and Mozart and Victoria's relationship is rendered possible by two fortuitous occurrences of his car breaking down.

Yet if Mozart's encounter is significant and symbolic for a number of reasons, including the fact that he decides to move to join Victoria in New York rather than return to France, the primary motivation for the voyage to Baton Rouge is to escape from the constricting norms of society and the related desire for exploration of spaces and places that have fueled their imagination (aided by the lyrics of a song by the Rolling Stones). The trio envisions America as an alternative to the limitations they face in France.[27] Befitting the film's status as a European production traveling to and through—and inspired by—America, the quest by the protagonists represents a hybrid of what are commonly theorized as the American and European road models. American protagonists "tend to be outcasts and rebels looking for freedom or escape" whereas European voyagers are more commonly "ordinary citizens."[28] While the three friends are not outlaws, they do seek to evade certain dominant and restrictive conceptions of culture and life in France, namely the spatial relegation to the suburbs that is central to many so-called *banlieue* or "*beur*" films. However, they only find temporary escape and limited freedom on the road. As is often the case in this film category, "the road leads to an exploration of the travellers' own sense of otherness," and *Baton Rouge* is no exception.[29] In other words, many of the same problems, restrictions, and social hurdles are reproduced on the road, from the ruthless neoliberal system that compels individuals to queue up for often exploitative employment (a visual and thematic echo with the earlier scenes in France) to the constant surveillance and policing of bodies. During their first stop on the driving portion of their itinerary, the trio witnesses an employee (presumably an undocumented immigrant) being led out of a restaurant in handcuffs to a waiting police car, a quick reminder of the flip side of the American dream that inspired their voyage.

This vignette of life for the underclass in America also foretells the fate of Abdenour and Karim, the film's two Maghrebi-French protagonists. They are arrested—also at a fast food restaurant—and deported after they are caught violating their tourist visas by working to fund their ongoing travels. Their return to France is therefore not of their own volition. Yet their desire to rebel against their place in French society is countered by the eventual choice to stay in the *cité* after their return to launch a business. As Will Higbee has argued, the ending "unambiguously" links the two Maghrebi-French youths' "future with France and, more specifically, the *banlieue*."[30] With the benefit of a wider view of Bouchareb's filmography, this interpretation might be reconsidered, given the irrevocable trajectory in his career away from the suburbs. Or, perhaps the idea of what France and the *banlieue* signify should be seen as fundamentally mobile/flexible and open to other spaces. The cooperative that is created by the duo to finance their project is made possible by a diasporic link engendered in travel—the choice of Mozart and Victoria to join the group as well, after a conversation via phone from New York. This network that links places and people—in solidarity in this case—would become a constant feature of Bouchareb's future films. Moreover, the fact that their undertaking is an American-style fast food restaurant suggests that they have drawn from their experience traveling and come back with new outlooks and ideas in addition to new points of contact, resulting in a more positive twist than one would have expected following the deportation back to France. Karim and Abdenour end up where they started, but they return with a more mobile perspective and a better understanding of their place in the world. Perhaps fittingly, the film closes with a twist on the classic road movie ending of travelers back on the road again, driving into the sunset. A freeze frame captures the two protagonists and their new business partners walking through what appears to be an underground transit passageway toward their new undertaking. They are all in motion, a group movement symbolizing collective action, and moving toward the camera, suggesting that they are staying in France rather than moving immediately toward new horizons.

FROM TRAVELING SHOTS TO TRANSFER POINTS AND "MOBILE VISION"

Having sketched out the spatial dynamics and the plot trajectory, I now turn to an analysis of how mobility is depicted in the film and of the types of borders that appear in the narrative. As argued above, *Baton Rouge* conforms to many of the typical elements of the road movie template. Arguably, the most crucial and ultimately defining manifestation of this is the traveling shot.[31] Such traveling shots have been theorized by David Laderman as a tracking shot intended to convey "a visceral sense of traveling at a hyper-human, modernized speed."[32] Laderman primarily has automobile travel in mind, but as I have argued elsewhere, the common preference in European road movies for slower modes of conveyance such as walking or public transit demands a broader conception of the traveling shot as a tracking shot that captures at any speed either the spirit or the disorientation involved in movement by foot, by bicycle, in trains and public transport, and by boat.[33] Although *Baton Rouge* does not stray far from Laderman's modernized/motorized conception, the more flexible categorization of traveling shots will be essential to my readings of subsequent examples.

THE ROAD FROM *BATON ROUGE* 47

Traveling shots serve two distinctive functions in *Baton Rouge*. The first category includes a number of sequences that use traveling shots and montages to express the exhilaration involved in discovering and traversing new landscapes. In an early moment of excitement generated by their travel, Karim exclaims that he wishes his father (who criticized his choice to quit what the younger man saw as a dead-end job in a factory bakery where the older man also worked) could see him as the group revels in the perceived freedom of racing through the Southern countryside on a freight train, enjoying the view from an open door. Later, the friends enjoy a festive ride on board the New Orleans-bound bus of a touring gospel group. The French travelers eagerly join the black Americans in a song before being dropped off near a highway sign indicating the exit for Baton Rouge.

Finally, the trio celebrates the acquisition of a car and the ready mobility it offers by driving outside the lines: they speed down a highway bound for Baton Rouge in the center of the road, ignoring the prescribed lanes and the constraints they represent. They had spent a period of time working under difficult conditions at an alligator farm to raise the funds for this vehicle, having realized that "without a car you are nothing here," and this aerial shot of the automobile visually represents their excitement and (temporary) sense of liberty. Working in a similar vein, another important traveling shot involves the moment that the trio first see their destination. While crossing a bridge,

Figure 2.1 The French travelers enjoy a moment of solidarity and song on the road aboard a touring gospel choir's bus

they catch a tantalizing glimpse of the skyline of Louisiana's capital city. Tellingly, the enthusiasm generated by this vista is short-lived. The presence of an oncoming truck in the exit lane compels them to abandon their attempt to get off the highway to visit the downtown. This will be the only time viewers witness them viewing the center of Baton Rouge. A highway bridge fits squarely in the category of what mobility theorist John Urry has termed "transfer points" and "places of in-between-ness"[34] and the symbolism of it as the site of their glimpse of the city will become clear over the following pages.

Instead of visiting the heart of the destination that bears the name of the film, the protagonists veer toward a roadside motel on a stretch of road replete with similarly dingy and dreary locales, including the fast food restaurant where they will find work and ultimately be discovered by immigration enforcement agents. Abdenour, Karim, and Mozart will spend the remainder of their time in the outskirts of Baton Rouge amid the dreary vestiges of American consumer society: oil refineries, gas stations, strip malls, roadside restaurants, and bars. This backdrop of roadside iconography and infrastructure of mobility is equally as endemic to road cinema as the exhilarating landscape shots described above,[35] and the traveling shots of these spaces serve an equally important purpose.

It is tempting to describe this setting as what Marc Augé theorizes as a "non-place," transient infrastructure built to facilitate movement, drive-through meals, and short stays by people on the road.[36] However, what at first glance seems like a mere transfer point is a place where people, often

Figure 2.2 The dreary roadside on the outskirts of Baton Rouge

minorities, work (those in the restaurant with the trio and a friendly African American housekeeper in the hotel) and socialize. It is on a drive through this space that Mozart hears Victoria Paine rehearsing a song by Billie Holiday inside an empty bar. He is asked to leave because the bar is not yet open, but when he returns for her performance we see that the bar is frequented by an almost exclusively black clientele. This roadside locale is a nod to the American road genre—the roadhouse bar is a seemingly requisite stopover in so many road movies—but also marked by its African American clientele as a place outside of the social mainstream in the American South. These factors mark it as a specific type of border on the outskirts of town: a possible contact zone for those willing and interested enough to stop. Victoria is not a local; she lives in New York and is on tour in the South, making the bar a meeting point for different travelers and also for local outsiders and traveling outsiders such as the French trio. Mozart will drive to see Victoria perform again, and his trip is constructed of a montage of roadside images that focus on neon lights (liquor stores, the Florida Girl Motel) that render the drab landscape at least momentarily more picturesque. This date is to be in Florida, across a boundary that is only significant because it marks a time change that causes him to miss their meeting. In the road cinema, however, the road gives (in the form of a "road event") as much as it takes away, and the following day the romance will continue after Victoria's bus, headed toward New York, fortuitously passes by Mozart as he checks on his broken-down automobile, which is parked on the roadside, spewing steam.

So far, I have discussed how *Baton Rouge* generally conforms to the classic road movie template. Now I will turn my attention to a discussion of why Bouchareb opted for this model for his first film. Put slightly differently, I will consider how he works with the road template and then transition into a broader discussion of how the key themes of *Baton Rouge* fit into his wider oeuvre. On one level, *Baton Rouge* reflects Bouchareb's interest in American genre cinema, something that continues to inform his work. And as I suggested, taking the narrative of three young *banlieue* residents onto the road toward Louisiana allowed the director to escape some of the typical parameters of French identity debates while remaining within an (albeit more distant) French colonial context. The road facilitates one ultimately transformative encounter, between Mozart and Victoria, but the trio does not seem to experience the transformative effects of travel or find the sort of enlightenment that one might expect from road cinema. This is reflected in the selection of generally uninspiring traveling shots discussed above (with the exception of a handful of fleeting moments of sensory enjoyment). The travelers are not immersed in nor awed by the spaces they traverse, a common result of road movie treks. Yet the outlook of the film is not, ultimately, gloomy and the protagonists are not solely defined by their outsider status.

A useful framework for thinking about how Bouchareb's voyagers experience space is the distinction that Dimitris Eleftheriotis makes between "panoramic perception" and "mobile vision."[37] "Panoramic perception" implies a certain privileged, or at least open and unobstructed, vantage point. Meanwhile, "the dizzying experiences of mobile vision challenge established and traditional certainties as they push travellers out of the stability of home and into unknown and uncertain territories." In both cases, the act of seeing while traveling plays a key role in the "knowledge acquisition" that often transpires in road narratives.[38] However, Bouchareb frames the opposition between purportedly stable home and "uncertain territories" in a rather complicated fashion. Arguably in road cinema, home is out of sight but never truly out of mind. Numerous critics have pointed out the essential function of home in road movies, where it serves as a basic point of comparison that travels and experiences are measured against. It has even been argued that "the trope of the road depends on home as a structuring absence."[39] The choice to devote a significant amount of time to Abdenour and Karim's post-return initiative signals that home has an important role in *Baton Rouge*. Moreover, the significance of home as a structuring idea is underscored by the fact that the characters barely see Baton Rouge, the intended destination. As mentioned, the distant glimpse they catch is from a highway overpass, one example of the recurring images of intermediate points in *Baton Rouge*. Examples include the overpass near Baton Rouge, exits on the highway, a bus station, numerous service stations and other roadside businesses serving travelers, and several airports. These include Orly, one serving New York, the unnamed Southern one where Abdenour and Karim are deported from, and another in that area that Mozart drives past after his friends have been deported that is perhaps the same.

These sites form a key aspect of "mobile vision" in the film. The sequence that narrates the two Maghrebi-French characters' deportation involves a series of images of movement that link Baton Rouge to their home, beginning with a drive back over the overpass from which they first saw the city from a distance. The sequence culminates with an ellipsis that frames them walking out of a passageway below a block of apartment buildings that immediately situates them back in their suburban Paris home after walking up the steps of the plane that is deporting them. This gesture might be interpreted in a variety of ways, starting with the irony of how quickly they were ushered back to France after investing so much time and effort to reach Louisiana in the first place. However, given the upbeat ending of the film, we might also read the rapid jumps between places and the constant in-between-ness in more positive terms. Randall Halle contends that while bridges are often viewed as non-spaces between two points, they also serve as "interzones," extranational zones of "contact and transfer" that involve complex interactions between highways, rivers, erstwhile bridges, border stops, mental maps, and visual media.[40] Virtually everything and everyone in *Baton Rouge* is part of an interzone. Notably, the cultures experienced by the trio are not fixed to a particular place. I have already mentioned the touring musician Victoria Paine. Another example is furnished by the traveling gospel choir, which they encounter on the road and which leaves them by the side of the highway near a sign indicating the road to Baton Rouge. The choir, although representative of one strand of regional culture (with roots in black spirituals, which by extension link it to the world), is not found in a place where we might expect, namely a church, but is encountered moving through space.

MOBILE MOVIES AND IMMOVEABLE BORDERS: ON THE BORDER OR CROSSING THE BORDER

In the opening pages of this chapter, I quoted Berghahn's observation on how road movies place an emphasis on "borders and border crossings" and in the process direct our attention to "the barriers that a territorialized understanding of nation and national belonging entails."[41] In *Baton Rouge*, as in Bouchareb's mobile movies in general, mobility serves to situate protagonists on the border or in relation to borders. Everyone is on a border in Bouchareb's cinema, a status that encompasses the positive and negative associations of borders. The complexity and protean nature of borders in the director's work call to mind theorist Manlio Graziano's assessment of borders as fundamentally "multidimensional and multifunctional" entities that simultaneously separate and bring together and whose political, social, legal, and psychological contours are constantly changing.[42] On the one hand, there is the borderland, a space (like interzones) of exchange. This is exemplified by the encounters with the gospel singers and Victoria Paine, both of which are representative of the positive revelatory experiences of leaving home and exploring new territories. On the other hand, the borderline is a site of exclusion exemplified in the passport check, a verification of someone's authorization to be in a particular place. Bouchareb's travelers have mobile outlooks, but borders in his films are sometimes immovable, whether physically or psychologically. The border as an immovable political, juridical, and mental construction is exemplified in *Baton Rouge* by passport checks and, more broadly, the recurring reference to police and policing of space. The French trio are never able to remain where they are or enjoy their state of being in motion. Every positive step or moment of enjoyment or revelation is countered by a reminder that their presence in American space is tenuous. The first scene in America is the border agent who scrutinizes the voyagers' French (Abdenour and Mozart) and Algerian (Karim) passports and warns them that they are not authorized to work. The next image of America is a police officer they encounter outside the airport as they celebrate their arrival, and one of their first experiences on the American road involves witnessing an employee of a fast food restaurant being arrested as they pause to eat. They are then chased by police after they hop off the train (presumably for riding in a freight car) and later detained by immigration agents who ask to see their passports at the bus station where they go to see Victoria off. These encounters are notable in a number of ways. For one, the official border is not only situated at a geographic boundary line, but can situationally appear in "transfer zones" such as the bus station. Moreover, the act of regulating the presence of "outsiders" in a given territory is not only the purview of the authorities. The act of kindness by the gospel choir (a ride on their bus) is followed by an encounter with an armed white farmer who exclaims that his barn is "no place for traveling" as he searches their bags, eminent symbols of mobility and travel. The farmer's suspicion toward outsiders and enforcement of sedentary norms suggests that Bouchareb views borders as complex social and cultural constructions as well as political or legal boundaries. They are mobile—that is, applicable in different places within territories and not just on their edges—and yet often psychologically immovable. As the subsequent analysis of traveling shots and borders in three later films demonstrates, Bouchareb is ultimately more interested in using cinematic mobility to place his characters in proximity to borders than to actually show how they experience the traversal of space.

THE ROADS FROM *BATON ROUGE*: ON THE MOBILE BORDER, FROM SENEGAL TO ISTANBUL

The uneasy imbrication of flexible, mobile outlooks on belonging that are conducive to border crossings and the inescapable specter of immovable borders provide a link between *Baton Rouge* and the other examples of what I classify as Bouchareb's transnational mobile movies. The protagonists and the overall outlooks of *Little Senegal*, *London River*, and *Road to Istanbul* are resolutely mobile, even though only the latter can clearly be categorized as a road movie. Considered together, these films suggest that Bouchareb views mobility and connectivity—whether physical or virtual—as an unavoidable norm in contemporary society.

Little Senegal follows the travels of Alloune, a Senegalese man who works as a historical guide on Gorée Island. The voyage narrative follows his quest in search of his ancestors who were victims of the slave trade, but it is not filmed like a road movie. There are very few traveling shots, and the movement between places is elliptical, more akin to the rapid cut from the Southern airport tarmac to the Parisian suburbs in *Baton Rouge* than to the road portions of that film. This can be interpreted through the fact that Bouchareb has opted to focus on movement that is forced rather than voluntary, and therefore the exhilaration of movement is far from Alloune's mind (see Chapter 9 for further discussion of this).[43] Alloune's search will take him to similar places—the American South (this time South Carolina) and then New York, where the American odyssey commences in Bouchareb's first film. Alloune is constantly shown walking, or sometimes riding on trains or buses, although his transatlantic voyage is not represented. Instead, the film cuts from Gorée's Door of No Return, the point of departure for slaves, to a pair of images of the Atlantic, and then to Alloune on a beach that is identified in an intertitle as Sullivan's Island, South Carolina.[44] Likewise, the travel from South Carolina to New York is not shown. We see Alloune walking down a small-town street before a cut takes us to an auto repair shop in New York. There, Hassan, Alloune's nephew, answers the phone and is surprised to learn that his relative is in Charleston. We next see Alloune on the MTA J train bound for Harlem. A brief series of shots on the train (similar to the scene in *Baton Rouge* after the trio arrives in New York) separated by a jump cut shows that all of the white passengers have disembarked before the train reaches Harlem.

Once again, Bouchareb has sketched out a scenario in which everyone is both mobile and at a border or occupying a border space. We see Alloune serving as a cultural-historical mediator in the opening scene, recounting the misery of slave voyages to a crowd of black American tourists. The sequence juxtaposes the image of an approaching boat seen through the island's infamous door, Alloune's office where he is researching his trip with a globe perched symbolically beside him, and a traveling image showing the tourists' vantage points on the water and Gorée as their ferry approaches. Beyond Alloune's voyage, the film's primary focus, points of transfer abound and mobility is depicted again as a fundamental reality. Hassan works as a cab driver to complement his job at the auto repair shop, and although we do not see a borderline or post in *Little Senegal*, citizenship and identity documents are central to a primary subplot of the film. Hassan's roommate Karim (played by Roschdy Zem, a French actor of Moroccan origin who has acted in six of Bouchareb's films) is in a complicated relationship with an African American woman named Amaralis, whom he planned to pay in exchange for a marriage that would allow him to obtain US citizenship. Amaralis thus makes possible Karim's official "border crossing" from one citizenship to another, a form of socioeconomic mobility. It is also significant that she is employed by the same taxi company that Hassan works at, where her job is to dispatch vehicles to all corners of the city.

Perhaps the most symbolically potent images of mobility are the ferries that open and close the film, the first delivering American tourists to Gorée and the second bringing Alloune away from the same place. As in *Baton Rouge*, the traveler returns to his starting point, but in this case he also retraces the "return" route of the tourists whose arrival at Gorée opens the film, and simultaneously connotes the initial departure by boat of slaves who were sent to the Americas from the island. It is notable that the same point-of-view traveling shot upon the approaching island is shown in the opening and the closing sequences. Alloune, unlike the tourists perched on the outside rails of the boat, demonstrates no interest in the spaces outside, instead sitting alone in the interior of the ferry, eyes forward fixed. This watery trajectory, beginning and ending at the Door of No Return, suggests that movement and circulation are inevitable. As Delphine Letort argues, the Atlantic "is no longer synonymous with rupture by the end of the film; it represents the link between the two continents . . . giving birth to the diasporic families that spread across the world."[45] The opening and closing images therefore situate the act of mobility, exemplified by the ferry as the initial and final stage of voyage and a metonymical reference to all other segments of the trip (if not a symbol of all mobility in general, present and past) on a borderland "link" between places, generations, and historical flows.

London River is another film that is fundamentally attuned to the mobile reality of contemporary life. Since the titular "river" never appears in the film, the title has been convincingly interpreted as the "flow" of people to and through the metropolis.[46] The film traces two voyages motivated by searches for people—and one aborted voyage—but is again not quite a road movie by most definitions of the term. This global coproduction assembles actors of various backgrounds, and an inherent transnationalism is recreated in the plot, which is in itself constructed around a narrative borderline that brings together two people from different places and with, at least initially, disparate outlooks.[47] Elisabeth (English actress Brenda Blethyn), a woman from Guernsey, and Ousmane (Malian actor Sotigui Kouyaté, who also played Alloune in *Little Senegal*) are linked by what eventually becomes the shared search for their respective children, both of whom are missing after the 7/7 London bombing attacks in 2005. The terrorist event is less the focus of the story than something that becomes a "catalyst for the exploration of cultural difference in London."[48] The quests of the parents, which will eventually merge into a shared endeavor, are as much about their attempts to make sense of a dynamic world that is no longer comprehensible to them.[49] Elisabeth will gradually get over one personally structuring ideational border, her initial suspicion caused by Ousmane's ethnic and religious difference, as it becomes clear that their children were in a relationship. Their initial encounter and gradual rapprochement is facilitated by their shared fluency in French, a linguistic connection that has been described as a "threshold" language.[50] That French is deterritorialized—neither character has French origins and they are conversing in that language in a space where it is not the official or primary language[51]—is another sign of Bouchareb's interest in reframing the borders that encompass identities and ideas about belonging.

Like *Little Senegal*, *London River* opens with a coastal vista and one is tempted to ask, particularly given the tragic event at the center of the narrative, if the water represents a borderline (limit) or a conduit. The question is answered after Elisabeth sets off by ferry from St. Peter Port, Guernsey, in search of her daughter. This particular island locale is a quintessential liminal space: geographically and culturally between the UK and France and with English and French as dual languages, Guernsey is spatially proximate to the Continent but not in the European Union, and is a Crown dependency but not in the United Kingdom.[52] It is therefore an apt starting point for a narrative that entails constant circulation and a steady diet of shots of the protagonists walking around or in transit. The camera tracks Elisabeth and/or Ousmane on the aforementioned ferry, on various buses, in a taxi, and, like in *Baton Rouge*, in a police car. The latter encompasses the longest single traveling shot in the film and is particularly poignant because the trip brings the two parents to the police station where they are informed that their children are dead. Other modes of transport and transfer have already brought the two characters together by this point. They unwittingly share a bus ride to a hospital where they are looking for their children amid the injured and, crucially, a pedestrian bridge from a rail station becomes the literal (as well as profoundly symbolic) link between the two characters. It is there that Ousmane identifies Elisabeth's daughter Jane from photos with his son. It then becomes part of the recurring route from his hotel to Jane's apartment, where Elisabeth is staying and where Ousmane is eventually invited to stay.[53] Mobility in *London River* is both the device that drives the search for the children forward and a highly charged symbol. After the parents learn that Jane and Ali (Ousmane's son) were spotted on the morning of the bombings with luggage (a symbol of travel and a recurring prop in *Baton Rouge*), they discover from a travel agent that the couple purchased tickets to travel to Paris on the Eurostar on the day of the bombing. Once again there is a certain circularity at play here; Jane, who is from an island between France and the UK, ends up dying on the way to take a train through the tunnel that was built to physically connect those two places. The multiple scenes showing Elisabeth and Ousmane on the bus are rendered retrospectively poignant when the truth is revealed: their children died when a bomb exploded on the bus they were taking to run an errand before catching their train. That the parents rely on the mode of transport that led their children to their death is another example of the ambivalence of and toward mobility in Bouchareb's mobile movies.

Unlike the previous two examples, the 2016 film *Road to Istanbul* fits more squarely in the road movie category. It tells the story of a single mother, Elisabeth (a name shared with the female protagonist of *London River*), who travels from her home in rural Belgium to Turkey in order to find her daughter, who converted to Islam and left to join a jihadi group in Syria. This framing once again demonstrates Bouchareb's interest in engaging with contemporary topics—it is his third film, along with *London River* and *Hors la loi/Outside the Law* (2010), to address terrorism in some way—from an atypical perspective. Belgium is certainly a conceivable starting point for youth who are lured to pursue jihad, but it is an interesting choice for a French director to not address it in relation to France. Furthermore, the bucolic setting counters the idea that radicalism is a particularly urban affliction. Likewise, the choice of a white European rather than one of Maghrebi origins challenges the stereotypical framing of social debates over the lure of terrorism for European youth.[54]

Elisabeth is shocked to learn that her teenage daughter, Élodie, has absconded to Cyprus with a young man named Kader and from there, the police believe, plans to travel to Turkey and then into Syria. She decides to go to Hatay, a Turkish province that borders Syria, to search for her. The now familiar images from the aforementioned films of walking through urban areas and transfer points (notably taxis and an airport in Turkey) also make appearances in *Road to Istanbul*. We also see numerous references to mobility. Elisabeth works as a nurse who makes house calls by automobile, and Kader's father owns a car repair garage, which Elisabeth visits while searching for her daughter. These seemingly insignificant references in fact perhaps signify a generational gap in which the parents enjoy economic and social mobility while the children have fallen out of the flow of society and the economy and reacted in an extreme fashion. However, unlike *Little Senegal* and *London River*, in *Road to Istanbul* the camera follows the protagonist along a significant portion of the road. Specifically, we see Elisabeth's quest to reach and cross the Syrian border from Hatay. This includes traveling shots of her walking along remote roads in the border region and a taxi ride with a driver who promises to take her across the border. This sequence elaborates multiple constructions of borders—cultural, political, ethical, and ideational—even before the actual geographic line is reached.

Figure 2.3 Soldiers inspect Elisabeth's passport at the closed border between Turkey and Syria in *Road to Istanbul*

Elisabeth is effectively turned away at the border twice, despite her protestations that her "papers are in order." After being dropped off by a taxi, she first walks toward a border crossing against the flow of refugees fleeing in the opposite direction. After she is refused passage at the border, Elisabeth walks slowly through a clearly distressed border landscape. Landscape plays a more prominent role in this film than any of those previously discussed. Elisabeth is framed amid fields and open roads captured in long and extreme long shots with a backdrop of mountains, passing military vehicles, and ramshackle residences. She sits among an anxious group of Syrians and others (including a woman from Tunisia) who are fixated on the border, waiting for loved ones on the other side. From their vantage point they witness explosions and gunfire in the distance, a stark reminder that this border does not just divide arbitrary political spaces but represents a barrier between war and peace, life and death. It goes without saying that her desire to cross in the opposite direction from the souls fleeing war stands out as unusual. The woman from Tunisia, however, takes sympathy with her plight and asks someone to connect Elisabeth with a taxi driver who does border crossings. This traveling sequence toward a different border crossing is accompanied by music that the driver sings along to in Arabic. When Elisabeth enquires about the meaning of the mournful-sounding tune, the driver recites some words in Arabic and answers that it is about "love" but suggests that she would not understand. Elisabeth is on the other side of at least one border (linguistic, emotional) that obscures the meaning of the song. This border does not correspond precisely to the geographic boundary line with Syria, although the implication is that one must be an Arabic speaker, and perhaps a Syrian exile, to truly understand the sad song. This time Elisabeth's quest will fall short of the physical borderline when the taxi is stopped at a pre-border military checkpoint. Although the context is very different, this recalls the reality on display in *Baton Rouge* that borders are not only at the frontier, but also effectively occur wherever the passage and identities of people are policed. Elisabeth is misclassified as a "tourist" and despite her protestations that her "papers are in order," she is detained by the police and brought back to the city where she started in an extended traveling sequence that echoes the police car drives in *Baton Rouge* and *London River*. Whether to offer admission to Europe to millions of refugees from Syria in particular, and migrants in general, who do not hold the requisite documentation to cross borders into (western) Europe has been the topic of a raging debate since 2015. More than simply an ironic reversal of fortunes experienced by someone carrying a European Union passport, which provides access to a vast number of territories in the world without a visa, this episode reinforces the idea that borders cannot simply be declined to physical or political boundary lines. In a number of ways, Elisabeth finds herself on the other side of the border, a reversal of roles for a European citizen.

The stark imagery and reality of the Turkey–Syria border is not the only geographic border engaged with in the film. Earlier in the film Elisabeth learned that Élodie was in Cyprus when she saw a photo sent to a friend via SMS of her daughter and Kader on the beach. Elisabeth presumed that their voyage was just an impromptu beach holiday until the police informed her that her daughter purchased two tickets from Cyprus to Istanbul and then to Hatay. Cyprus is symbolically similar to Guernsey in *London River*, although its liminality is markedly more fractious. The island is geographically proximate to the Middle East but is a member of the EU (since 2004). Like Guernsey, it is officially bilingual (Greek and Turkish) but is also partitioned between Greek and Turkish sectors. In other words, then, it is a borderline between Europe and Asia. As an EU member in close proximity to the Middle East, Cyprus has also been an epicenter of the refugee crisis and since 2015 has been processing record numbers of asylum claims. The seemingly playful images of the young couple as tourists before they become jihadis, on the beach, the site of countless poignant images of refugee and migrant travails, strangely belie the seriousness of their undertaking. They also underscore the contrast inherent in Elisabeth's border encounter between those desperately headed toward Europe and the much smaller flows in the opposite direction. If mobility is ultimately rewarding or fruitful—if certainly not entirely positive—in the previous three films discussed here, *Road to Istanbul* poses some serious questions about what ends mobility—generally perceived as a positive attribute—serves for Europeans. The narrative concludes in Istanbul, where Elisabeth is sent on a flight by the police in Hatay to meet Élodie, who is recovering from grave injuries suffered from a missile explosion that occurred while she was crossing into Syria. If the tenor is more pessimistic than the previous films, the centrality of borders remains a constant. In contrast with all three previous films, the geographic trajectory is not circular, and unlike in *Baton Rouge*, where the city named in the title is never seen in close-up, here we do briefly see central Istanbul in a series of establishing shots of famous sights (including several iconic mosques). This brief focus on the geographic and symbolic point where Europe and Asia meet (and often clash), when juxtaposed with the tranquil opening scene in rural Belgium, suggests that borders are both abundant and omnipresent in contemporary Europe.

CONCLUSION: MAPPING BOUCHAREB'S TRANSNATIONAL MOBILE MOVIES

Each of Bouchareb's mobile movies includes at least one map, a subtle prop that provides some insight into the director's ideas about "where we come from and where we may be going," as Tom Conley describes the symbolism of cartography in cinema.[55] In *Baton Rouge*, there is a map of the United States on the wall of Abdenour's apartment, a vast map of the world dominates the background at the organization where the trio chances upon the free tickets to New York, and a roadmap is a constant prop that accompanies the travelers in America. In *Little Senegal*, a globe shares the frame with Alloune as he researches his family history and travel itinerary. In *London River*, a map of the world figures prominently on the wall in the apartment that Jane and Ali shared just as their parents (who are seated in the foreground with the map behind them) come to understand that their children lived together. In *Road to Istanbul*, a map of Europe is prominently displayed on the wall of a classroom where Elisabeth attends a support class for relatives of youth who have departed to join jihadi groups. Each of these maps suggests interrogations over either individual or collective identities and, when connected together across Bouchareb's work, indicate that the director sees his various stories and protagonists as linked by space, culture, spirit, and the past, notably colonialism and slavery.

What does a map of Bouchareb's mobile movies look like? What kind of maps of the world does Bouchareb's work chart out? We could begin by looking at the titles of the four mobile films. Baton Rouge is a city that is hardly seen and that is certainly not essential to the plot but connotes French colonial history. The London "River" is not the iconic Thames, which we never see, but a metaphorical river. Little Senegal is an actual neighborhood in Harlem, populated by migrants from former French colonies and other nations in West Africa. It is not explored in depth as a diasporic space in the film and the

Figure 2.4 A large world map looms in the background at the moment when the trio from *Baton Rouge* finds a way to get to the United States

"Little" appellation that has been attached to numerous other ethnic enclaves instead seems to connote a tradition of flows of immigrants to New York in the fashion that *London River* would later evoke multiculturalism in London. The road to, or from, Istanbul in the final film refers to a city that was not anyone's intended destination, but which is the site of the last scenes of the film and a series of images that highlight the geographic in-between-ness of the city. These examples encapsulate the complexity of Bouchareb's vision of places, and the identities associated with them. Everything is mobile, askew, and names or titles do not precisely correspond to static notions of place. Borders abound, and Bouchareb's protagonists are constantly confronting or confronted by them—whether to cross or to not cross—and reside in often, but not always, uneasy proximity to others.

Travel in these films, by extension, does not involve an attempt to immerse the characters or the spectators in interconnected spaces, the "panoramic perception" discussed above. Bouchareb does not deploy the road movie template to highlight the continuity between places, as in two notable French-language road movies that address issues of identity, Tony Gatlif's 2004 *Exils/Exiles* and Ismaël Ferroukhi's 2004 *Le Grand Voyage/The Grand Voyage*. Those films trace voyages between France and Algeria and France and Mecca, respectively, by focusing attentively on the intermediary spaces and the gradual transformations of the protagonists as they cross those spaces—Andalusia in one case and the Balkans, including Istanbul, in the other—a focus that softens the contrast and confrontation between spatio-cultural binaries such as France and Algeria and Europe and Islam.[56] Bouchareb's mobile movies instead thrust their protagonists into contact or sometimes confrontation with borderlands and transit zones.

As I have argued, delving beyond the titles of these films demonstrates that France—although present in layers of historical and cultural background—is peripheral to the maps imagined in Bouchareb's films. Each narrative intersects with a francosphere, but those are at least one degree of spatial or temporal separation away from France: Belgium, Guernsey, New York via Senegal, or Louisiana. For this reason, Bouchareb's films are conducive to a kaleidoscopic reading, in a fashion similar to how cinéma-monde has been theorized. Looking back over Bouchareb's mobile movies as a group—the road he has taken from *Baton Rouge*—reveals a particular interest in the sites of borders, which function at times both as boundaries and as contact zones. Put differently, the physical maps are just a part of the story; in Bouchareb's films, the places that appear on them are not as clearly demarcated as cartographers suggest. His mobile protagonists incessantly encounter connections and barriers that belie the static lines and solid hues that demarcate national spaces. It is fitting that the title and destination of his first feature film derives from a boundary line. The origin story of the city of Baton Rouge, which is partly recounted in the film by a Native American who befriends the traveling trio, is that the Houma Indian tribe and the Bayogoula tribe used a bloody stick to mark the border between their respective hunting grounds. The French name for that "red stick" would become the name of the outpost established by Pierre Le Moyne d'Iberville, founder of the French colony of La Louisiane. This tale encapsulates the complexities inherent in Bouchareb's cinematic mapping of space: "New France," an oft-forgotten history of exploitation (of Native Americans and slaves), and a French "explorer" who was not actually from France but was born in Montreal. The trio did not truly find Baton Rouge, but in retrospect this is all the more appropriate given the way that Bouchareb sees places not as static entities but as mutable, complex, and historically and spatially multilayered.

NOTES

1. Alec Hargreaves, "From Ghettos to Globalization: Situating Maghrebi-French Filmmakers," in *Screening Integration: Recasting Maghrebi Immigration in Contemporary France*, ed. Sylvie Durmelat and Vinay Swamy (Lincoln: University of Nebraska Press, 2011), 29.
2. Delphine Letort, "Introduction: Postcolonial Migration Stories on Screen," *Black Camera* 6, no. 1 (2014): 92–5.
3. Ipek A. Celik Rappas, "Tracing a History of Terrorism in Rachid Bouchareb's Films: *London River* (2009), *Hors la loi* (2010) and *La Route d'Istanbul* (2016)," *Studies in French Cinema* 19, no. 3 (2018): 10.
4. By "francosphere," I am referring to a sphere of influences or interaction of the French language, France, and other at least partially French-speaking nations. Among other things, this includes former colonies and possessions of France and Belgium, Quebec, and other Canadian provinces with French-speaking communities.
5. Carrie Tarr, "The Mediation of Difference in *London River*," in *Bicultural Literature and Film in French and English*, ed. Peter I. Barta and Phil Powrie (New York: Routledge, 2016), 60.
6. Michael Gott and Thibaut Schilt, "Introduction: The Kaleidoscope of Cinéma-Monde," in *Cinéma-Monde: Decentred Perspectives on Global Filmmaking in French*, ed. Michael Gott and Thibaut Schilt (Edinburgh: Edinburgh University Press, 2018), 10.
7. Elizabeth Ezra and Terry Rowden, ed., *Transnational Cinema: The Film Reader* (Abingdon: Routledge, 2006), 1.
8. Dimitris Eleftheriotis, *Cinematic Journeys: Film and Movement* (Edinburgh: Edinburgh University Press, 2010), 15.
9. David Laderman, *Driving Visions: Exploring the Road Movie* (Austin: University of Texas Press, 2002), 15.
10. Daniela Berghahn, *Far-Flung Families in Film: The Diasporic Family in Contemporary European Cinema* (Edinburgh: Edinburgh University Press, 2013), 66.
11. Bill Marshall, "*Cinéma-monde*? Towards a Concept of Francophone Cinema," *Francosphères* 1, no. 1 (2011): 42.
12. See Alison J. Murray Levine, "Mapping Beur Cinema in the New Millennium," *Journal of Film and Video* 60, no. 3/4 (2008): 42–59; Will Higbee, "Re-Presenting the Urban Periphery: Maghrebi-French Filmmaking and the 'Banlieue' Film," *Cinéaste* 33, no. 1 (2007): 38–43.
13. Levine, "Mapping Beur Cinema in the New Millennium," 44.

14. Ibid., 46.
15. Michael R. Gott, "'Bouger pour voir les immeubles': *Jeunesse dorée* (2001), *L'Année suivante* (2006) and the Creative Mobility of Women's *Banlieue* Cinema," *Modern & Contemporary France* 21, no. 4 (2013): 453–72.
16. James F. Austin, "Destroying the Banlieue: Reconfigurations of Suburban Space in French Film," *Yale French Studies*, no. 115 (2009): 82.
17. Ibid., 81.
18. Higbee, "Re-Presenting the Urban Periphery," 38.
19. Ibid., 39.
20. Gott, "'Bouger pour voir les immeubles,'" 3–4.
21. Luce Vigo, "Au fast-food des beurs," *Révolution*, 13 December 1985.
22. Jason Wood, *100 Road Movies* (London: British Film Institute, 2007), xv.
23. Ibid., xix.
24. Ewa Mazierska and Laura Rascaroli, *Crossing New Europe: Postmodern Travel and the European Road Movie* (London: Wallflower Press, 2006), 166–8.
25. Carrie Tarr, "Maghrebi-French (Beur) Filmmaking in Context," *Cineaste* 33, no. 1 (2007): 32–7, 51.
26. Michael Gott, *French Language Road Cinema: Borders, Diasporas, Migration and "New Europe"* (Edinburgh: Edinburgh University Press, 2016), 7.
27. Tarr, "Maghrebi-French (Beur) Filmmaking in Context," 38. More information on this context is also provided in Chapter 5 of this volume.
28. Mazierska and Rascaroli, *Crossing New Europe*, 5.
29. Thibaut Schilt, "Hybrid Strains in Olivier Ducastel and Jacques Martineau's *Drôle de Félix* (2000)," *Contemporary French and Francophone Studies* 11, no. 3 (2007): 361–8.
30. Higbee, "Re-Presenting the Urban Periphery," 39.
31. Gott, *French-Language Road Cinema*, 10.
32. Laderman, *Driving Visions*, 15.
33. Ibid., 12; Gott, *French-Language Road Cinema*, 11–15.
34. John Urry, *Mobilities* (Cambridge: Polity Press, 2007): 42.
35. Walter Moser, "Le road movie: un genre issu d'une constellation moderne de locomotion et de médiamotion," *Cinémas: revue d'études cinématographiques* 18, no. 2–3 (2008): 21.
36. Marc Augé, *Non-lieux: introduction à une anthropologie de la surmodernité* (Paris: Seuil, 1992).
37. Eleftheriotis, *Cinematic Journeys*, 15–16.
38. Ibid., 77–8.
39. Gott, *French-Language Road Cinema*, 119.
40. Randall Halle, *The Europeanization of Cinema: Interzones and Imaginative Communities* (Urbana: University of Illinois Press, 2014), 4–9.
41. Berghahn, *Far-Flung Families in Film*, 66.
42. Manlio Graziano, *What Is a Border?* (Palo Alto, CA: Stanford University Press, 2018).
43. For an extensive discussion of unseen voyages or limited "mobile vision" in migrant and refugee travel narratives, see "The End of the Road? Dark Routes and Urban Passageways," Chapter 7 in Gott, *French-language Road Cinema*.
44. Islands have a central place in these films: Gorée and Sullivan's Island in *Little Senegal*, and then Guernsey in *London River*.
45. Delphine Letort, "Rethinking the Diaspora through the Legacy of Slavery in Rachid Bouchareb's *Little Senegal*," *Black Camera* 6, no. 1 (2014): 149.
46. Alison Smith, "Crossing the Linguistic Threshold: Language, Hospitality and Linguistic Exchange in Philippe Lioret's *Welcome* and Rachid Bouchareb's *London River*," *Studies in French Cinema* 13, no. 1 (2012): 78.

47. See the Introduction and Chapter 1 of this volume for discussions of Bouchareb's approaches to casting and production.
48. Tarr, "The Mediation of Difference in *London River*," 61.
49. See Chapter 7 of this volume.
50. Smith, "Crossing the Linguistic Threshold."
51. Gemma King, *Decentring France: Multilingualism and Power in Contemporary French Cinema* (Manchester: Manchester University Press, 2017), 163.
52. In Chapter 7, Mireille Rosello suggests that the island's "position allegorizes the geographical and political ambiguities of the borders of Europe."
53. Tarr, "The Mediation of Difference in *London River*," 64.
54. Celik Rappas, "Tracing a History of Terrorism in Rachid Bouchareb's Films," 10.
55. Tom Conley, *Cartographic Cinema* (Minneapolis: University of Minnesota Press, 2007), 3.
56. Gott, *French-Language Road Cinema*, 64–5.

CHAPTER 3

Questions of Gender and Embodiment in the *Intimiste* Films of Rachid Bouchareb

Kaya Davies Hayon

Rachid Bouchareb began his career making small-budget auteur films, but has since gained national and international recognition with the success of his Hollywood-inspired epics *Indigènes/Days of Glory* (2006) and *Hors la loi/Outside the Law* (2010). Bouchareb's diverse corpus transcends national distinctions and showcases a range of subjects from different backgrounds. However, Carrie Tarr criticizes his early film *Bâton Rouge/Baton Rouge* (1985) for the limited space it allows women,[1] while Anne Donadey takes issue with *Outside the Law*'s "problematic gender politics" and with the lack of agency it attributes to (marginalized) women.[2] According to Donadey, Bouchareb's corpus can be divided into two broad categories: *intimiste*, introspective films that highlight women's perspectives, and those that are more male-centered, which include the epic films *Days of Glory* and *Outside the Law*.[3] She focuses on the latter films and argues that they offer stock roles to their female characters, especially those of North African heritage.[4] As Donadey explains, Bouchareb's Hollywood-style films "rely on the epic mode, focus on male subjectivity and only offer a set of reductive roles for women."[5]

Building on Donadey's analysis, this chapter examines the representation of Arab women and their bodies in three of Bouchareb's more introspective films: *Cheb* (1991), *L'Honneur de ma famille/My Family's Honor* (1998) and *Just like a Woman* (2012). These films have been largely neglected in academic studies of Bouchareb's work, despite their interesting and, in many ways, progressive treatment of women of North African Arab heritage. Though set in different national locations and time periods, all three films privilege female viewpoints and represent their characters in ways that confront dominant negative stereotypes of Arab women. Whereas *Cheb* explores a young "*beur*" woman's conflicted response to the sex-gender system in Algeria, *My Family's*

Honor and *Just Like a Woman* use the trope of intercultural female friendship to examine the intersections of gender and cultural difference in France and America respectively.[6] These three films differ from Bouchareb's epics insofar as they offer complex constructions of female subjectivities. However, this chapter questions the extent to which their representation of women and their bodies reinforces the Western feminist perspectives that position the West as more liberated than the supposedly oppressed and patriarchal cultures of North Africa and the Middle East. In this chapter, I examine each film in turn, focusing on their genres, aesthetics, and representational strategies, while also situating them in relation to their sociopolitical contexts and to national and transnational cinematic trends.

GENDER AND DISEMPOWERMENT IN *CHEB*

Cheb (which means "youth" in Arabic) is Bouchareb's second feature film and an example of his early style of filmmaking. It adopts a largely realist aesthetic to tell the story of a young "*beur*" man named Merwan (Mourad Bounaas) who is sent back to his parents' homeland in Algeria after being convicted of committing two petty crimes in France. Having grown up in Roubaix in the north of France, Merwan struggles to adapt to life in Algeria, where he does not speak the language and where he is forced to serve in the hyper-masculinized space of the Algerian military. About halfway through the narrative, Merwan is contacted by his Maghrebi-French girlfriend Malika (Nozha Khouadra), whose father has tricked her into coming to Algeria for an arranged marriage. Merwan helps Malika escape, and the two protagonists journey across the Algerian desert in an attempt to return to France. Along the way, they experience Algeria as a deeply patriarchal society that is totally different from the one they have left behind in France. Malika, in particular, struggles to express her westernized feminine identity and experiences restrictions on her ability to move and act in the public sphere.

Cheb was cofunded by France and Algeria, shot on location in Algeria, and produced with the cooperation of the Algerian army.[7] However, the film was never released in Algeria, as its largely negative portrayal of the country was seen as an act of *trahison* (betrayal) by the Algerian state.[8] Though Bouchareb claims that this criticism of the film in Algeria was unexpected,[9] his comments in an interview on French television suggest that *Cheb* was always intended to appeal to a French, rather than an Algerian, audience, as it criticizes France's *double peine* law and explores the feeling of exile among young Maghrebi-French people who have been forcibly sent to a country and culture that are unfamiliar to them.[10] As Bouchareb explains, the film uses the characters of Merwan and Malika to represent "all the children who were born here in France and who have grown up here and who find themselves thrown back to Algeria and a . . . fairly violent situation . . . This isn't a touristic trip."[11] The film also seeks to expose what Bouchareb terms "intolerance in Algeria,"[12] a condition that is experienced not just by the "*beurs*" who go to Algeria, but also by the women and men who live in the country.[13] He thus portrays Algeria as a country that is inhospitable for the film's young "*beur*" protagonists, but that also appears to be oppressive for the people who live there, especially the women.

Though ultimately unreleased in Algeria, *Cheb* was shot at the end of a particularly tumultuous decade in Algeria's history that saw the rise of Islamist politics and the passing of legislation that limited women's bodily freedom in the public sphere. Following Algerian independence in 1962, Algerian "women's liberation, their public prominence, and the recognition of their political achievements . . . became associated with French values and a return to colonial rule."[14] Emphasis was therefore placed on recuperating women's traditional role and reassigning them to the domestic sphere. This process was reinforced by legislation that limited women's rights, including, most notably, President Chadli Bendjedid's changes to the Algerian Family Law Code in 1984, which legalized problematic practices like polygamy, matrimonial guardianship and repudiation, and upheld unfair inheritance laws.[15] Not only did the Family Law Code reinforce a vision of women as homemakers and procreators, but, as Zahia Smail Salhi notes, it also "facilitated violence against women, legitimized discrimination in practice, and made it particularly difficult for women to deal with the consequences of widespread human rights abuses."[16]

The rise of Islamism in Algerian society in the 1980s also posed a threat to women's rights. As early as the 1970s, women who behaved in ways that contravened conservative interpretations of the Qur'an were subjected to bullying and segregation in the workplace, verbal harassment on the streets, and even physical attacks.[17] The perpetrators of these attacks faced few to no repercussions from Bendjedid's government, who instead "co-opted the 'conservatives, and later, Muslim fundamentalists, to safeguard their interests and stay in power.'"[18] The close relationship between the Islamists and the state reignited the Algerian feminist movement and united a diverse array of women's rights groups whose aim was to abolish the Family Law Code. However, the ability of these groups to effect political change was hampered by the rise of the Front Islamique du Salut (FIS), a fundamentalist party that campaigned on a radical platform of populist politics, which gained them the support of Algeria's disenfranchised youth.[19] The rise of the FIS changed the fabric of Algerian society and made the public sphere more hostile to women: public places began to be populated by pious men and women wearing veils (such as the burqa and the niqab) that covered their bodies completely. When the FIS won the presidential elections in 1992, the army staged a coup, which led to the Algerian Civil War and increased gender-based violence against women.

Though it was made and released before the start of the Algerian Civil War, *Cheb* clearly references the growing intolerance in Algeria in the late 1980s and early 1990s. The film takes place in a male-dominated country that is constructed as hostile to women. Early on, we learn that the dominant Islamist political rhetoric prevails among everyday citizens: one of Merwan's comrades in the army tells him that he believes that women should stay at home and look after the children, and Malika's father and uncle treat her body as their personal property by controlling her movements and forcing her to cover up in public spaces. Indeed, we see very few women for the first half of the film, which is mainly focused on Merwan's attempts to integrate into the highly masculinized space of the Algerian army. When we do see Algerian women, they appear in marginal roles and are almost always fully covered by veils. Outside of the army, the streets are lined with men who abide by the country's dominant Muslim values. In one early scene, the camera settles on shots of hundreds of men kneeling down and praying in the direction of Mecca. Together, these scenes function to construct an image of Algeria as a patriarchal religious country that is heavily dominated by men. This point is later confirmed by Malika when she states that Algeria is "truly a men's country."[20]

Given its patriarchal religious structures, Algeria is a particularly difficult place for Malika to navigate. Like Merwan, Malika has grown up in Roubaix and fashions herself as an independent, liberated, and westernized young woman. The first time we see Malika on screen, she is framed behind a barred window in a house where she is being imprisoned by her father. One of the first things she says to Merwan is that women in Algeria have no power and that she desperately needs to return to France. Once she escapes from the familial home, Malika's clothes and physical appearance (that is, her sunglasses and trendy Western trousers and top) mark her out as different from the veiled Algerian women seen up to this point and emphasize "how totally out of place she is" in Algeria.[21] This is made abundantly clear in an early scene in which Malika and Merwan take a bus and Malika sits next to a local woman who is completely covered by a black veil. Her difference to the local Algerian women is highlighted by their clothing and physical proximity, but also via a medium close-up of a group of male travelers looking at Malika with confusion and disapproval. When she later descends from the bus, Malika's body becomes the explicit object of a number of critical male gazes. She is jeered at by the groups of men and boys who populate the streets, and is verbally harassed by some male onlookers in traditional white Muslim robes and taqiyahs for dressing in a way that shows her body. Moreover, Malika experiences restrictions on her ability to occupy public spaces because of her gender and her marital status. As an unmarried woman, she is unable to stay in a hotel room with Merwan and is forced to pose as his younger brother. Algeria thus emerges as a patriarchal space where women have very little freedom and where their bodies are subjected to discipline and control in the public domain.

Figure 3.1 A close-up of Malika's tearful face as Merwan cuts her hair in *Cheb*

As a result of the intimidation that she experiences, Malika quickly realizes that her gendered body is a hindrance in Algeria and that she will be able to move more freely if she cross-dresses as a boy. In one key sequence, she strips her body of its signifiers of her femininity by dressing in traditionally male attire and by cutting off her long, wavy hair. The distressing nature of this act is rendered by the intimate close-ups of Malika with tears running down her face as Merwan cuts her hair. When Merwan has finished, Malika recounts a story of a girl from her class who committed suicide after being imprisoned in Algeria by her family. The juxtaposition of these scenes is important, as it illustrates the extent to which Malika feels that her identity and her bodily existence are threatened by her location in Algeria. The film thus gives visual representation to Salhi's argument that the delegitimization of women's presence in the public sphere in the 1980s and 1990s constituted a form of physical and psychological violence that "[codified] their subjugation and [rendered] them more vulnerable in the face of growing conservatism."[22]

Malika's cross-dressing does initially imbue her with more agency and bodily freedom in Algeria. As mentioned already, she is able to stay in a hotel room by posing as Merwan's younger brother, she crosses a checkpoint without hassle, and she can walk in the street without experiencing constant verbal harassment from the men around her. However, Malika's newfound freedom is short-lived, and she is harshly punished for transgressing Algeria's patriarchal gender laws. After the hotel owner discovers that Malika and Merwan are not brothers, he calls the police, who forcibly return Malika to her father.

Merwan tries unsuccessfully to rescue Malika a second time, and is finally forced to leave her confined to the prison that is her familial home. The last shot we see of Malika is inserted into what appears to be Merwan's dream. Her body is completely covered by a white veil, and she walks with her back to the camera, before turning around and looking directly at it in an accusatory fashion. Whereas Merwan does manage to find his way back to France, albeit on a stranger's passport and to serve in the nationalistic, male-dominated space of the French army, Malika remains trapped in Algeria, a country that has been shown to be a dangerous and disempowering place for women. In the end, Malika emerges as the main victim of the film, precisely because her gender renders her powerless to escape Algeria and to change her situation.

In her analysis of *Cheb*, Carrie Tarr argues that "the film vividly demonstrates the conflicts between Malika's emancipated ideas about women's roles, and the puritanical and oppressive attitudes to women she experiences in Algeria."[23] Without doubt, the film represents the hardships for women in Algeria by exposing the country's unequal gender hierarchies and by condemning its turn toward religious conservatism in the late 1980s and early 1990s. At the same time, its representation of Algeria (and of local Algerian women in particular) does risk reinforcing Western feminist ideas about Arab Muslim women as oppressed and in need of liberating by their Western/westernized counterparts. These ideas have been criticized by the Algerian feminist critic Marnia Lazreg in her book *The Eloquence of Silence: Algerian Women in Question*, in which she discusses Western feminism's tendency to position "'different' women as . . . the embodiment of cultures presumed inferior and classified as 'traditional' or 'patriarchal.'"[24] In order to debunk these assumptions, Lazreg shows how localized practices—some of which are very rare, such as polygamy—are often seized upon by Western feminists as "normative absolutes."[25] Lazreg thus concludes that Western feminist perspectives not only play into sensationalist fears of the Arab Muslim world as inherently patriarchal, but also reinforce stereotypes of Arab Muslim women as oppressed and in need of liberating by their Western/westernized sisters.

In *Cheb*, Bouchareb arguably reinforces the distinction between Western/westernized women as liberated and Algerian women as oppressed. As mentioned, very few Algerian women are present in the narrative and those that do appear tend to function as foils for Malika's modernity and liberation. While the film does not offer an idealized vision of France (an argument that is reinforced by the opening documentary footage of anti-racism riots and police brutality in the Parisian *banlieues*), it does suggest that French society is more progressive in its treatment of women and their rights. As argued, Malika feels disempowered in Algeria and repeatedly struggles to reconcile her westernized femininity with the expectations placed upon Arab Muslim women in the film. Given the turbulent political context in Algeria at the time that *Cheb* was made, it is perhaps unsurprising that Bouchareb paints it in such a negative light. However, his film's representational strategies do bolster problematic and often decontextualized views of Algeria as a deeply patriarchal country and of Algerian women as irrevocably oppressed. In the end, *Cheb* upholds the North-South, Algerian-French binaries that reinforce the idea that Algerian women are disempowered by a patriarchal religious culture and that their bodies are regulated and controlled in the public domain.

FAMILY, FRIENDSHIP, AND FEMALE HONOR IN *MY FAMILY'S HONOR*

In contrast to the serious approach of *Cheb*, *My Family's Honor* is a humorous *téléfilm* that was first broadcast in France in 1998. It focuses on a young Maghrebi-French woman named Nora (Seloua Hamse) who lives with her traditional Maghrebi parents in Roubaix in the north of France. She works in a bar on the Belgian border and saves her hard-earned wages to fulfill her dream of traveling to India with her white French best friend, Karole (Karole Rocher). However, Nora and Karole's travel plans are thwarted when Nora finds out that she is pregnant and decides to keep the baby without the support of its white French father. Rather than lying to her family, and seeing few other options, Nora decides to tell her mother about the pregnancy, which sparks a comic chain of events that begins with Nora's mother fainting. Fearful that Nora's predicament will bring shame to the family unit, her mother attempts to marry her to a local Muslim man named Hamid (played by Roschdy Zem) before anyone else (including her father) can discover that she is pregnant. The film's comical approach conceals a darker criticism of the extent to which the traditional Maghrebi family unit controls female sexuality and negotiates honor across women's bodies.

My Family's Honor was first aired on French television toward the end of the 1990s, a decade that had been dominated by reductive stereotypical representations of Maghrebi-French women in the French media. Following the 1989 headscarf affair, in which three Muslim girls were expelled from school for wearing their veils to class, French media and political discourses routinely portrayed women and girls of Maghrebi descent as victims of a patriarchal culture that hindered their ability to integrate in France. During this decade, heinous—if in reality uncommon—occurrences, such as "honor killings, sequestrations, forced marriages, and other violent acts," were reported on as routine practices in Arab Muslim communities in France.[26] This media coverage elicited sympathy for young Maghrebi-French women. However, as Leslie Kealhofer argues, it also "contributed to the portrayal of Maghrebi cultures as 'other' and cast the traditional Maghrebi family structure (including religious and cultural traditions)—and in particular Maghrebi migrants and men of Maghrebi descent—in an unfavourable light."[27]

Negative media depictions of Maghrebi-French women were often reflected in French films. While most French films featuring Maghrebi-French people tended to focus on the experiences of men, those that did feature women often placed them in stereotypical roles by constructing them as victims of a patriarchal culture or as sex objects who were punished "for attempting to assert [their] autonomy."[28] These stereotypes also featured in French *téléfilms* like *My Family's Honor*, and were compounded by what Joseph McGonagle identifies as French television's difficulties representing "ethnic diversity across all sectors of programming, particularly with regard to incorporating characters of Maghrebi heritage in fiction-based programming."[29] It was not until 2006 that the French state officially recognized the importance of imposing quotas to ensure diversity on screen; however, this issue did first come to light in the late 1990s (around the time of *My Family's Honor*'s release) when critics and scholars began to call attention to the notable absence of ethnic minorities, particularly women, in French television and film.[30]

When analyzed in relation to this contextual history, it becomes clear that *My Family's Honor* was fairly exceptional in its decision to foreground a young Maghrebi-French woman and to represent her in three-dimensional terms. This latter argument is clear from the establishing sequences of the film, which show Nora working in a bar, smoking, taking illegal drugs, and attending raves, all of which are frowned upon in traditional Maghrebi households. Moreover, it is evident from the outset that Nora has had sex before marriage, and with a white man from outside of the Arab Muslim community at that. Like Malika in *Cheb*, Nora is constructed as an independent young woman who does not subscribe to the traditional values of her Maghrebi parents and who is clearly well integrated in France. Her representation not only countered dominant French stereotypes of Maghrebi-French women as passive victims or sexualized objects, but also confronted the limited visibility of ethnic minority women on French screens in the 1990s.

Tarr argues that the main conflict in *My Family's Honor* arises from Nora's inability to accept the "traditional Arabo-Berber-Islamic culture of [her] parents' generation, with its insistence on male authority, female virtue, arranged marriages and women's destiny."[31] In conservative Maghrebi households like the one represented in the film, women's bodies are viewed as the property of the male members of their family unit and as the primary sites across which familial and patriarchal honor are obtained.[32] As women's behaviors are so closely allied to family honor in traditional Maghrebi families, female purity is viewed as a valuable (economic) property and female sexuality must be carefully controlled.[33] These principles are evidenced clearly in *My Family's Honor*, in which Nora's body is positioned as the primary means by which her family's honor is negotiated. As mentioned in the Introduction, Nora's unborn child's illegitimacy sparks fear in her overbearing mother that she will not only bring shame to the family, but will also render herself undesirable as a wife. Nora's mother therefore sets about saving the family's potentially sullied reputation by asserting control over her daughter's body and sexuality. She sets up a marriage between Nora and Hamid, a local man who is also controlled by his manipulative mother. Hamid immediately falls head over heels in love with Nora and his attempts to win her affections—by becoming vegetarian, studying Buddhism, and buying her multiple desserts to satiate her cravings—generate much of the film's comedy. Hamid is a far cry from the stereotype of the patriarchal Maghrebi man seen in the French media (and recycled by Bouchareb in parts of *Cheb*). In fact, in this film, it is primarily older women who enforce patriarchal values about female sexuality and who engage in practices that could harm the wellbeing of their children. As Tarr explains, the film "contrasts Nora's defiant attempts to live a free, independent life with the hypocrisy and narrow-mindedness of the older generation" of Maghrebi women.[34]

Nora finds relief from her oppressive mother through her friendship with Karole. The portrayal of the women's friendship avoids falling back onto stereotypes of white French women as the saviors of oppressed Maghrebi women that have so often been seen in French films like Coline Serreau's *Chaos* (2001), which portrays an unusual intercultural friendship between a wealthy white French woman (Catherine Frot) and a prostitute of Algerian origin (Rachida Brakni), and in the Western feminist discourses discussed in relation to *Cheb*. Instead, the film portrays Nora as the more level-headed and pragmatic character, and as the one who guides and helps her wayward friend. In one scene, Nora tells Karole to be wary of her handsome new lover (Alex Descas) after he makes advances toward her in the cinema. Karole pays scant attention to her friend's concerns and gives all of their savings to her new boyfriend, who turns out to be a conman posing as an illegal immigrant in need of papers. The two women argue, and Karole takes an overdose, as she is unable to deal with the consequences of her argument with Nora. Here, it is Karole who needs saving, which arguably inverts the Western feminist tropes that position white women as the rescuers of their oppressed Arab sisters. Nora not only saves her friend from a toxic relationship, but also forgives her for losing their savings and diverts her ensuing existential crisis.

The final scene of the film shows Nora rejecting her mother's plans and regaining control over her body. Following Hamid's mother's discovery of the real reason for the marriage, Nora reaches breaking point and decides that her only option is to abort her baby. At the hospital, she discovers Karole, who has been admitted for taking an overdose. The women rekindle their friendship and decide to run away together so that Nora can have her baby without pressure from her family. They use Hamid's keys to steal wedding jewelry from his mother's shop, before accidentally setting the entire shop alight, and then driving off. On the one hand,

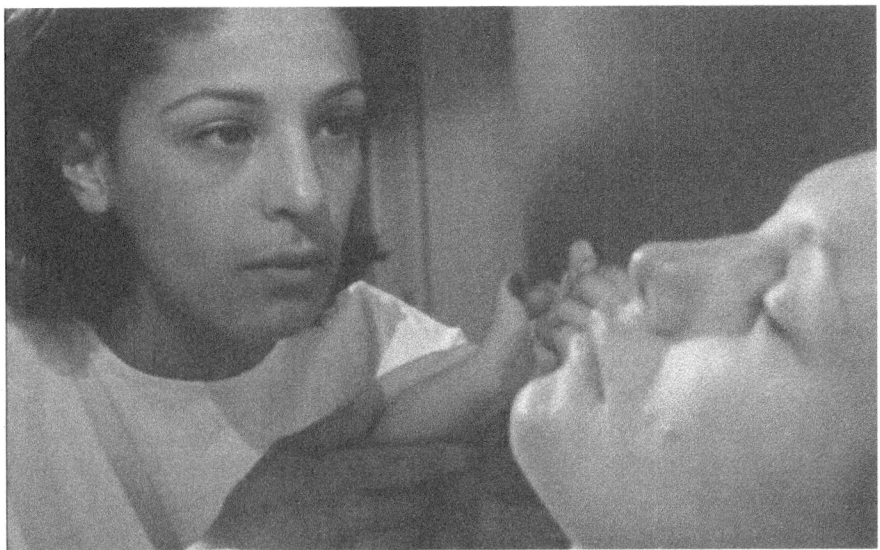

Figure 3.2 Nora at Karole's bedside in *My Family's Honor*

this final scene is progressive, as it shows Nora taking control over her body and her sexuality and deciding to raise her baby out of wedlock and in an unconventional family setup. On the other hand, it rather pessimistically implies that young French women of Maghrebi heritage can only find freedom by breaking ties with their immediate family and by escaping the constraints imposed upon them by their families. As the two women drive off into the distance, Bouchareb's camera cuts to a shot of Hamid, who has followed them from the hospital and hidden himself in the trunk of their car. For Tarr, this final shot, "however light-hearted, suggests that Nora may not be able to abandon her ethnic heritage or the weight of the masculine expectations as easily as she had hoped."[35] In the end, despite its humorous approach, *My Family's Honor* fails to challenge dominant negative French stereotypes about the Maghrebi family as patriarchal and about Maghrebi-French women as victims of their cultural heritage. The young woman at the center of the narrative does maintain a strong degree of agency and is finally able to regain control over her body and her existence, but this comes at the expense of breaking ties with her family and abandoning her culture of origin.

INTERCULTURAL FRIENDSHIP AND FEMALE LIBERATION IN *JUST LIKE A WOMAN*

In contrast to the two films discussed above, *Just Like a Woman* is set in the US and does not focus on Franco-Maghrebi relations or on French women of Maghrebi heritage. Instead, it draws on the generic tropes of the road movie to examine the friendship that forms between a white American woman named Marilyn (played by Sienna Miller) and a woman of Egyptian heritage named Mona (played by the Iranian actress Golshifteh Farahani). Unlike the heroines in *Cheb* and *My Family's Honor*, Mona is in an arranged marriage with Mourad, an Arab man (again played by Roschdy Zem) whom she appears to love but who is controlled by his overbearing mother (played by Chafia Boudraa, who also played Hamid's mother in *My Family's Honor*). Mona experiences an extremely tense and conflicted relationship with Mourad's mother, who is frustrated that Mona has been married to her son for five years and has yet to produce an heir. One day, Mona accidentally gives her mother-in-law an overdose of the wrong medication, and she dies. Distraught, Mona decides that her only option is to flee her husband and the family home. At the same time, Marilyn loses her job and decides to leave her terminally unemployed, emotionally abusive, husband (Jesse Bob Harper) after she finds him sleeping with another woman in their bed. She takes up her dance teacher's offer to perform in some bars on the route to Santa Fe, where she intends to enter a belly dance competition in the hope of joining a troupe. The women meet by chance at a rest area where they unite over their shared break-ups and decide to travel together to Santa Fe in Marilyn's car. Along the way, Marilyn and Mona develop a friendship that is based on shared points of commonality and that breaks down the perceived distinctions between their two cultures.

Over the past few decades, people of Arab Muslim descent have faced increasing demonization in America (and elsewhere). A number of events have impacted relations between America and its Arab Muslim subjects, including the Arab oil crisis of the 1970s, the Iranian revolution, 9/11 and the "War on Terror," and successive US governments' support for the state of Israel. In his book *Reel Bad Arabs*, Jack Shaheen argues that political events such as the ones listed above have helped to shape how Arab Muslim people are represented in visual media like film. Over the course of his analyses, Shaheen uncovers the extent to which mainstream Hollywood film has distorted "at every turn what most Arab men, women, and children are really like."[36] Whereas most Hollywood films portray Arab men as "brute murderers, sleazy rapists, religious fanatics, oil-rich dimwits, and abusers of women,"[37] women tend to be relegated to the margins of the plot or represented as "humiliated, demonized, and eroticized" characters.[38] They hardly speak and are very rarely seen in the workplace as "doctors, computer specialists, school teachers, print and broadcast journalists, or as successful, well-rounded electric or domestic engineers."[39] Rather, Arab women in Hollywood tend to be confined to stereotypical parts—such as submissive veiled women or radical terrorist threats—that are heavily influenced by Orientalist and neo-colonial stereotypes and that give them little agency or autonomy.

Given the broader political and representational context in the US at the time of its release, *Just Like a Woman* appears to be quite a progressive film insofar as it constructs its central Arab American character in complex and rounded terms that challenge the stereotypes that have circulated in Hollywood film and in dominant media and political discourses in the US. Like Malika in *Cheb* and Nora in *My Family's Honor*, Mona is given a fully developed space in the narrative and is imbued with a voice and mind of her own. However, as with the other two films discussed in this chapter, *Just Like a Woman* does initially seem to reiterate some outdated stereotypes about the Arab family as oppressive for younger women. From the very first sequence, which opens with a close-up of Mona's bare tummy, it is clear that Mourad's mother exerts control over her daughter-in-law's body and reproductive capacities. She takes Mona to a local faith healer, who enacts a ritualistic practice on her body, before prescribing her some herbal medicine to boost her fertility. Mona's inability to conceive is positioned as a source of stigma, and it is framed as a specifically female problem by her mother-in-law. In fact, Mourad's virility is not called into question until much later in the film, when Marilyn asks Mona whether her husband might be the cause of their fertility problems. To an even greater extent than in *My Family's Honor*, then, the mother in *Just Like a Woman* monitors her daughter-in-law's sexuality and views her childless body as a source of shame for the family. She even threatens to bring over a second wife if Mona does not fall pregnant soon.

The above scenes combine to create a fairly conventional vision of Mona as an oppressed character, and of the Arab family as inherently patriarchal. However, Bouchareb's repeated crosscutting to Marilyn's narrative shows that she also experiences her home life as oppressive and claustrophobic. Unlike Mona, Marilyn is the primary breadwinner in her relationship. Her husband is unemployed, yet seems happy to spend her money in bars in the evening. Moreover, as mentioned earlier, he is unfaithful to Marilyn and treats her disrespectfully. Though Marilyn eventually leaves him, she initially appears to be scared to assert her independence because of how her husband might react. In an early scene, she tells her dance teacher that she is ambivalent about entering a belly dance competition, as she does not think her husband would approve. By showing Marilyn's home life to be just as claustrophobic as Mona's, Bouchareb avoids demonizing one particular culture. Furthermore, as with *My Family's Honor*, he refuses to construct the male Arab character in stereotypical terms. Instead, it is Marilyn's husband who is shown to be the more patriarchal character: he is controlling of his wife's body and movements, treats her with disrespect, and does little to contribute to domestic life.

Given the stifling nature of the two women's lives in Chicago, it is unsurprising that they find the space of the open road to be both liberating and empowering. Whereas the initial sections of the film are mainly filmed indoors and in the small, claustrophobic, spaces of the women's homes and workplaces, the scenes on the open road are characterized by long shots, bright colors, upbeat music, and wide camera angles. Not only do these techniques emphasize the women's freedom, but they also indicate the extent to which *Just Like a Woman* references Ridley Scott's feminist take on the road movie in *Thelma and Louise* (1991). Just like the two characters in Bouchareb's film, Thelma and Louise (played by Geena Davis and Susan Sarandon, respectively) take to the road not, as Steven Cohan and Ina Rae Hark explain, "to escape socially coded notions of the feminine, but rather to flee patriarchy and its effects on their lives."[40] Here, Bouchareb also foregrounds the narratives and subjectivities of two women who feel stifled at home and who are escaping the constraints of their domestic lives. However, he goes a step further than Scott does in *Thelma and Louise*, by focusing on an intercultural female friendship that is born out of his two protagonists' rejection of the patriarchal underpinnings of their cultures and a shared interest in aspects of Arab music and culture, namely belly dance.

Belly dance is an expressive dance form that originated in the Middle East and North Africa, but is now also practiced in cities across North America, Japan, Europe, and Australia. Though belly dance remains steeped in stereotypes inherited from the European colonial era, it has seen a spike in popularity in America since the 1990s. For Sunaina Maira, this increased interest in belly dance offers an opportunity for white liberal American women to show their tolerance for Arab cultures through "the consumption of cultural commodities."[41] Other critics suggest that the appeal of belly dance among women from diverse cultural backgrounds stems from its ability to offer them a feeling of personal transformation and a specifically feminist form of leisure. For Angela Moe, for example, many women report feeling empowered by belly dance because it not only awakens them to their bodies' physical capacities, but also allows them to challenge embedded societal norms. As Moe attests, belly dance allows women of different cultures and creeds to "find ways to celebrate their bodies and movement, and to find joy among the company of other women, while often challenging public perceptions and assumptions about women's occupation of space."[42]

Figure 3.3 Marilyn and Mona belly dance on stage together for the first time in *Just Like a Woman*

In *Just Like a Woman*, belly dance is represented as a site of empowerment and cross-cultural connection for the two main protagonists. Despite their different cultural backgrounds, Mona and Marilyn both share an interest in the dance form and are shown at various points throughout the narrative dancing for their own personal pleasure and to escape the mundanity of their everyday life. For instance, the first time we see Mona on screen, she is belly dancing to music playing in Mourad's shop, while the first time we see Marilyn dance is at a class led by a white male instructor and attended by a group of women from diverse cultural backgrounds. In both of these scenes, the women dance for their own enjoyment and not that of an audience of (male) onlookers. However, once they take to the road, they begin to dance in public bars and restaurants in order to earn some money. In these scenes, the two women dress in brightly colored, sequined belly dance costumes that accentuate their waists and exposed tummies. The primarily male audience members look at both of their bodies desirously, but Bouchareb refuses to replicate their objectifying gazes and instead captures the energy of the women's performances. Repeated shots of the women's smiling faces suggest that they feel exhilarated, rather than objectified or disempowered, by their dancing.[43] The film thus suggests that (re)connecting with their bodies through belly dance is liberating for the central characters and allows them a momentary escape from their mundane patriarchal existences. While Bouchareb does not shy away from showing the commoditization and eroticization of the belly dancing body, he refuses to reinforce neo-colonial stereotypes and instead constructs the dance form as a site for the articulation of a transnational feminist politics.

Despite the fact that belly dance allows the women to unite across cultural divides, *Just Like a Woman* could still be seen to assert the problematic assumption that Arab women need to be liberated from oppression by their free-spirited white American counterparts. From the outset, the plot of the film is driven by the white American female character: it is Marilyn who invites Mona along on the road trip and it is Marilyn who encourages her initially reluctant friend to perform in public. Furthermore, Marilyn is portrayed as the more liberated character, a point that is reinforced by Sienna Miller's star persona and by Bouchareb's decision to call her character Marilyn, a name that immediately conjures up images of one of America's most famous female sex icons, Marilyn Monroe. In one scene, she is shown to be fiercely protective of Mona and defends her against the advances of a predatory male bar owner. Marilyn also saves Mona from drowning after she jumps into a deep river, and later defends her friend against some narrow-minded Midwesterners who verbally attack her using racist slurs. Though these plot devices are intended to illustrate Marilyn's devotion to her friend, they also risk reinforcing the trope of the oppressed Arab woman who needs rescuing by her more liberated white Western sister.

However, it is also possible to argue that the film invokes the stereotype of the white woman savior in order to invert it and reveal its lack of grounding in reality. This argument is evidenced most clearly toward the end of the film. As the women near their destination, they stop off at a local Indian reservation to camp and give Marilyn an opportunity to prepare for her upcoming dance competition. Here, they bump into the aforementioned racist family who violently beat Marilyn for traveling with and defending an Arab woman. Marilyn's injuries prevent her from performing in the competition, so Mona secretly travels to Santa Fe, poses as Marilyn on stage, and secures her friend a role in the dance troupe. This scene suggests that Mona is the one who saves her friend by participating in the dance competition and thereby making Marilyn's dream of dancing in a troupe possible. Like *My Family's Honor*, the film therefore inverts the trope of the white female liberator and portrays the cross-cultural female friendship in more even and progressive terms. Despite their different cultural and ethnic backgrounds, Mona and Marilyn are able to create a form of sisterhood that is not rooted solely in what bell hooks has termed their "common oppression"[44] as women, but rather is structured around their love, "shared interests and beliefs," and "appreciation for diversity."[45]

The final scene of the film is open-ended. Mona leaves Mourad by telephone and decides to hand herself into the police for accidentally killing his mother. Though Marilyn initially intends to continue traveling with the dance troupe, she is unable to leave Mona and decides to return to Chicago with her. The final shot shows them reuniting on the train platform and dancing to the music playing on the station radio. The women find solace in one another's company, which shows that sisterhood across ethnic and cultural divides is possible and can be empowering. Though *Just Like a Woman* does not always escape stereotypes about the Arab family unit or the older generation of Arab women, its transcultural focus does suggest that patriarchal imbalances of power are not unique to Arab cultures and can be found in Euro-American societies too. To a greater extent than *Cheb* or *My Family's Honor*, *Just Like a Woman* avoids painting Arab culture in a wholly negative light and instead shows its two main protagonists finding a sense of identity and empowerment through their shared passion for belly dance and through their intercultural friendship.

CONCLUSION

Charting the representation of women across three of Bouchareb's more *intimiste* films, from the beginning of his career through to the present day, reveals the director's enduring interest in gender politics in Arab cultures. The three films discussed in this chapter all foreground strong female characters of North African or Middle Eastern Arab heritage who live or have grown up in Western countries and who feel oppressed by their families and elements of their culture. This sense of oppression is particularly acute for Malika in *Cheb*, whose father traps her in Algeria, a country that is constructed in the film as being disempowering for women. Nora in *My Family's Honor* lives in France but feels suffocated by her mother's attempts to preserve the family's honor by concealing her pregnancy and arranging her marriage to a Muslim man in her community. Her solution is to break ties with her family and live an independent life. In *Just Like a Woman*, Mona must also escape the claustrophobic confines of the Arab household in order to experience a sense of liberation and freedom. Her journey across the American landscape with her white American friend Marilyn allows Mona to develop her independence, which ultimately leads her to refuse to return to her husband and previous life. The implicit message in all of these films is that Arab women cannot possess agency within the confines of the traditional family and that their only true option is to escape.

If the films portray the traditional Arab family unit in a negative light, they refuse to reiterate stereotypes about women from North Africa and the Middle East as passive victims. All three films represent their central female characters as independent and unafraid to make their own decisions. However, *Cheb* does tend to uphold the Western feminist perspectives that posit Western/westernized women as more liberated than their Arab sisters. The representation of intercultural female relationships is more nuanced in *My Family's Honor* and *Just Like a Woman*, which both invert the stereotype of the Arab woman as in need of liberating by her supposedly more progressive white Western friend. This significant difference notwithstanding, it can be concluded that all three films reiterate the problematic assumption that women of North African or Middle Eastern heritage cannot experience true autonomy and bodily freedom if they retain a strong connection to their culture of origin. The comparative analysis conducted in this chapter therefore suggests that the portrayal of women and gender in the context of Arab cultural traditions remains largely unchanged in Bouchareb's films and that the topic continues to be a contentious issue for the director. Though these *intimiste* films offer more nuanced representations of women and their bodies than Bouchareb's Hollywood-style epics, they ultimately reinforce the perception that Euro-American societies are more progressive in terms of their treatment of women's rights.

NOTES

1. Carrie Tarr, *Reframing Difference:* Beur *and* Banlieue *Filmmaking in France* (Manchester: Manchester University Press, 2005), 38.
2. Anne Donadey, "Gender, Genre and Intertextuality in Rachid Bouchareb's *Hors la loi*," *Studies in French Cinema* 16, no. 1 (2016): 50.
3. Ibid., 50.

4. Ibid., 58.
5. Ibid., 50.
6. Though the term "*beur*" has fallen out of favor in recent years and "Maghrebi-French" is a more generally used term, I adopt it here because of its cultural resonance at the time that *Cheb* was released. For more on changing attitudes to the term, see Will Higbee, *Post-Beur Cinema: North African Émigré and Maghrebi-French Filmmaking in France since 2000* (Edinburgh: Edinburgh University Press, 2013).
7. Tarr, *Reframing Difference*, 41.
8. "Rachid Bouchareb à propos de son film 'Cheb,'" INA Culture/YouTube, 9 July 2012, www.youtu.be/b7e8bmIcOwo.
9. Ibid.
10. The *double peine* law refers to a highly punitive legal practice that allows France to "repatriate" non-citizens after they have served time in France for committing a crime.
11. "Rachid Bouchareb à propos de son film 'Cheb.'"
12. Ibid.
13. Ibid.
14. Maria Flood, *France, Algeria and the Moving Image: Screening Histories of Violence, 1963–2010* (Cambridge: Legenda, 2017), 61.
15. Zahia Smail Salhi, "Gender and Violence in Algeria: Women's Resistance against the Islamist Femicide," in *Gender and Diversity in the Middle East and North Africa*, ed. Zahia Smail Salhi (Abingdon: Routledge, 2014), 168.
16. Ibid., 167.
17. Ibid., 167.
18. Louisa Ait-Hamou, "Women's Struggle against Muslim Fundamentalism in Algeria: Strategies or a Lesson for Survival?" in *Warning Signs of Fundamentalisms*, ed. Ayesha Imam, Jenny Morgan, and Nira Yuval-Davis (London: Women Living under Muslim Laws, 2004), 118, quoted ibid., 168.
19. Salhi, "Gender and Violence in Algeria," 172.
20. "vraiment un pays de mecs."
21. Tarr, *Reframing Difference*, 42.
22. Salhi, "Gender and Violence in Algeria," 161.
23. Tarr, *Reframing Difference*, 42.
24. Marnia Lazreg, *The Eloquence of Silence: Algerian Women in Question* (London: Routledge, 1994), 7.
25. Ibid., 10.
26. Leslie Kealhofer, "Maghrebi-French Women in French *Téléfilms*: Sexuality, Gender, and Tradition from *Leïla née en France* (1993) to *Aïcha: vacances infernales* (2012)," *Modern & Contemporary France* 21, no. 2 (2013): 185.
27. Ibid., 185.
28. Tarr, *Reframing Difference*, 87.
29. Joseph McGonagle, *Representing Ethnicity in French Visual Culture* (Manchester: Manchester University Press, 2017), 117.
30. Ibid., 54–65.
31. Tarr, *Reframing Difference*, 87.
32. Leila Ahmed, *Women and Gender in Islam: Historical Roots of a Modern Debate* (New Haven, CT: Yale University Press, 1992), 12.
33. Ibid., 12.
34. Tarr, *Reframing Difference*, 138.
35. Ibid., 140.

36. Jack G. Shaheen, *Reel Bad Arabs: How Hollywood Vilifies a People*, rev. ed. (Northampton, MA: Interlink, 2012), 172.
37. Ibid., 172.
38. Ibid., 184.
39. Ibid., 184.
40. Steven Cohan and Ina Rae Hark, ed., *The Road Movie Book* (London: Routledge, 2002), 63.
41. Sunaina Maira, "Belly Dancing: Arab-Face, Oriental Feminism, and U.S. Empire," *American Quarterly* 60, no. 2 (2008): 327.
42. Angela M. Moe, "Reclaiming the Feminine: Belly Dancing as a Feminist Project," *Congress on Research in Dance Conference Proceedings* 40, S1 (2008): 190. I have written at length about the feminist revival of belly dance in films and culture from the MENA region; see Kaya Davies Hayon, *Sensuous Cinema: The Body in Contemporary Maghrebi Film* (New York: Bloomsbury Academic, 2018), 59–63.
43. This representation of belly dance as a form of feminist empowerment is not uncommon in films featuring Arab women. For a discussion of films such as *Satin Rouge* (Raja Amari, 2002) and *La Graine et le mulet/Couscous/The Secret of the Grain* (Abdellatif Kechiche, 2007), see Davies Hayon, *Sensuous Cinema*, 66–81.
44. bell hooks, "Sisterhood: Political Solidarity between Women," *Feminist Review* 23 (1986): 127.
45. Ibid., 138.

CHAPTER 4

Genre and Universalism in the Films of Rachid Bouchareb

David Pettersen

Rachid Bouchareb is a central figure in the so-called *"beur"* generation of French-Maghrebi filmmakers who came of age in the 1970s and 1980s.[1] This loose grouping includes filmmakers like Mehdi Charef and Abdellatif Kechiche, who were either born in France to immigrant parents or born in former French colonies and immigrated to France at a young age. Bouchareb is best known for two big-budget films that revisit neglected moments in the history of French colonialism and decolonization: *Indigènes/Days of Glory* (2006) and *Hors la loi/Outside the Law* (2010). The former is a war film that relies on Hollywood-style spectacle to bring into public memory the contributions of North African soldiers to French war efforts during World War II. The latter brings visibility to the massacre of Algerian civilians by French soldiers at Sétif in 1945 in part through the iconography of the Western. Indeed, the film's massacre sequence shares many echoes with the opening of Sam Peckinpah's *The Wild Bunch* (1969). The beginnings of both films play on the ambiguity of whether or not the soldiers are the forces of order or outlaws. The shootouts in both films unfold in two spatial planes, the street level and the upper level of buildings where, in *Outside the Law*, armed men shoot at protestors from the windows. Both anchor the transition from the quotidian to violence in a peaceful street march that becomes a horrific scene of civilian casualties. Even the street boxing match in Bouchareb's film echoes the children playing with scorpions and ants outside town in *The Wild Bunch*. *Outside the Law* also recounts the history of National Liberation Front (FLN) militancy in immigrant shantytowns around Paris during the Algerian War of Independence through references to American gangster films, especially Francis Ford Coppola's *Godfather* trilogy (1972–1990). One of the central debates around these films is the appropriateness of Bouchareb's use of Hollywood genres to treat delicate questions of historical violence and memory. Indeed, some have criticized Bouchareb's use of genre traditions on the grounds that it sacrifices historical truth for spectacle in a bid to reach mainstream audiences.[2]

Bouchareb is not the only Maghrebi-French or Maghrebi filmmaker to turn to popular modes in order to connect stories of colonial history, diaspora, and displacement to mainstream audiences in France. To give just one example, Merzak Allouache, a contemporary of Bouchareb, was already doing this in the 1990s with films like the comedy *Salut Cousin!/Hi Cousin!* (1996).[3] What is distinctive about Bouchareb is the wide range of genres he employs in his films and the many spatial and cultural contexts in which he embeds their narratives. Bouchareb does not hide his fascination with the United States and Hollywood cinema.[4] Indeed, in a documentary about the US–Mexico border fence that is included on the DVD of *La Voie de l'ennemi/Two Men in Town*, Bouchareb explains that it was hard to grow up as an immigrant in France and that the Maghrebi-French people of his generation always had in mind the idea of an elsewhere. For Bouchareb, America was one of those elsewheres, a place that in his view was more open to immigration. Indeed, his first film, the small-budget auteurist *Bâton Rouge/Baton Rouge* (1985), is about three young men who travel to the United States to escape unemployment and the dreariness of their lives in a housing project on the outskirts of Paris.

While the question of genre and references to American genre films has been somewhat discussed with respect to *Days of Glory* and *Outside the Law*, it has not been part of the criticism of Bouchareb's other feature films. Indeed, much of Bouchareb's body of work has suffered from critical neglect. Analysis of his lesser-known feature films has tended either to treat individual examples[5] or to connect several films thematically, for example through questions of terrorism[6] or missing children.[7] In this chapter, I will focus on Bouchareb's use of three specific genres—the war film, the Western, and the interracial buddy comedy—across several of his feature films that come from different moments in his career. This approach brings into view the ways in which he employs the cinematic language of genre to reframe questions of migration, immigration, diaspora, and colonial history for mainstream audiences. I will leave out a consideration of *Days of Glory* and *Outside the Law* because these two films have already been widely discussed. Tracking Bouchareb's use of genres helps us to understand how he uses cinema to rearticulate a shared sense of the universal to include experiences that have been excluded from it. By universal, I reference the notion of French Republican universalism that has historically been conceptualized through an abstract notion of citizenship that purports to go beyond particularisms such as race and ethnicity. This conception of universalism has been the object of many critiques since the rise of postcolonial studies in the Anglo-American academy.[8] These critical voices have challenged the notion of universalism altogether because of its reinforcement of power inequalities, and they have shown how universalism has never had only one meaning or history.

The French political philosopher Étienne Balibar has sought to inventory the possibilities and pitfalls of universalism as a Western political and philosophical concept. He prefers to think of cultures as "open systems" that consist of "phrases, texts, discourses, and dialogues rather than 'visions of the world.'"[9] Universalism, in his view, is defined by acts of translation that seek to mediate between cultures, and he makes the case for an expansion of those with the power to translate.[10] He ultimately understands universalism as a mode of speech, one that he argues is a *procès*, which in French can mean both a process and a trial.[11] Bouchareb does not engage directly with the cultural or philosophical notion of universalism. Nevertheless, his films centrally explore questions of migration and belonging that reflect on the porous physical and cultural borders of nation-states in the contemporary world. Furthermore, his films arguably represent acts of translation in Balibar's sense through their juxtaposition of languages, cultures, and histories.

Film genres, I would argue, are central to understanding how Bouchareb's films are an example of Balibar's "process" of rearticulating the universal and translating between cultures. Genre traditions can be used to connect the familiar and the unfamiliar, and Mikhail Bakhtin's writings about genre can help us understand how these two poles relate. While his writings about genres focus mostly on speech and literature, they can be productively applied to cinema as well. Bakhtin understands genres as impersonal accretions of concepts, behaviors, events, and worldviews. Rather than view each new work in a genre as a repetition of the past, he argues instead that each new work is generating something new and unrepeatable.[12] Genres for Bakhtin represent a patchwork of uses: imperfect but good enough for the purpose at hand.[13] They both carry a history of the past, what he sometimes refers to as "genre memory," and open onto a future of unintended usages. This future potential is what enables them to help rework the present. As Gary Saul Morson and Caryl Emerson explain:

> Because genres are so often adapted from previous genres, they may carry the potential to resume their past usage and so to redefine a present experience in an additional way. Some genres easily lend themselves to this kind of "double-voicing"; they recover old contexts or intimate the possibility of new ones.[14]

Bouchareb's use of genres across his career seeks to enact double-voicing, that is, activating the historical contexts and embedded memories of these genres and then making them speak to a new context, whether it is the close-mindedness of Algerian society in *Cheb* (1991) or the linguistic pluralism of *multiculture* in

Belleville Cop/Le Flic de Belleville (2018). Morson and Emerson describe this process as double-voicing and reaccentuating:

> The unsuspected potential of a genre may also be used to "reaccentuate" a voice. This process is a common part of both individual psychic life, in which we arrive at our own inner discourse through reaccenting the discourses of others, and of collective social life, in which it serves as a method for adapting the lessons of one kind of experience to another.[15]

The recognizability of a film genre's style or even individual references to specific genre films allows for different historical experiences to be presented as already a part of the genres' historical memory.

Bouchareb's relationship to genre conventions is distinct from the ways in which French filmmakers have typically engaged with genre. When genre is broached in France, it is often subservient to the category of the auteur.[16] That is, genre is simply one element among many in an auteur's artistic palette. In part, this is the afterlife of the *Cahiers du cinéma* directors of the French New Wave who championed Hollywood genre directors like Hitchcock or Ford in their magazine's pages. When it came time for them to make genre films, for example Godard's gangster film *À bout de souffle/Breathless* (1960) or science fiction film *Alphaville* (1965), or Truffaut's gangster film *Tirez sur le pianiste/Shoot the Piano Player* (1960), the result is much less about the recognizable pleasures of genre conventions and more about an exercise in artistic expressivity and modernist reflexivity. Indeed, the pleasure of genre conventions in such films is analogous to the pleasures of cinephilia: it is the satisfaction of recognizing intertextual citations and being a part of the community that is able to recognize such citations. This has become a standard account of the pleasures of genre filmmaking in the age of postmodernism and pastiche, as seen in the reception of filmmakers like Quentin Tarantino.[17] There, irony and a sense of play prevent Tarantino's use of genre conventions from seeming oppressive.

Bouchareb, by contrast, often opts for a literal use of genre that is arguably closer to the mechanisms of remake, adaptation, or even fan fiction than it is to the knowing pleasure of cinephilic citationality. For example, unlike Godard's deconstructed war film *Les Carabiniers* (1963), Bouchareb's *Poussières de vie/Dust of Life* (1995) is a conventional prisoner-of-war film. Similarly, his so-called immigration trilogy, which includes *Days of Glory*, *Outside the Law*, and an as-yet unmade third film about the history of immigration in France from 1980s to the present, opts for straightforward genre exercises in the war film and the gangster film, respectively. Following *Outside the Law*, Bouchareb began work on a trilogy of films that explores the United States' relationship to the Arab world: *Just Like a Woman* (2012), *Two Men in Town* (2014), and *Belleville Cop* (2018). It is not clear exactly how the last film connects to the

Arab world, but Jamel Debbouze was originally supposed to play the lead role instead of Omar Sy, so perhaps these connections were lost when the casting changed.[18] What is important is that all three of these films are straightforward genre exercises: female friendship film/road movie, Western, and interracial buddy comedy. Importantly, these films were coproduced with American production companies and shot entirely or in part in the US.[19]

In his engagement with genres, Bouchareb corresponds neither to the model of the French auteur who makes European art films, like Abdellatif Kechiche, nor to the "*beur*" filmmaker who makes low-budget realist films or popular comedies about the realities of *multiculture* in contemporary France. Bouchareb makes big- and small-budget films set in and about places as diverse as the US, the UK, Belgium, and Africa. What is more, he has on occasion made films entirely in English, and he regularly produces films with production companies from around the world. Many of his films are multilingual, such as *Little Senegal* (2001), which takes places partly in the US and is in English and French. Despite the clear interest in genre one can see in his films, Bouchareb does not self-identify as a popular or genre filmmaker. Indeed, it is clear in interviews that he can speak the discourse of auteurism that conditions the French industry and the worldwide festival circuit.[20] Furthermore, in an interview on the *Road to Istanbul* DVD, he suggests that he likes to alternate between big-budget and smaller-budget films that are more personal.[21] However, even his supposedly smaller, seemingly auteurist films are also entangled with genre. Across the interviews included on his DVD releases, it is clear that he often thinks in terms of genre, either referencing a genre category like the Western or individual films that are well-known instances of a genre. In an interview included on the *London River* Blu-ray, he describes how his type of films make "a political proposition," but he grants that popular genre films can also have a political dimension. Bouchareb explains that while some films by Spielberg and Scorsese, or Andy Davis's *The Fugitive* (1993), might seem on the surface to be merely action films, they nevertheless contain a "denunciation at [their] deepest level."[22] This combination of genre filmmaking and a "political proposition" is something we find across his feature films.

Bouchareb's big-budget, genre-oriented films like *Days of Glory*, *Outside the Law*, and *Belleville Cop* are thus not a betrayal or a break from his smaller, auteurist or seemingly more realist productions like *Little Senegal* or *London River* (2009). Rather, his work invites us to consider how film genres can help rearticulate what counts as universal and who belongs. Bouchareb neither rejects nor criticizes the shared imaginary that Hollywood genres represent for audiences around the world. Instead, his films deploy a multitude of strategies that harness the language of Hollywood genres and redirect it to other ends. Attention to a few examples of the genres with which Bouchareb engages will reveal that genre filmmaking is not an occasional feature of his work. Rather, it is an essential component to Bouchareb's identity as a filmmaker.

TALES OF WAR: *CHEB* AND *DUST OF LIFE*

Like many genre categories, the war film has proved difficult to define. In the Hollywood context, Stephen Neale notes that some critics prefer to define it as any film that takes place in the broad context of a war, including service comedies and films about the home front.[23] Others, such as Jeanine Basinger, have taken a narrower approach, arguing that combat unifies those films that should count as war films. At its most narrow, Basinger's account suggests that each conflict produces its own genre, as in how films about World War II differ in tone and style from those about the Vietnam War.[24] Robert Eberwein offers the most inclusive definition, arguing that a war film can focus variously on "war itself," on the "activities of the participants off the battlefield," and on the "effects of war on human relationships."[25] This capacious definition allows us to consider films that may not even be set during a period of war but that nevertheless focus on the recruitment and training of soldiers, as is the case in Bouchareb's *Cheb* (1991). Here, the focus is not so much armed conflict but rather how military service mediates national identity and belonging.

Cheb takes up the question of the "*beur*" generation's double dislocation between the France in which many were born and raised and the country (or countries) of origin of their parents in the Maghreb. Bouchareb explains in an interview that the idea for the film came to him when he was vacationing in Algeria and he read a newspaper article about a young man with Algerian nationality who had grown up in France but was deported to Algeria after committing a crime and serving time in France. He suddenly realized that if he were expelled from France and forced to live in Algeria, the country would be totally foreign to him.[26] *Cheb* tells the story of a young man, Merwan (Mourad Bounaas), who grew up in Roubaix, near Lille, but is not a French citizen (he was born in Algeria). After being arrested for some petty crimes, the French penal practice of *double peine* sees him expelled back to Algeria, a country he does not know. *Cheb* mixes the open-ended wandering structure of the road movie with the war film and the Western. The customs officers send him to serve in the army as a means of reforming him, but he does not speak Arabic and does not know the culture. Nearly half of the film takes place in a military barracks near Oran in which we see Merwan training and interacting with officers and fellow enlisted soldiers. *Cheb* is far from the patriotic Hollywood war movies of the World War II and Korean War eras and is perhaps closest to the critical films of the Vietnam War period. In its focus on basic training and the boredom of being a soldier, it resembles the opening section of *Full Metal Jacket* (1987).

In Stanley Kubrick's film, the sequence at Parris Island features a US Marine drill sergeant, played by R. Lee Ermy, who humiliates and intimidates recruits in order to transform them into soldiers. Kubrick ensures that viewers are not sure whether to laugh or to be shocked by events until one of the intellectually disabled recruits suffers a breakdown and kills the drill sergeant before committing suicide. The conflict between the soldiers and the officers in *Cheb* does not approach Kubrick's dark humor. However, Bouchareb highlights how the rigid hierarchy of the military is alternately humorous and frustrating depending on one's perspective. The soldiers treat Merwan like an immigrant at first, and though he eventually makes friends, he becomes so exasperated with this new life that he decides to make a run for it and return to France.

Merwan eventually does make it back to France, though the final scene reveals him to be going through basic training in the French army. Just before leaving Algeria, he meets an *insoumis* or conscientious objector from Nanterre who had refused to appear for his obligatory French military service and fled to Algeria.[27] He eventually gives his papers to Merwan, though returning to France will mean time with the army. Once again in basic training, Merwan now understands the language (French), but his forlorn look causes the drill sergeant to yell at him to keep his head raised high. The film's ending calls attention to the ways in which military service mediates national identity and citizenship. Like the French Foreign Legion, which foreigners could join as a means of securing French papers, the armies in the film seek to produce national identity through discipline and service. At the beginning of the film, it is meant both as punishment and integration. However, when Merwan adopts the objector's identity, he uses the system against itself, that is to say, he reintegrates himself when the French system has already rejected him once. However, this reintegration is ambivalent. When Merwan remains silent as the other recruits sing "La Marseillaise," he reveals his uncertainty at how he fits into the supposedly universal French republic.

In his next feature film, Bouchareb takes up the war film more directly than in *Cheb* to bring attention to elements of colonial history in Vietnam that have been neglected. *Dust of Life* (1995) can be read as a kind of trial run for *Days of Glory* in terms of how to modulate narrative suspense and violent spectacle. *Dust of Life* is an example of the prisoner of war (POW) film, a subgenre of the war film that, as Paul Springer points out, is significantly cheaper to make because it often focuses on a single set.[28] The film, inspired by true events, tells the story of the son of a Vietnamese mother and an African American soldier near the end of US involvement in Vietnam. After the Americans leave in 1975, North Vietnamese troops take over Saigon. They ship the children of American soldiers and other orphans to camps in the North where the children will be "re-educated" through clearing jungle to make way for farming. The main character, Son Nguyen (Daniel Guyant), is a young man who is wrongly sent to the camp. Son is out buying food one night, and as he exits the store, he finds himself in the middle of a military round up and the soldiers throw him on the bus. Like the Jim Graham character in Steven Spielberg's *Empire of the Sun* (1987), Son is educated and comes from relative privilege. He can write, and he bears witness to life and death in the camp by keeping a journal. He eventually makes an escape attempt with two other boys but is recaptured. One of the camp guards, Un-Deux (Eric Nguyen), takes a liking to Son and sets him free at the end of the film for reasons that are not fully explained.

Bouchareb follows many of the classic stages of POW films, including first arrival, decoding the motivations of the other prisoners, and interactions with the guards. Charles Young argues that Hollywood POW films generally do not explore questions of collaboration with the enemy, despite the overwhelming presence of it in the historical record. While World War II and Vietnam-era Hollywood films ignore the question of collaboration, the majority of POW films set during the Korean War directly engage with it.[29] Bouchareb sets the question of collaboration and resistance at the center of the narrative of *Dust of Life*: some guards are friendlier than others, and some boys choose to collaborate while others resist. Viewers come to empathize with young Son not just because the film is focalized on him but also because he is falsely accused and because he is so principled in his dealings with the other boys. Indeed, before his escape attempt, he considers staying because he could become the head of a house and try to change the rules for the better.

Young explains that Hollywood POW films have most often been adventure films that feature a daring breakout. In part, adventure returns heroism to characters who have otherwise failed and been captured. Springer explains that even if Vietnam-era POW films do not feature breakouts, resistance is often a means of redemption for soldiers who have been captured.[30] Writing about post-World War II British POW films, Gill Plain suggests that the genre can employ a variety of tones that include the bleakness of *film noir* when it focuses on inescapable prisons or the levity of comedy and farce when it dramatizes the pleasures of escape.[31] *Dust of Life* opts for an overall serious tone that carefully manipulates suspense and character identification. In addition to scenes of resistance, Bouchareb dramatizes several escape attempts. We see several escaped boys returned to the camp by local tribes, and we hear them agonizing in the "tiger cage," foreshadowing Son's own confinement in a gentler version of the "oven" from David Lean's *The Bridge on the River Kwai* (1957) or the extreme kinds of prisoner torture seen in Michael Cimino's *The Deer Hunter* (1978). Son and another boy from Saigon plan and execute the escape attempt, and they keep it secret by killing one boy and allowing another to come along. The escape itself is a suspense sequence modulated with moments of freedom, quiet, and tense encounters with pursuing soldiers. By focalizing on Son, the film highlights his virtue and selflessness as distinct from the evil and selfishness of some of the other boys. It evokes some of the tropes of melodrama with its focus on the embodied emotions of suffering (beatings, starvation, illness) and its final recognition of virtue, when Un-Deux pulls Son from the tiger cage and frees him. The film's final subtitles affirm the "true" origins of the film's narrative. Like *Days of Glory*, *Dust of Life* seeks to memorialize events that have faded from memory through the narrative scaffolding of the POW film and an appeal to the moral absolutes of melodrama. Unlike some of the other classic POW films mentioned above, *Dust of Life* is not so much about an argument over the interpretation of events as it is a reminder that these events took place. Here, the "genre memory" of the POW film enables these events in Vietnam at the end of the war to become part of the audience's historical memory.[32]

THE WESTERN: *CHEB* AND *TWO MEN IN TOWN*

The Western has long been understood as the quintessential instance of the genre film for its highly coded iconography, especially its use of landscape. The genre has also been marked as fundamentally American for its connection to US frontier myths, both imagined and real, despite the fact that Western films have been made all over the world.[33] Recent scholarship on the Western has sought to situate the genre in terms of US imperialism and genocide. For example, Matthew Carter has argued that throughout its history the Hollywood Western has, as a genre, both reinforced a nationalist myth of the West and exposed the darker sides of US exceptionalism and imperialism.[34] In a related vein, Janet Walker argues that the Western is profoundly historical in the sense that it often tells history from the settler perspective.[35] Ella Shohat and Robert Stam draw explicit connections between the Hollywood Western, colonial cinema, and what they call "imperial adventure films."[36] What is important for our purposes here is the extent to which the Hollywood Western is arguably a colonial film genre that explores questions of economic conquest and exploitation and the forms of violence and displacement that accompany them.

Cheb connects to the iconography of the Western through its visual treatment of the Algerian landscape. Bouchareb repeatedly uses long tracking shots of desert landscapes and small isolated towns. At one point in the film, Merwan meets up with a young Maghrebi-French woman named Malika who has been locked up by her father and had her passport confiscated. At several moments during their run, Malika calls attention to how culturally and economically backward Algeria seems. In her view, it is a society for and about men at the expense of women. With this critical eye, Bouchareb invokes the Western's opposition between civilization, the frontier, and the uncivilized lands that lay beyond it. Merwan's desire to get back to what he considers to be "civilization," namely France, brings a critical eye to Algeria in the early 1990s. In a televised interview with Bouchareb from 1991, the journalist Henry Chapier notes how some people saw the film as a betrayal of Algeria when it premiered at Cannes. The interview dates from several months before the start of the civil war, and Chapier remarks that many in the Hexagon feared a coming Islamic turn in Algeria. Ultimately, Chapier argues that the film contains just as much love for Algeria as criticism, and Bouchareb goes on to explain how he sought to present a balance of perspectives, some of which he acquired through direct observation during his location scouting.[37] When Merwan is deported from France, he ultimately arrives at a desert that he has never seen before and that might as well be the unfamiliar yet impossibly beautiful landscape of a Western. Algeria is the land of his family origins, now his new home. When viewers observe Merwan looking at the landscape, it is not always clear what it is meant to signify. What he sees could be images of desolation, images of cinematic beauty, and spaces open to settlement. In this, Bouchareb signals the ways in which genre traditions can construct the spatial imaginary of places far from the locations in which they are set.

After Merwan's decision to flee the army, the film turns into a road movie while maintaining the setting and visual style of a Western. Indeed, the Western and the road movie are not as opposed as they might first appear. David Laderman argues that the Western is the "grandparent" of the road movie because of its emphasis on borders and journeys.[38] From this perspective, a classic road movie like *Easy Rider* (1969) simply exchanges horses for motorcycles. Michael Gott explains that narratives in road movies are defined by events that happen to the characters but that they do not always choose or initiate.[39] Merwan helps Malika escape, and as the pair wander through Algeria, trying to secure papers and get to Morocco, Bouchareb depicts just how conservative, misogynist, and religious 1990s Algerian society had become, at least to someone from France. Police recapture the couple, and Malika is sent back to her father. Through this ending, *Cheb* highlights the opposition between different notions of civilization that is at the heart of the Western. However, this opposition is mapped not spatially, between city and frontier, but culturally, between the Hexagon and a former colony, now an independent country. As argued above, Merwan has ties to both places but does not fully belong to either. In this, Bouchareb, challenges the ways in which most forms of nationalism seek to speak in the universal.

Bouchareb returns to the Western again with *Two Men in Town* (2014), which is a remake of *Deux hommes dans la ville*, a 1973 French-Italian coproduction by José Giovanni that starred Alain Delon and Jean Gabin. Bouchareb relocates the story to contemporary New Mexico along the US–Mexican border. Forest Whitaker plays William Garnett, a criminal who killed a sheriff's deputy and spent eighteen years in jail. While there, he converted to Islam and earned parole for the last three years of his sentence. Once Garnett is released, the local sheriff, played by Harvey Keitel, does not believe that he has changed and spends much of the film harassing him, waiting for him to slip up. His parole officer, Emily Smith (Brenda Blethyn), believes in him and helps him get back on his feet. Garnett gets a job at a local cattle ranch and even moves in with a new girlfriend that he met at the local bank. However, his past catches up with him, and his former criminal associate, Terence (Luis Guzmán), finds him and attempts to draw him back into his border trafficking scheme.

Bouchareb initially intended his film to be a story of redemption in the context of border trafficking. Indeed, he spent three months researching US-Mexico border relations, interviewing many locals in the American Southwest from different political parties. In the documentary on the border fence that accompanies the DVD release, Bouchareb admits that this aspect of the narrative fell away during production.[40] In terms of the film's genre, it is a mix of the ex-con film and the Western. Indeed, Blethyn explains in an interview on the DVD that after *London River*, Bouchareb talked about wanting her to be in a Western. In her mind, *Two Men in Town* is that Western.[41] This is certainly true if we are thinking about the Western in terms of setting. As in *Cheb*, Bouchareb chose to present the landscape throughout the film in wide shots with an eye toward beauty and desolation. Indeed, the filmmaker decided to shoot the film in Cinemascope, whose aspect ratio is often used to highlight vast open landscapes.

Two Men in Town also centers loosely around the conflict between the former criminal and the local sheriff. However, the film does not offer many of the traditional thematic concerns of the Western: the opposition between civilization and the frontier, geographic expansion as a form of American colonialism, or the showdowns between criminals and the law as a means of exploring notions of justice. Instead, the film concentrates on ordinary moments of work, prayer, domestic life, and love. In this, it is much more about who is allowed to make a home in the town than it is about conquest. The film opens with a scene in which migrants are captured, and throughout the film the sheriff never fully accepts that Garnett has paid his debt to society. Ultimately, the film reveals an unjust hierarchy between who can and cannot be a part of society.

The film sets out to be a tale of redemption, but in its conclusion, it opts for vengeance. In an effort to put pressure on Garnett to rejoin the criminal gang, Terence attacks his girlfriend, and in the final scene of the film, Garnett murders Terence in the same way that he killed the sheriff's deputy: bludgeoning his head with a rock out in the desert. In an extreme long shot, Garnett then walks out into the sunset as the film draws to a close. While this trope generally marks the narrative resolution of a Western in which the cowboy has successfully done his job, here it marks something darker. Indeed, this ending represents a twist on the original. In the 1973 version, the former criminal murdered the sheriff that tormented him. José Giovanni's film was meant to be an indictment of France's criminal justice system in the 1970s. Ultimately, Bouchareb intends *Two Men in Town* to be a topical Western about border relations, but it does not cohere around this possibility. The intended social critique of this film remains unclear. *Two Men in Town*, indeed, might reveal the limits of a filmmaker working outside his own social, cultural, and historical contexts, challenges that even extensive research could not overcome.

BELLEVILLE COP AND THE BUDDY COP GENRE

Bouchareb's most recent film as of this writing is *Belleville Cop* (2018). As a pure genre exercise, it is among his most enjoyable films to watch. In part, this is due to Omar Sy's magnetic star personality, but the film's charm also results from its genre: the mismatched buddy comedy, especially its 1980s Hollywood interracial versions in films like the Lethal Weapon (four films, 1987–98) and Beverly Hills Cop (three films, 1984–94) franchises. In interviews, Bouchareb has expressed how much he loves police comedies. What is more, he wrote the screenplay with Larry Gross, the screenwriter of *48 Hrs.* (1982), an early Eddie Murphy vehicle. Despite the cultural distance one might expect between Bouchareb and the American and Cuban-American cultures he dramatizes in *Belleville Cop*, the director describes himself as feeling "rooted" while making the film.[42] He does not explain what he means by this comment, but it could be as much about genre as about cultural context. However, the film did not do well with some critics in France who saw its use of genre as the empty repetition of clichés.[43]

In the film, Sy plays Baaba Keita, a detective in the culturally diverse and historically working-class Parisian neighborhood of Belleville. When a close friend of his, Roland (Franck Gastambide), is gunned down for his investigation into a network of African drug traffickers, Baaba heads to Miami to investigate what got his friend killed. Baaba teams up with a local Miami detective, Ricardo Garcia (Luis Guzmán), who is assigned to work with Baaba as punishment for harassing a rich Miami socialite who turns out to be one of the ringleaders of the drug trafficking ring. The pair initially struggle to work together, but by the end, they have become fast friends. In addition to the mismatched detectives, much of the comedy turns on Baaba's discovery of America. He brings his mother Zohra (Biyouna), who is content to sit by the pool, sip drinks, and embarrass her son. Baaba apparently has mommy issues, and his girlfriend, Lin (Diem Nguyen), who also works in law enforcement, is unhappy with his inability to move out of his mother's apartment and in with her. The drug trafficking plotline imitates that of *Lethal Weapon 2* (1989) and centers on a criminal gang who use their diplomatic immunity and an African charity organization to move drugs between a fictitious African nation, Miami, and France. In the climactic ending, Baaba and Garcia travel to "Daloa" and catch the Africans red-handed. The combat scenes reveal Baaba's Kung Fu abilities, and the ending leaves his mother in a romantic relationship with their Cuban-American driver and Baaba finally able to commit to Lin.

As I have argued elsewhere, echoes of Eddie Murphy are a central component of Omar Sy's star persona.[44] Even though the film references the *Lethal Weapon* franchise, it also operates as a loose remake of the first *Beverly Hills Cop* film (1984) wherein Baaba goes from the working-class neighborhood of Belleville to the glitz of Miami. Indeed, in a scene of dragon dancers (including Baaba) celebrating Chinese New Year in Belleville, one of the extras wears a black coat with the iconic sign of Beverly Hills in white on the back, but with "Beverly" replaced by "Belleville." What stands out in *Belleville Cop* is how multicultural it is, almost improbably so. In this, the film is not unlike Bouchareb's representation of multicultural London in *London River* in which several of the characters speak English, French, and Arabic.[45] In *Belleville Cop*, the Algerian actress Biyouna plays Baaba's mother. Baaba's girlfriend is Chinese, and he speaks the language with no trouble. Indeed, one of the film's early fight sequences takes place in a Chinese supermarket. After Baaba incapacitates the thief, one of the patrons starts yelling at him in Chinese that they should fight outside and that she is going to call the police. Baaba tells her not to worry, he *is* the police. When the police arrive, they ask Baaba what he is doing in that "costume." He tells them that it is not a costume; it is camouflage. Once the film shifts to Miami, characters repeatedly joke about how Cuban Miami is and several of the characters repeatedly speak Spanish, including Baaba. When Baaba first arrives at the Miami police station, his new partner, Detective Garcia, jokes with the front desk officers in Spanish about how France has sent a low-level street cop to the US for a high-profile mission. Baaba does not let on that he speaks Spanish. It is only later, during a scene in which Garcia and his mother come over to Baaba and his mother's house for dinner, that he reveals his Spanish-language abilities. Now that they have built trust, Garcia apologizes for making jokes at Baaba's expense.

The film in its original soundtrack is thus quadrilingual, though there are dubbed versions for French and American audiences that remove some of the play with language by making the dialogue track more monolingual. In its play with multilingualism and multicultural casting, the film enters the territory of color-blind casting in which actors are cast "without regard to their race or ethnicity."[46] Unlike the Cuban-Americans in Miami and the leaders of the African drug ring, the French characters do not have strong cultural identities in the film, and thus anyone could be cast into them. Ultimately, the fact that Bouchareb does not thematize this issue in the film naturalizes the diverse casting choices. *Belleville Cop* thus pushes the parameters of the interracial and international buddy cop comedy genre to the point of self-conscious parody, which in its very improbability can be read as the film's most inclusive gesture. Indeed, Baaba's method as a detective is always to act as if he belongs in whatever situation in which he finds or puts himself, whether this is an American police station, a high-profile news conference for the African aid organization, or the microphone on the dance stage of a nightclub. He knows others are discriminating against him, as in the case of Garcia and the American cops' sarcasm, or the French consular officials who loan him a Twingo to get around Miami, suggesting that they see his investigation as a joke. Nevertheless, Baaba perseveres and by acting as if he belongs, others come to see him as belonging, and he ultimately succeeds in toppling the African trafficking operation. The tropes of the mismatched interracial buddy comedy in which Garcia comes to accept and value Baaba's qualities foster an inclusive sense of belonging because of, not despite, the narrative improbabilities of the film and its genre.

CONCLUSION

This journey through some of the genres that Rachid Bouchareb employs highlights how he is an eminently transnational filmmaker who is especially interested in Hollywood genre traditions. Scholarly discussions of transnationalism have often struggled with how to understand imitations of Hollywood cinema and its genre-inflected traditions in Europe.[47] Considering the desire of Hollywood cinema to court audiences all around the world, can it even be said to be properly American? Given its commercial hegemony at the box office in many distribution contexts around the world, can it even be said to be transnational? Indeed, the seeming ubiquity of Hollywood cinema on screens around the world led Thomas Elsaesser to write in 1987 that "Hollywood can hardly be conceived, in the context of a 'national' cinema, as totally other, since so much of any nation's film culture is implicitly 'Hollywood.'"[48] For many, this hegemony is reason to craft laws, protections, and funding structures to protect culturally specific forms of national cinemas and coproduced regional cinemas that offer viable alternatives to Hollywood.[49] These issues and efforts are indeed fundamental. I raise them here, however, because I think Bouchareb's films, especially when considered through the lens of genre, suggest another way of relating to Hollywood. Instead of taking a critical stance toward Hollywood genre traditions, Bouchareb sees them as a shared language through which it is possible to translate between cultures and rearticulate what national cultures mean when they seek to speak in the universal. At times, this can take the form of invoking and subverting genre expectations, as one finds elsewhere in European art cinema. At others, it can involve reproducing genre conventions sincerely, seemingly uncritically, as a means of introducing diverse experiences to mainstream audiences. Bouchareb's films and career make global Hollywood genres local to different social, cultural, and historical contexts while also calling into question notions of locality. His films reimagine how individuals and communities attach to or are excluded from belonging, identity, and affinity across different cultures and spaces. This is how Bouchareb's films, and their use of genre traditions, represent an instance of rearticulating the universal in mainstream cinema.

NOTES

1. For a history of the term and the films and filmmakers grouped under it, see Will Higbee, *Post-Beur Cinema: North African Émigré and Maghrebi-French Filmmaking in France since 2000* (Edinburgh: Edinburgh University Press, 2013), 9–17.
2. For a discussion of these issues, see Anne Donadey, "Gender, Genre and Intertextuality in Rachid Bouchareb's *Hors la loi*," *Studies in French Cinema* 16, no. 1 (2016): 49; Ian Merkel, "Rachid Bouchareb's *Outside the Law*: Aesthetics and Reception in France," *Nka Journal of Contemporary African Art* 32 (2013): 64–5. About *Days of Glory*, see Panivong Norindr, "Incorporating Indigenous Soldiers in the Space of the French Nation: Rachid Bouchareb's *Indigènes*," *Yale French Studies* 115 (2009): 129, 140.
3. For a history of this move into the mainstream, see Higbee, *Post-Beur Cinema*, 26–60.
4. See Chapter 5 of this volume for further discussion of the American dimensions of Bouchareb's cinema.
5. Alison Smith, "Crossing the Linguistic Threshold: Language, Hospitality and Linguistic Exchange in Philippe Lioret's *Welcome* and Rachid Bouchareb's *London River*," *Studies in French Cinema* 13, no. 1 (2013): 75–90; Delphine Letort, "Rethinking the Diaspora through the Legacy of Slavery in Rachid Bouchareb's *Little Senegal*," *Black Camera* 6, no. 1 (2014): 139–53.
6. See Chapter 7 of this volume, as well as Ipek A. Celik Rappas, "Tracing a History of Terrorism in Rachid Bouchareb's Films: *London River* (2009), *Hors la loi* (2010) and *La Route d'Istanbul* (2016)," *Studies in French Cinema* 19, no. 3 (2019): 1–15.
7. Bennet Schaber, "Missing Children: Merzak Allouache and Rachid Bouchareb or, 2005 Ten Years Later," *Journal of North African Studies* 22, no. 5 (2017): 741–60.
8. Ernesto Laclau describes this shift as follows: "The spectacle of the social and political struggles of the 1990s seems to confront us . . . with a proliferation of particularisms, while the point of view of universality is increasingly put aside as an old-fashioned totalitarian dream." Ernesto Laclau, *Emancipation(s)*, new ed. (London: Verso, 2007), 26. See also Maurice Samuels, *The Right to Difference: French Universalism and the Jews* (Chicago: University of Chicago Press, 2016), 9–10; Patrice Maniglier, "L'Universel contrarié," *Critique* 833 (2016): 775–6.
9. Étienne Balibar, *Des Universels: essais et conférences* (Paris: Galilée, 2016), 124.
10. Ibid., 122–4.
11. Ibid., 37–41.
12. Gary Saul Morson and Caryl Emerson, *Mikhail Bakhtin: Creation of a Prosaics* (Stanford, CA: Stanford University Press, 1990), 290–1.
13. Ibid., 292–3.
14. Ibid., 293.

15. Ibid., 293.
16. This is not unique to France, and as Christine Gledhill notes, the auteur functioned in some early genre criticism in the 1970s and 1980s as a heuristic way to tie together interpretations of individual genre films. See Gledhill's essay in *The Cinema Book*, ed. Pam Cook, 3rd ed. (London: British Film Institute, 2007), 258–9.
17. Michelle Cho, "Genre, Translation, and Transnational Cinema: Kim Jee-Woon's *The Good, the Bad, the Weird*," *Cinema Journal* 54, no. 3 (2015): 45–6.
18. Jérôme Vermelin, "Omar Sy fait sa loi dans 'Le Flic de Belleville,'" LCI, 6 July 2018, https://www.lci.fr/cinema/video-omar-sy-fait-sa-loi-dans-le-flic-de-belleville-la-bande-annonce-2092506.html. Thank you to Leslie Kealhofer-Kemp for pointing this out.
19. Steve Pond, "Rachid Bouchareb Kicks Off Arab-American Trilogy With Sienna Miller Road Movie," *The Wrap*, 12 August 2011, https://www.thewrap.com/award-winning-filmmaker-direct-trilogy-arab-american-films-exclusive-30064.
20. "C'est quoi populaire? Rachid Bouchareb: réalisateur du *Flic de Belleville*," *Première*, October 2018, 59.
21. Rachid Bouchareb, *La Route d'Istanbul*, DVD (Blaq Out, 2016).
22. Bouchareb does not specify which films by Spielberg or Scorsese he means here. Rachid Bouchareb, *London River*, Blu-ray disc (Cinema Libre Studio, 2012).
23. Stephen Neale, *Genre and Hollywood* (London: Routledge, 2000), 125–33.
24. Jeanine Basinger, *The World War II Combat Film: Anatomy of a Genre* (Middletown, CT: Wesleyan University Press, 2003), 9.
25. Robert Eberwein, *The Hollywood War Film* (Malden, MA: Wiley-Blackwell, 2009), 45.
26. "Cheb, un pont entre deux cultures," *UniversCiné*, 30 November 2010, https://www.universcine.com/articles/cheb-un-pont-entre-deux-cultures.
27. The reference to Nanterre, one of Paris' historically Communist suburbs, is probably a reference to Communist refusals to serve during the Algerian War of Independence. For an account of this history and a discussion of the juridical regimes of refusing service, see Tramor Quéméneur, "Les 'Soldats du refus': la détention, la campagne de soutien et la répression des soldats communistes refusant de participer à la guerre d'Algérie," *Histoire de la justice* 16 (2005): 189–201.
28. Paul J. Springer, "Prisoners of War on Film and in Memory," *Orbis* 54, no. 4 (2010): 671.
29. Charles S. Young, "Missing Action: POW Films, Brainwashing and the Korean War, 1954–1968," *Historical Journal of Film, Radio & Television* 18, no. 1 (1998): 49–50.
30. Springer, "Prisoners of War on Film and in Memory," 681.
31. Gill Plain, "Before the Colditz Myth: Telling POW Stories in Postwar British Cinema," *Journal of War & Culture Studies* 7, no. 3 (2014): 278, 280–1.
32. See Chapter 8 of this volume for further discussion of the questions of history and memory in *Dust of Life*.
33. Neale, *Genre and Hollywood*, 133–4.
34. Matthew Carter, *Myth of the Western: New Perspectives on Hollywood's Frontier Narrative* (Edinburgh: Edinburgh University Press, 2014), 1–6.
35. Janet Walker, "Introduction: Westerns through History," in *Westerns: Films through History*, ed. Janet Walker (New York: Routledge, 2001), 7–13.
36. Ella Shohat and Robert Stam, *Unthinking Eurocentrism: Multiculturalism and the Media*, 2nd ed. (Abingdon: Routledge, 2014), 114–15.
37. "Rachid Bouchareb à propos de son film 'Cheb,'" INA/YouTube, 9 July 2012, https://www.youtu.be/b7e8bmIcOw0. The interview originally aired on France 3 on June 9, 1991.
38. David Laderman, *Driving Visions: Exploring the Road Movie* (Austin: University of Texas Press, 2002), 23.

39. Michael Gott, *French-Language Road Cinema: Borders, Diasporas, Migration and "New Europe"* (Edinburgh: Edinburgh University Press, 2017), 10.
40. Rachid Bouchareb, *Two Men in Town*, DVD (Cohen Media Group, 2015).
41. Ibid.
42. "C'est quoi populaire?" 59.
43. Théo Ribeton, "'Le Flic de Belleville': une comédie surproduite et informe," *Les Inrockuptibles*, 18 October 2018, https://www.lesinrocks.com/2018/10/18/cinema/actualite-cinema/le-flic-de-belleville-une-comedie-surproduite-et-informe; Thomas Sotinel, "'Le Flic de Belleville': Omar Sy sur les traces d'Eddie Murphy," *Le Monde*, 19 October 2018, https://www.lemonde.fr/cinema/article/2018/10/19/le-flic-de-belleville-omar-sy-sur-les-traces-d-eddie-murphy_5371962_3476.html.
44. David Pettersen, "Transnational Blackface, Neo-Minstrelsy and the 'French Eddie Murphy' in *Intouchables*," *Modern & Contemporary France* 24, no. 1 (2016): 51–69.
45. For a discussion of language use in the film, see Smith, "Crossing the Linguistic Threshold."
46. Angela C. Pao, *No Safe Spaces: Re-Casting Race, Ethnicity, and Nationality in American Theater* (Ann Arbor: University of Michigan Press, 2010), 4.
47. See, among other essays, Tim Bergfelder, "National, Transnational or Supranational Cinema? Rethinking European Film Studies," *Media, Culture & Society* 27, no. 3 (2005): 315–31; Stephen Crofts, "Reconceptualising National Cinema/s," in *Theorising National Cinema*, ed. Valentina Vitali and Paul Willemen (London: British Film Institute, 2006), 44–58; Paul Willemen, "The Nation Revisited," in *Theorising National Cinema*, 29–43.
48. Thomas Elsaesser, "Chronicle of a Death Retold," *Monthly Film Bulletin* 54, no. 641 (1987): 166. Cited in Crofts, "Reconceptualising National Cinema/s," 44.
49. See Jonathan Buchsbaum, *Exception Taken: How France Has Defied Hollywood's New World Order* (New York: Columbia University Press, 2017).

CHAPTER 5

The American Dimensions of Rachid Bouchareb's Cinema

Nabil Boudraa and Ahmed Bedjaoui

Transnationalism is perhaps the most obvious aspect of Rachid Bouchareb's cinema. Examining his filmography, one easily notices its multinational, global and hybrid characteristics, not just financially (production) but also, and most importantly, aesthetically and thematically. Several scholars have already written on this subject of transnationalism in relation to Bouchareb's cinema.[1] However, little has been written about the American dimensions of Rachid Bouchareb's films. Our aim in this chapter is to highlight the relationship between this Franco-Algerian filmmaker and the United States. We will examine several questions: How does this American imprint appear in his films? When and how does this fascination for the United States come about? How did it evolve throughout his filmmaking career? How does this American perspective come through in Bouchareb's work? How critical is he *vis-à-vis* American culture and politics? Does Bouchareb's fascination for the United States reveal something about his persona? By tackling these questions, we hope that, in the end, we will better understand both the filmmaker and his cinema.

CONTEXTUAL BACKGROUND

A good number of Bouchareb's films take place in the United States, including his very first feature film, *Bâton Rouge/ Baton Rouge* (1985), *Little Senegal* (2001), *Just Like a Woman* (2012), *La Voie de l'ennemi/ Two Men in Town* (2014), and his latest film to date, *Le Flic de Belleville/ Belleville Cop* (2018). This chronology actually helps trace the evolution of Bouchareb's rapport with the United States. In other words, he has evolved from using the country as a backdrop and as a place of fascination to a critical examination of American society, with its multiple issues and contradictions.

In order to understand Bouchareb's fascination with the United States, it is worth starting with an analysis of his own biography. Several aspects in Bouchareb's life find resonance in his films. We will weave some of these aspects into our analysis below and will emphasize that his family's uprooting, his experience in France as a child of immigrants, as well as the discrimination from which he suffered, pushed him to look elsewhere for a comfortable and comforting place. This is exactly where the United States became relevant, by providing an alternative to the prevalent identity politics in France, where the French assimilation policy was too suffocating. This is not to say that Bouchareb has naïvely ignored the tensions around identity issues that exist in the United States. On the contrary, as we will illustrate later, some of his films tackle the very same issues in the American context. There is no need for us to rehash here the whole debate about assimilation versus integration in the French context. Rather, our aim is to explain why and how Bouchareb sees in the United States a ground on which he can explore his thoughts and ideas on important issues, such as identity, ethnicity, nationhood, religion, women's roles in society, miscegenation, and coexistence.

A POINT OF DEPARTURE: THE *BANLIEUES*

Rachid Bouchareb is a second-generation Franco-Algerian, born and raised in a cosmopolitan Parisian suburb. He belongs to a generation of bi-cultural youths, born in France to Maghrebi parents. They are sometimes referred to as *"beurs"* (a term viewed as derogatory by many), a word formed by inverting the syllables of "Arab" using a kind of backslang known as *verlan*. This is itself a misconstrued designation, as many Maghrebi-French people are of Berber descent.[2] Navigating between their parents' heritage and majority French culture is no simple task for Maghrebi-French people of this generation. They suffer from discrimination that stems from the legacy of colonialism and the subsequent Algerian War of Independence, even if they were not directly involved in it. Most children of Maghrebi migrants were born either during this war or after it. Their integration into French society has also proved to be a Herculean task, notably because the French immigration system is one based on assimilation, a policy that denies them their family heritage.

It is common knowledge that in the 1970s and 1980s, American culture started to exert a huge impact on marginalized minority groups in France, particularly in the disadvantaged French suburbs known as *banlieues*. Among these influences, one can cite rap music, the dress code, the use of slang, and the way of talking, among other expressions and attitudes. As Alec Hargreaves explains:

> Anglophone spaces, above all the United States, have long dominated globally circulating cultural flows of this kind, which often exert a powerful attraction among younger members of minority ethnic groups. That attraction is visible in many aspects of "banlieue" culture, including language, dress codes, music (notably hip-hop), and street art such as "tagging" (i.e., graffiti). Thus, even when the action takes place entirely in the physically closed space of the "banlieues," films set in this milieu need also to be seen as located in wider, global spaces. Moreover, in their cinematic practices filmmakers raised in this milieu are often influenced by American models and from a very early stage, North America has featured as a real or imagined location in some of their most significant films.[3]

This American influence has obviously touched Maghrebi-French filmmakers, including Malik Chibane, Karim Dridi, Mehdi Charef, Abdelkrim Bahloul and Rabah Ameur-Zaïmeche, among many others. We argue, however, that of all the Maghrebi-French directors, Rachid Bouchareb is, without a doubt, the most influenced and fascinated by American culture. Furthermore, he is the most transnational. Bouchareb has "deterritorialized" his cinema,[4] by taking his stories and characters out of the national boundaries of France to other locales, including Vietnam (*Poussières de vie/Dust of Life*, 1995), Algeria (*Cheb*, 1991), and especially the United States (*Baton Rouge*, *Little Senegal*, *Just Like a Woman*, *Two Men in Town*, and *Belleville Cop*). As Mireille Rosello puts it, Bouchareb "was never national."[5] In fact, he has never confined himself to a specific category, be it national, linguistic, religious, or even ethnic. Bouchareb seems to perceive his identity as being hybrid, multiple, and always in the making.

The difficulties that Bouchareb had to endure because of his identity, especially during his childhood in a Parisian *banlieue*, enticed him to look for alternative places, where one's identity does not automatically collide with society. In Bouchareb's mind, America could be such a place.[6] The melting-pot nature of American culture obviously contrasts with the obsessive assimilation model of the French system, where hyphenated identities are not welcome because of the mindset that, first and foremost, everyone is French.

BATON ROUGE: AMERICAN DREAM OR MERE REFUGE?

After basking in this American culture in France, the time came for Bouchareb to experience America. The opportunity for him to make a film in the United States came in 1985, when he made his first feature, *Baton Rouge*, in the city of the same name. The question "Why Baton Rouge?" is raised a few times in the film, but no apparent response is offered. Instead, one character simply says: "Why not Baton Rouge?" Obviously, one can cite the American dream as a motivating factor, as well as curiosity about the Louisiana French names. We believe, however, that Baton Rouge as a destination is more the result of a desire for escape than the lure of this particular place.

The story revolves around three friends who want to leave their *banlieue* at any cost. Karim and Abdenour are French of North African descent. Their accomplice, Mozart, an amateur musician, is a "white" Frenchman. While Mozart dreams of running off to New Orleans for its jazz and blues, Karim and Abdenour do not seem to have a specific reason. They are out of place and restless. They certainly have a desire to go to Louisiana, but they do not exactly know why. The first scene illustrates this willingness to break away from both the place and the past. Karim works in his father's bakery, making burger buns (a reference to American fast food culture), and wants to leave his job and his father (and hence his origins) in search of something else, something new. The weight of both cultures (his North African roots and the constraints of French identity) push him to dream of another place.

For Bouchareb, almost everything in his filmmaking career started with *Baton Rouge*. In our conversations with him, Bouchareb told us that this first film is heavily influenced by American musicals, particularly Miloš Forman's *Hair* (1979) and Robert Wise's *West Side Story* (1961). This is clearly reflected in the scenes where the three protagonists perform a spontaneous dance in the streets of their *banlieue*. Despite their respective challenges (such as unemployment and family issues) these youths know how to break free from their conditions, albeit momentarily, through American cultural artefacts. In an interview, Bouchareb explains the context for this American influence on his cinema:

> If my first film expressed a drift toward the United States and not toward the Maghreb, it was because I felt involved in a culture based on America (music, cinema . . .). I was then in the shoes of the American immigrant, of the African American, of the uprooted. I listened to Black music.[7]

The influence of the part of American culture to which Bouchareb refers could be examined at many levels. An analysis of it would certainly allow for a better understanding of the culture of the *banlieues*.[8]

In a way, Baton Rouge is the dream for these Maghrebi-French youths to escape their conflicting identity issues and to free themselves from their condition as members of uprooted immigrant families. Although they do seek employment and new opportunities, what attracts them to the United States is not so much the American dream, but rather the dream of America. Simply put, America's melting pot here becomes the antithesis to the French obsession with assimilation.

NOT THE AMERICAN DREAM, BUT THE DREAM OF AMERICA

Rachid Bouchareb's interest in the United States is by no means fortuitous. Aside from Hollywood's stylistic influence, there is a philosophical reason based on his own biographical experience. Bouchareb understood early on that the United States has a tradition as a melting pot and is therefore a setting where a harmonious mixing of cultures is possible. He sees in the United States, despite all its flaws, an alternative to the Eurocentric way of thinking and dealing with race and ethnicity. As we explained above, Bouchareb belongs to a generation of Franco-Maghrebis for whom the centralist and assimilationist system in France prevents harmony between the two cultures that compose their dual identity. The tormenting issue of belonging and their discomfort in French society push many of them to look for other affective links. For many, the full return to their parents' culture is one such alternative, but for Bouchareb, this is not only a step backward, but also an exact duplication of the exclusivist system that they are trying to reject. His second film, *Cheb* (1991), is a perfect illustration of one such doomed attempt. Establishing rootedness in the ancestral land turns out to be not just difficult, but impossible. In fact, the protagonist in the film realizes the necessity of *errance* (wandering) when he says: "A man should be free to go anywhere he wants. Maybe one day, I'll go to the States. We are men, after all."[9] It is then through *errance* that Bouchareb embarks on his exploration of this prickly theme of identity, and not through a return to an "imagined community" or to a mythical source of origins.[10]

Bouchareb seems to advocate for a nomadic identity, or what Édouard Glissant calls "rhizomatic identity," whereby one could "exchange something with the other without losing or diluting oneself, without vanishing into a kind of non-space."[11] The problems of emigration, identity, and violent conflicts in Europe (and France, in particular) emanate from this centuries-old Eurocentric mind-set, linked to this atavistic notion of single and pure root, whether ethnic or linguistic. These atavistic and "tribal" attitudes are the main source of violence and exclusion for not just migrants in general, but also second- and even third-generation Franco-Maghrebis. How then do these philosophical reflections play out in Bouchareb's cinema?

Bouchareb is obviously not naïve. He knows too well that these ethnic tensions not only exist, but can even be worse in the United States. He believes, however, that the new world could be a place where the relation with the Other is not based simply on tolerance and coexistence, but better yet, on mixing and creolization. In fact, he announced this attitude early on in his filmmaking career. In *Baton Rouge*, Mozart, the majority ethnic French musician, ends up living with Victoria Paine, an African American singer, while his friend Abdenour dates (albeit briefly) Becky, a white American young woman. In *Little Senegal* (2001), Karim, the Franco-Algerian character, decides in the end to establish a real and lasting relationship with an African American woman, rather than see in their marriage of convenience just a chance to get a green card.

Bouchareb's Oscar-nominated *Dust of Life* (1995) narrates the story of racially mixed children in Vietnam, abandoned by their American fathers and harshly mistreated by the Communist regime. While this film is set in Vietnam and focuses on the post-war regime, there still is a connection to the United States through miscegenation. The fathers of the protagonists are US soldiers who had relationships with local women in Vietnam during the war. This heritage could also be interpreted as an indirect criticism of the American intervention in the region. In *Two Men in Town*, meanwhile, Garnett (played by Forest Whitaker) falls for Teresa Flores, a Hispanic woman, whom he wants to marry just a few days after their acquaintance.

In this context of *métissage* (creolization or racial mixing), Rachid Bouchareb seems to be pushing a bit further than some Hollywood films. His films are not

Figure 5.1 Forest Whitaker and Dolores Heredia in *Two Men in Town*.
Source: 3-b-productions.com

just about black and white tandems, but include many other ethnicities, as we have outlined above. In this regard, Bouchareb takes the American buddy movie genre and gives it a different outlook. Let us examine this perspective through his latest production to date, *Belleville Cop*.

THE BUDDY FILM GENRE AND THE ISSUE OF INVISIBLE MINORITIES

Bouchareb does not hide his admiration for the American buddy cop movies of the 1980s. Walter Hill's *48 Hrs.* (1982) and the Lethal Weapon series of four films (1987, 1989, 1992, and 1998), as well as the TV series *Miami Vice* (1984–90), have had a huge impact on Bouchareb's filmmaking. All of these include the classic duo of a white and a black character. While this film genre provided Bouchareb with a stylistic model for *Belleville Cop* (2018), he purposely goes beyond and expands this genre to include other minorities, thus making the buddy movie genre more in tune with the current context. This comedy-drama includes an American Latino (played by Luis Guzmán), a French man of African descent (Omar Sy), and two women from different minority ethnic populations in France (Algerian and Chinese, played by Biyouna and Diem Nguyen, respectively). Furthermore, Omar Sy's character is himself a product of *métissage*, as his mother is Algerian and his father is black African. To take this perspective one step further, creolization implies the unpredictable. According to Édouard Glissant, this lack (or absence) of control is exactly what scares the West, because the prevalent way of thinking is based on certainty, predictability, and control. In Glissant's view, mixing, be it cultural or ethnic, is simply too threatening to the dominant (white) ideology and power. So, Omar Sy's character becomes, in a way, the multicultural, multiethnic model of the twenty-first century. Unlike the actors/characters of the twentieth century, who were sometimes one-dimensional in terms of ethnicity, the protagonist of *Belleville Cop* is the epitome of the creolized and globalized world.

The buddy genre has provided more than simply stylistic inspiration for Bouchareb. During a press conference at the International Film Festival of Algiers (1–9 December 2018), journalists asked the director about his first comedy (*Belleville Cop*). He insisted that the influential buddy movies of the 1980s carried both political and social messages. *Lethal Weapon*, Bouchareb argued, is also a criticism of the apartheid situation in South Africa, while *Beverly Hills Cop* is full of references to racism and segregation against African Americans in the United States.

In sum, by championing mixed couples and diversity, Bouchareb challenges traditional and exclusionary modes of thinking, which characterize not just the United States, but Europe as well. In the context of today's globalized world, it is important to examine these perspectives on ethnicity, religion, cultural diversity, migration, and gender. Given that these concerns (among many others) are central in Bouchareb's cinema, one can wonder why he has been overlooked, by critics in particular.

THE IMPRINT OF SUNDANCE AND HOLLYWOOD'S WAR FILMS

Depending on the theme at hand, Bouchareb borrows from diverse Hollywood sources for his productions. The influence of both Hollywood and independent film (Sundance) on Bouchareb's cinema is not limited to the buddy movies of the 1980s and to the musicals of the 1960s and 1970s. On a thematic level, Bouchareb often starts off with the influence of an American film (or films) and then goes in different directions, hence affirming his own signature. In *Days of Glory* (2006), for example, Bouchareb draws from Edward Zwick's *Glory* (1989) to tackle the theme of North African soldiers and their participation in WWII. While *Glory* focuses on the participation of African American soldiers in the US Civil War (1861–5), Bouchareb's film examines the role of North African and Sub-Saharan African soldiers in the Allied forces. In drawing these connections, Bouchareb creates a link between two places (Africa and the United States) and between two eras (early twentieth century and mid-nineteenth century). The contexts are obviously different, but the problems remain the same. Segregation and injustice are universal issues. In this regard, the multiple problems faced by Franco-Maghrebis and by other minorities in the French *banlieues* are not that different from those one finds in American society. Bouchareb's vision is indeed much more global in scope than it first appears. He successfully interweaves issues from different cultures and eras, which makes his films universal in nature.

While the inspiration for this theme (participation of ethnic minorities in wars) comes partly from Zwick's *Glory* and from Stanley Kubrick's *Paths of Glory* (1957), Bouchareb chose to align his film with Spielberg's aesthetics, from his epic film *Saving Private Ryan* (1998). All of the Hollywood features in Bouchareb's film, including the battle scenes, the heroic characters, the closing sequence, and the narrative structure, contributed to making *Days of Glory* an epic film. In addition, Bouchareb has explained that in order for him to make *Days of Glory*, he had to watch many American war films, and several times, namely *The Longest Day* (Ken Annakin, Andrew Marton, and Bernhard Wicki, 1962), *The Big Red One* (Samuel Fuller, 1980), *The Bridge on the River Kwai* (David Lean, 1957), and *All Quiet on the Western Front* (Lewis Milestone, 1930).[12]

THE IMPACT OF THE ROAD MOVIE GENRE

Bouchareb acknowledges that early in his career, he became fascinated by American road movies.[13] In *Baton Rouge*, as soon as the three French youths land in New York, their adventure starts on the road. They travel by freight trains, hitchhiking, and taxi, and even buy a used car for the last part of their trip to Baton Rouge. *Cheb*, which takes place in the Algerian desert, also includes all the ingredients of a road movie. Bouchareb, who has a predilection for barren deserts and open spaces, chose the Sahara as the setting for this film on the quest for identity. The protagonist, a Maghrebi-French man, like Bouchareb himself, attempts to find roots and a sense of identity in his parents' homeland. Through the desert landscapes of southern Algeria, we see the influence of American road movies such as *Easy Rider* (Dennis Hopper, 1969), *Wild at Heart* (David Lynch, 1990) or even *Paris, Texas* (Wim Wenders, 1984). In *Cheb*, Bouchareb also uses endless roads that seem to lead nowhere. They resemble the roads in the Southwest of the United States, which we see in his later films, namely *Just Like a Woman* and *Two Men in Town*. In sum, to use a car analogy for these American influences on Bouchareb's cinema: he uses American models for the exterior design, but the engine, the interior, and the power are his own brand. To illustrate further the idea that Bouchareb draws on Hollywood's influences, and yet creates his own style of filmmaking, let us examine a case study.

THE GODFATHER: A MODEL YOU CAN'T REFUSE

When Bouchareb was asked specifically about the titles that influenced his controversial film *Outside the Law* (2010), he said:

> It was a mix. A lot of political movies, like *Z* by Costa-Gavras and Gillo Pontecorvo's *The Battle of Algiers*. Also, *The Grapes of Wrath*, the John Ford movie of Steinbeck's novel that starred Henry Fonda. Other epics too, like *Doctor Zhivago* and *Once upon a Time in America*, as well as various films from Italy, Greece, France and America. One very important movie was Jean-Pierre Melville's *L'Armée des ombres/Army of Shadows*, about the French Resistance in World War II.[14]

While Bouchareb did not mention *The Godfather* (1972) in this interview, we believe that Francis Ford Coppola's opus is perhaps the biggest influence on *Outside the Law*. Several critics have already noted the influence of gangster movies on Rachid Bouchareb's cinema, but *Outside the Law*, in particular, is perfectly modeled as a Hollywood gangster movie, even though the theme (or the many themes) of the movie are not necessarily conducive to such a genre.

Figure 5.2 The three brothers in *Outside the Law*. Source: 3-b-productions.com

To reach a broad audience with *Outside the Law*, Bouchareb structured it like a family saga, in the tradition of films like *The Godfather* and *Once upon a Time in America* (Sergio Leone, 1984). His Oscar-nominated drama is a follow-up to *Days of Glory* (2006), which is about the untold role of Maghrebi and West African soldiers in World War II. *Outside the Law* tells the story of a family fighting for Algeria's independence from France after World War II. After having their land taken away by French colonizers, the three brothers find themselves separated. Messaoud joins the French army in Indochina; Abdelkader becomes a political activist working for the Algerian independence movement in France; while the youngest, Saïd, chooses the profitable business of nightclubs and boxing in Paris. A cause soon brings them all together, and it is the Algerian War of Independence, which serves as the backdrop to this action-packed, historical drama, filled with crime, betrayal, violence, patriotism, and resistance.

While the context is dissimilar, from beginning to end this film evokes Coppola's *The Godfather: Part II* (1974). The two stories of iniquity and injustice are almost identical, and the viewer can also easily notice a similarity in the *décor*, the scenery, and the act of revenge. After all, the Sicilian/Italian culture in the Godfather trilogy is not that different from Algerian culture. The values of honor, dignity, family, and revenge at work in the film belong to the same geo-cultural space: the Mediterranean basin. We can readily identify many key scenes in *The Godfather* that inspired the making of *Outside the Law*, but let us start with the car bombing in Sicily, which killed Michael's newlywed wife. Abdelkader (the alter ego of Michael Corleone) also witnesses the killing of his new girlfriend in the exact same fashion. Following the scene when he has finally decided to accept his love affair with Hélène, he witnesses her atrocious death in a car bomb, which had been set for him.

In order to capture the intensity and the violence that characterized the conflict between the two Algerian factions[15] operating in France at the dawn of the Algerian War of Independence, Bouchareb draws from the war between the mafia families in *The Godfather*. For instance, the killing of the MNA member by the FLN in an empty café is identical to the scene in Coppola's film in which Frankie Pentangeli (played by Michael Gazzo) is strangled in a restaurant. Furthermore, the scene in which Vito Corleone (played by Robert De Niro) avenges the killing of his family by the village lord, back in Sicily, resembles Saïd's vengeful killing of the village *kaid* in *Outside the Law*.

In a way similar to Michael Corleone's assassination of both the New York police chief and the mafia boss, Virgil Sollozzo (also known as the "The Turk"), Abdelkader starts his criminal acts by killing the French superintendent (and torturer) in the police station. Interestingly enough, the hiding of the gun inside the restaurant restroom in *The Godfather* is also used, albeit in a slightly different manner, in this same sequence. In addition, *The Godfather: Part II* starts with Connie's wedding, and at a particular moment, the wedding ceremony is partly interrupted by the FBI. Similarly, Messaoud's wedding is interrupted and ended by the police. He and his brothers, however, did not have the power to resist, unlike the Corleone family. The wedding was also in the context of an anti-colonial war, which is not the case for *The Godfather*.

The other Hollywood blockbuster that has an impression (albeit small) on *Outside the Law* is Michael Mann's crime drama *Heat* (1995). The central scene, featuring a discussion between the police lieutenant, Vincent Hanna (played by Al Pacino), and Neil McCauley (the gang chief, played by Robert De Niro), finds resonance in Bouchareb's *Outside the Law*. Here, Colonel Faivre (Bernard Blancan) and Abdelkader (Sami Bouajila) meet each other in a hotel lounge and discuss their opposing respective causes, as if they were friends.

Alongside Michael Mann, Brian de Palma is another major influence on Bouchareb. Anne Donadey has addressed this connection in a recent article in which she examines specific scenes from *Outside the Law*, which she links with de Palma's *The Untouchables* (1987):

> Hollywood cinema, notably action films and cop and gangster movies, is ... constantly referenced in *Hors la loi*. For instance, two larger-than-life action sequences are filmed in that vein. The first is an improbably over-the-top shoot-out in a Paris police station in retaliation for a

police inspector beating up Algerian prisoners and throwing them into the Seine to drown. Although *The Battle of Algiers* also featured a very short scene in which FLN (Algerian National Liberation Front) militants went into a police station and killed a police officer, the style of Bouchareb's scene comes right out of Brian de Palma's violently stylized *The Untouchables* (1987) rather than from Pontecorvo's realistic style. Messaoud and Abdelkader infiltrate a police station from which Messaoud ends up shooting their way out, a gun in each hand. . .[16]

BOUCHAREB'S AMERICAN TRILOGY: A CRITICAL GAZE AT THE US

With the release of *Outside the Law*, Rachid Bouchareb faced a lot of criticism and scorn from both French media and politicians, especially conservative right-wingers, who accused him of falsifying history. Their blind nostalgia for French Algeria and their resentment of Algeria's independence prevented them from accepting a civil and peaceful debate around these issues. In any case, Bouchareb decided to move to the United States and open a cycle of films that tackle some important issues pertaining to American society. In this American trilogy, he specifically wanted to examine American relationships with the Muslim world.

Two Men in Town: A Modern-Day American Tragedy

Two Men in Town (also known as *Enemy Way*, 2014) is, without a doubt, the most American of Bouchareb's films. One could even argue that this is a typical Hollywood movie, not just because of its aesthetics, use of English (almost exclusively), cast (some of Hollywood's best actors), and setting (New Mexico), but also because of its themes, among which are American conservatism and Islamophobia. This film tells the story of William Garnett, an African American prisoner (played by Forest Whitaker), who converts to Islam and takes the new name of Djihad. Thanks to his good behavior in prison, where he spent eighteen years for the killing of a police officer, he is released on parole. As he tries hard to readjust to society and lead a normal life, he is constantly harassed by Sheriff Bill Agati (played by Harvey Keitel). He soon realizes that in addition to facing racism, he is also being persecuted for his conversion to Islam. Agati represents a caricature of the conservative American, who does not hesitate to persecute any minority, be it the Hispanic migrants trying to cross the border or the Muslims who lead simple lives but are always suspected of terrorism. In fact, the persecution of migrants and Islamophobia are two of the most important themes in Bouchareb's work.[17]

This film is the second part of a trilogy in which Bouchareb examines American perceptions of not just Muslims and African Americans in the United States, but also of Native Americans, albeit in a superficial way. In fact, *Enemy Way* (the other title of the film, which, in our view, better captures the essence of the story) refers to a traditional ceremony among Navajos, whereby medicine men help returning soldiers heal from the atrocities of war, and thus better reintegrate society without upsetting the balance and harmony of their community.[18]

Even though *Two Men in Town* is a loose remake of the 1973 French drama of the same name, Bouchareb gives this story his own touch. For example, he films it as a modern Western, which takes place in rural, as opposed to urban, locations. The magnificent and barren landscapes of the Southwest recall John Ford's Westerns. Bouchareb confirms that "there is [in this film] all the ideas of the Western, updated today with all the problems that the United States is facing."[19] Garnett's motorcycle replaces the cowboy's horse, but otherwise, *Two Men in Town* has all the ingredients of a Western, blended with elements of *film noir*. The landscape lends itself to this idea, but so does the culture of the Southwest, with issues of border crossings, illegal migration, human rights issues, white supremacy, and the plight of Native Americans, among other concerns.

More importantly, through the character of Garnett, Bouchareb wanted to recreate the culture of the Muslim African Americans of the 1960s.[20] By his conversion to Islam and his sharp look (he is always dressed in a suit and wearing glasses), Garnett becomes the alter ego of Malcolm X. Like so many young people of Maghrebi origin in France, Rachid Bouchareb felt rejected because of the color of his skin and his relation to Islam, even if he adopts quite a moderate approach to the religion. Garnett is a means by which to express this hatred of racism and Islamophobia. Also relating to the context of the 1960s and 1970s was the fascination with black American movements, such as the Black Panthers (present in Algiers during the 1969 Pan African Festival) and personalities like Malcom X and Martin Luther King. The latter was, one might add, the inspiration behind the peaceful March of the "*Beurs*" in 1983.[21]

In this film, Bouchareb also addresses multiple issues pertaining to clandestine migration and border crossings. The scene about the illegal migrants who died of thirst in the desert, with one of their babies eaten by coyotes, was inspired by actual events.[22] Similarly, there is a reference to the Minutemen, a militia group that takes it upon itself to control the borders, but that commits atrocities against poor, undocumented, migrants. Lastly, Bouchareb recently told us that he once saw the construction of a partial wall on the American–Mexican border, which inspired him to shoot one of the confrontation scenes between Garnett and Sheriff Agati at that location.[23] It is a premonitory hint at one of the most pressing issues in the United States today: clandestine immigration. In sum, these are all relevant topics, which are now of concern not just to the United States, but to the world at large.

Just Like a Woman: Gender, Religion and Cross-cultural Relations

Just Like a Woman (2012), obviously inspired by Bob Dylan's song of the same title, was originally intended to be a remake of Ridley Scott's *Thelma & Louise* (1991), but at the last minute, Bouchareb decided to take his film in a different direction. Scott's film puts two women behind the wheel to subvert the masculine gaze of road movies. It was very innovative for the road movie genre, and proposes a dialogue with its precedents, like *Bonnie and Clyde* (Arthur Penn, 1967) and *Easy Rider*.[24] Bouchareb's movie adds another layer through the use of references to ethnicity and religion. This is another example of our previous point about Bouchareb's tendency to depart from an American prototype to make something totally different out of it. Keeping the general background of *Thelma and Louise*, Bouchareb opted to use the story of two women from different cultural contexts in order to reiterate his favorite themes. It is true that the film still resembles *Thelma and Louise* in a number of ways. While Ridley Scott insists on feminism, Bouchareb goes further to denounce machismo, unemployment, the place of women in society, the condition of Native Americans, and racism (represented by a family of rednecks in a motorhome who are bothered by "Arabic" music and describe it as "barbarian").

Just Like a Woman is another buddy, road trip, and fugitive film, but with a different perspective and subtext. Bouchareb, who has traveled a lot in the United States, has said that he loves road movies, and through this film one can see that he has successfully mastered this genre, and even given it a personal cachet. More importantly, he deliberately added aspects of his own North African culture, namely music, belly dancing, and the Arabic language. He also used this story as a springboard to offer his perspective on some of America's ills: misogyny, xenophobia, anti-Islam rhetoric, and puritanism.

Bouchareb's version is an East-meets-West story, in which a white American woman (Marilyn, played by Sienna Miller) befriends an Arab woman (Mona, played by Iranian actress Golshifteh Farahani). They are oppressed at home (Marilyn by her husband, and Mona by her mother-in-law), but they both manage to free themselves through belly dancing. Everyone they meet seems to abhor and condemn them, except for the Native American character, which represents a leitmotiv in Bouchareb's filmmaking (*Baton Rouge* and *Two Men in Town*). It is our hope that Bouchareb will someday devote a film to Native Americans.

Set in sumptuous American landscapes, the film is also an ode to gender equality, respect of minorities, tolerance of the Other, and cross-cultural unity. The fear of the Other, mostly the non-white and the immigrant, is effectively

Figure 5.3 Golshifteh Farahani and Sienna Miller in *Just Like a Woman*.
Source: 3-b-productions.com

portrayed by Bouchareb in his film to show how it both dehumanizes its protagonists and prevents social harmony.

Little Senegal: The Search for Africa in America

Rachid Bouchareb, whose origin is North African, has always been interested in the search for African roots. His short animated film *L'Ami y'a bon/ The Colonial Friend* (2004) and feature film *Cheb* (1991) attest to this connection, but his breakthrough with Africa came with his 2001 drama, *Little Senegal*.[25] Little Senegal is the name of a tiny neighborhood in Upper Manhattan, New York, on 116th Street, between 5th and 8th Avenues, which is home to thousands of African immigrants, particularly Senegalese, who left their country in the 1980s due to economic hardships.

Little Senegal can actually be examined as a reverse version of the classic American TV series *Roots* (1977), in which the search for the African ancestors takes place in America instead of Africa. The film starts with a gospel song as a backdrop of a visit to the Slave Museum on Gorée Island in Senegal, where Alloune, the protagonist, is trying to find "the traces of an ancestor." To his dismay, he soon discovers that once the slaves were sold, they immediately lost their names and took their master's. Thanks to his persistent searching of the records, Alloune manages to trace back his lineage to the Robertson family. This name will take him to Ida, a descendant on his genealogical tree. Ida is a grandmother who manages a small kiosk in New York City. During the first encounter with Alloune, she rejects him vehemently. This segues to the multiple references to identity tensions in the film, and particularly anti-African racism, which Bouchareb had noticed when he was filming *Baton Rouge* fifteen years earlier. In *Little Senegal*, African immigrants are subject to constant invective from African Americans.

From one film to the next, Rachid Bouchareb asserts himself around the question of identity and of his African roots. He always highlights the link with his dream of America, which appears in one way or another in the three of his feature films that preceded *Little Senegal* (*Baton Rouge*, *Cheb*, and *Dust of Life*). But with the latter, the film director went further in tackling this subject, which has been an obsession for him. Without making any concessions, Bouchareb confronts eternal Africa and black America with a vision characterized by fluidity, sometimes by violence and derision, and constantly oscillating between optimism and disillusionment. After the fast-paced *Baton Rouge* and *Cheb*, we discover in *Little Senegal* a great serenity and a real maturity in both form and content. The pace is slower and with much less choppy editing. The cultural references are subtle, appropriate, and accurate. We find this same pace a few years later in *London River*, which examines similar themes: racial, religious, and ethnic prejudices. For critic Serge Kaganski, "the originality of *Little Senegal* is to move away from the usual white/black fault line to explore the different visions of negritude through the cultural divide between Africa and America."[26] *Little Senegal* reverses the process by bringing Africa to New York with the intent of instilling historical consciousness and a concept of Otherness. In a way, *Little Senegal* could be eye opening for the African American community (as well as other audiences). It breaks away from the traditional binary mold of Black and White to suggest a more mature vision of humanity and thus combat racial, ethnic, and religious prejudices. In this context, the character of Alloune (Sotigui Kouyaté) brings with him to New York not just African wisdom, but also a different way of accepting and dealing with Otherness.

CONCLUSION

In conclusion, our point is not to contest or ignore Rachid Bouchareb's Frenchness or transnationalism, nor his Algerianness or Africanness. In fact, one only has to examine the universal themes in his filmography to notice all of these aspects. We contend, however, that the American dimension in his filmmaking must not be understated. Both Hollywood and independent films have had huge impact on his cinema. But, as we have explained, Bouchareb goes beyond American culture. He uses it as a springboard to reach a universal dimension and appeal. He also sees in the United States a dream of an America where the old issues of ethnicity and religion could be jettisoned once and for all. His experience with these problems of belonging, identity, and discrimination allows him the possibility to offer an interesting outsider's perspective on American culture, with its burning issues regarding minorities, including Native Americans, African Americans, Hispanics, and Muslims, among others.

Lastly, despite his three Oscar nominations (for Best Foreign Language Film) and his long affair with the United States, Rachid Bouchareb's work remains little known in American circles, be it Hollywood, the media, or even academia. The aesthetics and concerns in his cinema should be ample reason to finally award him the full credit and acknowledgment that his work merits.

NOTES

1. Will Higbee and Song Hwee Lim, "Concepts of Transnational Cinema: Towards a Critical Transnationalism in Film Studies," *Transnational Cinemas* 1, no. 1 (2010): 7–21; Alec G. Hargreaves, "From 'Ghettoes' to Globalization: Situating Maghrebi-French Filmmakers," in *Screening Integration: Recasting Maghrebi Immigration in Contemporary France*, ed. Sylvie Durmelat and Vinay Swamy (Lincoln: University of Nebraska Press, 2011), 25–40; Anne Donadey, "Gender, Genre and Intertextuality in Rachid Bouchareb's *Hors la Loi*," *Studies in French Cinema* 16, no. 1 (2016): 48–60. See also Chapter 7 of this volume.
2. We will be using the term "Maghrebi-French" to designate this group instead of "*beur*."
3. Hargreaves, "From 'Ghettoes' to Globalization," 28.
4. We are borrowing Deleuze and Guattari's term to mean that certain cultural aspects transcend territorial boundaries.
5. Chapter 7 of this volume.
6. Rachid Bouchareb, interviewed by the authors in Algiers, 4 December 2018.
7. "Entretien avec Rachid Bouchareb, réalisateur de *Cheb*," in *Cheb: un film de Rachid Bouchareb—dossier pédagogique* (Liège: Les Grignoux, 2008), 8, available at https://www.grignoux.be/dossiers/12/Cheb.pdf.
8. Several scholars have worked on the culture of the *banlieues* and that of the so-called "*beurs*," such as Michel Laronde, Alec Hargreaves, Paul Silverstein, and Mustafa Dikec, among others.
9. "Un Homme doit être libre d'aller où il veut. Un jour, j'irai peut-être aux Etats-Unis. On est des Hommes après tout." The word *Homme* (Man) is used here to imply the freedom of mobility for humankind, and not in terms of gender.
10. We borrow this expression from Benedict Anderson's seminal work *Imagined Communities: Reflections on the Origin and Spread of Nationalism* (London: Verso, 1983).
11. Lorenz Khazaleh, "An Alternative to the Classical Eurocentric Way of Thinking," Department of Social Anthropology, University of Oslo, 3 October 2014, https://www.sv.uio.no/sai/english/research/projects/overheating/news/2016/van-haesendonck.html.
12. Fabien Lemercier, "Rachid Bouchareb, Director: 'Cinema Is a Crazy Business,'" *Cineuropa*, 20 September 2006, https://cineuropa.org/en/interview/67289.

13. Rachid Bouchareb, interviewed by the authors, Algiers, 4 December 2018.
14. "Interview with Rachid Bouchareb," Doha Film Institute blog, 18 October 2010, http://www.dohafilminstitute.com/blog/interview-with-rachid-bouchareb.
15. The MNA (Algerian National Movement) and the FLN (National Liberation Front).
16. Donadey, "Gender, Genre and Intertextuality," 50.
17. Ahmed Bedjaoui, *Le Cinéma à son âge d'or* (Algiers: Chihab, 2018), 95.
18. See "Coming Home: Strength through Culture," National Museum of the American Indian website, accessed 24 March 2020, https://americanindian.si.edu/education/codetalkers/html/chapter5.html.
19. Rachid Bouchareb, interview with Patrick Simonin, aired 30 April 2014, on TV5 Monde, available at https://www.youtu.be/xHicoxEICyk.
20. In Bouchareb's mind, Forest Whitaker is now the logical replacement for his favorite African actor, Sotigui Kouyaté, with whom he made *Little Senegal* and *London River*. Rachid Bouchareb, interviewed by Ahmed Bedjaoui, Oujda, Morocco, 11 June 2019.
21. *La Marche des beurs* (originally called the "Marche pour l'égalité et contre le racisme" [March for Equality and Against Racism]) was a march across France in which many Maghrebi-French youth participated.
22. Bouchareb was told about these events by some people in New Mexico while he was exploring the area for his film project. Rachid Bouchareb, interviewed by Ahmed Bedjaoui, Oujda, Morocco, 11 June 2019.
23. Ibid.
24. This idea was partly suggested to us by the editors of this book.
25. In 2009, he cowrote (with historian Pascal Blanchard) and directed a short documentary film entitled *Exhibitions* in which he denounced the human zoos of nineteenth-century Europe, when colonized black Africans (and other colonized peoples) were brought to European fairs as objects of exhibition.
26. "Little Sénégal," *Les Inrockuptibles*, 30 November 2000, https://www.lesinrocks.com/cinema/films-a-l-affiche/little-senegal.

CHAPTER 6

We Could Be Heroes: "Arabs" Becoming Brave in Rachid Bouchareb's Cinema

Julien Gaertner

The first scene unfolds on 5 September 2006. Jacques and Bernadette Chirac have attended a private screening of Rachid Bouchareb's film *Indigènes/ Days of Glory* (2006). Deeply moved, the presidential couple leave the movie theater determined to introduce a new law to put an end to discrimination against the colonial veterans who fought for the liberation of France in 1944.[1] The film not only establishes Rachid Bouchareb as a leading filmmaker capable of influencing a political decision, but also achieves an additional *tour de force*. For the first time, four descendants of North African immigrants portray Arab heroes on screen, who defended and liberated France. The social climate was tense in the wake of the riots of 2005 and the debate around Article 4 of the Law of 23 February 2005, which specified the "positive role of colonization," a law that was to be repealed by the president of the republic after one year of debate. *Days of Glory* was released in September 2006 and achieved a remarkable box office success with more than three million tickets sold in France. It also earned a certain critical acclaim and was rewarded by an Oscar nomination in the Best Foreign Film category, where it represented not France, but Algeria. This choice led to a controversy around Rachid Bouchareb's nationality—a French citizen, born in France to Algerian parents—which mostly went unnoticed because the film was untouchable, politically and artistically.[2] A few months before, in the euphoria of the moment, *Days of Glory*'s main actors—Jamel Debbouze, Roschdy Zem, Sami Bouajila, Samy Naceri, and Bernard Blancan—had won a collective Best Actor award at the Cannes International Film Festival.

The second scene takes place four years later, once again on the red carpet of Cannes. With almost the same cast, Rachid Bouchareb presents *Hors la loi/Outside the Law* (2010), a film about three brothers who escape the Sétif massacres in 1945 and experience the upheavals caused in France by the

Algerian War of Independence. This time, Bouchareb's film receives a cold welcome. On the very morning of the screening, demonstrators gather *en masse* in the streets of Cannes to protest against the film, calling for a "Crusade on the Croisette." Led by the Alpes-Maritimes regional representative, Lionnel Luca, several hundred people echo the opinion that right-wing politicians have been fueling for several weeks. These politicians accuse the film of being "pro-FLN,"[3] "falsifying history and reopening wounds," and even "using public money to insult the Republic."[4] Forty years after the controversy sparked by the film *Élise ou la vraie vie/Élise, or Real Life* (Michel Drach, 1970), Rachid Bouchareb was reopening the Algerian wound in France's collective memory. In 1970, several observers had found it

> shocking that, in the midst of the Algerian War, Elise protected and assisted Mohamed, a *fellagha*. Would censorship not be opposed to a film that holds up as an example the love story of a Frenchwoman and a Nazi? The film portrays French and Algerian workers, and the latter are represented in a much more favorable light than the former.[5]

The cast of *Outside the Law* climbed the steps of the Cannes Film Festival in spite of the political protest and pressure, but within a few days, the goodwill that Rachid Bouchareb and his heroes had won with *Days of Glory* seemed to have eroded. The press hesitated to praise a film it considered less accomplished from an artistic point of view. Audiences did not rush to see this feature film, whose ticket sales barely topped 300,000, or ten times fewer than what the heroes of *Days of Glory* had achieved. The characters that had brought tears to the eyes of spectators when they liberated France seemed much less desirable when they portrayed Algeria's independence.

Can Arabs be heroes in French cinema? Rachid Bouchareb seems to be able to maintain their heroic stature only to a certain extent, as confirmed by the public's reaction. A comparison of his two films *Days of Glory* and *Outside the Law* sheds light on the work of the filmmaker, the changes he brings to French cinema, and especially the way he rubs salt—via his heroes—into the deep wound that the Algerian War of Independence has left in the collective memory. Both feature films question the public's capacity to consider their Arab heroes as fully French. They also demonstrate the extent to which memories are still raw when the colonial past resurfaces.

AMERICAN-STYLE ARAB HEROES

In the 1980s, the debate around immigration in France, in politics and on the news, focused essentially on populations originating from the Maghreb (Algeria, Morocco, Tunisia), which dominated migratory flows after World War II. Among the different names given to these populations—Maghrebi, "*beur*" (French slang for Arab), North African, Muslim—the word "Arab" is most prominent in people's minds.[6] Far from defining a stable objective group, the word represents a social construction and cultural stereotype (something indicated in this chapter by the use of quotation marks around the word) that evolves in space and time and reflects social and political attitudes, discourses, and prejudices.[7] These "Arabs," who bring back memories of colonial times, also become the symbol of an Islam that is constantly presented as a threat. The word "Arab" serves as a common denominator in public opinion, and French cinema has never hesitated to use it either. From the early 1920s to the late 1960s, for example, the colonial-cinema genre erased any trace of Maghrebi fighters or resistors when referring to "Arabs." As such, on screen, North Africa became a virgin space to be conquered.[8] Resistance to the legionnaires was essentially depicted by a few "rebellious prostitutes"[9] or by shadows fleeing the fighting.[10] Even French films that reinterpreted the Algerian War of Independence[11] offered only subordinate roles to "Arabs." As Benjamin Stora points out:

> It has always been extremely difficult to portray the Other, the former native of colonial times, in French cinema. This absence is obvious both in entertainment cinema, where an exotic representation of the Other is maintained, and in the cinema of the 1960s, which condemned colonialism but neglected to show the fighters on the other side. As soon as these fighters started to act on their own, it presented a problem.[12]

In *Days of Glory*, Rachid Bouchareb not only upsets the representation of "Arabs" previously imposed by French cinema, but also transforms these formerly marginal characters into true heroes inspired by obvious film references. Comparisons are inevitable between *Saving Private Ryan* (Steven Spielberg, 1998) and *Days of Glory*. Bouchareb's film follows the codes of war movies as defined by American cinema. Spectacular and ultra-realistic fighting during the Normandy landing on one side can compare to the equally striking murderous assault of Monte Cassino on the other. The heroes of both films finish their journey defending an Alsatian village, where the snipers come to a tragic end. References abound, both narrative and visual, to the American model. Where Steven Spielberg draws the portrait of a multiethnic America, Rachid Bouchareb portrays colonized fighters from diverse social origins. They include:

> Yassir, a stubborn, sandal-clad mercenary who does not hesitate to rob corpses; Said, a tall child who leaves the skirts of his mother to become a man; Messaoud, a lover of France who wants to flee the misery of his country; and Abdelkader, a very young, well-educated, ranked soldier, thirsty for social revenge.[13]

The two works have other shared or similar aspects: the love of the flag, the praising of bravery, and especially the sense of sacrifice for a greater cause. Both films conclude with shots of cemeteries, for American fighters in one film and North African ones in the other. All of them died for freedom and were able to put aside their social condition and sacrifice their lives for a higher purpose.

Besides allusions to Steven Spielberg's film, one cannot help but observe influences and references to American films on the Vietnam War. The comparison between Algeria and Vietnam as theorized by Benjamin Stora[14] finds a cinematographic echo in Rachid Bouchareb's film. The heroes with immigrant origins who were sacrificed for their country in *The Deer Hunter* (Michael Cimino, 1978) can be seen as models for the bands of brothers of *Days of Glory* or *Outside the Law*. Like their American counterparts, Yassir, Said, Messaoud, and Abdelkader show bravery as they defend a sometimes ungrateful nation. "It should no longer be ignored," writes Olivier Séguret in the daily *Libération*, "that Rachid Bouchareb's film tells the story of four young Algerians [*sic*] who volunteered in the French army in 1943 to free the mother country from the Nazi yoke. They discover all at once a country, a people, and the war."[15] The newspaper *La Croix* considers the sacrificial journey of these Maghrebis as "the missing link in the history of France."[16] *Télérama* makes a similar observation:

> What is it to be French? It is, among other things, to be a "*bougnoule*" [derogatory French word for a Maghreb native] and ready to die for France. It took some time to be able to state this truth. It corresponds to a hidden page of history that Rachid Bouchareb is exhuming and brandishing in broad daylight in a beautiful gesture of recovered dignity.[17]

If drawing inspiration from American models works in *Days of Glory*, it shows its limits in *Outside the Law*. In *Le Monde*, the critic Thomas Sotinel points his finger at the film's "conventional rebels" and considers that "the scenario deliberately unwinds its string of moral and political dilemmas that the two older brothers always resolve in favor of the cause, and against the individuals."[18] Others point out the not-too-subtle ambition to measure up all at once to *Once upon a Time in America* (Sergio Leone, 1984) and *Gangs of New York* (Martin Scorsese, 2002) as a historical fresco, to *Raging Bull* (Scorsese, 1980) as a pugilistic saga, or even to *The Godfather* (Francis Ford Coppola, 1972) as a story of brothers torn apart. The magazine *Première* notes that the film offers "a nicely polished, not unpleasant, moment of entertainment, but is nevertheless light years away from the *Once upon a Time in Algeria*, *Independence Now* or *Gangs of Sétif* that a Leone, a Coppola, or a Scorsese might have created from the same story."[19] This fascination with American cinema would become more and more evident in the filmography of Rachid Bouchareb, who would either shoot future films in the United States[20] or continue to draw inspiration from America, as in his most recent film, *Le Flic de Belleville/Belleville Cop* (2018). After all, his first feature film, *Bâton Rouge/Baton Rouge* (1985), was already the story of an American dream.

Rachid Bouchareb seems to repeatedly borrow from American cinema to make his Arab characters recognizable to viewers and to provide them with a clear dramatic path that will make them perfectly identifiable. The heroes of *Days of Glory* and *Outside the Law* are cinematographic archetypes that defend the same values as their American counterparts while still being specific to French cinema.

"IN HISTORY BOOKS, THE HEROES DO NOT LOOK LIKE US"[21]

To be a film hero, and at the same time to claim an Arab identity, is not an easy equation in French cinema. Yet it seems to be Rachid Bouchareb's full intention. The promotional campaign for *Days of Glory* gave its actors ample opportunity to address the issue. For *Le Nouvel Observateur*, "one year after the riots in the suburbs," the actor Jamel Debbouze is a "new soldier of the Republic."[22] In *Le Monde*, Jean-Luc Douin believes that the film

> not only invites France to recognize the merit of these men considered as sub-patriots, or recall that at the beginning of the 1960s their pensions and invalidity benefits were frozen, but pushes our country to search its conscience and examine the way it looks at and treats its red, white and Arab citizens.[23]

Questioned by *Le Nouvel Observateur*, Jamel Debbouze points out the veterans' lack of resentment and links this to ongoing debates about the level of integration of Maghrebi-French youth in France:

> When we see their state of mind, we see what a mistake it is to keep talking to us about integration. We are legitimate in this country; we grew up here; we are "*icissiens*" [from "*ici*," from here]. This is our country. I love France . . .
> No politician will make us change our minds about our home and our roots. They must take us into account. We are the lifeblood of this country. I hope that people who go see the film will understand that the face of France also looks like ours.[24]

Roschdy Zem, who plays the role of Messaoud, believes that "racists criticized us for being Arabs; now they are criticizing us for being French."[25] After reminding the audience of the bravery shown in the service of a republic that was colonial at the time, the "Arab" heroes claim the full right to be French, with a shared history, shared memories, and the demands of citizens. The strength of *Days of Glory* therefore lies in Rachid Bouchareb's capacity to use cinematographic codes—especially character development—for the purpose of advancing a new narrative and a vision of the history of France that was unprecedented on screen.

In interviews with historians,[26] debates, opinion pieces, TV reports, and documentaries,[27] the film attracted significant attention and dominated the public debate for several weeks. The press largely echoed the debate around the military pensions paid to these veterans while at the same time giving the spotlight to actors who defended their identity throughout the different interviews. *Le Nouvel Observateur*, which devoted several articles to the film and its actors, quoted in its title the one who represents them best, Jamel Debbouze, who declared "the '*beur*' does not exist" and "why I love France."[28] For the heroes of *Days of Glory*, the question is no longer about being loyal or not to the country that they allude to as "the motherland," but about claiming their rightful place on French soil after a sacrifice for France. Through these "Arabs," who by virtue of their heroic actions can claim French nationality as a full right, the historian Marc Potier considers that the film fills "a hole in collective memory" and that it can hope "to have a beneficial impact on the content of schoolbooks."[29] Luc Gruson believes that the film "adopts the right tone: it bears witness to history without embellishing it, without settling scores or placing memories or victims in competition."[30] Throughout France, the film became an object of historical interest. The newspaper *La Croix* reported that before a preview of the film in a Bordeaux cinema,

> around one hundred Moroccan veterans, in djellaba, cane in hand, with military medals on their chest, were silently waiting for the film to start. In their speeches, Rachid Bouchareb and Jamel Debbouze seek to set a resolutely political tone. Immigration is not only an economic issue, insists the director. Not all immigrants are road sweepers: some were also liberators.[31]

The first dialogues of the film set the tone for this heroization, pointing to the commitment to France and the heroes' ultimate moral choice, their sacrifice. In an Algerian village, a local official urges the men to voluntarily enlist. "We must liberate France from the German occupation! Our blood will wash the French flag!" he shouts to those who do not hesitate to climb into the French army trucks.[32] Despite the fears of his mother, Saïd—portrayed by Jamel Debbouze—wants to join them: "I want to help France," he says. Once in Provence, Saïd kneels down and remarks on the quality of the soil. His friend Messaoud confirms, in a statement that leaves no room for discussion: "The soil of France is better." Moments later, upon their arrival in a village, Saïd, exhilarated by his first battle, recounts his exploits to a pretty French woman. In his broken French, he insists: "I liberate a country, it is my country! Even if I never see it before!" His character seems to constantly need to reaffirm that the presence of Maghrebi immigration on French soil has become legitimate by right of blood, by right of war.

Participation in the liberation could, in a way, make migration from the Maghreb to France legitimate. When questioned by a France 2 journalist during a televised interview, another actor in the film, Samy Naceri, follows the same reasoning: "When my son goes to school, I want his history teacher to say to him: 'There were Maghrebis, Jews, *pieds-noirs* (European settlers in Algeria), who defended France . . . We were the cannon fodder.'"[33] On the same TV program, Jamel Debbouze emphasizes that "in history books, the heroes do not look like us, or very little." Sami Bouajila then adds: "When people say that this is a chapter of our history, they don't say that it's ours, the French people of Maghrebi origin. It's our history, our shared history."[34] But this history is not always easily shared, and sometimes it awakens a certain guilty conscience. On its front page, *L'Express* wonders: "Should we be ashamed to be French?"[35] Because in the final scene of the film, an aged Abdelkader—the only survivor of the tragic epic that ends in an Alsatian village where the local population had given them a warm welcome—wanders in the middle of a cemetery, looking for the graves of his former companions under the tricolor French flag floating in the wind.[36] Without a word, the elderly man returns to the housing complex for single workers where he has been living for decades, separated from his family. With this bitter ending, "*Days of Glory* becomes a great national cause"[37] and *La Croix* points out that "the fact that men exposed to death, who can no longer accept the unfair treatment imposed on them, awaken desires of emancipation, is one of the most fruitful contributions of this film."[38]

Even though *Days of Glory* denounces an injustice and a discrimination against Maghrebi soldiers, Rachid Bouchareb seems to choose not to cross other lines. The ideology behind the independence of the countries of the Maghreb is never expressed. Abdelkader is the spokesperson for it throughout the film, but the dialogues only address this indirectly: "Captain, with our French brothers in arms, we are fighting under the same flag, on the same ground, against the same enemy . . . the German bullets do not distinguish us, Captain." Later, in front of a crowd of soldiers gathered around him, he explains that they are there "to obtain the same rights as [their] French brothers in arms," before being interrupted by his superiors, who do not appreciate his speech. This taste for liberty, gained in combat and in contact with the "motherland," will be costly for Abdelkader, who will be condemned to a life of isolation and poverty. But far from directly expressing any aversion to the French system, the film only exposes the facts, and the actors, in their interviews, continually emphasize the veterans' lack of bitterness.[39] In *Days of Glory*, Rachid Bouchareb seems to keep his heroes, who were sacrificed in war, on the threshold of what can be said and is acceptable in a French society recently shaken by post-colonial debates on its identity.[40] By claiming French citizenship for his heroes without asserting a desire for independence for the Maghreb countries, the director marks not only the history of French cinema but also the history of immigration, and his film has become a key milestone for both. But after this masterstroke, Rachid Bouchareb seemed determined to go further and to overcome the taboos in collective memory that he had only alluded to thus far.

A CONTROVERSIAL HEROISM

For the critic Olivier Barlet, *Outside the Law* follows the trajectory set by *Days of Glory*:

> There is perfect continuity between the two sagas. They share the same enveloping music that arouses emotions at the chosen moment, use the same epic lyricism to describe the era, show the same desire to historically document the Franco-Algerian relation by means of an effective fiction designed for the general public, and pull the same big heavy strings to convey a message with every shot. The same actors carry the same names in both films, even if most of them had died by the end of *Days of Glory*.[41]

The filiation between the two stories is not only clear in the way the auteur constantly explores the place of Maghrebis in the history of France, but is also obvious in the filmmaker's desire to stage these two narratives as cinematographic frescoes that borrow heavily from American films.

Outside the Law opens with the tragic scene of the spoliation of an Algerian family's farmland by colonists in 1925, but then sends us forward—for the length of the credits—to archived images of the liberation parade of 8 May 1945 on the Champs-Élysées, images of public rejoicing that could have been included at the end of *Days of Glory*. These black and white images scramble the border between history and fiction and soon dissolve into color to carry us back to Algeria, in Sétif, on the same day. Rachid Bouchareb uses this film technique to place two key moments in French history face-to-face, and also to present his new film, *Outside the Law*, as a continuation of *Days of Glory*. Using this symbolic date as a starting point—when France celebrated liberation and the end of World War II at the same time as violently repressing desires of independence in Algeria—Rachid Bouchareb begins *Outside the Law* where he had left off with *Days of Glory*. Unvoiced aspirations for independence give way to the unambiguous depiction of the first upheavals in the fight for the end of colonization in Algeria. The scene that follows the credits, and which was the main cause of the controversy surrounding the film, takes us to a demonstration—no longer held on the Champs-Élysées but on the streets of Sétif. An Algerian flag is brandished. A shot goes off. An Algerian demonstrator collapses. Repression begins.

Paris is liberated, while Sétif is subject to colonial rule. The symbolism has an impact on screen, but it also gave rise to protest in France, even before the first public screening of the film. Because no feature-length fiction film had yet dared to address the subject of the repression in Sétif,[42] a part of public opinion was offended by Rachid Bouchareb's attempt to do so. With *Outside the Law*, the heroization of three Algerian brothers (portrayed by Jamel Debbouze, Roschdy Zem, and Sami Bouajila), who have kept the same given names as their characters in *Days of Glory*, provoked a completely different debate than its predecessor. Before the screening at the Cannes International Film Festival, an ideological controversy was fueled by member of parliament Lionnel Luca, secretary of state for veterans Hubert Falco, and the mayor of the city of Cannes and his deputies, who organized a gathering in front of City Hall. A movement called "Truth History—Cannes 2010" was also created to call people to demonstrate and disrupt the festival. The film was accused of supporting the FLN with the financial backing of the French state. What it really did was shed light on an unvoiced chapter in the history of French colonization in Algeria. Until then, and unlike Algerian films,[43] most French fictions dealing with the Algerian War of Independence had exclusively focused on the period from 1954 to 1962, thus ignoring the earlier events and massacres. The film was criticized for showing the repression of the massacre of Sétif by the French troops, and in addition, the director was accused of having produced, under the pretense of fiction, a work of art that defends a particular vision of history. Rachid Bouchareb does indeed blur the line between fiction and history, but so do many films, if not all fictions. While *Platoon* (Oliver Stone, 1986) or *Apocalypse Now* (Francis Ford Coppola, 1979) plunge the spectator into a metaphysical vision of war, this universal dimension that is present in the American models is absent from *Outside the Law*.

Critics also did not hesitate to point out the heroes' failings. When Sami Bouajila's character publicly rallies support for the FLN among the workers of a factory, the sequence is not only very demonstrative and ideological, but also, and above all, not very credible. In reality, the FLN had decided to conduct only clandestine operations on French territory. Similarly, allusions to the struggle between the FLN and the rival MNA (National Algerian Movement) of Messali Hadj were considered hardly more convincing by most of the critics, as were the scenes of violence. When the characters engage in spectacular armed raids against the *harkis* or police officers, Rachid Bouchareb continues his heroization of the FLN.[44] These scenes of violence, which are specific to the codes of the gangster film, are historically problematic because only once did the FLN bring the war officially to French soil (in August 1958), before changing its strategy. Finally, this heroization has the further disadvantage of obscuring an anti-colonial France that is almost entirely absent from the movie, and it seems to reinforce the idea that the entire French nation was against the independence of Algeria. Thus, for Benjamin Stora, *Outside the Law* "suggests a little too easily that the France of the time was a uniform block, entrenched behind its good post-Vichy consciousness."[45] The brief allusion to those who at the time were called "suitcase carriers" raises questions, because it also seems to be staged to reinforce the heroization of the main characters.[46] In *Outside the Law*, the French leftists who help the FLN seem to be motivated exclusively by feelings of love, while the vast majority of these suitcase carriers actually had a clearly ideological objective. Indeed, a young French woman who falls in love with Abdelkader (Sami Bouajila) will take any risks for him without any explanation of a possible political commitment.

"From brave fighters, Said, Abdelkader and Messaoud have become sad heroes," adds Olivier Barlet.[47] In *Libération*, which had widely covered and supported *Days of Glory*, Didier Péron emphasizes the difficult comparison between *Outside the Law* and its forerunner, which

> was based on simple identification mechanisms: it followed various soldiers coming from colonial territories in their long march to liberate France during the Second World War. The unjust fate that awaited them, and the asymmetry between the treatment received by colonials and French soldiers, allowed spectators to identify with these heroes from the shadows who had been excluded from the great national narratives. With *Outside the Law*, which describes how the intellectual Abdelkader and his brother, Messaoud, who returns wounded from Indochina, organize a network of FLN resistance in the shantytown of Nanterre, the surge of sympathy is not as easy to create. Abdelkader and Messaoud, who assassinate by strangulation compatriots affiliated with the Algerian national movement and a good father who does not pay the revolutionary tax, are fighters for a freedom that remains abstract.[48]

Contested for their actions by some politicians, criticized by historians as much as by film critics, and shunned by audiences, the heroes of *Outside the Law* were the perfect countermodels for those of *Days of Glory*. But despite the critics who disapproved of his narrative choices, and a segment of public opinion that remained opposed to this film, Rachid Bouchareb nevertheless found a few weighty supporters. At the height of the turmoil, several leading figures, including the historians Gérard Noiriel, Benjamin Stora, and Mohammed Harbi, expressed their support for the film against the current of those who remained nostalgic for colonialism:

> The work of a director is not that of a historian and does not have to be judged by the state. Nobody asked Francis Ford Coppola to tell the story of the Vietnam War in *Apocalypse Now* with historical precision. A tragic page of history can just as well be told through fiction, with its inevitable shortcuts, as through the necessary work of historians. In the case of Bouchareb's film, the fundamental problem is elsewhere: pressure was exerted on the channels of France Télévisions not to coproduce the film and on the officials of the Cannes Film Festival not to include the film in the official selection.[49]

But the matter of *Outside the Law* did not stop with the demonstrations, or with the debates in the news, and even less with the quarrels about history and memory. Having been approached by an association of repatriates from Algeria, the Superior Council of the Audiovisual—the national body that regulates the media, but that overstepped its bounds here—called on the leaders of France Télévisions to organize a debate around the movie.[50] Although this recommendation did not lead to any result, in the end, this unprecedented gesture by a public authority cast doubt not only on the quality of the film but also, and above all, on the honesty of Rachid Bouchareb's intentions.

ARAB AND ANTI-COLONIALIST, AN IMPOSSIBLE FRENCH FILM HERO

Ten years after the controversy, it remains disturbing to see how *Outside the Law* is continually judged by its potential historical errors or artistic failures. This critical bias seems to be an attempt to obscure the dramatic intent of the filmmaker and the emotional trajectory of his heroes. By starting his film with the expropriation of an Algerian family and the feelings of injustice that stemmed from the different realities in Paris and Sétif on 8 May 1945, and finally the images of the repression of the demonstration in favor of independence, the director introduces an extremely simple cinematographic mechanism. What Rachid Bouchareb portrays at the beginning of the film is no longer the blind commitment to France held by the Maghrebis in *Days of Glory*, but rather, the main reasons for the anti-colonial rage of his heroes. This is a rage that justifies, throughout the scenario, the choices and the commitment of the heroes for the armed struggle promoted by the FLN and against the political game of Messali Hadj. In *Outside the Law*, the heroes seek revenge and fight against French Algeria. In *Days of Glory*, the heroes fight against Nazism to liberate France. By depicting the Maghrebi soldiers who liberated France and then transforming these same characters into FLN militants, Rachid Bouchareb opts to tell two episodes of the same story. However, it is clear that the filmmaker touches on a taboo subject by transforming his heroes into supporters of Algerian independence and ending French colonization in Algeria. Through these two films, the work of Rachid Bouchareb reveals the extent to which the relationship to the colonial past and the Algerian War of Independence remains a delicate issue, regardless of the abundance of work done by historians. In this regard, it appears that *Outside the Law* was as politically necessary as *Days of Glory* had been four years prior. Thanks to the collaboration with successful actors of immigrant descent, the film contributes to breaking a wall of silence and oblivion, as *Days of Glory* had done. In donning the costume of heroes, the sons rehabilitate the history of their fathers and thwart the national silence on the events of 8 May 1945 in Sétif, as well as the repression of the demonstration of 17 October 1961 in Paris, which closes *Outside the Law*.

Despite the controversy around this film, it opened—thanks to its heroes—a necessary debate that seemed nevertheless to tear apart an increasingly inward-looking France. While the emotion created by *Days of Glory* led to political promises, *Outside the Law* contributed to the political mourning process initiated by Nicolas Sarkozy in Constantine on 5 December 2007, when he called the colonial system "a profoundly unjust enterprise of servitude and exploitation." But this same Nicolas Sarkozy very soon reversed his position, repeatedly refusing repentance, when faced with revolted deputies obsessed with the idea of safeguarding the "honor" of France.

Beyond the political turmoil, the public debate, and the questions raised about the artistic qualities of Rachid Bouchareb, which continue to be discussed in the French press, *Days of Glory* and *Outside the Law*, the two key films of his career, reveal his purpose as an auteur. If he seems to have abandoned his early political ambitions more recently, he nevertheless stands out as the French filmmaker who made a major contribution to the debate on the role of the children of Maghrebi immigrants in French society. Above all, by highlighting the decisive role of colonized soldiers in the liberation of France in 1945, the massacres of Sétif, and Algerian independence, Rachid Bouchareb has offered the public heroes that challenge the collective imagination of what "Arabs" should be. Can these characters be heroes? Just for one film.

*

The research for this chapter was funded by the French government: UCA-JEDI project ANR-15-IDEX-01.

NOTES

1. In an article entitled "Pour la sortie d'*Indigènes*, Chirac harmonise les pensions des anciens combattants coloniaux," Jean-Dominique Merchet adds that "the President of the Republic has decided to unfreeze the pensions of colonial veterans on the very day that *Days of Glory* was released to all theaters." *Libération*, 26 September 2006.
2. Jean-Luc Wachthausen, "*Indigènes* est-il français ou algérien?" *Le Figaro*, 25 January 2007.
3. The FLN—National Liberation Front—remains the main political party in Algeria and was the principal nationalist movement during the Algerian War of Independence.
4. Clarisse Fabre, "La polémique enfle autour du film 'Hors la loi,'" *Le Monde*, 4 May 2010.
5. Pierre Mazars, *Le Figaro*, 16 June 1970. During the Algerian War of Independence, the Arabic term *fellagha* was used to designate an Algerian fighter.
6. Yvan Gastaut, *L'Immigration et l'opinion en France sous la Vème République* (Paris: Seuil, 2000), 109.
7. For further discussion of the representations of "Arab" characters in French cinema, as well as the construction of the idea of the "Arab" in this context, see Julien Gaertner, "Aspects et représentations du personnage arabe dans le cinéma français: 1995–2005, retour sur une décennie," *Confluences Méditerranée* 55 (2005): 189–201. The author explains that using the term "Arab" in his analysis is a deliberate choice and one that serves to underscore how French cinema has generally not distinguished between Moroccan, Lebanese, Algerian, or Saudi characters. For Gaertner, therefore, it signifies a "cultural stereotype, a pre-established concept, in sum . . . a role that has already been played" (91).
8. Abdelkader Benali, *Le Cinéma colonial au Maghreb: l'imaginaire en trompe-l'oeil* (Paris: Cerf, 1998), 155.
9. Christelle Taraud, *La Prostitution coloniale: Algérie, Tunisie, Maroc, 1830–1962* (Paris: Payot, 2003), 35.
10. Pierre Boulanger, *Le Cinéma colonial: de "L'Atlantide" à "Lawrence d'Arabie"* (Paris: Seghers, 1975), 57.
11. For example, *Avoir vingt ans dans les Aurès/ To Be Twenty in the Aures* (René Vautier, 1972).
12. Benjamin Stora, "'Hors la loi', une héroïsation problématique," *Marianne*, 18 September 2010.
13. Jacques Morice, "Cinq soldats d'Afrique du Nord se battent pour la France. Au-delà de l'hommage, la guerre au plus intime," *Télérama*, 30 September 2006.
14. Benjamin Stora, *Imaginaires de guerre: les images dans les guerres d'Algérie et du Viêt-nam* (Paris: Découverte, 1997).
15. *Libération*, 25 May 2006.
16. Marie Boëton, "L'Honneur rendu aux 'Indigènes,'" *La Croix*, 26 May 2006.
17. *Télérama*, 27 September 2006.
18. Thomas Sotinel, "'Hors-la-loi': rebelles académiques," *Le Monde*, 21 September 2010.
19. Bernard Achour, "*Hors-la-loi*," *Première*, 22 September 2010.
20. *Just Like a Woman* (2012) and *La Voie de l'ennemi/ Two Men in Town* (2014).
21. Jamel Debbouze during a news report on France 2, 27 September 2006.
22. *Nouvel Observateur*, 27 May 2006. The article is subtitled: "The most beloved comic of the French public lends his popularity to promote Rachid Bouchareb's film *Days of Glory*. He wants to give African soldiers and their descendants the place they deserve in the history of the nation."
23. Jean-Luc Douin, "'Indigènes': une page oubliée de l'histoire de France," *Le Monde*, 27 May 2006.
24. Jacques Morice, "*Indigènes* recueille tous les suffrages," *Nouvel Observateur*, 27 May 2006.

25. Ibid.
26. For example, Benjamin Stora's article in *Le Monde*, 27 September 2006.
27. See *Jamel, Rachid, Roschdy, Samy . . . petits-fils de tirailleurs/Jamel, Rachid, Roschdy, Samy. . . Grandsons of Riflemen* (Morad Ait-Habbouche and Hervé Corbière, 2006).
28. Interview, *Nouvel Observateur*, 28 September 2006.
29. Marie Boëton, "'Indigènes,' le film de leur vie," *La Croix*, 27 September 2006.
30. Ibid.
31. Ibid. The historian believes that the film "will disrupt the traditional way that history is taught . . . Its intent is to transcribe the facts as they truly are and to say, in this case, that Africans and North Africans have contributed to the liberation of our country. I believe that this truth was forgotten in a France traumatized by the Algerian War."
32. Benjamin Stora points to a question that stems from the way recruitment is represented: "We see a native dignitary coming to the villages to convince the men to go defend France. And then the volunteers enthusiastically climb into the trucks. That was not the case everywhere." *Le Monde*, 27 September 2006.
33. News report on France 2, 27 September 2006.
34. Ibid.
35. Christophe Carrière, "*Indigènes*, quelle histoire!" *L'Express*, 21 September 2006.
36. In *Télérama*, this scene was particularly appreciated: "Two exhausted Maghrebi soldiers swallow the steaming soup given to them by an elderly housewife. A beautiful sequence, reflective of the film more broadly, that does nothing less than completely challenge, in a gentle way, a traditionally French image." 27 September 2006.
37. *L'Express*, 21 September 2006.
38. *La Croix*, 27 September 2006.
39. See in particular the France 2 news report, 27 September 2006.
40. Here I refer to the debate around Article 4 of the Law of 23 February 2005, which specified the "positive role of colonization."
41. Olivier Barlet, "*Hors-la-loi*," *Africultures*, 25 May 2010.
42. This repression led to a debate on the number of fatalities.
43. For example, *Chronique des années de braise/Chronicle of the Years of Fire* (Mohamed Lakhdar-Hamina, 1975).
44. A *harki* is an Algerian native soldier who served alongside the French army.
45. *Marianne*, 18 September 2010.
46. These "suitcase carriers" were French citizens, mostly anti-colonialist, and mainly involved in carrying money and papers for the FLN.
47. Barlet, "*Hors-la-loi*."
48. Didier Péron, "'Hors-la-loi,' une saga sans souffle," *Libération*, 22 May 2010.
49. *Le Monde*, 4 May 2010.
50. Emmanuel Berretta, "'Hors la loi': le CSA réclame un débat sur France Télévisions," *Le Point*, 25 August 2010.

CHAPTER 7

Globalization, Cinema, and Terrorism in Rachid Bouchareb's Films: *London River*, *Baton Rouge*, and *Little Senegal*

Mireille Rosello

What does Rachid Bouchareb's *London River* (2009), but also the director's earlier films, tell us about the intersection of globalization, terrorism, and cinema? Given the intimate relationship between recent forms of terrorism and the media, cinema, one of the most powerful distributors of popular stories, does not have a choice but to participate in a cultural struggle about how to understand and represent terrorism.[1] Many voices have suggested that the terrorist attacks against the twin towers in New York were instantly legible as a typical Hollywood movie.[2] Wheeler Winston Dixon, author of a collection of essays on film and television after 9/11, cites film critic David Thompson and Lawrence Wright, author of the script of the 1998 film *The Siege*. The former is reported to have said "There was a horrible way in which the ghastly imagery of September 11 was stuff we had already made for ourselves as entertainment first,"[3] while the latter stated that the events were "cinematic in a kind of super-real way. It was too Hollywood."[4]

Thus 9/11 is constructed as a turning point in the history of cinema and of the world. All future terrorist attacks are now supposed to have their original cinematographic script: some kind of generic Ground Zero is the standard for future stories. Conversely, all future media performances including movies now have to reckon with an implicit benchmark. The cinematographic spectacularization of the attacks on US soil has had irreversible consequences for global cinema. First of all, two powerful myths about the globalization of cinema and terrorism have backed each other up: "Hollywood," aka CNN, was the reference for international news coverage sending images of terrorism around the world. As a result, even more than before, Hollywood imagined itself as the mandatory global norm. All films about terrorism would now by default be compared to such performances. Secondly, terrorism as an object of representation became both taboo and inescapable: its absence in contemporary films is structuring and remarkable—they fall into the categories of about or not about terrorism.[5] Thirdly, and perhaps even more distressingly for filmmakers or creators in general, the idea that the terrorist attack "was" cinematic erased the distinction between what happened and all the obviously but invisibly politicized representations. The simultaneous occurrence of the event and of the distribution of images erased the process of narrativization that goes into the creation of any story, fiction or non-fiction film. In terms of representational politics, "mass-mediated" terrorism and "terrorist spectaculars"[6] hijack the distinction between the story and storytelling techniques and challenge movies to achieve the same illusion of effective pseudo-self-evidence.

To exaggerate, I could say that all films are now global because terrorism imposes an artificially global (US-driven) grammar over cinema. And it is not very reassuring to refine the formulation by saying, perhaps more accurately, that films are now potentially all global in the face of terrorism because they are made for audiences who will be expected to be familiar with an event that many describe as cinematic: 9/11. Cinema, the global, and terror are now inextricably entangled.

London River, Bouchareb's 2009 film, seems to be the perfect example of this phenomenon. Terrorism could have been both the theme and the narrative grammar capable of explaining the global character of that work of art. Bouchareb's choice to set the story in London right after the July 2005 attacks makes the timeliness and topicality of his film both unremarkable and potentially controversial. It would seem counterintuitive to claim that *London River* is not a film about terrorism. After all, the title of the interview that the director granted to Stuart Jeffries for *The Guardian* is "Rachid Bouchareb: My Film about the 7/7 London Bombings."[7] The film follows two characters that desperately look for their missing children after the bombings. When Brenda Blethyn (whom Bouchareb had already noticed in Mike Leigh's *Secrets and Lies*) was asked to play the role of one of the main protagonists, she hesitated to participate in the mediation of the tragedy. Alerted by her agent that Bouchareb was making a film "about 7/7," she remembers thinking: "Oh no, I don't want to do that. It's too recent history, and it seemed like sacrilege."[8] She implies that the film was breaking a taboo: her formulation suggests that fiction has a sacred duty to not intervene too early. On the other hand, many reviewers criticized the film for its sentimental plot and absence of solid political analysis.[9] Stephen Holden, writing for the *New York Times*, goes as far as saying that "This movie is not concerned with history or politics."[10] As for Kaleem Aftab, he accuses the film of pandering to an international audience and of being suitable for six-year-olds.[11] In other words, there was no "sacrilege" but rather a selling out to a form of globalization that individualizes and depoliticizes.

Most of the negative comments are, however, paradoxical: critics are favorably impressed that Bouchareb replaced sensationalism with an intimate and personal story, but then, they criticize that individual story for being apolitical. And this apparent contradiction has to do with the fact that their readings focus exclusively on the plot and then find the film predictable, didactic, or too politically correct.[12] To be fair, if the plot is the only object of scrutiny, it is difficult to disagree: if we summarize *London River* as the story of a Christian European and a Muslim African who get to know each other, overcome their differences and become friends, it is hard to be excited about the allegorical structure of the binary opposition between two stock characters of contemporary history. The mother is prejudiced and Islamophobic, assuming that her daughter was manipulated by her Muslim lover. And only slowly will she accept that the man whom she encounters is, like her, looking for a missing child, a victim of the terrorist attack.

My point is that this film is political in a way that is not acknowledged by such criticism. *London River* approaches the fraught terrain of terrorism/global/cinema from an angle that is precisely "political" if we adopt Jacques Rancière's definition of "*le politique*" and understand it as the moment where the stakes of the debate and the distribution of the sensible are being negotiated.[13] If we do not read or watch for the plot but become aware of the protocol that governs the perspective and enables a certain story to unfold, then it is possible to examine the ways in which the film refuses to let global terror function as a generic constraint or at least resists the pressure to adopt such grammar. What I call here grammar, protocol, or generic constraint add up to the overall frame that will instruct the spectator either to ignore those who are not deemed worthy of our attention or to focus on individuals that we will construct as victims or perpetrators. The frame is what, generally, makes concepts and object appear or disappear. More generally and perhaps more crucially, the frame accounts for who counts as what Judith Butler calls "grievable lives" in her 2009 *Frames of War*. At the beginning of the introduction ("Precarious Life, Grievable Life") she explains that she is

> seeking to draw attention to the epistemological problem raised by this issue of framing: the frames through which we apprehend or, indeed, fail to apprehend the lives of others as lost or injured (losable or injurable) are politically saturated. They are themselves operations of power. They do not unilaterally decide the conditions of appearance but their aim is nevertheless to delimit the sphere of appearance itself.[14]

In the case of cinema, the camera constitutes one of what Butler calls the "operations of power" to the extent that it implicitly asks the spectator to agree with what is treated as relevant, important, worth seeing, or relegated to invisibility.

The film offers us the possibility to define terrorism as a discourse that insists on becoming the primary logic of any narrative. In order to take advantage of that possibility, however, it is necessary to watch the film politically, by which I mean obliquely: focus on the framing device rather than the plot, and on details rather than the global picture. If we do so, *London River* becomes a film that chooses to make sense of the world from a vantage point that refuses to be compromised by the myth of global terrorism, and that shares that vantage point as a gift to the audience. *London River* is therefore less "about" terrorism than about the possibility to resist the cinematographic storytelling conventions that overdetermine the terror/global/cinema nexus.

THE FUNCTION OF TERRORISM AND THE NATIONAL IN BOUCHAREB'S FILMS

The overdetermination in question functions as the equivalent of perspective in a Renaissance painting. We do not even have to agree on how to define terrorism for it to occupy the function of a vanishing point on the canvas that films will only then have to fill. Like an Oulipian constraint, a perspective line does not predict what the theme of the painting or the poem will be. It is, however, a structure that both limits and enables the deployment of certain narrative elements.

Therefore, I propose to focus more specifically on those elements of *London River* that are more vulnerable to the presence of a pre-imposed cinematographic frame: the representation of space and of the characters' religious practices. Space, or rather the spatial rootedness of the protagonists, is crucial because, as in a painting, some places in the film will seem closer to or further from an imagined center, smaller or more relevant, or relegated to the status of unimportant detail. As for the filmic construction of religious practices in a transnational setting, it intervenes in a situation where Islam, as the chaotic point where culture meets religion and race, has become one of the mandatory building blocks of any narrative influenced by global terrorism discourses. Yet, before focusing on the spatial framing and the representation of religion in *London River*, I propose to look back at Bouchareb's earlier films because they provide clues as to how the director can successfully occupy a different place in this fraught landscape.

Terrorism, when used as the name of a paradigmatic global frame, occupies a function analogous to that of the concept of the nation(al). National cinema supposes a naturalization of the bond between a national culture (presumed relatively homogeneous in terms of historical legacy, geographical contours, and linguistic abilities) and a corresponding public. A national audience is imagined as implicitly sharing such references. Terrorism is one of the concepts that functions both as a representational matrix and a theme. And for Bouchareb, the necessity to work against a constraining hegemonic frame is not new: he belongs to a community of filmmakers who already had reasons to question their relationship to the idea of the national. His relationship to the idea of the national—and specifically to France and Frenchness—has never been straightforward. For a director of Algerian origin born in France during the Algerian War, France was never the implicit and naturalized home whose hegemonic culture and values are expected to be shared, even if only as references. Bouchareb's French films all have an "accent."[15] He was never national.[16]

And even more interestingly, his "accent" is not immediately recognizable. On the one hand, Bouchareb belongs to a generation of directors whose works have questioned the hegemonic French perspective line and who have (sometimes) been provisionally reincorporated into the system of representation. It was the case in France in the 1980s and 1990s when a cluster of directors troubled the idea of Frenchness by focusing on disenfranchised *banlieues* and on the figures of (at first male) children of African immigrants.[17] The dissident national French hero was a young male disenfranchised by his ethnicity and/or class and the spatial signature of that type of figure was the depressing high-rise neighborhoods where spectacular or endemic violence is expected.

Bouchareb could have been a part of that movement. Instead, his way of filming his relationship to Frenchness was never quite in sync with that of his contemporaries. His first feature, *Bâton Rouge / Baton Rouge* (1985), so often cited as one of the first "*beur*" films, is in fact slightly idiosyncratic: the director's focus is on *banlieue* youths but he precisely takes them out of the ghetto. The geography of this rearranged national space is transnational: Bouchareb films three Parisian *banlieue* friends in the United States, far from the archetypal French peri-urban zones. *Baton Rouge*, instead, is the backdrop of their adventure. It is also the city of blues rather than of urban rap (the audioscape that accompanies so many *banlieue* films). Here *Baton Rouge* is not constructed as an alternative francophone space where the protagonists would be more French because perceived as more authentic by a historically displaced French minority. Instead it is an elsewhere where the relationship to the national may be reinvented, a space, as Bouchareb puts it in an interview, where the "characters would not be seen as *beurs* but as individuals with all their hopes and dreams."[18] Bouchareb's early films (and plots) are already examples of transnational rather than minority French cinema, which sets him apart from the movement of "*beur*" directors who, as Lanzoni suggests, have achieved national and therefore indirectly international recognition by now, but as French directors.[19]

When he filmed *Baton Rouge*, Bouchareb was not, however, turning his back on the preoccupations of his contemporaries and looking for a (probably illusory) escapist cinematographic or supra-national space. He explored the same cultural, political and ethnic issues as *"beur"* directors.[20] His rethinking of the national was already global in a very idiosyncratic way since rather than reinterpreting Frenchness through the more and more recognizable postcolonial prism, he carefully avoided the potentially binary Maghreb-France axis. He never proposed some cosmopolitan version of the global as a solution to his questions about the national: in *Baton Rouge*, the characters are quickly confronted with the limits of the American dream: when money runs out, they have to bum train rides or steal and they end up being deported by the immigration police. In *Poussières de vie/Dust of Life* (a 1995 film produced in France and set in Vietnam), Bouchareb also highlights local difficulties rather than exploring an exotic destination, focusing on the children born to Vietnamese women and American soldiers who had returned to the United States. Global mobility is not presented as a form of liberation and is not the alternative to the issues that *banlieue* youths confront in France. Yet, the narratological building blocks and especially the filming of space and the focalization are different from what is typically found in *"beur"* or *banlieue* films of the period.

Little Senegal (2001) is an interesting model of what will later happen in *London River*. Here America is both the destination and the origin since the film is about the main protagonist's quest to find his ancestors, taken from Senegal to the new world more than two hundred years before the story starts. Alloune, who has long worked as a tour guide in a slavery museum, will now embody the history that he has been explaining to tourists. *Little Senegal* thus begins in Gorée, currently one of the districts of Dakar, Senegal, but also an island from which slaves were shipped to the new world. For Bouchareb, that liminal space is the organizational principle of a struggle over what constitutes a nation (historically and geographically). The film starts in Africa and continues in the US, yet the 2001 film was subtly but firmly participating in the French debate about the function and place of the colonial past, and especially the legacy of slavery.[21] But there again, Bouchareb complicates a Franco-French or francophone debate. The main protagonist, whose job is to guide American tourists around the museum of slavery, ends up rewriting the Middle Passage, retracing the steps of one branch of his enslaved family. The character's trajectory combines and therefore defamiliarizes two grand narratives picked up in books written more than ten years apart: Paul Gilroy's *The Black Atlantic* (1993) and Christopher Miller's *The French Atlantic Triangle* (2008). *Little Senegal* refuses, however, to imagine transnational racialized lines of alliance. Delphine Letort notes that the character of African origin is shown to be alienated from the African American community and that the film is skeptical about the ability of a globalized diaspora to come to terms with the legacy of French colonialism, the history of slavery, and the postcolonial condition.[22]

One element of *Little Senegal* is worth mentioning here as a transition to *London River* because the two films share the same lead actor: just as Bouchareb both deals with the issues that *banlieue* youths confront but also refuses to systematically assign them to what could be misconstrued as their "natural" environment, he chooses, as the main protagonists of his films, actors who sabotage any attempt to map identity politics over the characters' trajectory. Both in *Little Senegal* and *London River*, the screen is powerfully occupied and defined by Sotigui Kouyaté, who does not fit the profile of the typically young, and sometimes amateur, actors found in films portraying ethnic minorities. Born in Mali to a long and illustrious family of griots,[23] he is famous for his work with Peter Brook (especially *The Mahabharata*). A tall and thin black body whose posture is always erect, Kouyaté's presence exudes dignity and a remarkable sense of entitlement. Contrary to the figure of the spontaneous male (and now female) *banlieue* youths, whose explosiveness is sometimes blamed, sometimes feared, and sometimes explained, translated, or justified,[24] Kouyaté appears as a timeless, almost mythical old wise man.

When one of the building blocks of the global discourse on terrorism is the profiling of ethnicized subjects or the racialization of cultural and religious factors, the choice of an actor by the film director testifies to the difficulty of navigating the troubled waters that separate the materiality of the body and representational politics. By stating that he wrote his scenario for his actors,[25] Bouchareb reminds us that there is no pre-existing empty frame that would have to be filled by people who correspond to our mental stereotypes of who, for example, is a potential victim and who is a potential perpetrator of terrorism.

THE REMAPPING OF GLOBAL AND LOCAL

London River is a global story that locally rearranges—rather than erases or reinforces—the traditional global opposition between the South and the North. The main protagonists of the films are the parents of two young people whom they have not been able to reach after hearing the news that a terrorist attack had been perpetrated in London. The film follows them on their quest for their missing children but also for a way to make sense of a world that has become incomprehensible to them. From one point of view, the two heroes may look like archetypes: black and white, the African man and the European woman, the Muslim and the Christian. But the male protagonist, who is originally from Mali, has lived in France for so long that he is completely estranged from his son, who was raised in Africa and is now studying in London. As for the representative of the global North, she lives in Guernsey, a tiny island situated in the English Channel off the coast of Normandy, whose position allegorizes the geographical and political ambiguities of the borders of Europe. London is thus identified as eccentric to these two regional points of reference: Guernsey and the south of France.

The film opens on the deserted green cliffs of Guernsey, accompanied by the sound of waves and of Elisabeth Sommers humming to herself as she walks alone on a small path overlooking the sea. That image is then matched by a bird's eye view of another rural landscape, and this time the soundtrack emphasizes cicadas. A black man is seen alone in the middle of an olive grove. In a series of tightly arranged crosscutting shots, the characters are then embedded in their symmetrical natural environments, the horizontality of the sea beyond Elisabeth responding to the verticality of the tall elms that surround Ousmane. The establishing shots that introduce the two protagonists are thus almost didactic in their insistence on constructing them as symmetrical: in these first scenes, both are presented as rural characters from the North. Both are presented as connected to the land: she takes care of a small farm; he is a forester in the South of France. They are alone in a landscape that constitutes a meaningful spatial identification marker. The traditional opposition between the rural poor from the global South and the Western(ized) inhabitants of the global cities of the North is replaced by a shared rootedness in the materiality of the soil. Elisabeth is shown to be feeding animals, picking salads. Later in the film, when the two characters have warmed to each other, this connection is officially recognized as what makes sense of their world: as tragic as they are, the events in London and terrorism in particular are not the paradigm of meaningfulness.

Whereas at the beginning of the film Elisabeth clearly mistrusts Ousmane and treats him as a potential terrorist, she eventually apologizes to him. This is one of the most interesting and perhaps optimistic scenes of *London River*. Both characters are seated on a public bench in a park (see Figure 7.1). Quietly, Elisabeth admits that she suspected Ousmane's son of having manipulated her daughter.

Figure 7.1 Ousmane and Elisabeth on a public bench in a park in London

To which he answers, with disarming honesty and a lack of defensiveness that confers dignity to this powerful character, that he had also feared the worst and did not rule out that his child was responsible for the attacks. Both characters are in fact acknowledging that they are estranged from their children. Jane never told her mother about her relationship and Ousmane did not raise his son and does not know him. Terrorism is what has brought them to a specific neighborhood in London, away from their rural homes. But in that particular moment, it is their relationship to the land that connects them in a differently global way.

In this scene filmed in a park, the two characters have managed to momentarily ruralize London by moving away from the bustling neighborhood where their children shared a flat. In this quiet area, the protagonists talk about their jobs as respectively farmer and forester.[26] Elizabeth comments on the fact that Ousmane's hands, like hers, are scarred by his work. Both parents know that their children would not have made the same choice. Elisabeth says that her daughter is ashamed of her mother's hands, the hands of an old farmer. And when Ousmane explains that his job consists of keeping elms alive, a battle he is losing, Elisabeth is capable of not only following the conversation but also adding a meaningful detail to that ecology of thinking: the last elms, she says, still grow in Guernsey. The allusion to "*griffures*" (scratches), "*blessures*" (wounds), the "fight against the death of trees" is a moment of diversion, a pause during which a new type of unspectacular war becomes important. Ousmane is confronted by and talking about the "slow violence" whose link with globalization is subtly and powerfully suggested in this scene.[27]

That conversation is also crucial for the globalized audience to understand the meaningfulness of the last two scenes of the film. Ousmane, asked by one of his colleagues what they must do about the elm, reluctantly gives him the order to fell it and refuses to watch. We now know what that episode means to him. The last shot shows Elisabeth hoeing her field with a strength that comes from anger and grief after a few seconds of contemplating the sea as the temptation of an ultimate refuge against her pain. The fight against the disappearance of the elms, the physically demanding preparation of a vegetable patch acquire a new dimension. The dynamic of terrorism, with its own logic of violent, spatial, and temporal reconfiguration, is pushed to the background, and the film invites us to reassess the importance of issues that were, until now, relegated to the status of meaningless details.

GLOBAL SIGNS OF THE RELIGIOUS

Just as places are filmed in a way that refuses to adopt contemporary frames of reference, Islam, and religion in general, are presented from the very first scenes from a very specific point of view. The place that religion occupies in the story is the object of a double re- and de-emphasis, a gesture that, far from being a movement away from political issues, constitutes *London River*'s political stance. A film about terrorism that does not talk at all about Islam or rather presents Islam as a difference that does not make a difference is itself remarkable because it refuses to fall into the trap of having to choose between accusation and justification.

The logic of the film insists that Islam only matters in the context of the terrorist/global/cinema nexus if one is already constrained by Islamophobic scripts that have, paradoxically, nothing to do with Islam. When the terrified mother discovers that her daughter's flat is in a neighborhood where the Arabic language is omnipresent and where bodies are darker than her own, she calls her brother and complains that the place is "crawling with Muslims." It is almost too painfully obvious to make the point that she does not know whether she has met a Muslim yet and is only paraphrasing the dominant discourse that conflates Arabic, Arabs, religion, culture, and race. It does not exonerate the character from the accusation of crass prejudice, but her reaction is contradicted by all the other visual elements that have introduced religion until then.

Long before Elisabeth meets Ousmane, the spectator has been told that he is a Muslim but has also been presented with his religion in a way that makes it strictly equivalent to Elisabeth's Christian background. Instead of treating Christianity as the obvious European religion and therefore the unmarked background on which Islam stands out as the foreign cultural element, *London River* uses the establishing shots to treat the characters' religions as differences that should not make more difference than the geographical settings in which they are contingently presented. The first scenes of the film, which have organized the protagonists' spaces, have already added the religious to the frame. Islam and Christianity were thus forcefully paired as symmetrical.

Contrary to a myth that treats Europe as secular and its immigrants as deeply and archaically religious, the film presents its characters as deeply engaged in their own religious rituals. The first time we see Elisabeth, she is walking toward a small church and we hear, in quick succession, a very short quotation from the minister's sermon and the voices of the small community singing in unison (although her voice is emphasized in the soundtrack). As for Ousmane, the first shot shows him praying among olive trees (see Figure 7.2) and two close-ups on his hands show his rosary and then ritual ablutions. He is physically alone and she is also symbolically isolated—no visual allusion is made to any interaction between Elisabeth and the other churchgoers. Both are religious but in a way that does not focus on communities and belonging. Bouchareb does not represent the dominant ethnic European as secular, a choice that is perhaps even more significant for a French audience than on the international scene.

Figure 7.2 Ousmane praying under olive trees in the south of France

Once again, Bouchareb departs from films whose representation of Islam is linked to a national discourse. As Michel Cadé showed in his study of the role of religion in "*beur*" and *banlieue* cinema, Islam, until the beginning of the century, is practically absent from representations of culturally Muslim communities.[28] Only gradually do allusions to religious practices appear in films, suggesting the possibility to accreditate the existence of a non-controversial "Islam de France."[29]

In *London River*, the treatment of religion is hardly realistic: the symmetry between Elizabeth and Ousmane's rituals is highlighted, stylized. Islam and Christianity are intertwined by a visual transition that no element of the plot justifies. Both in Guernsey and in the South of France, Christianity is the pretext to mention both love and persecution. In Guernsey, the minister is heard reading a text from Matthew (5:43) about loving those who persecute us. In a crosscutting shot, we see Ousmane, who has just been introduced as a Muslim, sitting alone, peacefully, in the shade of an old chapel. Islam and Christianity are seen as inseparable to the extent that both religions are also cultural references in the same region. *The Voice of History*, a disembodied didactic narrative, intervenes from the outside: we hear the voice of a tour guide commenting on the fact that in the twelfth century, whole communities were eliminated in Flanders, the Rhineland, and Champagne. The historical reference to the Cathars (whose sites have now become tourist destinations) may well be unrecognizable to an international or even national audience, but visual clues still suggest violence in that peaceful chapel: Ousmane is sitting in front of a medieval painting representing the persecution of people thought to be heretic. And due to the tight editing, the image is still very close to the allusion to the "love your enemies" sermon but also to the vision of a beautiful black body praying alone in an idyllic landscape. A further connection between Christianity and Islam, as well as between the characters who have not yet met each other, is deliberately established by a confusing and rather unrealistic visual transition: as the guide announces that they are going to visit the "garden," a close-up on stone crucifixes removes the spectator from the geographical space that Ousmane occupies and takes us to the island. When the shot becomes larger, we realize that we are in the little cemetery where Elisabeth came to talk to her dead husband. The symbol of Christianity has been used as a mode of transportation between the two spaces, the two protagonists, and the two religions.

Later in the film, the allusions to Islam and Christianity practically disappear altogether. Ousmane is seen praying once more in his hotel room for a few seconds, but any other reference is indirect and linked to the search for the two children. The visits to the mosque are part of the quest: the imam distributes flyers with the addresses and telephone numbers of hospitals. His main dramatic function is that he can speak French and can therefore work as a hyphen between Ousmane (who speaks no English) and the men and women who might have known his son. Just as the crucifix created a relatively artificial and therefore all the more remarkable visual bridge between the South of France and the island and between the two faiths, the imam's unexplained native fluency connects that which other traditional scenarios would present as a priori separate and self-contained.[30]

The camera is not visually interested in the mosque as a place of worship. At no point does Bouchareb present us with the stereotypical image of a community of Muslim men praying together. Religion is clearly articulated as one of the possible identification markers of a multicultural and internally diverse Europe.[31] But the film proposes one of the most idealized definitions of secularism: a system that allows religions to coexist and cohabit. The earlier allusions to love and hate nuance this apparently optimistic picture but the representation is also an implicit response to or a comment about militant forms of French *laïcité* that tend to focus on and object to the most public manifestations of Islam. *London River* neither ignores its characters' faiths nor turns their religion into a cultural identity.

CONCLUSION

What are the consequences of altering the frame of global terrorism? Bouchareb's intervention into what remains a conceptual minefield suggests that if cinema alters the parameters used to represent the actors, it participates in a reorganization of the world defined as a concept that competes with the state, the nation, the local, the global, or *le monde* in French.

The ways in which *London River* frames terrorism posits the existence of an implied audience that is neither French nor francophone but global in very specific ways. The presence of two parents whose children will never be seen because they have already disappeared before the beginning of the story interpellates us spectators as either dead (like the young victims) or in mourning (like the parents).[32] Such modes of identification are more relevant than categories such as Africa and Europe, the global South and the global North, minority or dominant ethnic, Islam and Christianity, or even male and female. This is not to say that religion, nationality, gender, or class are treated as irrelevant. On the contrary, we are asked to become more aware of how such constructions constitute framing devices and to connect with them in more nuanced and self-conscious ways. To that extent, Bouchareb's films contribute to the emergence of a kind of transnational cinema that privileges what Higbee calls movements of "transvergence."[33] If we are capable of empathy with the main protagonists, it has to happen on the basis of alliances that are not national, nor even post-colonial. If this film is "francophone," it is not in the sense that has been used to describe films made by or about minority speakers of French who need to question the supremacy of the Hexagon, the former *métropole*, in a word, Paris, as having appropriated the place of the center. Bouchareb manages to make us understand what francophone means when it is distinct from anglophone, rather than as opposed to (hexagonal) French. In *London River*, when the characters express themselves in French, they speak neither as the representatives of the old imperial center (France) nor as the former colonized francophone periphery. French is a sort of imperfect lingua franca between the two characters only because one of them (Ousmane) does not understand English, the national language of the country where the story takes place. Paradoxically, Elisabeth's rudimentary French is presented as the bridge that connects her to Ousmane, whose French connects him as much to Africa as it does to France.

But Ousmane and Elisabeth are also global in specifically local ways. No one in the film is entitled to speak for the universal; both protagonists are simultaneously extremely local and globalized by forms of grief that are compounded by the difficulty of making sense of their spatial, conceptual disorientation.

The categories that generate stereotypes (religion, place of origin, ethnicity) are never ignored, and the film is not an attempt to universalize the representation of mourning. Instead, it globalizes mourning in a way that precisely takes into account the historical and political situation of the main characters.[34] If *London River* succeeds in troubling the cinema/global/terrorism nexus, it is not so much because of what the film shows as what it chooses not to show, and also because it makes the spectator aware of the structuring absences—a possibility itself opened up by the change of perspective inaugurated by the very first scenes. By inviting the viewer to become aware of what is or could be a center, a periphery, an identity or a coincidence, a detail, or the main point of a story, *London River* avoids a number of archetypal narratives.

Bouchareb's focus on two grieving parents who did not know each other before the beginning of the story enables him to relegate the figure of the terrorist to a visual and political elsewhere. The perpetrators never become characters. Narratologically speaking, after an attack covered by global media and works of fiction, a number of generic conventions are attractive because they allow the storytellers to talk about the terrorists who must be found, named, and accounted for. They become the main protagonists of the tale that subsequently needs the conventions of detective fiction. Bouchareb articulates a critique of the dominant Western gaze on terrorism by representing the terrorists in a certain way.[35] The issue of thematization is yet another narratological level.

By refusing to even mention the terrorists, Bouchareb frees the spectators from a recognizable set of options: we do not have to choose between, or combine a number of, plausible scripts: neither the film nor the audience must demonize or "humanize" the suicide bombers,[36] nor does *London River* provide a narrative of causality that would make their actions historically or politically understandable. I argue that this impossibility is precisely what creates a politicized global audience: the film avoids to work from within narrative logics that are, regardless of their attempt to condemn or understand the terrorists, both authorized and limited by a perspective of surveillance.[37] As spectators freed from that particular set of options, we are left with the task of reinventing what it means to grieve politically from a different perspective.

NOTES

1. Douglas Kellner, *From 9/11 to Terror War: Dangers of the Bush Legacy* (Lanham, MD: Rowman & Littlefield, 2003); Douglas Kellner, *Media Spectacle and the Crisis of Democracy* (Boulder, CO: Paradigm, 2005); Tomasz Pludowski, *How the World's News Media Reacted to 9/11: Essays from Around the Globe* (Spokane, WA: Marquette, 2007); Lisa Finnegan, *No Questions Asked: News Coverage since 9/11* (Westport, CT: Praeger, 2007).
2. Geoff King, "'Just Like a Movie?' 9/11 and Hollywood Spectacle," in *The Spectacle of the Real: From Hollywood to "Reality" TV and Beyond*, ed. Geoff King (Bristol: Intellect, 2005): 47–59.
3. Wheeler Winston Dixon, *Film and Television after 9/11* (Carbondale: Southern Illinois University Press, 2004), 10.
4. Ibid., 9.
5. The force of the taboo is clear when the blurring between fiction and the reality of politics is judged unbearable. After the attacks in Paris in November 2015 the theatrical release of Nicolas Boukhrief's *Made in France* (2015) was canceled.
6. Brigitte L. Nacos, "Terrorism as Breaking News: Attack on America," *Political Science Quarterly* 118, no. 1 (2003): 23–52; Brigitte L. Nacos, *Mass-Mediated Terrorism: The Central*

Role of the Media in Terrorism and Counterterrorism, 2nd ed. (Lanham, MD: Rowman & Littlefield, 2007).
7. Stuart Jeffries, "Rachid Bouchareb: My Film about the 7/7 London Bombings," *The Guardian*, 6 July 2010, https://www.theguardian.com/film/2010/jul/06/rachid-bouchareb-london-river-interview.
8. "*London River*—Brenda Blethyn interview," *IndieLondon*, accessed 24 March 2020, http://www.indielondon.co.uk/Film-Review/london-river-brenda-blethyn-interview.
9. Philip French, review of *London River*, *The Guardian*, 10 July 2010, https://www.theguardian.com/film/2010/jul/11/london-river-film-review; Susie Thomas, "Film Review: *London River* (2009), directed by Rachid Bouchareb; screenplay by Bouchareb, Zoé Galeron and Olivier Lorelle," *Literary London: Interdisciplinary Studies in the Representation of London* 8, no. 2 (2010), http://www.literarylondon.org/london-journal/september2010/thomas2.html.
10. Stephen Holden, "In Wake of Terror Attacks, Unlikely Bonds," *New York Times*, 6 December 2011, http://www.nytimes.com/2011/12/07/movies/london-river-stars-brenda-blethyn-review.html?_r=0.
11. Kaleem Aftab, "London River: The Film of the 7/7 Bombing," *The Independent*, 17 February 2009, http://www.independent.co.uk/arts-entertainment/films/features/london-river-the-film-of-the-77-bombing-1623696.html
12. Jean-Luc Douin, "'London River': une rencontre sous le signe du deuil," *Le Monde*, 22 September 2009, http://www.lemonde.fr/cinema/article/2009/09/22/london-river-une-rencontre-sous-le-signe-du-deuil_1243397_3476.html#oeypI3zgJZbR7xMS.99.
13. Jacques Rancière, *The Politics of Aesthetics: The Distribution of the Sensible*, trans. Gabriel Rockhill (London and New York: Continuum, 2004).
14. Judith Butler, *Frames of War: When Is Life Grievable?* (London: Verso, 2009).
15. Hamid Naficy, *An Accented Cinema: Exilic and Diasporic Filmmaking* (Princeton, NJ: Princeton University Press, 2001).
16. Here I am deliberately creating an echo to the title of Bruno Latour's 1991 book, *We Have Never Been Modern*, trans. Catherine Porter (Cambridge, MA: Harvard University Press, 1993).
17. Examples of this trend include *Prends 10.000 balles et casse-toi/Take Your Ten Thousand Francs and Get Out* (Mahmoud Zemmouri, 1981), *Le Thé au harem d'Archimède/Tea in the Harem* (Mehdi Charef, 1985), *La Haine/Hate* (Mathieu Kassovitz, 1995), *Hexagone* (Malik Chibane, 1994), *Douce France* (Malik Chibane, 1995), *Raï* (Thomas Gilou, 1995), *Bye-Bye* (Karim Dridi, 1995), *Salut cousin!/Hi Cousin!* (Merzak Allouache, 1996), *Le Gone du Chaâba/The Kid from Chaaba* (Christophe Ruggia, 1997). For films that focus on female protagonists, one has to wait until the turn of the century: *Inch'Allah dimanche/Inch'Allah Sunday* (Yamina Benguigui, 2001), *Dans la vie/Two Ladies* (Philippe Faucon, 2007), *Tout ce qui brille/All That Glitters* (Géraldine Nakache and Hervé Mimran, 2010). See also: Carrie Tarr, "Community, Identity and the Dynamics of Borders in Yasmina Yahiaoui's *Rue des Figuiers* (2005) and Karin Albou's *La Petite Jérusalem* (2006)," *International Journal of Francophone Studies* 12, no. 1 (2009): 77–90; Carrie Tarr, "From Riots to Designer Shoes: *Tout ce qui brille/All That Glitters* (2010) and Changing Representations of the Banlieue in French Cinema," in *New Suburban Stories*, ed. Martin Dines and Timotheus Vermeulen (London: Bloomsbury Academic, 2013), 31–40.
18. Richard Derderian, "The *Banlieues* as *Lieux de Mémoire*: Urban Space, Memory, and Identity in France," in *Géopolitique et mondialisation: la relation Asie du Sud-Est/Europe*, ed. Pierre Lagayette (Paris: Presses universitaires de la Sorbonne, 2003), 107–20, 115.

19. Rémi Fournier Lanzoni, "A National Recognition for *Beur* Cinema: Rachid Bouchareb and Abdellatif Kechiche," in *French Cinema: From Its Beginnings to the Present* (New York: Bloomsbury Academic, 2015), 465–79.
20. Alec G. Hargreaves, "From 'Ghettoes' to Globalization: Situating Maghrebi-French Filmmakers," in *Screening Integration: Recasting Maghrebi Immigration in Contemporary France*, ed. Sylvie Durmelat and Vinay Swamy (Lincoln: University of Nebraska Press, 2011), 25–40; Will Higbee, "Re-presenting the Urban Periphery: Maghrebi-French Filmmaking and the 'Banlieue' Film," *Cinéaste* 33, no. 1 (2007): 38–43.
21. 2001 is also the year of the so-called Taubira law that recognizes the slave trade and slavery as a crime against humanity. See also Pascal Blanchard, Nicolas Bancel, and Sandrine Lemaire, ed., *La Fracture coloniale: la société française au prisme de l'héritage colonial* (Paris: Découverte, 2005); Renaud Hourcade, "L'Esclavage dans la mémoire nationale française: cadres et enjeux d'une politique mémorielle en mutation," *Droit et cultures* 66 (2013): 71–86.
22. Delphine Letort, "Rethinking the Diaspora through the Legacy of Slavery in Rachid Bouchareb's *Little Senegal*," *Black Camera* 6, no. 1 (2014): 139–53.
23. A griot is defined as a member of "a class of musician-entertainers of western Africa whose performances include tribal histories and genealogies." *Merriam-Webster Dictionary*, accessed 5 April 2020, https://www.merriam-webster.com/dictionary/griot
24. See Abdellatif Kechiche's *L'Esquive/Games of Love and Chance* (2004): the focus of the film is on adolescents who must memorize Marivaux's *Le Jeu de l'amour et du hasard* to perform the play at school. Oscillating between Marivaux's eighteenth-century French and contemporary French, the film debunks the stereotype of the illiterate and uncouth youth whose language is rudimentary at best and often aggressive. The film presents the exchanges between the characters as highly ritualized language games. See also Ari J. Blatt, "The Play's the Thing: Marivaux and the 'Banlieue' in Abdellatif Kechiche's *L'Esquive*," *French Review* 81, no. 3 (2008), 516–27; Boris Bastide, "Review of Abdellatif Kechiche's *L'Esquive*," *Artelio*, January 2004; Colin Nettelbeck, "Kechiche and the French Classics: Cinema as Subversion and Renewal of Tradition," *French Cultural Studies* 18, no. 3 (2007), 307–19.
25. Jeffries, "Rachid Bouchareb."
26. For a compelling and precise analysis of how London itself is filmed (and how the symbol of the bridge is emphasized in a decidedly unspectacular way), see Carrie Tarr, "The Mediation of Difference in *London River*," in *Bicultural Literature and Film in French and English*, ed. Peter I. Barta and Phil Powrie (New York: Routledge, 2016), 60–74.
27. Rob Nixon, *Slow Violence and the Environmentalism of the Poor* (Cambridge, MA: Harvard University Press, 2011).
28. Michel Cadé, "Hidden Islam: The Role of the Religious in *Beur* and *Banlieue* Cinema in France," in *Screening Integration: Recasting Maghrebi Immigration in Contemporary France*, ed. Sylvie Durmelat and Vinay Swamy (Lincoln: University of Nebraska Press, 2011), 41–57.
29. Cadé mentions films such as Philippe Faucon's *Dans la vie/Two Ladies* (2007) and Rabah Ameur-Zaïmeche's most recent work: whereas Islam is simply absent from the director's first film, *Wesh Wesh, qu'est-ce qui se passe?/Wesh Wesh, What's Happening?* (2001), the connection between religion and workplace is integral to *Dernier maquis/Adhen* (2008). Cadé, "Hidden Islam."
30. Critics have of course noticed that the Londoners' ability to speak French in this film is slightly implausible or "contrived," as Gary Collinson puts it. "British Cinema: London River," *Flickering Myth*, 9 October 2010, flickeringmyth.com/2010/10/british-cinema-london-river-2009.html. Having cast some of the actors who already worked with him

on *Indigènes/Days of Glory* (2006), Bouchareb could take advantage of a francophone Muslim police officer (Mathieu Schiffman) and of a francophone imam (Sami Bouajila). For a remarkably rich and precise analysis of how French, English, Arabic, and Mandinka function in the film, see Alison Smith, "Crossing the Linguistic Threshold: Language, Hospitality and Linguistic Exchange in Philippe Lioret's *Welcome* and Rachid Bouchareb's *London River*," *Studies in French Cinema* 13, no. 1 (2013): 75–90.

31. Africa is never filmed, never shown, not even as the subject of dreams or flashback sequences.
32. In Bouchareb's *La Route d'Istanbul/The Road to Istanbul* (2016), the main role is again occupied by the figure of a parent but this time the film focuses on another aspect of the terrorism/global cinema—radicalization. Here, Elisabeth is a Belgian mother whose teenage daughter has vanished. When the police discover that she is headed for Turkey, the mother decides to follow her to what seems to be the most plausible destination: Syria and Islamic State territory.
33. Will Higbee, "Beyond the (Trans)national: Towards a Cinema of Transvergence in Postcolonial and Diasporic Francophone Cinema(s)," *Studies in French Cinema* 7, no. 2 (2007), 79–91.
34. "Many people think that grief is privatizing, that it returns us to a solitary situation and is, in that sense, depoliticizing. But I think it furnishes a sense of political community of a complex order, and it does this first of all by bringing to the fore the relational ties that have implications for theorizing fundamental dependency and ethical responsibility." Judith Butler, *Precarious Life: The Powers of Mourning and Violence* (London: Verso, 2004), 22.
35. Elaine Martin argues that by "subtly shifting concepts of 'we' and 'they' while stressing causality, history and temporality," Third Cinema films implicitly respond to the critique made by Edward Said in "The Essential Terrorist"—a text in which he points out that the terrorist is always the other and the concept is based on an erasure of history and causality. Elaine Martin, "Films about Terrorism, Cinema Studies and the Academy," in *Terror, Theory, and the Humanities*, ed. Jeffrey R. Di Leo and Uppinder Mehan (Ann Arbor, MI: Open Humanities, 2012), https://quod.lib.umich.edu/o/ohp/10815548.0001.001/1:4.1/--terror-theory-and-the-humanities?rgn=div2;view=fulltext; Edward W. Said, "The Essential Terrorist," in *Blaming the Victims: Spurious Scholarship and the Palestinian Question*, ed. Edward W. Said and Christopher Hitchens (London: Verso, 1988), 149–58.
36. Elaine Martin, "The Global Phenomenon of 'Humanizing' Terrorism in Literature and Cinema," *CLCWEB: Comparative Literature and Culture* 9, no. 1 (2007).
37. Compare with the well-known scene in Gillo Pontecorvo's *La Bataille d'Alger/The Battle of Algiers* (1966) in which recruits are taught how to deal with terrorism and are made to watch the film of a checkpoint: at the very moment when soldiers are bullying an old man because they suspect that his suitcase contains explosives, they allow the woman who carries the bomb to walk right past them. The spectator has, by then, become an insider and recognizes that unless one knows who the terrorists are, it is impossible to identify them. Similarly, Philippe Faucon's *La Désintégration/The Disintegration* (2011) narrativizes the gradual evolution of an ordinary citizen who slowly becomes a jihadist. In both cases, the purpose of the camera is to make the spectators understand how "they" function, regardless of what this knowledge would imply.

PART II

Case Studies

CHAPTER 8

Aesthetics of Confinement: Space, *Memento Mori*, and the Recording of History in Rachid Bouchareb's *Poussières de vie/Dust of Life*

Michael O'Riley

Like other films in Rachid Bouchareb's corpus such as *Cheb* (1991), *Little Senegal* (2001), and *Indigènes/Days of Glory* (2006), *Poussières de vie/Dust of Life* (1995) traces the contours and dilemmas of individual subjects caught between cultures, memories, and national histories. An adaptation of Duyên Anh's autobiographical novel *La Colline de Fanta/Fanta Hill* (1989),[1] Bouchareb's film was nominated for an Academy Award for Best Foreign Language Film as an Algerian submission. *Dust of Life*, however, does not tackle these issues through the prism of the African diaspora like the other films but, rather, through the often elided or repressed question in Vietnam and elsewhere of Vietnamese American identity and the Vietnam War.[2] In particular, the film focuses on the children that were born of the union of American GI soldiers and Vietnamese women. *Dust of Life* returns to the Fall of Saigon on 30 April 1975 and the departure of American troops alongside the North Vietnamese conquest of South Vietnam and the rise of the Provisional Revolutionary Government. The film aligns itself with the memory work germane to the excavation of shrouded national histories in much the same ways that films like *Days of Glory* and Bouchareb's short film *L'ami y'a bon/The Colonial Friend* (2004) seek to rewrite the national collective history of France by underscoring the role of West and North African subjects within the forging of that narrative. However, as we will see, it also distinguishes itself slightly in this regard from films such as *Days of Glory* in its engagement with the instrumental underpinnings of memory, history, and national space.

Dust of Life engages with what Paul Ricoeur refers to as the "matrix of memory" and the ways that memory is manipulated by historiography to serve ideological ends.[3] In the case of the narratives and subjects represented by *Dust of Life*, it is clear that history has simply forgotten or expunged them from the official record, left them behind as it were. While *Days of Glory* and *The Colonial Friend* seek to reinscribe colonial African subjects and their complex multicultural history into French national collective history, from which they had been excluded, *Dust of Life* centers on street children, the so-called *bụi-dời*, later also called *poussières de vie* or "dust of life."[4] These children were assigned the same pejorative term, along with orphans and others left behind after the Vietnam War, and they were sent to re-education camps in northern Vietnam by the new government.[5] Viewed as souvenirs of the enemy and markers of the American imperialist presence, they were perceived as threats to the nationalist regime in Vietnam at the close of the war. In *Dust of Life*, these forgotten children are not so much reinscribed into the historical record through memory work as actually brought back from their absence in it with an accompanying representation of the dynamics of how they were forgotten. By this, I mean that although the memory of these individuals and their particular experience is represented, the actual conditions and ideological underpinnings that led to their erasure from the national historical record are also examined and queried in the film as part of the memorialization process.

As their name suggests, the "dust of life" remain the invisible excess of history, the very embodiment of what Ricoeur describes as the threatening silhouette of forgetting: "Forgetfulness remains in fact the disturbing threat outlined behind the phenomenology of memory and the epistemology of history."[6] Ricoeur acknowledges the act of forgetfulness in collective memory as having an ideological underpinning, what he calls "memory manipulated" to a nation's political ends.[7] However, his suggestion that the manipulation of memory through an intentional forgetting in the establishment of historical records poses an additional threat is particularly useful in the context of Bouchareb's work and, specifically, in the ways that *Dust of Life* brings to the screen these forgotten children. Indeed, their very embodiment on the screen, as we will see, poses a threat to the conception of the dialectic of memory and history as it relates to the national record of history.

While the Vietnamese re-education camps have by and large come into wider historical consciousness, with estimations of hundreds of thousands of prisoners incarcerated in numerous camps located primarily in the extreme northern regions of Vietnam, very little attention has been paid to the specifics of these camps and even less to the thousands of children interned, an unknown number of whom died. Indeed, the nature and conditions of these camps have been the subject of great debate. Officially, the Vietnamese government did not and still does not consider these camps to be prisons but, rather, places where individuals could be rehabilitated into society through constructive labor and social education. It is generally acknowledged by the Vietnamese government that in the summer of 1975, after the fall of Saigon to the Communist regime of Ho Chi Minh, individuals involved in the previous government were ordered to register under the new government and were then transported to camps throughout the newly united country. Life in the camps consisted of hard labor, including road building and land mine clearance, as well as political indoctrination denouncing Western imperialism.[8] A memorandum to Amnesty International in 1981 from the Socialist Republic of Vietnam asserted that the incarcerated were criminals guilty of acts of national treason punishable by life imprisonment or the death penalty.[9] The Vietnamese government argued, moreover, that it was allowing these individuals to be re-educated and, thus, treated more humanely than what they deserved. What has been expunged almost entirely from the official record is not only the deaths and treatment of these prisoners, but also the record of scores of children subjected to incarceration, mistreatment, and death in the re-education camps.

In many ways, *Dust of Life* constitutes a *memento mori*, a tribute to death and to the death of memory itself in relation to these children. Yet, it is through the remembrance of them that the film also engages with multiple layers of traumatic and repressed histories of imperialism in Vietnam—French, American, and neo-colonial Vietnamese in the form of the Communist government that acceded to power after the war. These histories were used, as the film shows, to forge a new national narrative through forgetting. As Benedict Anderson states, such amnesia or active forgetting is a characteristic of strong narratives of nationalism: "All profound changes in consciousness, by their very nature, bring with them characteristic amnesias. Out of such oblivions, in specific historical circumstances, spring narratives."[10] Anderson's assertion of the role of forgetting and amnesia in the creation of narratives of nationalism and national identity is important in the case of Vietnam, as *Dust of Life* demonstrates.

This chapter explores how the film underscores the interwoven relationship of memories of imperialism in Vietnam, with one representation of an imperialist regime being supplanted by or merged into another. The film suggests how multiple memories of imperialism and oppression are related to one another and may ultimately coalesce into one, interchangeably reactivating one another at the same time through an occasionally traumatic re-enactment. These moments function as *memento mori* in the film, yet within the cinematographic spaces of the film they also highlight the problematic structure of the memory of oppression and the way it functions ideologically to forget or leave behind the trauma of imperialism. By incorporating traumatic *memento mori* of imperialism and subsequent reactions to this past in different cinematographic loci across the national space and landscape of Vietnam represented in the film, *Dust of Life* engages with the very problem of memory and its manipulation. It does not simply record lost or occluded history, but comments on the act of historiography itself as it relates to inscribing national loss. In so doing, the film bears witness to the disillusionment of post-colonial

Vietnam, representing its confinement in the competing memories of imperialist loss and the failed promises of both Western capitalism and nationalist communism.

REPETITION AND SYMBOLIC SPACES OF CONFINEMENT

Dust of Life deploys what one might call an aesthetics of confinement in its cinematographic and editorial representations of national space in the film.[11] Many of the cinematographic spaces of the film symbolically signal a confinement or imprisonment in a history of loss and societal decomposition. Editorial and cinematographic symbolisms reveal a societal entrapment in the *memento mori* of imperialism and oppression. Indeed, the symbolism of the Vietnam War and American imperialism becomes equated with the rise of Vietnamese nationalist oppression. The two repressed memories often become one within the cinematographic space of the nation, one traumatic and spectral memory haunting another.

The opening scene representing the chaotic withdrawal of American forces from Saigon provides a complex yet salient example of this. Accompanied by Jimi Hendrix's version of "The Star-Spangled Banner," the film's long opening montage is composed of short rhythmic cuts. It depicts the protagonist, Son, a thirteen-year-old boy, and his mother as they make their way through the streets of Saigon to the US embassy. Son N'Guyen, as we learn, is the son of a Vietnamese woman and an African American soldier. The scenes of Son and his mother rushing to the US embassy to seek asylum, along with the masses of other Vietnamese American children and their mothers, only to be turned away, are intercut with brief depictions of departing American troops, throngs of frightened Vietnamese, the ravaged cityscape of Saigon, and symbols of the Provisional Revolutionary Government. As the montage progresses, we witness the film's signal that the nation and its people will simply retrace the horrors of the war it has just experienced, this time at the hands of the new government.

This occurs in a sequence of images that confine the Vietnamese people and children like Son between the icons of oppression represented in cinematographic space. As Son and his mother hurry through the streets, the camera cuts to a low-angle shot of an overhead US helicopter that we witness from the perspective of the streets of Saigon. After the shot of the hovering helicopter, we encounter a close-up of children in the street loading a magazine into a military rifle, suggesting a symbolic transfer of war itself into the hands of the Vietnamese people. The film then cuts to the chaos of the US embassy rejecting the pleas of Son's mother and other women who seek asylum for their children. Medium and extreme close-up and panning shots reveal the desperation of masses of Vietnamese clamoring behind the bars of the US embassy and ultimately being rejected. The signs of US imperialism and abandonment frame the people on the ground, as war is symbolically transferred directly to them. They are framed by the prisonlike bars of American nationalism that rejects their pleas for help, thus confining them to the consequences of the new regime. Here, the signs and symbols of the failed promises of American imperialism function as editorial bookends that confine the people represented in the streets of Saigon.

The next sequence of shots mirrors the theme of confinement in the previous sequence that began with the hovering US helicopter. As if to spatially mimic the symbols of failed and fatuous US imperialism, it frames and surrounds the Vietnamese men and children taken prisoner by the new government. A low-angle shot captures the 1975 provisional government flag fluttering in the air. The next shot cuts to children on the ground, their hands in the air as they are taken prisoner by the new regime. We then cut to another low-angle shot of the provisional flag followed by an eye-level view of prisoners in the round-up. The montage finally ends on a family photo of Son next to his mother and American father in uniform. Like the sequence before it, this sequence suggests the subjugation and confinement of the people to a form of distorted nationalism that simply mimics the imperialist undertones of the first. Hendrix's distorted national anthem sutures and further reinforces the representation of the two forms of nationalistic imperialism as interchangeable.[12]

Abandoned, ravaged, and forgotten, the Vietnamese remain confined to repeat the cycle of oppression suffered at the hands of the US presence. The repetitive symbols of overhead authority depicted here—whether of US military presence, a national embassy, or the flag of the new provisional government—will ultimately fail the Vietnamese people, and the distortions of nationalism and oppression that reverberate in the soundtrack simply transfer themselves from one regime to another. In both cases, the Vietnamese remain subject to these icons of imperialism, visually confined in the rapid-fire images of their chaotic wake. The film's opening montage thus signals this transfer from one regime to another, suggesting that a symbolic recoding of the nation space will amount to nothing more than the literal and metaphoric confinement of its people. Here, as elsewhere in the film, the nation is condemned to relive the imperialism of the past, subjugated to the commandeered space and hovering icons of authority that reign over it. It is important to note that these images also constitute unresolved memories of national trauma forgotten and brought to the screen. They suggest that the memories of the Vietnam War and American imperialism were simply supplanted by a new form of oppression that, itself, will leave more memories of death and disillusionment in its wake. We will see that these memories, like those of the Vietnam War before them, will symbolically be buried almost as soon as they are produced.

SOVEREIGN POWER, SPECTRAL MEMORIES, AND THE BODY

As the filmic narrative skips ahead three months to the renaming of Saigon, Son and other children are rounded up on the streets of what is now Ho Chi Minh City and taken prisoner in the night. The children are transported to a preliminary re-education center where government officials tell them in Vietnamese that the "heroic path" of the people in their "fight against American aggression has saved us." In a series of telling shot reverse shots, the fate of these boys' condition and the national memory of it is signaled by editorial and cinematographic styling. Medium close-ups of the boys, as they speak to one another about their plight, alternate with wide-angle shots of them from the point of view of the provisional government officials until we see one boy attempting escape. The subjugation of the boys' lives to the new nationalist discourse is made clear in the next sequence of shots and countershots. A close-up of the loudspeaker from which the discourse of freedom from American oppression is transmitted cuts to the authorities of the provisional government wielding machine guns. We then see the escapee running off from the perspective of the soldier who shoots him. Here, deep focus allows us to see the victim and his killer clearly in the night, underscoring the event and bringing it into the historical narrative the film is creating. However, it also places us in the position of the masses of boys who witness the act from behind. This, too, is their fate, in a way. While not a foreshadowing of the actual physical death of all of these boys, this parallel matching does communicate the position these prisoners will later hold in the eyes of the state and national memory. The shots then alternate between the boys and the victim as the dead boy, shown in a close-up, is dragged to the tarmac, face down. In the interim, the other boys are herded past the corpse into military transport trucks. Continuing shots alternate of the victim on the ground and the boys in the back of a convoy truck—its gate closed upon them—further establishing the relationship between these prisoners and the dead body on which the camera lingers momentarily, as the sequence ends and the prisoners are transported northward. Here, the camera lingers on the dead boy, thus underscoring the excess of the gaze. As spectators, we witness not only the murder and the way the physical subject is discarded, but also the mechanisms underpinning this national narrative. The suggestion is not only that the memory of this act is left behind by the state, but that these boys share the same condition, albeit of death in life, or what Giorgio Agamben calls "bare life."[3]

The ending shots of this sequence equating or suturing the dead body with the other prisoners provide an illustration of Agamben's discussion of the conditions that produce "bare life." Agamben argues that the political machinery of modern sovereignty reduces the human to a liminal state between the symbolic death of the subject and the physical death of the body, a state between life and death. In *Dust of Life*, the symbolic death of the subject and the physical death of the body are represented in turn, one equated with the other through the symbolic language of the shots. In both these cases—in death as in life—the boys' condition reflects Agamben's conception of the state of exception characterizing sovereignty in which there is

> a new decision concerning the threshold beyond which life ceases to be politically relevant . . . and can as such be eliminated without punishment. Every society sets this limit; every society—even the most modern—determines who its "sacred men" will be.[14]

According to Agamben, the sovereign state establishes the state of exception and determines with impunity the conditions of life and death of its subjects. Moreover, the memory of the creation of this state of exception—of the production of bare life without impunity—is symbolically erased, left behind, as the convoy moves forward.

The grand irony of this sequence, in its representation of the state of exception, is that the national trauma and death caused by the Vietnam War becomes the spectral presence against which new forms of oppression and their memories are forged and then immediately left behind to linger as forgotten shadows. Bouchareb's film not only brings these occluded memories to the screen in this case, but also points out the vicissitudes inherent in official forms of memory itself, which can be used to forge new ideologies of oppression and victimization. The Communist government's commemoration of the victory of the Vietnam War through its transmitted discourse of freedom from the American oppressor is represented in this way in the above sequence. The complexities, ambiguities, and national traumas of a nation at war with itself as much as with the American presence are forgotten in the name of a new nationalist agenda, the traumas of which in turn are forgotten and left behind.[15] Collective memory—inclusive of remembering and forgetting—becomes part and parcel of the state of exception and its sovereign structure. What remains, in a state of decomposition and imprisonment, as the ending shots of the sequence suggest, is the space of the nation itself, traversed by the spectral presence of national traumas left behind.

This equation between memory, forgetting, and the state of exception in which the boys find themselves between life and death is reinforced throughout the film. As Son befriends Bob, an older, stronger boy who serves at first as protector and menace (perhaps the ultimate incarnation of imperialism), the convoy continues onward to the Phu Van camp in the North. Prior to its arrival, we see the starving boys given food by local villagers at a stop along the way. Here, the fate of the caravan of prisoners is linked to that of the liberated people in a series of shot reverse shots alternating between the boys imprisoned behind the gates of the truck and the villagers peering in at them. Physically free, the villagers look on helplessly as the convoy recedes into the distance, as if to signal that they, too, share the same condition as these boys. Upon arrival, a dead body is laid on the ground, left behind as the prisoners fall into line with other children already at the camp. A victim of the heat and malnourishment, this boy is placed face down, just like the aforementioned escapee. Soon, we learn that of the eighty boys taken prisoner in Saigon, only sixty-nine arrived. As the boys stand as a group in front of the commanding officer, they are addressed as guilty criminals and told that American imperialism has led them and the nation to this fate. As the discourse continues, a wide-angle shot shows the boys listening in rank order as another dead body is carried past in the foreground. Similar to the wide-angle shots of the group of boys at the preliminary camp sutured with the image of the dead escapee, these shots of the group of prisoners further establish the parallel between their death as subjects and the physical death of the body. Though physically alive, the prisoners share the same fate as the passing body brought to decompose, as Son will later discover, on what is referred to as "Fanta Hill." As the dead body passes, we hear the commanding camp officer inform the prisoners that "the sooner you make amends, the sooner you'll be sent back to your families." Here, the irony of the scene highlights the state of exception as it forges a new narrative that ultimately will eliminate the children in the background. As the boys stand together in a group, devoid of agency, their physical bodies are already symbolically marked as forgotten as well. They, too, will pass on into the pockmarked history of the jungle where their fellow prisoner is being carried. *Dust of Life* remembers these boys but ultimately demonstrates how one form of imperialism is remembered and forgotten in exchange for new forms of neo-imperialist narratives and oppression that will also leave behind the memories of bodies strewn throughout the countryside.

SURVEILLANCE, IMPERIALISM, AND MEMENTOS OF SACRIFICE

The repossession of the land in reaction to the "century of slavery" that Vietnam endured (in the words of the commanding officer) is a principal theme of the new regime's discourse and yet, this repossession itself is predicated on confinement, forced labor, and surveillance reminiscent of French colonialism. The prisoners are beaten and forced to do meaningless tasks of hard labor. In one particular scene representative of many other scenes of forced labor depicted in the jungle, the boys are forced to repeat the mantra that "work is the standard for measuring man's value" as they are shown a tree that they must cut down by hand. Here, a high-angle shot looks down upon the prisoners positioned in front of the tree as the commanding voice utters mantras to be repeated about labor and its value. The wide, high-angle shot of the exploitation captures the boys' confinement and subjugation within the vastness of the jungle. The scene is reminiscent of the exploitation of labor and resources that took place during French colonialism in Vietnam, where Vietnamese workers toiled away for little recompense. Shot from above as a long take, like many of the scenes of labor in the film, this scene recalls the surveillance to which the Vietnamese were subject under French colonialism; the prisoners at work are nearly always under the watchful eye of authority. The land itself becomes a space of confinement for the prisoners, one seemingly caught in a cyclical pattern of colonial surveillance.

Throughout the scenes set in the camp, policies reminiscent of French colonial ideology are used to the ideological ends of the new regime. Most of these involve an attempted erasure of the memory of French and American imperialism. Son and other Vietnamese American children are reminded continuously that their fathers have abandoned them. Son, who carries with him a photo of his father, is ultimately compelled to destroy the photo.[16] Son understands that any connection to his father under this regime represents a racial and cultural taboo that must be hidden. As Christina Elizabeth Firpo has shown, French officials in Indochina systematically uprooted *métis* children—those born of Southeast Asian mothers and white fathers—as they were viewed as a threat to the colonial order, security, and white French dominance.[17] In a similar manner, here the new regime uproots and attempts to erase all signs of racial and cultural miscegenation.

Similarly, all emblematic traces of Western influence must be expunged. Son, along with other boys in the camp, such as Little Hai, raised in a Catholic orphanage, is punished for being Catholic. In a scene where Son is denounced by one opportunistic boy leader, his crucifix is discovered and ripped from around his neck. He is then subject to beatings. Elsewhere in the film, Son and Little Hai, always in danger for their beliefs, pray in private, away from the eyes of the camp leaders. Throughout their time in the camp, the boys are subject to the neo-colonial ideology of the Communist regime in its attempt to eradicate all traces and overt mementos of other forms of culture, race, and ideology. The film records both this erasure and the boys' attempts to resist it. Witnessing the destruction of Son's crucifix, Bob carves him another out of wood as a gift. This portrayal of the *memento mori* and its destruction constitutes a sort of *mise-en-abyme* of the film's engagement with the very idea of memory and the *memento mori* itself. As symbolic reminders of mortality, *memento mori* function as an injunction to remember—replete with a cautionary narrative about the potential death of memory—and thus serve as a sort of meta-reflection on the nature of recall. The emphasis on the erasure of the crucifix and its replacement in the film serves to underscore the very issues surrounding the themes of memory, sacrifice, and the preservation of narratives that the film engages.

In a larger sense, Bob's replacement of Son's crucifix after its removal by the regime reflects the film's engagement with and commentary on the totalitarian manipulation of memory itself, in particular in relationship to the sacrificed figures constituting the "dust of life." Although the Communist regime attempts to erase all forms and memory of difference, the traces of the *memento mori*—the symbolic representation of mortality—nonetheless re-emerge in different ways. Their re-emergence conveys not only the history of the acts committed by the regime, the deaths of countless child prisoners as well as others, but that of the apparatus of the state of exception that attempted their erasure as well. Although the government certainly operates through control of the people, it is also shown to exercise total control of memory. In his reflections on *memento mori*, Thomas Docherty makes reference to Tzvetan Todorov's understanding of totalitarian regimes as exercising just such control: "One important aspect of totalitarian regimes is the control not of language or of people but of memory."[18] In *Dust of Life*, the control and erasure of the *memento mori* constitute a destruction of the injunction to remember mortality and, symbolically in this case, a destruction of the memory of the national sacrifice of these boys at the hands of the regime.

WITNESSING, RECORDING, AND THE EXCESS OF TRAUMA

Perhaps the most important aspect of the film's engagement with the totalitarian control of memory and national space comes in the thematic importance it accords to witnessing and recording. Since Son can read and write, he is given paper and a pencil to record basic camp information by Mr Can Bô, one of the camp leaders. Mr Can Bô speaks in French with Son and attempts to reason with him throughout the film. As an embodiment of the author, Son records not only the basic names and information of the boys in his brigade as instructed, but also the details of the horrors he witnesses in the camp (see Figure 8.1). Son becomes a central witness in the film and a leader of sorts.[19] As the film progresses, the boys devise a plan to escape by building a raft they believe will enable them to navigate the river to Saigon. Son's ability to read and write finds him stealing into the headquarters where a map of the nation hangs on the wall. A close-up shot of Son using the map to trace the escape route to the South demonstrates the symbolic connection between national space, resistance, and the figure of the author/witness. The route to the South that Son traces is the converse of the very route the new regime took in conquering the country and taking him prisoner.

Yet, the film signals that this cartographic information is not sufficient for the boys' act of resistance. Moreover, it signals symbolically that any

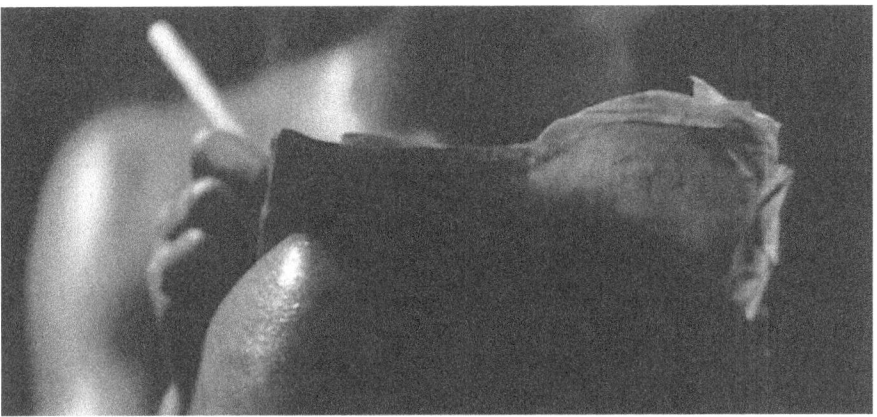

Figure 8.1 Son records the history of the internment camps

representational act of resistance through memory work, such as the film itself, cannot simply retrace the lines of territoriality; it cannot simply replace memories of loss within the space of the nation. Any symbolic recoding of space must take place through a radical act of witnessing, one that will ultimately bear witness to the very attempt to destroy any trace of the history of the camps and prisoners. When Son returns with the information to discuss escape plans with Bob and Little Hai, who soon thereafter falls ill and will be replaced by Shrimp in the escape attempt, another corpse is carried past. This point-of-view shot places the dead body directly in the line of sight of the boys. In the night, the boys see what is very likely the body of Darkie, a snitch who earlier in the film surprised them making the raft and is consequently drowned by them in a desperate act of self-preservation. The very next shot, in daylight, marks the beginning of a long sequence of discovery in the makeshift cemetery of Fanta Hill. A tracking shot follows Son from behind as he passes by a sign in Vietnamese that reads: "Pathway for the Restoration of Human Dignity." As Son enters, we see bottles of Fanta partially buried in the ground along the pathway, their bottoms turned upward. Inside are pieces of paper with the names of boys who perished in the camp. A close-up shot reveals the name Nam and the date of his death, November 1975. A second close-up reveals another victim. Son places these paper mementos in his journal as a high-angle shot from behind reveals him in the midst of a cemetery of hundreds of bottles sticking out of the ground. The camera then reverses to a low-angle shot that slowly pans upward across the sea of bottles, stopping on Son and his journal. Confined here in the middle of the dead, the author-witness figure must bear the memory of the deceased. With this information and burden, the boys attempt their escape.

Throughout this escape, however, Son is doomed to witness and relive other traumatic histories that merge the boys' own personal experiences of an oppressive regime with those of the Vietnam War as well.[20] As they make their way through the jungle, the boys are discovered by an indigenous group shown to be sympathetic with the new regime (and portrayed earlier in the film). As the trio of Bob, Shrimp, and Son is chased by the camp officials, aided by indigenous informers, we witness the death of Shrimp as he steps on an explosive land mine. A series of shot reverse shots captures Son and Bob, as well as the disfigured and bloody body, seemingly still breathing. The camera lingers on the heaving body as Son implores Bob that they must continue. Like soldiers in the Vietnam War, from either side, the boys must flee danger while leaving their fallen comrade behind. The unresolved horrors of one form of imperialist oppression merge with another in this scene, and the heaving corpse of Shrimp incarnates the spectral bodies of the Vietnam War.

In many ways, the camera's focus on the body conjures multiple historical traumas from Vietnam's histories of imperialist oppression and is akin to what Thomas J. Connelly has identified as an important tenet of a "cinema of confinement." Connelly argues that central to many films that turn around the themes of confinement, imprisonment, or limited space is the role of the excess of the gaze. For Connelly, "the excess of the gaze not only demonstrates the attraction and appeal of confinement cinema, but can provide insights into the mechanisms of power and ideology."[21] Although Connelly's discussion addresses the dynamics of desire that mediate the spectator's affective relationship to scenes and themes of spatial confinement, it also applies to this scene as well. The lingering shot of Shrimp's abandoned corpse, like that of the escapee in the film's earlier scene, draws attention to the excess of the gaze as it lingers on the discarded physical bodies of these boys strewn across the nation. In so doing, the camera signals how national space remains trapped in the nation's unresolved memories of oppression, not only those of the Vietnam War and French colonialism, but also of the re-education camps. The excess of the gaze here records the spectral presence of what has been expunged from official record.

The confinement of Son and Bob soon moves from a form of metaphorical imprisonment to literal physical confinement as the boys are captured, beaten, and taken to the "Tiger Cage," a hole in the ground reserved for punishment. Like war prisoners, the boys are thrown into the ground without food. Son's first thought in this space is to record what he has witnessed and to write down the names of the dead. In close proximity, Bob then dies next to Son. In a sequence reinforcing the relationship between confinement, witnessing, and the nation space, the shots cut from the scene of recording taking place in the dark hole to Bob's body being carried to Fanta Hill for burial. We then cut back to a long take of Son in the Tiger Cage, as he records these events in his journal. This sequence reinforces not only the equation between the buried and repressed memories of the boys' physical deaths and the nation space, but also that of the relationship between the official acts of the nation and the role of individual testimony. Son, like Bob, is in many ways already buried and erased, a figure of "bare life" confined to the recesses of national space and its narrative. Yet, his act of witnessing and recording threatens from this confined space. The camera makes this clear in its long take of the close-up of his journal and the pencil scrolling across in darkness (Figure 8.1). The physical body is already nothing more than a spectral presence haunting this space, yet the recording of its history is of central importance. This scene, then, constitutes an embodiment of the film's engagement with Duyên Ahn's autobiographical novel. The author's memories come to embody the space of the nation on screen and its representation of the historical record.

ENDINGS

The film's ending invites comparisons with those of other films by Bouchareb, but none more so than *Days of Glory*. Freed by Mr Can Bô, who has seemingly come to a realization about the cruelty of the camps, Son is loaded into a cargo truck with other liberated prisoners. The film's final shots alternate between the remaining prisoners seen against the backdrop of Fanta Hill as it burns, and Son, clenching the crucifix Bob gave to him, as he is taken away. This scene is taken up in analogous ways at the end of *Days of Glory*. The final scenes of *Dust of Life* end on the symbolism of sacrifice and loss through *memento mori*. In *Days of Glory*, the military graveyard in Alsace and the tombs of fallen comrades Said, Messaoud, Yassir, and Martinez visited by an aged Corporal Abdelkader represent the loss, sacrifice, and memory of the North African soldiers who served France in World War II. Like Son, Abdelkader is the surviving witness to this history. That scene serves as a prelude to an extradiegetic commentary on the history of the North African soldiers' pensions and their ultimate disregard by the French nation. Likewise, in *Dust of Life*, these final shots establish a relationship between Son and the sacrifice of the boys left behind at the camp. They convey the sacrifice and memory of Son's fallen comrades, and serve as a prelude to an extradiegetic commentary that appears on screen, informing us that the film is based on a true story and that several thousand Amerasian children remain in Vietnam with the hope of leaving for America. Both films thus establish a relationship to what has been left behind.

Both *Days of Glory* and the earlier *Dust of Life* end on the themes of impossible union, sacrifice, and commemoration. In *Days of Glory*, however, an attempt to incorporate the soldiers into the narrative of French national identity dominates the film. The narrative of belonging and identity within the framework of French national history conditions the film's treatment of memory and history. *Days of Glory* attempts an incorporation of loss into the fabric of French national identity and expresses a desire for belonging within its narrative.[22] As I showed, in *Dust of Life*, however, the very underpinnings of the national narrative in Vietnam and its instrumentality, its entrapment in the memories of Western imperialism and loss, are queried and underscored. *Dust of Life* demonstrates that the national narrative in Vietnam is predicated upon a repetitive cycle of oppression and exclusion. It is a narrative trapped in the past that deploys forms of oppression and ideology resembling those of French and American imperialism in Vietnam. While in *Days of Glory* the national narrative and space are validated as worthy of the characters' belonging, in *Dust of Life* they are problematized. Nonetheless, even though *Dust of Life* can be seen to engage more directly with the instrumentality of national memory than *Days of Glory*, both films show the recording of history to be a national narrative of forgetting, one punctuated at the end by a longing for the validation of identity by a seemingly absent yet influential paternalistic ideal, a space of belonging that indeed remains outside narratives of the nation directly experienced by Bouchareb's characters.[23]

NOTES

1. Duyên Anh, *La Colline de Fanta*, trans. Pierre Tran Van Nghiêm and Ghislain Ripault (Paris: Belfond, 1989).
2. It should be noted, however, that the African diaspora is nonetheless represented in this film through the main character's African American father, a soldier who served in the Vietnam War.
3. Paul Ricoeur, *Memory, History, Forgetting*, trans. Kathleen Blamey and David Pellauer (Chicago: University of Chicago Press, 2004), 172. See also Ayo Coly, "Memory, History, Forgetting: A Review of Rachid Bouchareb's *Indigènes* (2006)," *Transition*, no. 98 (2008): 150–5.
4. On the issues of memory and the incorporation or rejection of North African characters in Bouchareb's work, see Anne Donadey, "'Wars of Memory': On Rachid Bouchareb's *Hors la loi*," *Esprit Créateur* 54, no. 4 (2014): 15–26. See also Alec Hargreaves, "*Indigènes*: A Sign of the Times," *Research in African Literatures* 38, no. 4 (2007): 204–16.
5. In the 1930s, the term referred to the starving people of the countryside who moved to urban areas to take refuge. It is intended to refer to a vagrant child moving about like dust. See Philippe M. F. Peycam, *The Birth of Vietnamese Political Journalism: Saigon, 1916–1930* (New York: Columbia University Press, 2012). The term became widely known thanks to the song of the same title in the 1989 musical *Miss Saigon* by Claude-Michel Schönberg and Alain Boublil. For an analysis of the use of the term in the musical, see Matthew Bernstein and Gaylyn Studlar, *Visions of the East: Orientalism in Film* (New Brunswick, NJ: Rutgers University Press, 1997), 167.
6. Ricoeur, *Memory, History, Forgetting*, 536.

7. Ibid., 102. On forms of memory in Ricoeur's work, Abdelmajid Hannoum writes that "Ricoeur reserves a distinct place for the manipulated memory, instrumentalized memory, so to speak, in which both memory and forgetfulness are subject to an intense manipulation by power." See Abdelmajid Hannoum, "Paul Ricoeur on Memory," *Theory, Culture & Society* 22, no. 6 (2005): 126.
8. See for instance, Le Hu'u Tri, *Prisoner of the Word: A Memoir of the Vietnamese Reeducation Camps* (Seattle: Black Heron Press, 2010).
9. *Report of an Amnesty International Mission to the Socialist Republic of Viet Nam* (London: Amnesty International, 1981), 23.
10. Benedict Anderson, *Imagined Communities: Reflections on the Origins and Spread of Nationalism* (London: Verso, 2006), 204.
11. I discuss these issues surrounding the themes of confinement in more detail below. The term "cinema of confinement" comes from Thomas J. Connelly: see his *Cinema of Confinement* (Evanston, IL: Northwestern University Press, 2019).
12. On Hendrix's "Star-Spangled Banner" in relation to nationalism, see Marck Clague, "'This is America': Jimi Hendrix's Star Spangled Banner Journey as Psychedelic Citizenship," *Journal of the Society for American Music* 8, no. 4 (2014): 435–78.
13. Giorgio Agamben, *Homo Sacer: Sovereign Power and Bare Life*, trans. Daniel Heller-Roazen (Stanford, CA: Stanford University Press, 1998).
14. Ibid., 139. Agamben also uses the space of the Holocaust camps as a compelling example of sovereign bio-power. The representation of the Vietnamese re-education camps is analogous in this regard.
15. Bouchareb's interest in a nation at war with itself is perhaps most apparent in his 2010 film *Hors la loi / Outside the Law*.
16. This is reminiscent of Messaoud and Sergeant Martinez in *Days of Glory*, who also carry with them "illicit" photos of their relationship to other ethnic and national backgrounds. See Michael F. O'Riley, "Mapping National Identity and Unrealized Union: Rachid Bouchareb's *Indigènes*," in *Cinema in an Age of Terror: North Africa, Victimization, and Colonial History* (Lincoln: University of Nebraska Press, 2010): 49–78.
17. Christina Elizabeth Firpo, *The Uprooted: Race, Children, and Imperialism in French Indochina, 1890–1980* (Honolulu: University of Hawaii Press, 2016). See also Kim Lefèvre's autobiographical novel *Métisse blanche* (Paris: Aube, 2001).
18. Thomas Docherty, "Memento Mori," in *Literature and Cultural Memory*, ed. Mihaela Irimia, Dragoş Manea, and Andreea Paris (Leiden: Brill, 2017), 59.
19. In this regard, Son recalls Abdelkader in *Days of Glory*.
20. It is important to note that *Dust of Life* displays the tendency in Bouchareb's work to focus on the experiences of boys or men. Anne Donadey has discussed the use of the epic genre and theme, which appears here, with reference to the role of gender in Bouchareb's work. See "Gender, Genre, and Intertextuality in Rachid Bouchareb's *Hors la loi*," *Studies in French Cinema* 16, no. 1 (2016): 48–60.
21. Connelly, *Cinema of Confinement*, 13.
22. On this topic see Panivong Norindr, "Incorporating Indigenous Soldiers in the Space of the Nation: Rachid Bouchareb's *Indigènes*," *Yale French Studies*, no. 115 (2009): 126–40.
23. In *Days of Glory*, this paternalistic ideal takes the form of epic, masculine warfare and the French narrative of heroism and resistance that ensues. In *Dust of Life*, it takes the form of a distant American father figure.

CHAPTER 9

The Door of No Return: A Cinema of (Up)rooting and Decentering in Rachid Bouchareb's *Little Senegal*

Gemma King

The histories of colonialism and slavery have carved triangular paths between Western Europe, West Africa and the Americas that continue to haunt the descendants of enslaved people and shape their movements across the Atlantic. This chapter focuses on Rachid Bouchareb's 2001 film *Little Senegal* to reveal the importance of transnational movement, translingual dialogue, and the decentered relationship with the anglo- and francospheres that defines Bouchareb's work. Coproduced by Algeria, France, and Germany and with dialogue in Arabic, English, French, and Wolof, the film charts the Senegalese man Alloune's pilgrimage to the United States in search of traces of his ancestors, who were enslaved in the early nineteenth century. Through his journey from the island of Gorée off the coast of Dakar to New York via Charleston and back again, Alloune not only discovers the fate of his forebears, but also locates their descendants living in the Little Senegal neighborhood of Harlem (the district's name unknowingly connecting them to their lost Senegalese past). Across these multilingual spaces, *Little Senegal* explores the characters' processes of (self-)discovery, drawing out the tensions between fixity and displacement that define their lives. Shifting between English and French, Senegal and the US, the nineteenth and the twenty-first century, *Little Senegal* takes a unique cinematographic approach to mobility that departs from the fixed, national sphere.

Mapping Alloune's journey against the decentered perspectives of cinéma-monde, this chapter reads Bouchareb's approach to anglophone and francophone spaces as representative of centuries of transnational movement. The film not only charts the post-colonial flows that shape migration patterns today, but retraces the paths that were trodden in earlier ages of globalization: the transatlantic trajectories of the slave trade. Through this journey, *Little Senegal* arrives at a complex understanding of space in which lingering colonial forces remain, but are not necessarily lived as hierarchical, hegemonic or Hexagonal; that is, dominated or defined by metropolitan France. Throughout the film, symbolic motifs, most importantly that of the tree, offer a means of understanding the tensions between home and homelessness that lie at the heart of the film. *Little Senegal* is both uprooted—its characters lost, migrating, and traveling across the world—and rooted—these same characters connected to earth and to one another via their family tree. In its representation of diverse languages, cultures, and patterns of movement, Bouchareb's film offers a new vision of the palimpsestic pathways that have existed between and across the African, European, and American continents for at least 400 years. This chapter provides an overview of the transnational trajectory of Rachid Bouchareb's filmmaking career, revealing the linguistic, cultural, and geographic hybridity of his films, before focusing in on *Little Senegal* as an emblematic example of his decentered cinema.

FILMMAKING ACROSS THE ANGLO- AND FRANCOSPHERES

Since the 1984 release of his first internationally recognized work, the short film *Peut-être la mer/Perhaps the Sea*, Rachid Bouchareb's cinema has been defined by border crossing. Born in France to Algerian parents, and a francophone filmmaker who has produced more films in France than in any other country, Bouchareb is frequently identified as a French, Algerian, or (most often) a Franco-Algerian director. Yet the majority of Bouchareb's films feature characters of varied origins, several coproduction partners and dialogue in multiple languages. His filming locations range from Colombia to Tunisia to Belgium, his coproduction partners from Hong Kong to Germany to Morocco, and his dialogue from Vietnamese to Mandinka to Spanish. Although his films are increasingly set and filmed beyond France, it remains Bouchareb's primary (co)production country, and French is the most frequent language used in his films. However, the labels of "French" or any other national cinema are insufficient to define or contain his oeuvre. Instead, Bouchareb's films can be viewed as an example of cinéma-monde, a francophone yet transnational cinema in which the metropolitan French nucleus is decentered to make way for a multitude of national, cultural, and linguistic forces.[1]

Of Bouchareb's eleven features to date, five are partly or even fully set in the United States.[2] Yet Bouchareb's American-set cinema does not conform to stereotypical narratives of the "foreign" director drawn to the magnetic center of Hollywood.[3] Instead, these films explore connections across the anglo- and francospheres. To borrow Mary Louise Pratt's term, Bouchareb's "American" cinema represents "language contact zones"[4] which both include, and extend far beyond, the cultural nuclei of Hexagonal France and the mainland US. By contrast with the US-based films of much earlier French directors such as Jean Renoir, René Clair, and Julien Duvivier,[5] for whom, in Hollywood, "a director was a mere *exécutant* [subordinate], stifled by the power of the producer,"[6] Rachid Bouchareb's American films are as geographically, culturally, and linguistically diverse as the rest of his work. Bouchareb's experience in the US is not that of a regional filmmaker drawn into the monolingual anglosphere of Hollywood, but one whose approach decenters dominant filmmaking nodes from within. Consideration of Bouchareb's full filmography, with production countries, languages, and plot summaries (see the Appendix), reveals the extent to which his oeuvre is both focused on, and created within, diverse spaces.

Transnational approaches to filmmaking raise questions about the categories of national cinemas. Cinéma-monde helps us to understand this trans-, supra-, or perhaps even post-national realm in which Bouchareb's films are set, made, and consumed. Coined by Bill Marshall in a 2011 article for *Francosphères*,[7] cinéma-monde has been picked up by several scholars (including the editors of this volume and myself)[8] as a means of better understanding a diverse cohort of contemporary films which engage either linguistically, financially, narratively, culturally, or politically with the French-speaking world, but in ways that decenter the traditional Hexagonal filmmaking space from the primary point of focus. As such, it offers a decolonial framework for approaching clusters of global cinemas that share a language and a colonial history.

In each of Bouchareb's films, France as contemporary nation and historical force of colonial power exerts its influence over production, characters, and narrative in diverse ways. Yet not one film takes place entirely in France, with French-only dialogue, or a cast, crew, or characters of solely Gallic (i.e. white French) origins. Instead, each of his films continually traverses geographical, linguistic, and cultural boundaries.

In their volume *Cinéma-Monde: Decentred Perspectives on Global Filmmaking in French*, Michael Gott and Thibaut Schilt use the term "franco-zones" to explore these crossings between decentered francophone spaces:

> In comparison to the "world cinema" and "transnational cinema" categories, cinéma-monde is slightly less broad in its purview. Cinéma-monde is transnational, and it is of the world or greatly concerned with the world and its others. However, our conception of *monde*, as the French term suggests, is more limited by design to include linguistic and cultural connections that belong to what we would like to call "franco-zones." Similar to "contact zones" (Pratt 2010), franco-zones are physical spaces within or across francophone or non-francophone countries or even virtual, ideational spaces where cultural and linguistic connections might occur.[9]

In Bouchareb's films, some characters speak French as a native language, some use it as a non-native lingua franca, while others do not understand it at all. Some scenes unfold on metropolitan French soil, some in African or Southeast Asian territories formerly colonized by France (Senegal, Vietnam), some in francophone European countries and regions (in Belgium, for instance), some in nominally non-francophone places such as the US (yet even there, culturally plural spaces such as Louisiana emerge as echoes of French imperial histories). Some films are mostly or entirely funded by French bodies, including the government's national CNC fund (Centre national du cinéma et de l'image animée), some are jointly funded by other French-speaking nations (Morocco, Algeria), while others are coproductions whose French or francophone financial contributions are joined by third players (Italy, Germany). As Gott and Schilt write, cinéma-monde is "a critical framework or optic through which to approach a flexible corpus of films that are linked to the francophone world by some combination of linguistic or cultural affinities, geographic contacts, production connections, or reception networks."[10]

Rachid Bouchareb's films are an ideal oeuvre for examining what a cinéma-monde might look like: diverse connections and traversals within, across, and beyond spaces in which France, French and francophonie play varying roles. Films like *Hors la loi/Outside the Law*, *Indigènes/Days of Glory*, and *Cheb* focus in large part on France, examining France's role in a shifting universe since the mid-twentieth century. US-based films like *Just Like a Woman*, *Le Flic de Belleville/Belleville Cop*, *La Voie de l'ennemi/Two Men in Town*, and *Bâton Rouge/Baton Rouge* open up questions about the rival filmmaking centers of France (so often reduced to Paris) and the US (so often reduced to Hollywood). These films represent dominant filmmaking spaces in alternative ways that focus on multicultural cities, regional spaces, urban peripheries, and national borders. Films like *Poussières de vie/Dust of Life*, *La Route d'Istanbul/Road to Istanbul*, and *London River* situate themselves across a mix of francophone territories (recently decolonized Vietnam in *Dust of Life*, francophone Belgium in *Road to Istanbul*) and non-francophone third spaces (Syria in *Road to Istanbul* and the UK in *London River*) but not in metropolitan France. In these films, the use of the French language reveals both remnants of colonial influence and a contemporary repurposing of lingua francas that "unanchor" language from the national.[11] But perhaps the most illuminating case of cinéma-monde to be found in Rachid Bouchareb's work is the transcontinental, quadrilingual post-slavery tale of *Little Senegal*.

FAMILY GRAVES AND FAMILY TREES: *LITTLE SENEGAL*

In the year 2000, the middle-aged Alloune (Sotigui Kouyaté), a multilingual guide at the Maison des esclaves, a Senegal slavery museum, sets off on a journey to the United States to search for traces of his ancestors, enslaved and transported as part of the slave trade in the early days of the nineteenth century. As Alloune seeks out whatever evidence he can, from archival microfiches to fading tombstones, he is led from the haunting plantations of South Carolina to the bustling metropolis of New York City. There, in the aptly named Harlem neighborhood of Little Senegal, he locates his own nephew, Hassan, recently migrated for economic reasons, as well as the Robinsons, an African American family he believes may be descended from his ancestors. As the film progresses, Alloune becomes close with Ida Robinson (Sharon Hope) and her pregnant adolescent granddaughter, Eileen (Malaaika Lacario). He only leaves this new family when Hassan is murdered and Alloune carries his body home to Senegal. As Alloune follows the paths trodden by his ancestors and finds a new home with his distant family, Bouchareb's camera lingers not on movement, but on images of trees, earth, and graves, foregrounding the theme of rootedness that is at the heart of the film. For, despite all the travel that the characters undertake, *Little Senegal* provides a compacted portrayal of space, in which the distances between continents are collapsed, and the deep-rooted connection between them is foregrounded. In *Little Senegal*, characters are in constant movement, but we rarely witness this. Instead, the camera shows us how these characters are attached to earth, territory, family, and home through literal and figurative roots and trees.

Little Senegal's opposing themes of home and homelessness, connection to earth and movement across it, are incarnated in Alloune's profession as a griot. The griot is a West African storyteller whose mantle is passed down through the generations ("any of a class of musician-entertainers of western Africa whose performances include tribal histories and genealogies").[12] The griot is not only an essential part of the character of Alloune, who is first seen recounting histories to visitors to the Maison des esclaves, and who ultimately travels the world so that the lost story of his ancestors may be told. The role is also an integral part of the life and identity of the actor who portrays Alloune, Sotigui Kouyaté, who is descended from generations of griots. In an interview with Kouyaté for *Télérama*, Louis Guichard notes that "for him, being an actor is but an echo of a deeper truth . . . when he holds out, by way of farewell, his business card, one notices that the title 'griot' precedes that of actor."[13] Alloune and Kouyaté are both perpetual travelers who elucidate the past through the stories they learn and tell.

The importance of travel and storytelling is also mirrored in the film's use of multilingualism. In *Little Senegal*, multiple languages circulate according to flows that mimic colonial trajectories (the French language brought to Senegal, Wolof and French brought to the US, English brought back to Senegal, and so on). Yet they also set off in new directions that reflect the dispersed nature of movement in the contemporary world. In all cases, code switching carries important cultural connotations, and fluency in at least one (but ideally both) of the lingua francas of French and English is essential for the economic and social advancement of the film's African characters. Among themselves, the Senegalese and Maghrebi characters speak French, Arabic, or Wolof. Yet English is the film's most commonly used tongue. It is even spoken by Alloune before leaving Senegal, as he guides African American tourists around the Gorée slavery museum. English becomes a greater point of contention on US soil, however. The film's African characters speak English with the African Americans in varying degrees of fluency. The former's struggles with English and the latter's resentment of French reveal the stark contrast between the different black identities that make up the Harlem population. For Delphine Letort, even Alloune's accent when he speaks English creates symbolic connections between diverse spaces: "Alloune's French accent is noticeable when he speaks in English, thus orally connecting the American story with the French colonial past."[14]

In fact, French is even used in some US scenes as a means of gendered oppression, isolating migrant women from their new host society. Alloune's nephew's partner Biram is perhaps the most oppressed character in the film: she appears in multiple scenes but barely speaks and is never seen outside the claustrophobic environment of the apartment. Despite her minimal dialogue and positioning on the fringes (of both the narrative and her new society), Biram utters one of the film's most illuminating lines. When challenged by Hassan for being absent from the home one evening, she reveals that she has been trying to integrate by taking English language classes, much to Hassan's disapproval. Earlier, she was seen writing in a journal, hiding it under her pillow when she heard Hassan approaching. Drawing distinct parallels between her own oppression and historical enslavement, she retorts in French: "Am I going to be your slave my whole life?" She then code-switches into unsubtitled Wolof in an angry outburst, raising her voice for the first time in the film. Her rebellion takes place in Wolof, her liberation in English. Taken aback by this response, Hassan drags Biram into the yard and beats her. In this scene, gender, culture, and language manifest as intersecting axes of power that both oppress Biram and offer her the potential for escape. Biram's pointed question reveals how little has changed for women in her position throughout history, but her pursuit of English classes in a transnational context also shows the possibility of independence, a possibility which is threatening to her oppressor. This tension reaches breaking point when she draws the link between her disenfranchisement in the present and the oppressions of the past.

Indeed, though Alloune's journey takes place in 2000, and the film does not include any flashbacks, the distinction between the era of slavery and the present day is often blurred, the two eras even overlapping. The film appears to transcend the fixity of time. Émile Breton describes Alloune as an ethereal transplant in the twenty-first-century United States. He is at once physically present and ontologically misplaced, an "African visitor come from another world and another time."[15] Like Breton, Letort sees Alloune not as a character anchored to his contemporary timeline, but one who "seems to cross the boundaries of time and space."[16] One African American character's later revelation that the tattoo on her buttocks means "ghost" is telling, for the film is haunted by the specters of the past. In this way Alloune is connected with the image of the tree, alive yet transcendental of time, and so often filmed in the contrasting environment of the cemetery (as shown in the figures which follow). Letort also identifies the symbolic link between the family tree and the time that Alloune metaphorically traverses:

> Alloune gains mastery over the past by retracing the route of his ancestors, recovering pieces of hidden history that allow him to further the drawing of his genealogical tree, which metaphorically evokes the desire for a past, articulating a fantasy of flow and mobility behind the travails of forced migration.[17]

The film frequently weaves imagery of trees and (grave)stones together in connection with the themes of physical movement and familial connection. From the stone doorway of the Maison des esclaves' Door of No Return (*Porte du voyage sans retour*), through which enslaved people passed on the island of Gorée before being transported to the Americas, to the gravestones of the treed cemeteries of South Carolina and New York in which enslaved people and their ancestors are buried (Figures 9.1 and 9.2), Alloune is frequently framed by stones and trees which evoke the paradoxical mobility and fixity of his ancestors' and his own movements through the world. Stones quite literally tell Alloune his family story, through the names inscribed on the Robinson family grave. Indeed, the importance of the tree and its connection with stones, bones, and the grave in *Little Senegal* should not be underestimated. For the metaphoric and political significance of these symbols has long been associated with colonial, familial, geographical, and even ontological rootedness in (post-) slavery francophone contexts:

> It has been argued that stones and bones in post-slavery writing function as traces, which constitute a material connection to an otherwise unavailable primeval past. Specifically, these ancient formations and relics provide a numinous link to a prelapsarian time and space that pre-exist the plantation. Here, in a very different construction, the lack of anteriority of stone, mineral, and ancestral bone is the geological corollary of the shallow arboreal roots described above. The bones of the grandfathers, relics of a recent past, the superficial roots of the island's trees, and the absence of any "montagne primitive" or "pierre dure" betoken precariousness, illegitimacy, and a lack of mastery of time and space.[18]

In a number of studies of *ancien régime* and Republican France, Giulia Pacini has explored the physical, political, and symbolic interpretation of trees as emblematic of nation and Empire, a powerful combination of stability and progress, rootedness in the Hexagon and *rayonnement* (influence) in the colonies.[19] Aging Versailles trees were sold to the navy in 1774,[20] and the link between boats and the transatlantic slave trade at that time cannot be ignored. In fact, this connection endures to the present day, for example in the wake of the 2019 Notre-Dame fire. In discussions of the reconstruction of the cathedral's historic wooden frame, nicknamed *la forêt* for the myriad Ile-de-France oak trees which composed it, the question of using French-grown trees quickly gained prominence: "Foresters wish for the *forêt* frame to be reconstructed using French oaks, with the traditions and quality of the original construction."[21] Pacini writes:

> The tree could be viewed as root or as growth, and as such it could be taken to signify both the stability of the ancien régime and the hopes of the new republic [. . .] As gigantic elements that link the earth to the sky and the past to the future, they appear to embody ideals of transcendence in ways that few other objects can rival.[22]

Elsewhere in Bouchareb's oeuvre, it is notable that the final scenes of 2009's *London River* juxtapose the shot of a French tree that the arborist Ousmane (again played by Sotigui Kouyaté) has decided must be cut down, with images of the Guernsey farmer Elisabeth as she visits the graves of her husband and recently deceased daughter. Ousmane is also seen praying in a French forest before undertaking his journey to the UK in search of his son. Indeed, Pacini's research on the power of trees in the era of slavery can help us understand their haunting presence in Bouchareb's film(s) and the contemporary age.

In *Little Senegal*, the tree serves a similar purpose, appearing often in American cemeteries and embodying the film's central theme of the connection between present and past. In fact, multiple reviews of the film reference this motif of the tree, both physical and genealogical, and the linked symbol of roots, both deeply embedded and traumatically torn up. In *Variety*, David Stratton remarks that *Little Senegal* "reverses the idea of 'Roots'" in the film's fractured portrayal of family.[23] In *Positif*, Françoise Audé describes the Harlem neighborhood of Little Senegal, where Alloune finds the living members of his family tree, as an "urban jungle."[24] In *Les Inrockuptibles*, Serge Kaganski and Raphaël Badache explain that Alloune "discovers the final American branch of his ancient family tree in the figure of Ida."[25]

As Alloune wanders through the eighteenth-century slave graveyard of South Carolina (Figure 9.1) and the twentieth-century New York cemetery (Figure 9.2), the frame is dominated by trees as much as it is by graves. In Figure 9.1, the gravestones are almost lost in an overgrowth of wild grass and

Figure 9.1 Alloune at antebellum cemetery, South Carolina

Figure 9.2 Modern cemetery containing Robinson family grave, New York

plants. Ancient oaks extend over Alloune's head and into the earth beneath, which may or may not house the remains of his ancestors. All appears lost in the past, as if Alloune is stepping back into the time during which the cemetery was active. The only sign of current human life in the picture, dappled light cast over his plodding frame, Alloune appears as a solitary figure transported into history. By contrast, in Figure 9.2, Alloune finds himself in a far more modern cemetery. Here, snow covers the ground but many of the polished headstones are wreathed with fresh flowers. In the middle ground, busy highways rise into bridges that almost seem to travel over the cemetery itself. In the background lies the Manhattan skyline, including the World Trade Center towers, captured just months before their destruction and rendered all the more eerily representative of the turn of the millennium when viewed post-9/11. Here are buried the American descendants of Alloune's ancestors, the Robinsons, the most

Figure 9.3 Alloune at Hassan's grave by the sea, Gorée

recent having died only a few years before. Yet in both spaces, the symbol of the tree defines the space. Captured in the center-left frame, deprived of leaves in its winter environment but very much alive, another old oak stretches from the earth into the sky, its branches reaching even higher than the city skyline. Here too, the past looms large, its tendrils reaching into the present.

Thus, time in *Little Senegal* collapses in on itself. Lynchings and acts of racial oppression in the present day evoke the crimes of the past. Sites of generational trauma and the rupture of familial ties continue to exert their influence on the Robinsons and others. Like the South Carolina cemetery, they are simultaneously haunted by the history of slavery, and rooted in the present day. The film often lingers on complementary yet opposing shots, such as the chains Alloune holds in the first scene, as he explains how enslaved people were transported to the Americas, and the chains used to lynch a black man in a recent KKK-reminiscent crime. Watching the televised footage of this crime as the newsreader explains that "the victim was sprayed with black paint before he died," we read the same solemn pain on Alloune's face as when he held the chains in the Gorée museum and told an all-too-similar story. Through its narrative, iconography, and cinematography, *Little Senegal* juxtaposes and draws together different spaces and times to reveal the lineage of trauma. As Françoise Audé writes, the film is linked by a chain, "not of iron, but of flesh, which unites generations."[26] This evokes a discussion between Alloune and Ida, before he reveals their shared ancestry.

> Alloune: Your great-great-grandparents. Where are they from?
> Ida: Why go back so far?
> Alloune: You're forgetting when and how they came.
> Ida: What's the point of thinking about the past?

Alloune: You've not had a lot of luck. I've had more than you. My ancestor wasn't taken as a slave, but that could have been me.
Ida: Who were my ancestors in Africa? I don't know. Who were they? I just want to know what I'm going to buy myself for dinner.

This lineage shapes many of the characters, but perhaps most poignantly that of Eileen. An African American descended from Senegalese slaves, her mother has recently died (her name etched on the Robinson grave Alloune visits) and she is soon to become a mother herself. Eileen is uprooted by the loss of her mother, the rupture of her relationship with her grandmother, the absence of a supportive father or partner, and the pregnancy she fears will expel her from society, all of which lead to her literal homelessness. But Eileen is also connected to a family tree that Alloune has progressively mapped out in his notebook, whose branches extend to a new generation with the birth of her daughter. Both attached and isolated, she incarnates the film's themes in opposite yet complementary ways.

RACHID BOUCHAREB'S DECENTERED CINEMA

Little Senegal cannot be defined as an American, French, Senegalese, or any other national film as we might traditionally understand one to be. Instead we find ourselves in the realm of a decentered cinema in which territory is both solid and fluid, and in which space is both historically situated and transcendent of time. If there is a linguistic, cultural, or ontological center in *Little Senegal* (and it could be argued that there is not), it is neither of the colonial territories which exert their influence over the film's languages and characters. It is not the France whose colonization of the protagonist's country leads him to speak the French language, even if the former colonial power is the majority financier of the film. Neither is it the English-speaking US to which generations of Africans have traveled, either by force under slavery, or by choice as present-day economic migrants.

Instead, despite what the title might suggest, the geographical focal point of the film is Senegal itself. The West African country is both origin and destination, literal home to the film's African characters and ancestral home to its African American ones. Senegal is the site at which the film's languages meet, from which all its characters ultimately originate and to which so many of them return. *Little Senegal* opens and closes with a shot of the Gorée museum's stone Door of No Return, through which enslaved people passed, leaving their homeland behind forever. Yet despite the moments Alloune spends contemplating the doorway, he is not confined to the binary movements of his ancestors. Instead, his movements are decentered and circular. He treads the paths of British, French, and American colonizers, of enslaved Africans, of contemporary African migrants that traverse the Atlantic in scattered yet interconnected ways. Yet unlike his ancestors, he returns home. This recalls my own work on multidirectional voyages in contemporary multilingual film, in which characters undertake post-colonial journeys that defy the conventions of Eurocentrism. In these films, characters do not only tread linear paths from former colonies (such as Senegal) toward metropolitan France. Instead, transnational movement is polycentric; journeys are enacted in myriad directions, between a multitude of franco-zones that may or may not include France.[27] In its production context, cast, filming locations, languages, and narrative, *Little Senegal* positions itself in a space both influenced by and transcendental of the national. Bouchareb's cinema is perhaps best understood as cinéma-monde more than any other label (French cinema, transnational cinema, world cinema, and so on). This is not to underemphasize the non-francophone elements that are so inherent in Bouchareb's films, but to recognize the persistent cultural, linguistic, and financial influence of the francosphere on Bouchareb's filmmaking practices, and within the narratives of his individual films. While cinéma-monde is born of the practices of globalization that arose with colonialism, it is not intended to operate along hierarchical lines, with all roads leading to the center of metropolitan France. Instead these films follow rhizomatic patterns, in which many franco-zones across the globe (including but not especially France) operate as centers of linguistic and cultural diversity.

Little Senegal's narrative is dominated by constant physical movement across these franco-zones. Yet despite the physical uprooting of the film's characters, the screen is dominated by images that evoke a seemingly paradoxical rootedness. For one, there is an almost complete absence of the representation of travel. Shots of the sea are taken from the viewpoint of an observer on land. Though there are many street scenes, Hassan works as a taxi driver, and Alloune is briefly seen on the subway, characters walk far more often than they ride. When they take public transport (such as the ferries between Gorée and Dakar), it is usually to circulate around one city, rather than to depart from it. Most strikingly, there is no footage of Alloune's journey by plane to the US and back again. We switch abruptly from one shot of him looking out over the water at Gorée, to an almost identical shot of him staring out to sea from a beach at Sullivan's Island, South Carolina. We know we have been transported from Senegal to the US only when the camera lingers on a plaque explaining the island's significance as a site where enslaved Africans first set foot in the Americas. Though Alloune has traveled the world between these two shots, within seconds the camera takes us from the Maison des esclaves on Gorée to the Old Slave Mart Museum in Charleston. It is as though the two places, the two ports at either end of the transatlantic journey, are both opposites and doubles, two sides of the same coin, impossibly distant yet intimately connected through space and time.

This is perhaps best summed up in the film's final cemetery image (Figure 9.3), after Alloune has carried his nephew's body home. The camera captures Hassan's grave in the foreground, the sea in the background, and Alloune's hand pressed against the earth in a gesture of familial connection. The shot foreshadows Bouchareb's later film *London River*, in which family graves are also filmed in a coastal setting. Though *London River*'s family graves are located on a very different island—Guernsey—and the camera looks out over a very different body of water—the English Channel—the pairing of the grave and the sea evokes the same tensions of anchoring and unmooring we see in the final scenes of *Little Senegal*. Alloune is framed in a space that is both fixed and moving, the backdrop of the sea across which he has traveled contrasting with the earth against which he presses his palm. The picture is one of paradoxical rootedness and decentering, connection to home and displacement from it.

CONCLUSION

Little Senegal tells a story of movement and homelessness, but also of connection and home. In its representation of a world in which characters constantly cross national borders, linguistic barriers, and cultural lines, the film is a quintessential example of the multidirectional filmmaking that characterizes Rachid Bouchareb's oeuvre as a whole. The cinematography emphasizes territory, earth, rootedness, touch. The story is marked by the trauma of slavery, the uprooting of bodies, the rupture of families, and the transgenerational impact of displacement that leads to physical and ontological homelessness in the contemporary age. The colonial lingua francas of English and French are mixed together in spaces as varied as Gorée and Harlem. Twenty-first-century lynchings are visibly linked (via chains) to seventeenth-century slave restraints. Nineteenth-century cemeteries in the South are visually linked to twentieth-century family graves in New York City. *Little Senegal*'s characters speak French and are impacted by the history of French colonialism, but do not pass through France. The film is mostly set in the eastern US, with majority-English dialogue and a half-American cast, but was produced by Algeria, France, and Germany (with no US funding). From Dakar to Charleston to New York (but never Paris), from Wolof to English to Arabic to French, from African Americans to Senegalese travelers to African migrants, Bouchareb's film expresses the myriad relationalities of the post-colonial world. In all these ways, *Little Senegal* offers us an inventive cinematic portrayal of culture and territory that is fundamentally decentered, (up)rooted and multilateral. In the film's final shot, as Alloune looks out through the Door of No Return to see a boat setting out from the Senegalese coast, his gaze—and with it, Bouchareb's camera—extends out beyond the limits of continents and centuries.

NOTES

1. Michael Gott and Thibaut Schilt, ed., *Cinéma-Monde: Decentred Perspectives on Global Filmmaking in French* (Edinburgh: Edinburgh University Press, 2018); Bill Marshall, "Cinéma-monde? Towards a Concept of Francophone Cinema," *Francosphères* 1, no. 1 (2011): 35–51.
2. *Le Flic de Belleville/Belleville Cop* (2018), *La Voie de l'ennemi/Two Men in Town* (2014), *Just Like a Woman* (2012), *Little Senegal* (2001), *Bâton Rouge/Baton Rouge* (1985).
3. This is despite Bouchareb's demonstrated interest in experimenting with the conventions of Hollywood genre film, as David Pettersen suggests in Chapter 4 of this volume.
4. Mary Louise Pratt, "Arts of the Contact Zone," *Profession* (1991): 33–40.
5. Ben McCann, *Julien Duvivier* (Manchester: Manchester University Press, 2017), 118–19.
6. Ibid., 136.
7. Marshall, "*Cinéma-monde?*"
8. Ibid. See for example, Gott and Schilt, ed., *Cinéma-Monde*; the "Cinéma-monde: Film, Borders, Translation" conference held at the University of Stirling, UK in May 2018 and attended by the above authors; Michael Gott, "Lost at Sea or Charting a New Course? Mapping the Murky Contours of Cinéma-Monde," in *Cinéma-Monde*, ed. Gott and Schilt, 131–54; Leslie Kealhofer-Kemp, "The Career of Actress Hafsia Herzi: Crossing Borders, Challenging Barriers," in *Cinéma-Monde*, ed. Gott and Schilt, 110–28; Gemma King, "Merry Christmas in No Man's Land: European Borders, Language Barriers and Front Lines in Christian Carion's *Joyeux Noël*," in *Cinéma-Monde*, ed. Gott and Schilt, 175–91.
9. Michael Gott and Thibaut Schilt, "Introduction: The Kaleidoscope of Cinéma-Monde," in *Cinéma-Monde*, ed. Gott and Schilt, 9, quoting Mary Louise Pratt, *Imperial Eyes: Travel Writing and Transculturation*, 2nd ed. (New York: Routledge, 2010).
10. Ibid., 2.
11. For the concept of the "unanchored language," as "a language which is not directly associated with its country of origin, and which thus functions beyond traditional cultural and linguistic politics," see Gemma King, "Langues désancrées: le rôle du français dans *London River*," in *Genre, Text and Language: Mélanges Anne Freadman*, ed. Véronique Duché, Tess Do, and Andrea Rizzi (Paris: Classiques Garnier, 2016), 318.
12. "Griot," *Merriam-Webster Dictionary*, accessed 5 April 2020, https://www.merriam-webster.com/dictionary/griot.
13. Louis Guichard, "Sotigui Kouyaté, acteur et griot," *Télérama*, 20 April 2001, updated 1 February 2018, www.telerama.fr/cinema/sotigui-kouyate-acteur-et-griot,54970.php.
14. Delphine Letort, "Rethinking the Diaspora through the Legacy of Slavery in Rachid Bouchareb's *Little Senegal*," *Black Camera* 6, no. 1 (2014): 148.
15. Émile Breton, "Les Racines et la vie: *Little Senegal* de Rachid Bouchareb," *L'Humanité*, 18 April 2001, www.humanite.fr/node/245015.
16. Letort, "Rethinking the Diaspora," 147.
17. Ibid., 143.
18. Maeve McCusker, "'We Were All Strangers Here': Time, Space, and Postcolonial Anxiety in Traversay's *Les Amours de Zémédare et Carina, et description de l'île de la Martinique*," *French Studies* 72, no. 2 (2018): 222.
19. Giulia Pacini, "A Culture of Trees: The Politics of Pruning and Felling in Late Eighteenth-Century France," *Eighteenth-Century Studies* 41, no. 1 (2007): 1–15. *Rayonnement* can be described as the cultural, political, and national "radiating influence" of France beyond the Hexagon, most often associated with the "glory" of the French

monarchy and later Republic. The *Dictionnaire Larousse* defines it as "influence exerted by a person or country, through their prestige" (www.larousse.fr/dictionnaires/francais/rayonnement/66761). The term originates from the literal definition of *rayonnement* as "radiation," i.e. that of beams or rays of light. Giulia Pacini, "Arboreal Attachments: Interacting with Trees in Early Nineteenth-Century France," *Configurations* 24, no. 2 (2016): 173–95; Giulia Pacini, "The Monarchy Shapes Up: Arboreal Metaphors in Royal Propaganda and Court Panegyrics during the Reign of Louis XV," *Journal for Eighteenth-Century Studies* 39, no. 3 (2016): 431–48.
20. Pacini, "A Culture of Trees," 5.
21. Mathilde Golla, "Notre-Dame: les acteurs de la forêt française prêts à reconstruire la charpente," *Le Figaro*, 17 April 2019, www.lefigaro.fr/societes/notre-dame-les-acteurs-de-la-foret-francaise-prets-a-reconstruire-la-charpente-20190417.
22. Pacini, "A Culture of Trees," 1.
23. David Stratton, "Film Review: *Little Senegal*," *Variety*, 26 February 2001, 44.
24. Françoise Audé, "'Little Senegal': L'invention d'Alloune," *Positif*, May 2001, 31.
25. Serge Kasanski and Raphaël Badache, "Little Sénégal," *Les Inrockuptibles*, 30 November 2000, www.lesinrocks.com/cinema/films-a-l-affiche/little-senegal.
26. Audé, "'Little Senegal,'" 31.
27. Gemma King, *Decentring France: Multilingualism and Power in Contemporary French Cinema* (Manchester: Manchester University Press, 2017), 190.

CHAPTER 10

Rachid Bouchareb's *Hors la loi/Outside the Law*: A Lesson in History, Reception, and Artistic License

Jennifer Howell

After the international critical acclaim and box-office success of *Indigènes/Days of Glory* (2006), the second installment of Rachid Bouchareb's announced trilogy, *Hors la loi/Outside the Law* (2010), came as a disappointment to many French critics and moviegoers who criticized its historical representation and gangster aesthetic. *Outside the Law* recounts the story of three Algerian brothers (Sami Bouajila as Abdelkader, Roschdy Zem as Messaoud, and Jamel Debbouze as Saïd) living in the Nanterre shantytown near Paris during the Algerian War of Independence (1954–62). The film begins in Algeria in 1925 when the protagonists, as young children, witness the confiscation of their father's land by French colonial authorities. While the film focuses on the workings of the Algerian resistance, specifically the National Liberation Front (FLN), in metropolitan France, it also includes a seven-minute scene depicting the massacre of Algerian nationalists in Sétif, Algeria, by French authorities during the celebration of VE Day on 8 May 1945. For this reason, Bouchareb and some of the film's actors consider *Outside the Law* to be a historical sequel to *Days of Glory*, which portrays the plight of North African colonial soldiers in the French army during World War II. *Days of Glory* and *Outside the Law* together form a historical continuum spanning the period running from World War II to Algerian independence. A planned third film in the trilogy would cover Maghrebi immigration in post-colonial France.[1]

Regardless of Bouchareb's insistence that *Outside the Law* did not have a political agenda, the film sparked a heated public debate. Among the film's most vociferous critics was Lionnel Luca, a deputy of the center-right Union for a Popular Movement (UMP). Luca had admittedly never seen the film before attacking its "falsification" of history, "revisionist" agenda, and "anti-French" sentiment.[2] Echoing Luca's concerns, other right-wing politicians and memory groups nostalgic for French Algeria (veterans, *pieds-noirs* [European settlers], and *harkis* [indigenous soldiers who served in the French army during the Algerian War of Independence]) argued that Bouchareb's representation of the Sétif massacre embodied the kind of historical repentance that the Sarkozy administration so adamantly condemned. Less virulent critiques highlighted the film's historical anachronisms, omissions, and errors. Despite attempts to have the film removed from the 2010 Cannes Film Festival, the selection committee allowed it to be screened. In protest, the mayor of Cannes, Bernard Brochand, mobilized approximately 1,200 individuals—including Luca—who gathered at the city hall to honor the French victims of the Algerian War of Independence.[3]

Press coverage of the film's release was to be expected given the media's portrayal of the political effect of *Days of Glory*, which resulted in the unfreezing and equalization of the pensions of France's colonial soldiers. This film made history not only because it was a commercial success, but also because it had significant political sway. Nicola Cooper contends that "the real impact of Bouchareb's film [*Days of Glory*] has . . . been more political than cultural. It provided a catalyst," she writes, "for a crucial thaw in France's attitude towards its indigenous veterans."[4] The French government initially froze colonial pensions in 1959 as African nations began declaring their independence. This decision would prevent the readjustment of colonial pensions to account for increases in the cost of living. Later, the then minister of finance, Laurent Fabius, would allow for the pensions of those veterans living on the African continent to align with the cost of living there. The disparity among pensions remained, with African veterans receiving on average 25 percent of that of their former brothers in arms living in France.[5] Though the French president, Jacques Chirac, and his wife Bernadette were moved to do more for former colonial soldiers after a private screening of *Days of Glory*, veterans and their families would have to wait until 2011 before the complete unfreezing of pensions.[6] That Chirac decided to act before the public became aware of the injustice does not lessen the film's impact on French spectators. Mireille Rosello argues that the political impact of *Days of Glory* retains its significance because "by proposing a new narrative that we are invited to accept as a new (even provisional) truth, the film changes a historical canon rather than our relationship to historical truth."[7] Since *Outside the Law* deals with a polarizing historical moment in French history, did the second film of Bouchareb's proposed trilogy have a similar effect on French audiences, despite negative reviews and lack of subsequent political reform? I argue that *Outside the Law* falls short of the impact that Rosello attributes to *Days of Glory*. The reason is twofold. First, by the time Bouchareb released *Outside the Law*, France had already entered a new "moment of memory" (defined below) colored by President Nicolas Sarkozy's anti-repentance rhetoric. Second, marketed as a gangster/crime film with a predominantly Maghrebi-French cast, *Outside the Law* does not have the same "polished" allure of historicity as *Days of Glory*, a genre difference that critics ultimately used to discredit the legitimacy of Bouchareb's counternarrative.

COLONIAL FRACTURE AND THE SARKOZIAN ERA OF ANTI-REPENTANCE

For Rosello, an "event of memory" sparks controversy because it challenges the accepted historical paradigms that have come to define the "moment of memory" during which the event occurs.[8] A moment of memory is "a provisionally stable period during which the paradigms that we accept as what is historical discourse and what we consider to be just noise are relatively set."[9] By way of comparison, "an event of memory is what modifies the whole paradigm and what makes us see that we were blind to the borders set by the hegemonic moment of memory."[10] Released just four years after *Days of Glory*, *Outside the Law* belongs to a new moment of memory ushered in with the election of Nicolas Sarkozy in 2007. Although Vincent Martigny has argued that Sarkozy's anti-repentance rhetoric does not constitute a radical change from previous administrations, he admits that Sarkozy's understanding of French national identity as a fixed concept (and not the dynamic product of "historical compromise") has become his hallmark.[11] And contrary to Chirac, whose presidency was marked by various acts of national contrition (he officially apologized, for example, for the state's complicity in the Vélodrome d'Hiver round-up of Parisian Jews, the 1945 Sétif massacre, and the slave trade), Sarkozy inaugurated his presidency by announcing that he would "bring an end to repentance."[12] The Sarkozy years would "favor an acknowledgment of facts, not repentance,"[13] and aim to "make the French proud of France again."[14]

In the spirit of anti-repentance, one of Sarkozy's first acts as president was to create the (now defunct) Ministry of Immigration, Integration, National Identity, and Cooperative Development, whose purpose was to articulate and promote a French national identity, as well as to regulate immigration and confirm the cultural assimilation of France's immigrant community through various language and citizenship exams. As a result of this decision, eight historians resigned from the National Museum of Immigration History's twelve-person advisory committee. In their letter of resignation, they denounced the creation of Sarkozy's new ministry because it negated the historical objectives of the soon-to-open museum, which had been created to "account for the diversity of histories and memories, both individual and collective, to make a history for all, including proud moments and gray areas, so as to help overcome prejudice and stereotypes."[15] For them, Sarkozy's inaugural political act defined "immigration as a 'problem' for France and for the very existence of the French."[16] Sarkozy's anti-repentance rhetoric continued to trigger controversy in the months following the election. Some critics saw in his political discourse traces of the infamous 23 February 2005 law that would have forced educators to teach the "positive role" of French colonization, particularly in North Africa,[17] had Chirac not required that this language be removed before the law's adoption. Both the original wording of the law and Sarkozy's espousal of one national historical narrative deny the coexistence of multiple competing narratives.

Since the diversity of contemporary French identity partially stems from France's colonial past, how this historical period is remembered has important implications for the present. An important example of this is provided by the 2005 youth riots that took place in the marginalized suburbs of Paris and other major cities and whose participants were primarily from minority populations (notably, Arab and black). The riots began after two teenagers were fatally electrocuted in the transformer of an electricity substation where they had been hiding from patrolling police officers. Even though they had done nothing wrong and did not have a criminal record, the boys allegedly feared police harassment. Nevertheless, during an official visit to areas most affected by the riots, Sarkozy, then minister of the interior, described rioters on camera as "riff-raff" (*de la racaille*) and "delinquents" (*voyous*).[18] Sarkozy's swift dismissal of the rioters demonstrated his failure to acknowledge that colonial prejudices could negatively impact minority populations in France today. His inability, or perhaps refusal, to recognize that together France's colonial past and post-colonial present constitute a historical and an ideological continuum is symptomatic of what historians Pascal Blanchard, Nicolas Bancel, and Sandrine Lemaire have termed France's "colonial fracture."[19] They argue that France's denial of colonial history—evident, for example, in high school curricula and the International Organization of La Francophonie, which promotes the French language and humanist values around the world—has negatively impacted the ways in which the state and those minorities whose histories have been excluded from France's grand master narrative interact. We should not be surprised that Sarkozy would equate the 2005 riots and other moments of suburban youth violence with the refusal of certain immigrant communities to integrate into French society, rather than with their indignation at police brutality and racial profiling, that is, at systemic racism whose origins are to be found in the colonial era. Thomas Martin maintains that "for Sarkozy . . . post-colonial thinking and [self-critical] colonial memory . . . are inherently incompatible with national identity."[20] It is therefore meaningful that Bouchareb often responded to critics who considered *Outside the Law* to be "anti-French" with the assertion that he was born in France.[21] Yet he also demonstrates through historical fiction that his perspective on French history differs from that of mainstream French society. He explains, for instance, that frequent visits to the Nanterre shantytown and his parents' involvement with the FLN in Paris marked his childhood: "That's why I made a movie about the Algerian War in France. Because it's my story too."[22] Bouchareb's narrative therefore includes episodes that are perhaps not to be found in Sarkozy-era historical discourse, but with which he and a large proportion of his spectators would personally identify.

The debate surrounding *Outside the Law*, which has since disappeared from the public eye, prompted an investigation into the historical responsibilities of filmmakers and other artists. As is to be expected, this new line of inquiry raised more questions than it answered. In a collective statement published in *Le Monde* on 5 May 2010, prominent historians of the Algerian War of Independence recognized that Bouchareb's case constituted an exception in French cinema because of its pre-release controversy and subsequent state attempts to interfere with its production. The document's twelve signatories denounced the pressure exerted on the film's coproducers to cut funding, as well as on members of the Cannes Film Festival's selection committee to exclude the film from that year's competition: "It does not bode well when political authorities want to write the history that our fellow citizens will see on screens tomorrow."[23] That the Defense Historical Service, affiliated with the French Ministry of Defense and the Armed Forces, invited historians to a private screening of the film prior to its release is cause for concern as this kind of intervention is uncommon, if not unprecedented. The twelve signatories of the aforementioned statement reminded readers that "no one asked Francis Ford Coppola to retell the history of the Vietnam War in *Apocalypse Now* with 'historical' precision."[24] Nevertheless, historians like Benjamin Stora who were perceptibly uncomfortable with *Outside the Law* would continue to publish commentaries several months after the film's initial release at Cannes on 21 May 2010. Throughout the controversy, Bouchareb maintained his position that his film was a work of fiction and should be understood as such. In her defense of the film, historian Malika Rahal asserts that historians have placed *Outside the Law* under scrutiny because it broaches a highly sensitive subject and, cinematically, does not compare to any of the films identified by Bouchareb as models, including Francis Ford Coppola's *The Godfather* (1972) and Sergio Leone's *Once upon a Time in America* (1984).[25] Rahal raises an important point here, suggesting that the controversy surrounding the film was partially due to Bouchareb's exercise of artistic license.

OUTSIDE THE LAW AS GENRE FILM: BOUCHAREB'S GANGSTER AESTHETIC

As a gangster film, *Outside the Law* exploits the various narrative tropes of crime fiction, including the triangulation of detective-criminal-victim, an investigation that leads to the logical resolution of an enigma, and the existence of two competing narratives (the investigation and the crime).[26] For the purposes of this analysis, the gangster film is understood as a subgenre of crime fiction, distinguishable from other subgenres (film noir, thriller) by its exploitation of specific visual tropes—such as its "recurrent iconography of urban settings, clothes, cars, gun technology and violence"[27]—and by its focus on organized crime. In addition, the spectator is made to identify with the criminal protagonist rather than with representatives of the law. Film critics often point to *Outside the Law*'s stylized visual aesthetic—one of the genre's more recognizable calling cards—as a major shortcoming. Didier Péron, for instance, describes Bouchareb's re-creation of the gangster film's visual code in the following way: "The action happens less in 1950s Paris than in a world saturated with the codes and archetypes of American cinema."[28] Throughout his critique, Péron enumerates specific examples that strictly adhere to the subgenre's more distinct characteristics; he cites *Outside the Law*'s costumes, machine guns, blonde femme fatale, and urban decor. Péron reduces the film to a collage of clichés without considering the ways in which Bouchareb's cast—as Maghrebi-French actors—subverts the traditional gangster aesthetic. Similarly, film critic Thierry Méranger underscores the film's artificiality with respect to historical representation, character development, and décor, despite its estimated €20,000,000 budget. He suggests that one would expect more from a budget of that magnitude even though, by Hollywood standards, the film cost relatively little to make. By placing undue importance on what he calls the film's "Paris de studio"—which suggests that spectators will know that the film was shot in a studio rather than on location—and the various fusillades and bombings, Méranger dismisses the possibility of reading crime (that is, the nexus of the gangster narrative) as a mode of resistance.[29]

For film scholar Dennis Broe, such readings identify crime as a problem rather than "questioning the entire framework in which [that] problem [is] defined."[30] Susan Hayward concurs, arguing that "the gangster was associated with the proletarian class ... Therefore the only way he [*sic*] could access wealth and thereby self-assertion—that is success ... was by stealing it."[31] Throughout her definition, Hayward describes the gangster film as an American genre that emerged during Prohibition and the Depression. When applied to other national contexts, as in Bouchareb's case, the gangster film centers on socioeconomic inequality, as well as the illegal activities used to circumvent it. Bouchareb makes use of the "classic" gangster narrative with Saïd, who initially grows his wealth and power via prostitution before turning to legal ventures like boxing. At the same time, the filmmaker subverts the gangster narrative with his focus on the clandestine FLN network, which operates in the Nanterre shantytown and whose inhabitants make a meagre living as Renault factory workers. Deemed illegal by French authorities, the FLN functioned outside the law in order to assert Algerian independence. However, as

Hayward clarifies, in the classic American gangster film, the gangster must fail for two reasons. First, the gangster's death confirms that the American dream cannot be fulfilled illegally. Second, it prevents the hypocrisy of the American dream—that success ultimately comes at someone else's expense—from being exposed.[32] In Bouchareb's film, French Republicanism—liberty, equality, fraternity—is as elusive as the American dream. Of the three brothers, only Saïd is spared at the end of the film, arguably due to his lack of commitment to the Algerian cause.

Bouchareb has commented that while *Days of Glory* had an explicit political objective—one that was achieved before its official release[33]—*Outside the Law* did not. In his detailed analysis of *Days of Glory*, Édouard Loeb argues that the film's trailer, official website, and movie posters contributed to its politicization. Not only did they highlight the film's cinematic appeal in a traditional sense (that is, by focusing on cast, plot, accolades), they also framed the film within a larger historical framework, that of World War II and the liberation of France from Nazi occupation. Loeb demonstrates that the film's paratext and media coverage paved the way for political action due to their open treatment of veterans' pensions.[34] In Loeb's assessment, *Outside the Law* "does not defend a social cause, but rather a historical point of view."[35] A brief comparison of theatrical trailers supports his hypothesis. At the beginning of the French trailer for *Days of Glory*, the historical context is made evident by a reference to the year 1943 and to the number of African soldiers who fought for the French during World War II. Dramatic music takes the viewer through a series of images typically found in war movies: gunfire, patriotic flag waving, soldiers marching, and so on. While the trailer relies more heavily on visual cues, short excerpts of dialogue demonstrate that the film is not only about liberating France. In one clip, Abdelkader—a colonial soldier—exclaims: "It's time things changed for us, too." The trailer played an important role in disseminating the film's political message in France between its screening at Cannes and its national release on 27 September 2006.[36] The official French poster reinforces the aforementioned themes. The four main characters—all played by actors that French audiences would easily recognize—are presented side-by-side in combat gear; the French title, *Indigènes*, appears in white bold lettering beneath them. The juxtaposition of word and image is powerful because it challenges the French spectator to reconsider the identity of national heroes, to rethink accepted historical narratives. *Days of Glory* clearly announces itself as a post-colonial counternarrative, one that recounts the history of World War II from a marginalized subject position.[37]

In contrast, the French trailer for *Outside the Law* does not openly reference the film's historical premise. Emphasis is placed instead on the fictional saga of the three central protagonists. Following a brief mention of *Days of Glory*—most likely a marketing tactic used to associate the two films as part of a series—the only words that appear on screen are "the destiny of three brothers." Cuts between action shots are faster than in the *Days of Glory* trailer and are syncopated by music. Yet there are moments when the camera lingers on actors, specifically on those who also appeared in the first film (another marketing strategy): Sami Bouajila as Abdelkader, the revolutionary idealist; Roschdy Zem as Messaoud, the muscleman; and Jamel Debbouze as Saïd, the shrewd businessman. Spectators who watch the trailer after having already seen the film will recognize historical scenes including the 8 May 1945 and 17 October 1961 massacres; however, these images appear fleetingly across the screen without historical references. Viewers who have yet to see the film may simply accept such scenes as part and parcel of *Outside the Law* as a genre film due to their suggestion of violence.

Bouchareb's utilization of the gangster film as a generic model nevertheless allows him to represent and question the violence of decolonization, which, in the film, is more openly associated with the FLN than with French authorities. Throughout its development, crime fiction and its various subgenres have played with the Manichean dialectic to the point that detective and criminal have become indistinguishable, even embodied in the same character, namely the "outsider" who "reemerges as a threat to the established order,"[38] especially when that order is problematized. The figure of the outsider or the *hors-la-loi* (in French, a noun that refers to an "individual who places themselves outside the law or who is declared an outlaw because of their behaviors and activities"[39]) supersedes the traditional detective when there is a perceived absence of justice. In this case, the outsider takes the law into their own hands, and their actions are deemed outside the law or *hors la loi* (adjective prepositional phrase, meaning "persons not subject to the law"[40]).[41] Bouchareb chose the title of his film because journalists frequently used the term "outlaw" in the 1950s and 1960s to describe FLN militants.[42] With its title and narrative structure, the film subverts the crime fiction genre in that the viewer questions preconceived notions of "good" and "bad" in French society. In *Outside the Law*, Bouchareb's "heroes" are deemed outlaws by a representative of the law (Colonel Faivre). And yet, because Faivre also belongs to a group that operates beyond the law (the Red Hand[43]), the line separating detective and criminal is increasingly blurred as the film progresses.

Furthermore, the historical context of decolonization forces the viewer to question moral judgments of violence. In his study on the legitimacy of violence in the literature of slave revolts, Joe Lockard argues that there is "an ethical charge to understand the legitimacy of demands for liberation and that the responsibility for counterviolence cannot be placed on the enslaved."[44] The lexical fields that describe crime and the violence of (de)colonization are similar. Frantz Fanon describes the final encounter between colonizer and colonized—that is decolonization—as "reek[ing] of red-hot cannonballs and bloody knives. For the last [the colonized] can be the first [the colonizer] only after a murderous and decisive confrontation between the two protagonists."[45] This "confrontation" is metaphorically reproduced in the film's final sequence when Colonel Faivre discovers Abdelkader's corpse among protestors and police officers in a Paris subway station. Realizing that his is a lost cause, Faivre concedes to his dead enemy with the words "You won." As protestors resume their chants of "Independence for Algeria," he walks away from the chaotic scene and leaves Abdelkader's only surviving brother, Saïd, to a fate unknown.

While the parallel between Fanon's words and the language of crime may seem far-fetched, it explains why Bouchareb relies so heavily on violence—more so than perhaps is necessary, as his critics contend. Benjamin Stora claims that the filmmaker distorts history, simplifies political complexities, and resorts to "pure violence" so as to cater "to the demands of the spectacular."[46] As Anne Donadey has pointed out, the film's depiction of violence is quite tame by Hollywood standards: spectators are subjected to neither gushing blood nor images of torture. She further argues that not all violence is portrayed equally, citing the ways in which internecine Algerian violence appears more personalized with close-ups of Messaoud strangling adversaries he knows well. By way of comparison, when the FLN targets the police or when the French target FLN militants, violence is represented on a larger scale and more anonymously, as when Abdelkader and his men shoot down a convoy of *harki* soldiers or when the police detonate bombs in the Nanterre shantytown. Donadey's observations lead her to conclude "that the film's point of view is more subtle" than Stora implies.[47]

Bouchareb's decision to create a genre film nevertheless has several noteworthy effects. First and foremost, Bouchareb and his team wanted to make a film that audiences would enjoy watching; they wanted *Outside the Law* to be "a true cinematic pleasure accessible to the general public."[48] Secondly, the familiarity moviegoers in France presumably have with the gangster genre allows Bouchareb's historical counternarrative to seem less unfamiliar—perhaps even plausible—to viewers who may have otherwise been less receptive to the film's subtext (that is, an Algerian perspective on French colonialism and the Algerian War of Independence). Thirdly, the gangster subgenre allows Bouchareb to subvert the gangster archetype. Alice Mikal Craven argues that "gangsters are criminals in any gangster genre film, but they are *glorious* criminals, and this is especially true for *Hors-la-loi*."[49] While I do not find Bouchareb's gangsters to be "glorious" in the sense that they do not—and, arguably, are not meant to—inspire admiration in the viewer, I do agree that Abdelkader, Messaoud, and Saïd surface as tragic heroes with whom marginalized populations could potentially identify. In fact, Bouchareb has been criticized for allegedly inspiring violence among France's disenfranchised youth. Historians Benjamin Stora and Renaud de Rochebrune argue, for instance, that *Outside the Law* proposes violence as the sole viable means of conflict resolution between colonizer and colonized. They question if such a takeaway is appropriate for a film whose intended audience includes immigrant youth from the French suburbs.[50] There are, however, reasons why "turbulent" youth would not fully idolize Bouchareb's gangster heroes. Neither Abdelkader nor Messaoud are sexualized or live in the lap of luxury. Instead, they remain connected to the shantytown, refrain from drinking alcohol, do not die in a blaze of glory, and have limited relations with women. Even though Abdelkader and Messaoud use violence to garner support for the FLN, they are a far cry from Coppola's Michael Corleone and Brian De Palma's Tony Montana (*Scarface*, 1983)—prime examples of the "glorious criminal."

Among the more problematic aspects of gangster cinema is its stereotypical and heteronormative representation of gender identity. Anne Donadey convincingly argues in her reading of *Outside the Law* that "although critics were bothered by the Hollywood epic, popular genre in which the film was shot, they did not seem to pick up on the genre's gendered overdeterminations, which Bouchareb proved unable to undermine."[51] One could argue—albeit less convincingly—that Bouchareb's failure to deconstruct gender binaries in his film reflects the genre's focus on challenged masculinities. Donadey's point is that, regardless of Bouchareb's aesthetic models, he could and should have created space for female agency. Hélène, for example, surfaces as a young ingénue, seemingly unaware of the stakes of her own political dissidence. As a failed femme fatale, this character does little more than tempt Abdelkader, who remains married to the Algerian cause. As a character that embodies sexuality and therefore transgression, Hélène must die in order for Abdelkader to succeed.[52] Algerian women, with the exception of the mother, are of lesser consequence. Throughout the film, each of the three brothers establishes a distinct yet problematic relationship with women: Abdelkader, the revolutionary, struggles to refuse Hélène's advances; Messaoud, the "muscle," marries an Algerian woman who respects the patriarchy; Saïd, the outwardly stereotypical gangster, uses women as a commodity to be sold. All three nevertheless respect their mother, who is the only female character to exercise a (limited) degree of agency. While she navigates narrative space with relative freedom—for instance, she visits Abdelkader in prison unaccompanied—she remains intimately tied to Algeria. Before leaving their home, she carefully wraps a handful of dirt to take with her, thereby becoming an allegory for Algeria. According to Donadey, the mother "comes to embody the lost ancestral land for whose recovery her sons are fighting and dying."[53] As second-class citizens, Algerian women can only contribute to independence by raising "future male citizens."[54] After the deaths of Abdelkader and Messaoud, the only remaining male figures are Saïd, who refuses to commit himself to the Algerian cause, and Messaoud's young unnamed son. At the end of the film, both remain tethered to a life in metropolitan France.

As the second film of Bouchareb's announced trilogy, *Outside the Law* only begins to explore the relationship between Maghrebi identity and integration into French society. If some critics find that Bouchareb's film too readily reproduces the tropes of American gangster films (for example, *The Godfather* and *Once upon a Time in America*), they fail to notice that such cinematic models often foreground community identity (Italian Americans in Coppola's film and Jewish Americans in Leone's). As Alec Hargreaves argues: "The American dimension of Bouchareb's oeuvre is by no means wholly detached from the kinds of issues—ethnic, cultural, and political—faced by young North Africans . . . in France."[55] He further suggests that Bouchareb could not have made films like *Days of Glory* (and, I would add, *Outside the Law*) without the participation and financial backing of notable Maghrebi-French stars, and especially Jamel Debbouze.[56] The director's recasting of other popular actors like Sami Bouajila, Roschdy Zem, and Samy Naceri also contributed to the commercial success of *Days of Glory*.[57] Regarding *Outside the Law*, we should note that star power and large budgets have been shown to help films that have received negative reviews.[58] What this suggests is that the existence of such Maghrebi-French individuals in the film industry provided Bouchareb with the opportunity to make films that, in an indirect way, address the very issue of integration. Following the rules of the gangster film, Bouchareb underscores the genre's ability to represent racial and ethnic prejudice. Marginalized outsiders can only attain "happiness" through various forms of transgression. The oppressed must therefore (re)act in ways that are outside the law because it is the only action available to them. This reality is reinforced by the legal status of Algerians in France during the 1950s; as colonial subjects, they were denied the rights reserved for citizens. At the same time, Bouchareb's casting of Maghrebi-French actors in leading (gangster) roles afforded him the freedom to play with gangster typologies:

> We're not making community-centered cinema. We're making untouched cinema. When have we ever seen a gangster movie starring North Africans, in the fifties, wearing fedoras, suits and ties, with cigars, the world of boxing? Where does this exist? So, we are completely free! Even if [the movie is] a failure, it's OK.[59]

The fact that Thierry Méranger believes that the film's only model for "successful" integration is Saïd reveals his misunderstanding of how this character functions in the film with respect to narrative and, more generally, of how Bouchareb subverts gangster tropes to proffer a subtle social commentary.[60] Saïd owes his upward mobility to his early beginnings as a pimp. While wealthier—and perhaps, more successful—than immigrants living in the Nanterre shantytown, Saïd remains on the fringe of French society as the owner of a cabaret and as a promoter of amateur boxing. When Faivre and his men shut down his club, Saïd first reassures them that his business is indeed legitimate before complying. His anxiety about the legitimacy of his business practices in Pigalle reminds spectators that he earned his place through illegal means in one of Paris's red-light districts. Furthermore, his affiliation with prostitution earlier in the film and, later, with alcohol, women, and cigars results in his marginalization within the Algerian community. Even though his activities allow him to make sizeable financial contributions to the FLN, they later become a nuisance to the same organization, whose leaders decide that he must be dealt with accordingly. Consequently, Saïd remains marginalized with respect to both French and Algerian societies as they are depicted in the film. Although Bouchareb should be criticized for not challenging the genre's problematic representation of gender, he does use the gangster film to create a historical counternarrative within which to situate contemporary French issues of social exclusion and inequality.

CONCLUSION

In many respects, the polemics surrounding *Outside the Law* are more intriguing than the film itself. However, this has little to do with the film's narrative and aesthetic attributes, but more with the film as an event of memory with the power to shed light on France's colonial fracture. We have seen that French critics focus more on the controversy surrounding the film's release than on its merits as a work of historical fiction. When they do, it is to underscore the film's weaknesses. Critics often attribute the film's shortcomings to its "questionable" historical representation and/or gangster aesthetic. Both lines of criticism raise questions (one historical, the other artistic) about the filmmaker's exercise of artistic license with respect to national history. As a French-Algerian artist, is Bouchareb not free to create works of fiction that call into question the very limits of historical representation? Although this question is somewhat rhetorical, in the context of *Outside the Law* it does lead to some important conclusions. First, the fact that a film about the Algerian War sparked controversy in France nearly fifty years after decolonization is argument enough that Bouchareb's film is historically significant. Second, the film's reproduction and, at times, subversion of a stylized genre aesthetic should not discredit the filmmaker's seriousness of purpose. Marketed with the allure of gangster cinema, *Outside the Law* has the potential to reach a wide and diverse audience. Bouchareb's film was unsettling because it successfully disseminated a critical, post-colonial counternarrative under the guise of mainstream cinema. That politicians attempted to prevent the film from being released demonstrates their fear that it would threaten the established order if it were to become an event of memory. Ironically, the controversy ensured that Bouchareb's film did just that. One can only hope that the controversy will not deter potential investors from backing the third and final installment of Bouchareb's planned trilogy.

NOTES

1. Éric Libiot, "Rachid Bouchareb: '*Hors-la-loi* est un film sur l'injustice,'" *L'Express*, 22 September 2010, https://www.lexpress.fr/culture/cinema/rachid-bouchareb-hors-la-loi-est-un-film-sur-l-injustice_921086.html
2. The FLN's secretary general, Ahmed Benkrim, reportedly defended *Outside the Law* "tooth and nail" before having seen it. See Nora Amir, "'Hors-la-Loi' de Rachid Bouchareb, ce n'est pas exactement ce qu'on croyait," 10 May 2010, http://www.algerie-dz.com/forums/archive/index.php/t-168615.html, quoted in Nedjib Sidi Moussa, "L'Histoire et la politique hors-la-loi? Réflexions autour d'un film sur des indépendantistes algériens," *French Politics, Culture and Society* 30, no. 3 (2012): 120.
3. For a detailed account of the controversy, see Will Higbee, *Post-Beur Cinema: North African Émigré and Maghrebi-French Filmmaking in France since 2000* (Edinburgh: Edinburgh University Press, 2013), especially 86–7.
4. Nicola Cooper, "Days of Glory? Veterans, Reparation and National Memory," *Journal of War and Culture Studies* 1, no. 1 (2008): 91.
5. Jean-Dominique Merchet, "'Indigènes' fait craquer Chirac," *Libération*, 25 September 2006, https://www.liberation.fr/evenement/2006/09/25/indigenes-fait-craquer-chirac_52394; Alec Hargreaves, "*Indigènes*: A Sign of the Times," *Research in African Literatures* 38, no. 4 (2007): 208; Mireille Rosello, *The Reparative in Narratives: Works of Mourning in Progress* (Liverpool: Liverpool University Press, 2010), 111–12; Mireille Rosello, "Rachid Bouchareb's *Indigènes*: Political or Ethical Event of Memory?" in *Screening Integration: Recasting Maghrebi Immigration in Contemporary France*, ed. Sylvie Durmelat and Vinay Swamy (Lincoln: University of Nebraska Press, 2011), 115.
6. "Décristallisation des pensions civiles et militaires de retraite, des pensions militaires d'invalidité et de la retraite du combattant," Assemblée des Français de l'étranger, 7 January 2011, https://www.assemblee-afe.fr/decristallisation-des-pensions.html
7. Rosello, "Rachid Bouchareb's *Indigènes*," 118.
8. Ibid., 119.
9. Ibid., 119.
10. Ibid., 121.
11. Vincent Martigny, "Le Débat autour de l'identité nationale dans la campagne présidentielle 2007: quelle rupture?" *French Politics, Culture & Society* 27, no. 1 (2009): 37.
12. Elain Sciolino, "Chirac Sets Apologetic Example for Sarkozy at Slavery Commemoration," *New York Times*, 10 May 2007, https://www.nytimes.com/2007/05/10/world/europe/10iht-paris.4.5655879.html.
13. "Sarkozy Refuses Repentance and Bets on the Future in Algiers," *FigaroVox*, 11 July 2007, http://www.lefigaro.fr/debats/2007/07/11/01005-20070711ARTWWW90317-sarkozy_refuses_repentance_and_bets_on_the_future_in_algiers.php.
14. Sciolino, "Chirac Sets Apologetic Example."
15. Marie-Claude Blanc-Chaléard et al., "Un amalgame inacceptable!" *Le Monde*, 21 May 2007, https://www.lemonde.fr/societe/article/2007/05/21/un-amalgame-inacceptable_912821_3224.html

16. Ibid.
17. Loi no. 2005-158 du 23 février 2005 portant reconnaissance de la Nation et contribution nationale en faveur des Français rapatriés, Article 4, accessed 26 March 2020, https://www.legifrance.gouv.fr/eli/loi/2005/2/23/DEFX0300218L/jo/article_4.
18. Benjamin Bonneau, "Les Présidents et la banlieue, 30 ans de politique et de... renoncement," Europe 1, 27 October 2015, https://www.europe1.fr/politique/les-chefs-de-letat-et-la-banlieue-30-ans-de-politique-et-de-renoncement-2536067
19. Pascal Blanchard, Nicolas Bancel, and Sandrine Lemaire, ed., *La Fracture coloniale: la société française au prisme de l'héritage colonial* (Paris: Découverte, 2005).
20. Thomas Martin, "SOS Racisme and the Legacies of Colonialism, 2005–2009: An Ambivalent Relationship," *Modern & Contemporary France* 23, no. 1 (2015): 68.
21. Libiot, "Rachid Bouchareb: '*Hors-la-loi* est un film sur l'injustice.'" Bouchareb's film was presented as an Algerian film at Cannes and the Oscars. While Luca was supposedly relieved that *Outside the Law* was not in competition as a French film, Yasmina Adi and colleagues dismiss the importance of the film's nationality. Since Bouchareb has dual citizenship, he could choose to submit his film as either French or Algerian. However, because there were already several French films vying for the Palme d'Or and the Oscar for Best Foreign Language Film, *Outside the Law* stood a better chance of winning as an Algerian film. See Yasmina Adi et al., "Le film 'Hors-la-loi' de Rachid Bouchareb: les guerres de mémoire sont de retour," *Le Monde*, 5 May 2010, https://www.lemonde.fr/festival-de-cannes/article/2010/05/05/le-film-hors-la-loi-de-rachid-bouchareb-les-guerres-de-memoires-sont-de-retour-par-yasmina-adi-didier-daeninckx_1346714_766360.html.
22. "Entrevue avec Rachid Bouchareb: réalisateur de 'Hors-la-loi,'" *Outside the Law*, directed by Rachid Bouchareb (2010; New York: Palisades Tartan Video, 2011), DVD. The translation is from the DVD's English subtitles.
23. Adi et al., "Le film 'Hors-la-loi' de Rachid Bouchareb."
24. Ibid.
25. Les Invités de Mediapart, "'Hors-la-loi,' un film dans l'Histoire," *Mediapart*, 13 October 2010, https://blogs.mediapart.fr/edition/les-invites-de-mediapart/article/131010/hors-la-loi-un-film-dans-lhistoire.
26. For a detailed study of the crime fiction "formula," see Jacques Dubois, *Le Roman policier ou la modernité* (Paris: Nathan, 1992); Tzvetan Todorov, *The Poetics of Prose*, trans. Richard Howard (Ithaca, NY: Cornell University Press, 1977), especially the chapter "The Typology of Detective Fiction," 42–52.
27. Susan Hayward, *Cinema Studies: The Key Concepts*, 2nd ed. (London and New York: Routledge, 2000), 128.
28. Didier Péron, "'Hors-la-loi,' une saga sans souffle," *Libération*, 22 May 2010, https://next.liberation.fr/cinema/2010/05/22/hors-la-loi-une-saga-sans-souffle_653692.
29. Thierry Méranger, "*Hors-la-loi* de Rachid Bouchareb," *Cahiers du cinema*, September 2010, 41.
30. Dennis Broe, "Class, Crime, and Film Noir: Labor, the Fugitive Outsider, and the Anti-Authoritarian Tradition," *Social Justice* 30, no. 1 (2003): 22.
31. Hayward, *Cinema Studies*, 154.
32. Ibid., 154.
33. Rosello, "Rachid Bouchareb's *Indigènes*," 115.
34. Édouard Loeb, *Cinéma et politique: l'effet* Indigènes (Bry-sur-Marne, France: INA, 2011).
35. Ibid., 68.
36. Ibid., 33.

37. The cover art used on the collector edition of the French DVD is different from the movie poster. On the DVD, a lone soldier is shown holding the French flag. In the background, the viewer can make out a combat scene through a haze of gunfire. See Chapter 6 of this volume for a discussion of the portrayal and reception of Arab heroes in Rachid Bouchareb's cinema.
38. Broe, "Class, Crime, and Film Noir," 38.
39. "Hors-la-loi," *Trésor de la langue française informatisé*, http://atilf.atilf.fr.
40. "Hors la loi," *Trésor de la langue française informatisé*.
41. Anne Donadey observes that critics often hyphenate the film's title. See her article for a thorough discussion of the film's French title, as well as its translation into English and Arabic. As a side note, the press kit, trailers, DVD covers, and French-, English-, and Arabic-language movie posters use the hyphenated French title even though the unhyphenated title appears at the beginning and end of the film. Anne Donadey, "'Wars of Memory': On Rachid Bouchareb's *Hors la loi*," *Esprit Créateur* 54, no. 4 (2014): 15–26.
42. "Entrevue avec Rachid Bouchareb."
43. The Red Hand was a counterterrorist organization charged with the elimination of FLN leaders and sympathizers. It operated with impunity under the auspices of the French government throughout the 1950s.
44. Joe Lockard, "Nat Turner, Slave Revolts, and Child-Killing in US Graphic Novels," in *Cultures of War in Graphic Novels: Violence, Trauma, and Memory*, ed. Tatiana Prorokova and Nimrod Tal (New Brunswick, NJ: Rutgers University Press, 2018), 105–22, 119–20.
45. Frantz Fanon, *The Wretched of the Earth*, trans. Richard Philcox (New York: Grove Press, 2004), 3.
46. Benjamin Stora, "À propos du film *Hors-la-loi*. Une héroisation problématique. In *Marianne*, 18–24 septembre 2010," https://benjaminstora.univ-paris13.fr/index.php/articlesrecents/limage/229-a-propos-du-film-hors-la-loi-une-heroisation-problematique-par-benjamin-stora-in-marianne-18-24-septembre-2010.html
47. Donadey, "'Wars of Memory,'" 20.
48. Rachid Bouchareb, "Les nouvelles générations ont besoin de connaître le passé colonial," *UniversCiné*, 12 May 2011, https://www.universcine.com/articles/rachid-bouchareb-les-nouvelles-generations-ont-besoin-de-connaitre-le-passe-colonial.
49. Alice Mikal Craven, "The Gangster in *The Devil Finds Work* as a Template for Reading the Parisian *Banlieues*," *African American Review* 46, no. 4 (2013): 584, original emphasis.
50. Benjamin Stora and Renaud de Rochebrune, "*Hors-la-loi*: enjeux secondaires et enjeux réels," *Cahiers du cinéma*, October 2010, 90. When Éric Libiot questioned Bouchareb about the relationship between immigration and delinquency, the filmmaker responded: "To my knowledge, delinquency does not have a specific origin." See Libiot, "Rachid Bouchareb: '*Hors-la-loi* est un film sur l'injustice.'"
51. Anne Donadey, "Gender, Genre and Intertextuality in Rachid Bouchareb's *Hors la loi*," *Studies in French Cinema* 16, no. 1 (2016): 58.
52. Ibid., 54.
53. Ibid., 53.
54. Ibid., 53.
55. Alec G. Hargreaves, "From 'Ghettoes' to Globalization: Situating Maghrebi-French Filmmakers," in *Screening Integration: Recasting Maghrebi Immigration in Contemporary France*, ed. Sylvie Durmelat and Vinay Swamy (Lincoln: University of Nebraska Press, 2011), 36.
56. Ibid., 36–7. For more on Debbouze's financial contribution and star power, see Hargreaves, "*Indigènes*"; Higbee, *Post-Beur Cinema*; Olivier Barlet, "*Days of Glory*:

Another Vision of French History," in *Film in the Middle East and North Africa: Creative Dissidence*, ed. Josef Gugler (Austin: University of Texas Press, 2011), 306–14.
57. Hargreaves, "From 'Ghettoes' to Globalization," 37. According to the Lumiere database (accessed 2 April 2020), *Days of Glory* made €3,172,625 at the European box office while *Outside the Law* made €478,518.
58. See, for example, Suman Basuroy, Subimal Chatterjee, and S. Abraham Ravid, "How Critical are Critical Reviews? The Box Office Effects of Film Critics, Star Power, and Budgets," *Journal of Marketing* 67, no. 4 (2003): 103–17.
59. "Entrevue avec Rachid Bouchareb." The translation is from the DVD's English subtitles.
60. Méranger, "*Hors-la-loi* de Rachid Bouchareb," 41.

CHAPTER 11

Postcolonial Feminism, Gender, and Genre in Rachid Bouchareb's *Just Like a Woman*

Anne Donadey

Rachid Bouchareb is one of too few male filmmakers who pays regular attention to women's issues and recurrently features prominent migrant or multicultural female characters. In this chapter, I discuss to what extent his *Just Like a Woman* (2012) can be seen as a postcolonial feminist film. I define postcolonial feminist films as including four interrelated characteristics. First, the films center on intersections of issues of race, gender, and colonialism. Second, they focus on female characters, on women's agency, and on female solidarity, including thematizing the difficulty of creating solidarity in the midst of a patriarchal world. Third, if the films include cross-cultural relations, they highlight interdependence among characters instead of (to paraphrase Gayatri Spivak) featuring white women saving brown women from brown men.[1] Finally, the films counter racist, colonialist, and sexist stereotypes while portraying complex characters and their relationships.

Bouchareb has also made a series of films in which male subjectivities are foregrounded. His tendency to include female subjectivities in some films but not others appears to be related to three primary factors: the gender of his coscriptwriters or their interest in women; whether the films are made for television or for theatrical release; and, as I have argued elsewhere, the genre of his films.[2] Bouchareb's epic war films, which are also his most famous ones (*Indigènes/Days of Glory*, 2006, and *Hors la loi/Outside the Law*, 2010), were cowritten by Olivier Lorelle and focus on male protagonists. They are influenced by Hollywood war and gangster films, whose conventions include an overwhelming reliance on male subjectivity, male agency, and male-male relationships. Except for *Little Senegal* (2001), Bouchareb's more *intimiste*, introspective films such as *L'Honneur de ma famille/My Family's Honor* (1998), *London River* (2009), *Just Like a Woman* (2012), and *La Route d'Istanbul/Road* to *Istanbul* (2016) tend to feature female protagonists.[3] Like Ridley Scott in *Thelma and Louise* (1991) and a number of other directors on both sides of the Atlantic, Bouchareb has also been able to feminize the traditionally male road movie genre, with films like *Cheb* (1991) and, more recently, *Just Like a Woman*.[4] The latter is one in a series of films Bouchareb has made in the United States. Building on my earlier argument about gender, genre, and intertextuality in *Outside the Law*, I analyze how the female-focused *Just Like a Woman* both alludes to Scott's iconic *Thelma and Louise* and avoids some of the pitfalls of its intertext. I examine Bouchareb's use of the *intimiste* genre, discuss the role of belly dancing, and critique some of the film's blank spots. I conclude with an assessment of the extent to which *Just Like a Woman* can be seen as a postcolonial feminist film.

FEMINIZING THE BUDDY/ROAD MOVIE GENRE: WHEN THELMA AND LOUISE MEET MONA AND MARILYN

Just Like a Woman focuses on the parallel situations experienced by two women from different backgrounds living in Chicago, a city with a fairly large Arab Muslim population. This is not the Chicago of tourists or upper-middle-class residents but a generic Midwestern or East Coast American city bereft of any identifying landmark except for the elevated train,[5] like Stephen Frears's London in *Dirty Pretty Things* (2002). White working-class American Marilyn O'Connor (Sienna Miller) and naturalized Arab American Mona Souni (Golshifteh Farahani) both take to the road to escape bad situations.[6] Like *Thelma and Louise*, *Just Like a Woman* starts with intercut scenes introducing the lives of the two women, highlighting both how different they are and their less than optimal circumstances. Marilyn and Mona are ethnically and culturally dissimilar, but they are both dealing with patriarchal contexts and long for an escape. As Thibaut Schilt describes it, in the buddy movie the buddies are "physically dissimilar and of different social and national backgrounds."[7] One is a fair-skinned blonde woman and the other a younger, olive-skinned brunette. They know each other because Marilyn shops in Mona's family-run convenience store. Their similarities are indicated by the fact that both their first names start with the letter M, perhaps a reference to the self (me/ *moi*), and they are highlighted in the intercut scenes through the repeated use of sound bridges (the same music or song, especially the women's theme song, Natacha Atlas's hauntingly elegiac "Adam's Lullaby"). The music connects the two women's experiences by starting at the end of a scene with one of the women and continuing into the beginning of the next scene with the other woman. Like Thelma and Louise, they are both childless. Marilyn is summarily fired from her dead-end job for no reason and finds her good-for-nothing husband Harvey (Jesse Harper) cheating on her in their marital bedroom. As for Mona, she lives with her husband Mourad (Roschdy Zem, whom Bouchareb has cast in many films) and his overbearing mother (veteran Algerian actor Chafia Boudraa, whom Bouchareb also cast as a stereotypical mother in *My Family's Honor* and *Outside the Law*). The mother makes Mona's and Mourad's lives miserable, ordering them around and menacing Mona because the latter has not had children yet, even though she has been married for five years. When Mona makes a mistake with the mother's heart medicine, the latter dies from an overdose. Unlike *Thelma and Louise*, in which the pre-trip scenes setting up the situation last less than ten minutes, *Just Like a Woman* develops the conditions leading to the trip gradually, spending more than twice that amount of time in Chicago. The road trip proper only begins almost half an hour into the film.

The film generally follows the conventions of the American road movie genre more than the European one, as defined by David Laderman.[8] It follows "an outlaw couple" driving a convertible car through the "vast empty spaces" of the American landscape; "soul-searching discussion occurs in mobility's pauses" (what Laderman calls "the 'campfire' approach").[9] *Just Like a Woman* features a move from the enclosed space of the Midwestern city to the wide American landscape of the Southwest. There are many shots of bucolic empty spaces, forests, farms, and small towns off the beaten path. During their pauses in deserted, wide open spaces, the women pitch their tent and bond over the patriarchal similarities in their lives. The film also uses what Thibaut Schilt enumerates as "techniques expected of travel cinema: the Widescreen format, a recurrence of extreme long shots, a healthy dose of tracking and panorama shots."[10] In particular, the camera is often positioned in another vehicle moving either next to, in front of, or behind the women's car. It is also positioned in the back seat, filming the women's backs, their faces in profile (when they look at each other), the reflection of their eyes and faces in the rear-view mirrors, and the view of the road from the windshield or other windows of the car. For Martin O'Shaughnessy, other "key traits of the genre" include the fact that "it is peopled by cars and other vehicles (notably heavy lorries), motorways and minor roads (and their interplay), service stations, motorway rest areas and anonymous hotels. But, at a deeper level, its fundamental thrust is towards revolt against social norms."[11] These features are central to both *Just Like a Woman* and its intertext. For instance, when Thelma and Louise start taking back roads to evade the police, they often stop at ramshackle gas stations with little traffic. The same is true of Mona and Marilyn, who stop at one such service station, ironically called "Busy Corner." While Thelma and Louise are trying to escape to Mexico, Marilyn and Mona are off to New Mexico. Further, "*Thelma and Louise*'s use of home as a metaphor for prison" is also a trope found in *Just Like a Woman*.[12] Mona has never before left her Chicago neighborhood. In the neighborhood in which they live, the women's lack of options is visually rendered through their placement in space. They are almost always seen indoors or in enclosed locations. Mona is filmed inside the home, the fenced-in backyard, or the family's overfilled convenience store, or she is seen with her husband and/or mother-in-law. Likewise, we observe Marilyn at home, in her cramped windowless office at the back of a warehouse, and walking to and from work through unattractive back alleys. Like the European road movie, the film also features characters using public transport.[13] Marilyn is shown riding the "L" through Chicago and when Mona leaves, she first takes a cab and then a bus. It is only when she meets Marilyn by chance in the liminal space of the rest stop (neither the city nor the open road) and hitches a ride with her in the latter's convertible that the possibility of escape opens up for both women. In many road films, chance encounters or narrative developments occur during stopovers, and Bouchareb follows this trope. Perhaps in a nod to the European location of the director, the car that ensures their escape is not a classic, American, blue-green 1966 Thunderbird but an aging, European, maroon-red Saab.

Like *Thelma and Louise*, the film feminizes the road/buddy movie genres. In both films, the road provides an escape as well as increased dangers. There are many visual and plot allusions to Scott's film throughout *Just Like a Woman*. For instance, like Thelma, Marilyn has been putting off telling her husband, Harvey, that she would like to go on a trip (to audition for a part in a dance company in New Mexico). Like Louise, Marilyn drives and smokes, and the women wear sunglasses on the road. As in *Thelma and Louise* after the attempted rape scene, when Marilyn finds out that Mona is wanted for questioning in the death of her mother-in-law, the two women argue over whether to go to the police and whether they will be believed or not. However, unlike in *Thelma and Louise*, Marilyn breaks the solidarity by leaving Mona because she is afraid of being jailed, although she ends up changing her mind and returning for her. As in *Thelma and Louise*, the police come to question Mona's husband (after his mother's death and his wife's disappearance). In that scene, the tone of the dialogue is initially neutral, until George, the white male police officer (Tim Guinee), starts voicing the Western stereotype of Arab Muslim women as always-already oppressed, which is then countered by Mourad:

>George: Did your mother beat her?
>Mourad: What?
>George: Did your mother beat her?
>Mourad: What kind of question is this?
>George: What do you mean?
>Mourad: I don't understand your question.
>George: It's a question.

Mourad: Does your mother beat your wife?
George: Relax! Yes or no, did your mother beat your wife? (*Silence, as Mourad looks at George disgustedly, shaking his head.*) You beat your wife?
Mourad: Do *you* beat your wife?

The dialogue is filmed in a shot reverse shot pattern, with each character's face in close-up, highlighting the opposition between the two men. In this exchange, the white cop assumes that the poor wife was a victim of domestic violence from either the mother or the son, or both, something he may not have so easily presumed had the family been white. Initially, Mourad is disoriented by the question. The fact that he is showing surprise alerts the audience to the question's problematic grounding in stereotypical pre-judgment, as it is not something he had ever considered as a possibility. When George starts hammering the point, Mourad reverses the racist gaze by returning the questions to their sender, which is an effective way to show the audience how problematic the questions are. This tactic is particularly successful since the audience has only seen Mourad as a calm and quiet man. This previous knowledge, coupled with his returning the question, opens up a space for the audience to understand the question as grounded in racist stereotype rather than being a neutral part of an investigation. George's female partner (Bahar Soomekh), an immigrant who may herself be of Middle Eastern origin, interrupts his line of questioning by pulling him aside. She pushes back against him, telling him that his questions could be "seen as prejudicial in court," thus reinforcing the anti-racist message of the scene. Unlike *Thelma and Louise*, *Just Like a Woman* thus addresses the issue of racism and its effects on the characters.

As in *Thelma and Louise*, the space of the open road is shown to be dangerous for women, both for gender reasons (the women escape from sexual harassment twice, as discussed in more detail below) and for racial ones. In the New Mexico campground where they are staying before Marilyn's audition, the women practice belly dancing under the disgusted eye of a white vacationing family. About seventy minutes into the film, the mother (Mary Woods) clashes with Mona and Marilyn and uses an extremely derogatory expletive generally used against Arabs in the United States. Her petty, racist worldview is in contrast with the beautiful, wide-open shots of the Southwestern landscape. Marilyn yells at her, and for a while we are under the impression that the women have won this fight. However, the family follows Marilyn, and the son (Galen Hutchinson) beats her up as his parents look on approvingly. *Just Like a Woman* does not solely focus on women's intercultural friendship and solidarity. It also showcases how white women can and do participate in racism and white supremacy, since the mother incites her son to violence. It highlights how racism is learned and transmitted intergenerationally. This scene—the most violent one in the film—counters the stereotype of violent Arab Muslim men addressed above by showing a young white American man beating up a woman, something that is not acceptable yet widespread in Western contexts. It is also interesting that it is Marilyn, the white woman who stood up for her friend, who is the victim of racist violence. In this way, the film both demonstrates that whiteness may not protect someone who takes a stand against racism and showcases the reciprocal support the two women engage in since Mona rushes to Marilyn's side. It is at this point that Marilyn loses all hope of achieving her dream of a career in belly dancing because of her physical injuries, saying: "It's over, Mona." As in *Thelma and Louise*, the breakdown of the older character occasions the rise of the younger one. However, Mona does not go on an outlaw spree but instead ends up replacing Marilyn in her audition and winning her a place at the dance company.

The film avoids some of the pitfalls of its primarily white intertext by staging the road trip as a multicultural one, homing in on the intercultural friendship that develops between the women, and working against racist, colonialist, and sexist stereotypes. For instance, Mona's husband, Mourad, is more like Louise's sweet boyfriend, Jimmy (Michael Madsen), than Thelma's husband, Darryl Dickinson (Christopher McDonald). An insensitive boor, Darryl is closer to Harvey, Marilyn's unemployed, drinking and partying white husband. In Ridley Scott's film, all men are bad, and stereotypically so—Thelma's middle-class husband, her grifter boyfriend, the rapist, the truck driver—except for officer Slocum (Harvey Keitel) and Louise's loving working-class boyfriend. In *Just Like a Woman*, working against the stereotype of Arab Muslim men's violence, it is Marilyn's white husband who is insensitively patriarchal and Mona's Arab husband who is gentle and loving. The film takes particular care to present Mourad as a nice man whose primary fault lies in his inability to stand up to his mother, just as Louise's boyfriend's main fault was being commitment shy. The against-type casting of Zem, with his impressive build and rugged face, as Mona's husband, could lead the audience to expect that he will seek power over his younger, smaller wife. Bouchareb plays with these expectations to highlight this character's peaceful nature. For example, in one of the first scenes a few minutes into the film, the family returns to their store only to find that someone has painted extremely racist graffiti on the window (the same expletive later used by the racist mother at the campground). Whereas his mother wants to call the police, Mourad refuses, saying: "It's just kids." In this early scene, the film establishes both the racism Arabs have to deal with in Chicago and Mourad's lack of response to the situation, which could be interpreted as a sign of his peaceful nature and/or passivity. Both Louise's boyfriend and Mona's husband end up standing by the women they love, but in each case that is not enough, and the women must continue their trajectory without them.

In the two films, the women turn away from heterosexual relationships to develop relationships of interdependence and solidarity with another woman. A lesbian subtext is present in both. Like *Thelma and Louise*, *Just Like a Woman* features a brief kiss between the women. Instead of occurring at the end of the film before the car leaps into the Grand Canyon, in *Just Like a Woman* the kiss occurs when Marilyn experiences a change of heart about leaving Mona behind, breaks up with Harvey over the phone, and returns for Mona, about an hour into the film. The kiss (initiated by Marilyn) is thus positioned in a more positive context that hints at a future for the women's relationship. A second, brief peck (initiated by Mona this time) occurs sixty-nine minutes into the film, as the women are going to sleep. The two women are often shown sharing close quarters in their tent. There is nothing overtly sexual about these situations, though. The lesbian subtext is also covered up by the two women discussing heterosexual relationships and their desire for children, as well as recurring shots of Marilyn's hand sporting her wedding band. The film stages the relationship between the women as one of joint solidarity, avoiding the white-savior complex. The two women help one another out in turn. For instance, after Marilyn loses her job, Mona does not make her pay for the items she was purchasing in the store. The first gesture of female solidarity in the film is of a woman of color helping a white woman and not the opposite. In the second half of the film, Mona also encourages and coaches Marilyn with her dance practice while on the road. Conversely, about forty-one minutes into the film, the women have stopped by a lake somewhere between the Midwest and the Southwest. Mona, feeling hopeless at her situation, breaks the bucolic peace of the scene by throwing herself into the lake. Marilyn has to dive in to save her, as Mona cannot swim. Soon after this, the women are discussing their failed marriages and Mona mentions that hers was arranged, yet Mourad "was so kind to me." Marilyn's first reaction is to be shocked at the mention of the arranged marriage, but she quickly rethinks her initial attitude, adding: "What difference does it make? I was crazy about Harvey. Look where it got me. He was cheating on me." Here, the white character models what a non-Orientalist approach to the topic could be. Although the women come from different cultural contexts, their gendered outcomes are the same, as both are wondering whether they are going to get divorced. As in *Thelma and Louise*, the two women support each other and while initially Marilyn appears stronger, the meeker and younger Mona undergoes an inner transformation that allows her to come into her own.

Most American reviewers emphasized the *Thelma and Louise* intertext, concluding that *Just Like a Woman* paled in comparison to Scott's iconic film. For instance, Justin Chang opened his review with "*Thelma and Louise* gets a bland cross-cultural update in *Just Like a Woman*" and Amy Nicholson titled hers "*Just Like a Woman* wishes it were *Thelma and Louise*."[14] However, it is helpful to remember that although *Thelma and Louise* now has the status of a classic feminist film, reviewers were also highly critical of it when it was first released.[15] Bouchareb's film avoids caricaturing its male characters, unlike Thelma's husband, the rapist, and the truck driver. Scott's film includes action scenes such as the convenience store robbery, the exploding truck, and various car chases. In *Just Like a Woman*, these are replaced by scenes of belly dance performance by the two heroines. It is true that *Just Like a Woman* is not as visually stunning as *Thelma and Louise* (although it does include beautiful cinematography by long-time Bouchareb collaborator Christophe Beaucarne), but stunning visuals were not what Bouchareb was primarily after in this film. The locations he used in *Just Like a Woman* are not quite as iconic as Scott's. We are treated to Midwestern farmland and less spectacular Southwestern landscapes.[16] Unlike other road movies, Bouchareb's film is less about the landscape (and certainly not about conquering the open space) and more about the characters and their relationship.

The tone of *Just Like a Woman* is more *intimiste* than that of *Thelma and Louise*. According to Isabelle Vanderschelden, *intimiste* film is "a genre specifically associated with French cinema," characterized by introspection, "slow narratives and domestic plots," and "psychological narratives," and it "is often, but not exclusively, associated with female directors and protagonists."[17] Bouchareb is a master of the *intimiste* tone, which is particularly well suited to rendering subtle intercultural and female relationships, as well as presenting characters moving in harmony with a landscape instead of conquering it. I would argue that it is in part due to the use of this minor key (purposefully less showy and more modest in scope) that reviewers may have found *Just Like a Woman* less satisfying than its intertext. Bouchareb expressed the hope that this film would strike an "understated tone."[18] Understated sobriety is a feature of all of his *intimiste* films. It contributes to making them effective in helping the audience relate to the characters but also has a held-back, modest effect that critics accustomed to either Hollywood-style movies or ambitious experimental films may not always fully appreciate.

All of Bouchareb's *intimiste* films that focus on women were made for television.[19] As Leslie Kealhofer-Kemp has demonstrated, films made for television in France share a number of characteristics. They tend to be lower budget, "seek to provoke an emotional response from viewers," are made to attract a large public, and often revolve around familial and schooling themes as well as issues of discrimination.[20] These are also features of Bouchareb's made-for-television, *intimiste* films, from *My Family's Honor* to *Just Like a Woman* and *Road to Istanbul*. Kealhofer-Kemp's description of films made for television also happens to dovetail with characteristics of films directed toward a female audience. As Ramona Mielusel notes, in Franco-Maghrebi films, the road movie is most often male-dominated and the made-for-television films tend to focus on "strong female characters."[21] There may be an expectation that theatrical film audiences are primarily male and that television film audiences are primarily female, perhaps in part due to the fact that men tend to make more money and are therefore able to spend more on entertainment than women, and based on stereotypical expectations of women being aligned with the private space of the home. As I discuss below, the minor key used by Bouchareb in *Just Like a Woman* also extends to his representation of belly dancing in the film.

A POSTCOLONIAL FEMINIST REPRESENTATION OF BELLY DANCING

One of the interesting aspects of *Just Like a Woman* is the role and representation of belly dancing, something many reviewers have commented upon. We first see Mona dancing to Arabic music in front of her husband in the family's store when there are no customers present except for Marilyn, three minutes into the film. A minute later, we are shown Marilyn belly dancing as well, practicing while working and in dance class. *Just Like a Woman* thus sets up belly dancing as a commonality between the two women. In a film interested in replacing stereotypes with more complex representations of diverse people and their evolving relationships, one might have expected the film to be more critical of the danger of cultural appropriation and Orientalizing involved when a white Western woman takes up belly dancing. Amira Jarmakani has critiqued the white liberal feminist appropriation of belly dancing for purposes of individual self-help and liberation in the United States.[22] The film initially appears to follow this potentially problematic trope, as Marilyn is taking belly dancing classes from Peter (Michael Ehlers), a white male instructor, and her classmates are mostly plump, middle-aged white women.

Before the women hit the road, Mona shows Marilyn a clip from a 1950s film in which actor Samia Gamal is dancing. Mona refers to Gamal as "the best dancer in Egypt." Gamal made fifty films in twenty-five years, between 1939 and 1964.[23] She was known for "combining Eastern dancing and Western dances," thus demonstrating the hybrid nature of belly dancing and reminding us that the search for authenticity can be an Orientalist trap.[24] The focus on cultural mixing is reinforced in a later scene in which Mona tells Marilyn that Gamal was briefly married to a Texas millionaire in the 1950s. Through the Gamal film clip, Bouchareb introduces Western audiences to the long tradition of Egyptian cinema. As critics have noted, his multiple influences position him as a global filmmaker and part of accented cinema. Interestingly, *Just Like a Woman*'s major actors also share global identities, as do the director and scriptwriter of that most American of road movies, *Thelma and Louise*. There is a long tradition of road movies set in the United States and made by European directors, such as Wim Wenders's *Paris, Texas* (1984).[25]

As the women drive down to Santa Fe, Marilyn's plan is to finance the trip by belly dancing in restaurants her dance instructor Peter has found for her. She asks Mona to perform with her. Mona is initially unconvinced:

Mona: Marilyn, I don't dance in restaurants.
Marilyn: You think I do? First time for everything, right?

This dialogue recalls an earlier one in which Peter had suggested that Marilyn dance in restaurants to practice her moves and pay for her trip, and Marilyn, like Mona, had expressed doubts by replying: "Peter, I can't dance in a restaurant!" With these short dialogues, the film responds to the stereotype (active in Arab Muslim contexts) of Western women as sexually available and insists on the parallel situation in which the two women find themselves. At this point in the film, belly dancing provides them with an economic opportunity more than with self-empowerment.

The film stages a number of belly dancing scenes, including three performances, each lasting about two minutes. In Laura Mulvey's classic formulation, in Hollywood-style cinema, the expected audience is male and is supposed to derive pleasure from looking at the female character as spectacle on the screen. Mulvey notes that a female performance is often included in such films, providing an opportunity for the main male character and the expected male audience to gaze upon the sexualized female object of desire.[26] Bouchareb's three performance scenes modify this script. In the first instance, thirty-two minutes into the film, the women are dancing in a Moroccan restaurant in southwestern Illinois. They are initially a bit tentative (especially Mona) but soon gain confidence and end up enjoying themselves. They look at each other more than at their audience. The camerawork generally avoids voyeuristic close-up shots of gyrating bellies, tending to film the women primarily in medium close-ups of their faces and chests or in medium long shots from mid-thigh up. In these cases, sometimes a customer's head or a shadow hides the gyrating belly. Even though we are shown male customers putting money in the women's belts, we also see some of the female patrons starting to dance along. By the end of the scene, many diners have joined the dance and the atmosphere is more good-natured than sexualized. The women are not under the gaze of a main male character. Although they are the objects of the spectators' and the restaurant patron's gaze, they are also the subjects of one another's gaze as they look at each other, and they return the customers' gazes. Further, the female patrons' participation and the good-humored atmosphere on the screen provide a model for the audience watching the film, encouraging us to figuratively join the women's dance rather than voyeuristically gaze at them.

In the second scene, forty-seven minutes into the film, the women are performing in a Southwestern bar.[27] They appear surer of themselves and of their performance. This scene features a few belly shots but generally uses long shots in which the women's entire bodies are visible from farther away. The primarily white male audience is shown to love the performance, which they appear to receive in a more sexualized manner than the audience in the first scene did. However, this is tempered by a white cowboy starting to imitate the women's moves, which changes the atmosphere to slightly comical and once again good-natured. Through the types of shots used, Bouchareb is careful to dull the sexualized aspect of the belly dance performance and to avoid filming it in a voyeuristic manner. He also explained that he used the restaurant and bar's actual customers instead of actors, giving the scenes a less polished, more realistic feel.[28]

In the third performance scene, toward the end of the film, Mona is auditioning with a belly dancing company in Marilyn's place. She is initially filmed in a long shot from backstage, where we can only see her from the back. She is wearing Marilyn's black wig and facing a panel of four judges who are sitting in the auditorium. At this point, the film's audience does not know with certainty that Mona is the one on stage. The camera then focuses on her face and arms (confirming that Mona has indeed taken Marilyn's place) and uses medium and extreme long shots. Once again, the performance is not sexualized, and the camerawork eschews voyeurism by avoiding close-up shots of her breasts, behind, or belly and privileging close-ups of Mona's face as she dances. Her facial expression is initially neutral, and she appears to concentrate on her dance moves. As she starts to feel more comfortable, a smile appears on her face. The inclusion of the dance company members judging the performance in the extreme long shots also encourages the audience to focus on the artistry of the dance instead of on its voyeuristic aspect. Further, the audience's eyes are drawn to the two female judges, who sit in the middle and start to smile and move to the music, as the restaurant and bar audiences did in the previous performance scenes. The two male judges, one of whom is black, are more obscured, sometimes more in the shadows, sometimes out of focus, and sometimes hidden by material from Mona's costume. Jarmakani indicates that in the US context, belly dancing is "a historically eroticized dance" and a "spectacle and commodity" that is connected to a colonialist legacy.[29] In his film, Bouchareb includes the commodity angle, but he modifies the spectacle aspect and pushes against the eroticized and colonialist contexts of the dance. Made-for-television films are supposed to be family friendly, which may be one reason for the toning down of the erotic aspect of the dance. Another reason could be related to a desire to counter Orientalist representations by avoiding overly sexualized exoticization of the dance. *Just Like a Woman* opens with a close-up shot of Mona's bare belly. However, this is not a belly dancing scene.

Mourad's mother had taken Mona to a black female Santeria healer in the hopes that Mona would get pregnant. Ironically, the scene in which a belly is most exposed thus relates to the expectation of reproduction for women, not to belly dancing. The directness of that first shot may be a way to get the audience to question compulsory motherhood for women, by showing Mona's belly as being more exposed there than in any of the belly dancing scenes. In general, *Just Like a Woman* modifies the classic Hollywood representation of women as spectacle and, through camerawork and *mise-en-scène*, models audience identification with the two female protagonists instead.

Bouchareb's modest representation of belly dancing in a minor key may be contrasted to that of Abdellatif Kechiche's in *La Graine et le mulet/Couscous* (2007). Kechiche's camera is literally in his actors' faces through his constant use of extreme close-ups, creating a claustrophobic feeling that corresponds to the lack of options experienced by his main character Slimane (Habib Boufares). In the now-famous final scene of the film, Slimane's stepdaughter Rym (Hafsia Herzi) engages in a lengthy belly dance performance during the pre-opening of Slimane's new restaurant in order to placate the restless diners who have been waiting for food to be served. The camera films her gyrating, shimmying round belly and her face in extreme close-ups.[30] Critics have interpreted this scene in very different ways. Most notably, Kaya Davies Hayon disagrees with Ginette Vincendeau and Will Higbee's position that this scene objectifies the dancer. For Davies Hayon, "the dance sequence . . . (re)claims the belly dancing body as a vehicle of agency and (female) empowerment."[31] Kechiche and Bouchareb use different filmic techniques to de-eroticize the dance. Kechiche makes the scene last so long that the audience (both diegetic and real), like the weary and sweaty performer, becomes exhausted rather than titillated.[32] He relies on intense filmic techniques that seem to push his actors to the limit—such as intrusive camerawork, extreme close-ups, fast-paced and lengthy dialogues, and very long scenes. The intrusiveness onto his actors makes me question Davies Hayon's interpretation that Kechiche is using these film techniques "to institute a new, more ethical way of looking that resists de-subjectification."[33] In contrast, Bouchareb's minor key camerawork is more classical, restrained, ethical, and generally respectful of his actors' space.

Just Like a Woman also portrays the danger of being subjected to sexual harassment stemming from the dance performance when after the first restaurant scene, manager Tarek (Sayed Badreya) wants to have sex with either one of the women. The women escape and end up sleeping in the car. One could critique the portrayal of Tarek as fulfilling stereotypical expectations of the lecherous Arab. He could also be seen as Bouchareb's attempt to portray a variety of Arab male figures, from loving if somewhat passive Mourad to a man trying to abuse his power. In this way, Bouchareb cannot be accused of providing too positive and unrealistic a portrayal of Arab men. Further, after the second performance in the Southwestern bar, the cook (Boots Southerland), an older white man, acts in a similar way to Tarek, asking Marilyn if the women do private dances. The film thus sets up a parallel between the two men, showing that sexual harassment is a generalized problem regardless of the ethnicity of the male perpetrators.

Most reviewers have interpreted belly dancing in the film as an expression of female self-empowerment.[34] However, I would argue that this interpretation primarily reflects the wider US understanding of belly dancing as outlined by Jarmakani.[35] In the film, while belly dancing does represent a dream of escape for Marilyn, it actually becomes a way for the women to eke out a living while on the road (since they make more money dancing than in other jobs Marilyn has had). However, its more sordid underside is presented through the heightened risk of sexual harassment for dancers. More than female empowerment, dancing becomes a vehicle to express female solidarity, when Mona auditions for Marilyn and gets her the job with the dance company. By the end of the film, Mona decides to return to Chicago and to turn herself in to the police, and Marilyn tosses her dance contract and chooses to go back with Mona instead of staying in Santa Fe. They are returning together, but not to their husbands. The film ends with the two women dancing and walking away together on the train platform, while an American Indian man looks on approvingly with a smile. As the credits roll, we are shown iconic shots of Chicago, including the landmark Willis (formerly Sears) Tower, perhaps indicating that the women's return to Chicago will provide them with access to a more expansive space beyond their former neighborhood. These are followed by shots of city streets with several Arab neighborhood stores. The film thus seems to intimate that although the women are returning to their geographical point of departure, they will be building a new life together there beyond familial constraints.

BLANK SPOTS

In two aspects, *Just Like a Woman* provides problematic representations that limit its scope as a postcolonial feminist film. Discussing Bouchareb's earlier made-for-television movie *My Family's Honor*, Leslie Kealhofer-Kemp argues that the Maghrebi mother uses her agency to bolster traditions "that reinforce patriarchy and the oppression of women" in ways that have "negative consequences for other people, especially their children or other Maghrebi-French youths."[36] This analysis also applies to the mother in *Just Like a Woman* (reinforced by the fact that the same actors, Chafia Boudraa and Roschdy Zem, play mother and son in both films). Mourad's mother is the perfect illustration of what scholar Deniz Kandiyoti has called "bargaining with patriarchy."[37] Women bargain with patriarchy when they accept their lower role in the family's hierarchy with the expectation that they will wield power through their sons and over their daughters-in-law in old age.[38] The film thus demonizes Mourad's mother and puts most of the patriarchal burden on her. Stereotypically negative portrayals of mothers-in-law are common in many cultures. Making older women appear directly responsible for the maintenance of patriarchy while their hapless husbands and sons are left off the hook is one of the ways in which patriarchy both functions and hides its functioning, which is problematically re-enacted in the film. However, the film also seeks to undermine stereotypes of Arab men as sexist and of Western men as open-minded, which is perhaps why the film's major villains are the traditional Arab mother, the callous white working-class husband, and the racist white family. Since Mourad's mother is the only fatality in the film, her entirely negative depiction also serves to make the audience empathize with Mona and not feel bad about the loss of her mother-in-law. Her coming disappearance is foreshadowed early on in the film, when both Marilyn and Mourad separately and casually mention that things would be better if she were gone.

Just Like a Woman not only feminizes but also ethnically diversifies the road movie. The road movie worldwide has generally moved in this direction in the past twenty years, and Bouchareb's film is part of this trend. In *Thelma and Louise*, people of color—American Indian and black—were solely part of the background of the story. Although one of the protagonists in *Just Like a Woman* is an Arab woman, the portrayal of American Indians unfortunately remains somewhat limited and stereotypical. As in *Thelma and Louise*, they wait, sit, and gaze impenetrably and silently. Only one American Indian character, the tribal security agent, is active. He first appears unfriendly (he makes the two women get off the reservation as they are camping there illegally) but then invites them to a community party, which they do not attend, and drives them around, as if he has nothing else to do than to take Mona to Santa Fe. Ahmed Bedjaoui views this character more positively as being "proud and authentic" and "the only one who helps the two women on the run."[39] Already, in *Baton Rouge* (1985), a Native American man befriended the protagonists, and in both cases he contributes to the characters' mobility (selling them a car or driving them). In *Just Like a Woman*, the tribal security officer is also briefly shown in the auditorium watching Mona during her audition, sitting motionless and expressionless. Bouchareb includes the space of the reservation in his film, highlighting its partially sovereign status by showing that it has its own institutions (tribal security) and laws (the security officer tells the women that camping is not permitted there). This can be interpreted as an acknowledgment of the history of oppression of indigenous people in the Americas, put in parallel with the oppression of the female protagonists. As the women flee from mainstream society, they end up on a reservation, a space that is a physical marker of both colonial conquest (the most arid lands into which indigenous people were pushed) and continuing partial sovereignty. The reservation is a safer space for the women but one in which they are not allowed to trespass; indeed, it is outside the reservation, in the campground, that Marilyn is attacked by the white racist family. The women are then welcomed back to the reservation and helped by its inhabitants. On the one hand, this support can be seen as a gesture of solidarity across genders and ethnicities. However, the landscape of the reservation and its inhabitants are only used as background to Marilyn and Mona's story. The reservation is important for the women because it represents the end of the road for them, a space of temporary reprieve, and one in which they both make the decision to face their issues and go back to Chicago together. Although it is true that in the road movie genre, people met along the way generally tend to remain vague figures, the way in which American Indians are filmed here recalls past ethnographic portraits and visuals from *Thelma and Louise*. American Indians in *Just Like a Woman* are somewhat stereotypical silent witnesses or helpers whose only purpose is to support the two women.

CONCLUSION

To what extent can *Just Like a Woman* be called a postcolonial feminist film? It certainly appears to be so in its portrayal of the two female protagonists and their relationships, its critique of racial, cultural, and sexual stereotypes, and its insistence on intercultural female solidarity as a two-way street. However, Bouchareb's film continues to reproduce some stereotypical portrayals of the immigrant mother as the main agent of patriarchy, a depiction that has not changed much since *My Family's Honor* of 1998. His portrayal of American Indians is mixed. Although the presence of the reservation can be interpreted as a critique of US colonization, American Indian characters are represented as background figures with little agency. In spite of these two somewhat problematic aspects, the *intimiste* tone of the film is particularly well suited to render the lives of working-class women from different backgrounds who take to the road and develop a relationship of mutual solidarity and love in a minor key.

NOTES

1. Gayatri Chakarvorty Spivak, *A Critique of Postcolonial Reason: Toward a History of the Vanishing Present* (Cambridge, MA: Harvard University Press, 1999), 284. I thank Amira Jarmakani and the editors of this volume for their helpful suggestions.
2. Anne Donadey, "Gender, Genre and Intertextuality in Rachid Bouchareb's *Hors la loi*," *Studies in French Cinema* 16, no. 1 (2016): 48–60. For the script of *Just Like a Woman*, Bouchareb partnered with two women, Lebanese scriptwriter Joëlle Touma and Marion

Doussot. In an interview, he also explained that he left room for the actors to improvise some of their dialogue. See Bijan Tehrani, "Rachid Bouchareb's *Just Like a Woman*," *Cinema without Borders*, 30 June 2013, https://cinemawithoutborders.com/3446-golshifteh-farahani-sienna-miller-rachid-bouchareb-just-like-a-woman. There are two versions of *Just Like a Woman*, an 87-minute version for theatrical release (on which this article is based) and a 110-minute made-for-TV version.
3. Donadey, "Gender, Genre and Intertextuality," 49–50.
4. For a summary of critics' analyses of the road movie as a male genre, see Ewa Mazierska and Laura Rascaroli, *Crossing New Europe: Postmodern Travel and the European Road Movie* (London: Wallflower Press, 2006), 161–2. For a discussion of the French-language road movie as being inclusive of female characters since its beginnings, see Michael Gott, *French-Language Road Cinema: Borders, Diasporas, Migration and "New Europe"* (Edinburgh: Edinburgh University Press, 2016), 31.
5. In *Just Like a Woman*, the location being somewhere in Illinois is mentioned twenty-five minutes into the film, and Chicago is only explicitly mentioned thirty-nine minutes in, thus creating an initial sense of indeterminacy in the location.
6. Creating a connection between his films, Bouchareb had also used the last name Souni for the characters of the three brothers in *Outside the Law*. Roschdy Zem, who plays Mona's husband, portrayed two different characters that were both named Messaoud Souni, first in *Days of Glory* and then in *Outside the Law*.
7. Thibaut Schilt, "Brittany, No Exit: Travelling in Circles in Manuel Poirier's *Western*," in *Open Roads, Closed Borders: The Contemporary French-Language Road Movie*, ed. Michael Gott and Thibaut Schilt (Bristol: Intellect, 2013), 59.
8. David Laderman, *Driving Visions: Exploring the Road Movie* (Austin: University of Texas Press, 2002). Bouchareb's first feature film, *Bâton Rouge/Baton Rouge* (1985), was also a road movie set in the United States. His interest in road cinema thus predates *Thelma and Louise*. However, the main characters in *Baton Rouge* are male.
9. Laderman, *Driving Visions*, 248, 253, 265.
10. Schilt, "Brittany, No Exit," 59.
11. Martin O'Shaughnessy, "Nowhere to Run, Somewhere to Hide: Laurent Cantet's *L'Emploi du temps*," in *Open Roads, Closed Borders*, ed. Gott and Schilt, 158.
12. Laderman, *Driving Visions*, 271.
13. As Mazierska and Rascaroli have noted, "whereas the main vehicles for traversing the North American expanse are the private car (preferably a convertible) and the motorbike (Harley Davidson), European films often opt for public transport (trains, buses), if not hitchhiking or travelling on foot." *Crossing New Europe*, 5.
14. Justin Chang, "Film Review: 'Just Like a Woman,'" *Variety*, 5 July 2013, https://variety.com/2013/film/reviews/film-review-just-like-a-woman-1200517290; Amy Nicholson, "'Just Like a Woman' Wishes It Were 'Thelma and Louise,'" *Los Angeles Times*, 3 July 2013, https://www.latimes.com/entertainment/movies/moviesnow/la-et-mn-just-like-woman-review-20130704-story.html.
15. See for instance Sheila Benson, "True or False: Thelma & Louise Just Good Ol' Boys?" *Los Angeles Times*, 31 May 1991, https://www.latimes.com/archives/la-xpm-1991-05-31-ca-2730-story.html. The pushback was so strong that Janet Maslin felt the need to write a counter-article on the topic for the *New York Times*, "Film View; Lay Off 'Thelma and Louise,'" 16 June 1991, https://www.nytimes.com/1991/06/16/movies/film-view-lay-off-thelma-and-louise.html.
16. Bouchareb is drawn to the region, having shot his subsequent film, *La Voie de l'ennemi/Two Men in Town* (2014) in New Mexico. A comparison of the treatment of space in both films would be intriguing but is beyond the scope of this chapter.

17. Isabelle Vanderschelden, *Studying French Cinema* (New York: Columbia University Press, 2013), 18, 136. The term *intimiste* was originally applied to the Post-Impressionist paintings "of quiet domestic scenes" inhabited by women, created by Pierre Bonnard and Édouard Vuillard. See "Intimism," Tate website, accessed 27 March 2020, https://www.tate.org.uk/art/art-terms/i/intimism. Interestingly, Bonnard's paintings were also an inspiration for Algerian writer and filmmaker Assia Djebar. See Anne Donadey, *Recasting Postcolonialism: Women Writing between Worlds* (Portsmouth, NH: Heinemann, 2001), 96–102 for more details. In the *dossier de presse* of *Just Like a Woman*, Bouchareb explained that he was ready to make a smaller, *intimiste* film after the larger-than-life *Outside the Law* (http://www.3b-productions.com/tessalit/justlikeawoman/download/just-like-a-woman-dossier-de-presse.pdf).
18. *Dossier de presse*, *Just Like a Woman*. Bouchareb used the term "*sobre*" in French.
19. Two of his *intimiste* films had a theatrical release in France: *Little Senegal* focused on a male character and *London River* on one male and one female character.
20. Leslie Kealhofer-Kemp, *Muslim Women in French Cinema: Voices of Maghrebi Migrants in France* (Liverpool: Liverpool University Press, 2015), 107, 109.
21. Ramona Mielusel, *Franco-Maghrebi Artists of the 2000s: Transnational Narratives and Identities* (Leiden: Brill, 2018), 49.
22. Amira Jarmakani, "Belly Dancing for Liberation: A Critical Interpretation of Reclamation Rhetoric in the American Belly Dance Community," in *Arabs in the Americas: Interdisciplinary Essays on the Arab Diaspora*, ed. Darcy A. Zabel (New York: Peter Lang, 2006), 145, 147, 159, 164.
23. "Samia Gamal," IMDb, accessed 27 March 2020, https://www.imdb.com/name/nm0303636.
24. Ibid.; see also Kaya Davies Hayon, *Sensuous Cinema: The Body in Contemporary Maghrebi Film* (New York: Bloomsbury Academic, 2018), 64.
25. Alec G. Hargreaves calls Bouchareb's vision "global" in "From 'Ghettoes' to Globalization: Situating Maghrebi-French Filmmakers," in *Screening Integration: Recasting Maghrebi Immigration in Contemporary France*, ed. Sylvie Durmelat and Vinay Swamy (Lincoln: University of Nebraska Press, 2011), 34. Hamid Naficy includes Bouchareb's films in his definition of *An Accented Cinema: Exilic and Diasporic Filmmaking* (Princeton, NJ: Princeton University Press, 2001). Sienna Miller is American and was raised in the UK by American and South African parents ("Sienna Miller," IMDb, accessed 27 March 2020, https://www.imdb.com/name/nm1092227). Golshifteh Farahani is an Iranian actor who lives in Paris. She was also cast in another Ridley Scott film, *Body of Lies* (2008) ("Golshifteh Farahani Biography," IMDb, accessed 27 March 2020, https://www.imdb.com/name/nm0267042/bio). Scott himself is actually British. He began his career in the United Kingdom and was in his early forties when he made his first US film ("Ridley Scott Biography," IMDb, accessed 27 March 2020, https://www.imdb.com/name/nm0000631/bio). Meanwhile, *Thelma and Louise*'s scriptwriter, Callie Khouri, is Arab American on her father's side ("Arab Americans: Callie Khouri," Arab America, accessed 27 March 2020, https://www.arabamerica.com/arabamericans/callie-khouri/), and the film's main producer, Pathé, was originally a French company.
26. Laura Mulvey, "Visual Pleasure and Narrative Cinema," *Screen* 16, no. 3 (1975): 6–18. For a discussion of how film techniques can be used to circumvent the voyeuristic, neocolonial male gaze in the specific context of belly dancing, see Davies Hayon, *Sensuous Cinema*, especially Chapter Three (59–90).
27. Bouchareb's first film, *Baton Rouge*, also features a number of bar scenes.
28. Tehrani, "Rachid Bouchareb's *Just Like a Woman*."
29. Jarmakani, "Belly Dancing for Liberation," 145, 148.

30. See Kaya Davies Hayon, *Sensuous Cinema: The Body in Contemporary Maghrebi Film* (New York: Bloomsbury Academic, 2018), 78–9.
31. Ibid., 77.
32. Ibid., 79–89.
33. Ibid., 77.
34. See Nicholson, "'Just Like a Woman' Wishes It Were 'Thelma and Louise,'" in particular, as well as Miriam Bale, "If Thelma and Louise Were Belly Dancers," *New York Times*, 4 July 2013, https://www.nytimes.com/2013/07/05/movies/just-like-a-woman-follows-sienna-miller-across-the-plains.html.
35. Jarmakani, "Belly Dancing for Liberation," 145, 147, 159, 164.
36. Kealhofer-Kemp, *Muslim Women in French Cinema*, 114. See also her analysis of the portrayal of the mothers in that film, 117–23.
37. Deniz Kandiyoti, "Bargaining with Patriarchy," *Gender and Society* 2, no. 3 (1988): 274–90.
38. Ibid., 278–9.
39. Ahmed Bedjaoui, *Cinéma et guerre de libération: Algérie, des batailles d'images* (Algiers: Chihab, 2014), 23.

CHAPTER 12

Relations of Disjuncture in a "World-in-motion": Rachid Bouchareb's *La Voie de l'ennemi/ Two Men in Town*

Valérie K. Orlando

Rachid Bouchareb's 2014 film *La Voie de l'ennemi/Two Men in Town* depicts our complicated era of globalization as defined by a "truism" grounded in the idea "that we are functioning in a world fundamentally characterized by objects in motion."[1] Arjun Appadurai notes that this chaotic "world-in-motion"[2] offers an apt description for how globalization operates, is fueled, and is sustained. Today's global forces set in "motion . . . objects, persons, images and discourses . . . [that] have different speeds, axes, points of origin and termination, and varied relationships to institutional structures."[3] In this chapter, I argue that in *Two Men in Town*, Bouchareb casts his cinematic net wide to encompass our era of global networks in a multitude of sociopolitically and culturally based messages that provide visual representations of Appadurai's world-in-motion, with all its constraints and challenges.

RELATIONS OF DISJUNCTURE IN A WORLD-IN-MOTION

Set in the United States, *Two Men in Town* tells the story of the marginalization and impossible societal reinsertion of an ex-convict, William Garnett, who spent eighteen years in a prison in New Mexico for killing a police officer in his hometown located in the desert southwest. In order to explore the socioeconomic and cultural landscapes of Bouchareb's film, I use a framework grounded in theories of globalization and citizenship as proposed in the work of Arjun Appadurai and Kwame Appiah; notably, Appadurai's *Modernity at Large: Cultural Dimensions of Globalization* (1996) and Appiah's *Cosmopolitanism: Ethics in a World of Strangers* (2006). Garnett's attempts at living a life of non-violence in the middle of a Mexican-American gang-infested town in the desert Southwest place the film in a unique category that reveals the stresses and negative influences of globalization in the twenty-first century. Even though *Modernity at Large* was published over twenty years ago, we can still feel the urgency of Appadurai's affirmation that "today's world involves interactions of a new order and intensity."[4] The twenty-first-century mobile world, powered by the constant transnational flow of goods and humans, is not equitable for all individuals, nations, and societies:

> To say that globalization is about a world of things in motion somewhat understates the point. The various flows we see—of objects, persons, images, and discourses—are not coeval, convergent, isomorphic, or spatially consistent. They are in what I have elsewhere called *relations of disjuncture*.[5]

Appadurai explains that these "relations of disjuncture" occur "between economy, culture, and politics." They are what makes "the complexity of the ... global economy"[6] or, as we have seen in recent years, the increasing inequality with respect to land, money, and security. These negative global forces stand as hindrances to the right to enjoy a "being-in-the-world,"[7] a position of the self that is positive and autonomous, operating in harmony with others and the environment.[8] This positive being-in-the-world connotes an active self that is cosmopolitan and fully invested in community citizenship, as Appiah suggests:

> There are two strands that intertwine in the notion of cosmopolitanism. One is the idea that we have obligations to others, obligations that stretch beyond those to whom we are related by the ties of kith and kind [sic], or even the more formal ties of a shared citizenship. The other is that we take seriously the value not just of human life but of particular human lives, which means taking an interest in the practices and beliefs that lend them significance.[9]

For Appadurai, the challenge to any conception of cosmopolitan individuals' being-in-the-world would lie in the relation of disjunctures on the global and local levels that constantly test access to citizenship and communal belonging. The framework for exploring these disjunctures in societies relies on five dimensions, designated as "ethnoscapes, mediascapes, technoscapes, financescapes, and ideoscapes."[10] As Bouchareb's film reveals, these different *scapes* interact, converge, and diverge on global and local levels and thus make us aware of the extent to which this "world-in-motion produce[s] fundamental problems of livelihood, equity, suffering, justice and governance."[11] Disjunctures are "deeply perspectival constructs, inflected by the historical, linguistic, and political situatedness of different sorts of actors: nation-states, multinationals, diasporic communities, as well as subnational groupings and movements."[12] Individuals like William Garnett must find their way through the landscapes of these disjunctures, realizing that some are navigable, while others are not, because each landscape "is subject to its own constraints and incentives (some political, some informational, and some technoenvironmental)."[13]

BOUCHAREB'S CINÉMA-MONDE: MULTIPLE DECENTERINGS

Two Men in Town is typical of Bouchareb's multifaceted cinematic oeuvre that situates local and global perspectives in relation to each other. With a cast that is international, and a script featuring multiple languages, ethnicities, and ways of looking at the world, the film highlights examples of Appadurai's relations of disjuncture on the levels of the sociopolitical, the economic and the cultural. As a film about our world-in-motion, Bouchareb's *Two Men in Town* is exemplary of the cinematic productions of the cinéma-monde.[14] As a transnational art form, the films of the cinéma-monde of the twenty-first century are influenced by the flows of globalization. Emanating from the former French colonial world, this category of cinema resonates transnationally across borders and national identities as its films reveal the disjunctures apparent within the local and global scapes described by Appadurai. As Michael Gott notes in the second chapter of this volume, Bouchareb's "'kaleidoscopic' vantage point on the world and his films have long been aligned with what scholars have recently theorized as cinéma-monde." The director's films challenge audiences to think about the differing scapes of the globe that "involve floating across fluid margins and facilitating lateral encounters" among people, things, and places.[15] Supporting the view that cinéma-monde is "no longer francophone, strictly speaking" but rather "post-postcolonial," Florence Martin observes that one of its most salient qualities is that plots and characters are constantly "decentered" from nations, languages, and ethnic ties of origin.[16] Bouchareb's *Two Men in Town* exemplifies the qualities and aspects of cinéma-monde films as defined by Dayna Oscherwitz, who notes: "These films ... aspire, through their own global circulation, to persuade us of the need for open borders, for a world in which human movement produces shared understandings and collective development."[17]

One of the most noticeable aspects of Bouchareb's dedication to the decentering of his francophone origins in *Two Men in Town* is his script, written in English, Spanish, and Arabic. In fact, this film in particular exemplifies what Florence Martin and Bill Marshall have noted is one of the most predominate qualities of cinéma-monde: filmmakers' departure from using French or making claims to being part of *la francophonie*.[18] Additionally, the multiple languages used make us aware that even in the most remote places, no one dominant narrative can exist, and even those that are the most imaginative are possible. This quality of the unusual as possible is demonstrated, for example, in Garnett's use of Arabic in the desert of the US Southwest. Discussing Bouchareb's often decentered scripts, Mireille Rosello suggests that the French-Algerian filmmaker makes audiences "aware of what is or could be a center, a periphery, an identity or a coincidence" in order to avoid "a number of archetypal narratives."[19] The credits for *Two Men in Town* roll in French, but the film script was cowritten in English, Spanish, and Arabic by Olivier Lorell and the famous Algerian author Yasmina Khadra.[20] The director uses well-known American actors Forest Whitaker and Harvey Keitel in the roles of the lead protagonists. Bouchareb's cast is multiracial and multilingual, with entire scenes in Spanish for which no subtitles are provided.[21]

William Garnett, played by Whitaker, converts to Islam while in prison and, upon his release, is convinced that his faith will help to set him on the right path in compliance with his parole and his search for a normal life. Unfortunately, Sheriff Bill Agati (Keitel) cannot forgive Garnett for the eighteen-year-old murder of a police officer on his force. The sheriff does not accept that Garnett is a changed man and, therefore, constantly harasses him, hoping to coax an incident in order to send the ex-convict back to prison. In Agati's eyes, Garnett will forever be a deviant. Although dedicated to Garnett's redemption, parole agent Emily Smith (Brenda Blethyn, also cast in Bouchareb's 2009 film *London River*) is powerless to protect him. She is constrained by Sheriff Agati's maneuvering against the ex-prisoner and her own outsider status (as a transplant from Chicago), which ultimately prevent her from challenging the sheriff's corrupt policing.

As with many of Bouchareb's films, *Two Men in Town* depicts uprooted characters like Garnett, who are often estranged from family, and who find themselves in opposition to others in landscapes that are devoid of familiarity.[22] Once Garnett is released from prison, even though he has paid his dues with prison time, he is still perceived as deviant by Agati and most of the town's white community because of his religion and his past. Sociologists John Cross and Alfonso Hernández Hernández remark in their 2011 article "Place, Identity, and Deviance" that deviancy is always "a product of social construction beginning with the act of labeling [by others]." This labeling forces the individual ultimately to decide "acceptance or rejection of the label."[23] In the film, Garnett is constantly confronted with the perception of others and the labels that are foisted on him. These hinder any new identity formation.

In the final moments of the film, Garnett is unable to fend off the past demons of rage and anger that haunt him in order to find redemption. He is also unable to stifle the deviant identity fabricated for him by Agati and the wider, local community. The ex-convict eventually succumbs to the violence surrounding him fomented by his former gang-leader "brother," Terence (Luis Guzmán), who operates a ring of drug trading and human trafficking across the US–Mexican border. The opening scene depicts Garnett bashing in Terence's head with a rock in the vast desert. This scene is almost exactly repeated (albeit with different camera angles) at the end of the film, thus revealing the story as a long flashback, a circle of violence that has engulfed Garnett. Trapped in a cycle of death that offers no exit, Garnett's tortured life is caught up in murder. The moral of the story is that history repeats itself and that despite transformation through religious devotion, destiny and/or fate as well as the power of others (Agati) dictate the outcomes for Garnett. The film offers an understanding of a contemporary, existential reality that underscores the fact that humankind is shaped by its environment. This fact mandates that individuals' destinies will always be defined by their surroundings. Bouchareb's film script harkens to the proverbial fatalism of *mektoub*—"it is written"—believed by Muslim cultures around the world. More precisely, "*Koulchi bel mektoub*" means nothing is left to chance, because chance does not exist. Everything has already been decided by a higher power beyond one's control.[24]

In general, whether or not viewers prescribe to the fatalism depicted in the film, what is particularly interesting is that its plot explores universal aspects of the human condition in our contemporary glocal era. A term that emerged in the 1990s, "glocal" describes how global sociocultural and economic networks influence local political policies, moral codes, and social interaction. It is a term "related [to] notions of hybridity, fusion, creolization, and mixture"[25] and often evokes ideas of insecurity in individuals and communities that arise from a sense of loss (of identity, tradition, language, and so on) in their local lives. Loss of these social attributes causes communities to feel that they are at the mercy of outside forces over which they have no control. Within the angst of the glocal, the chaos of Appadurai's disjunctures of a world-in-motion becomes apparent.[26]

The border space depicted in *Two Men in Town* suggests thinking of border and order (b/order) as intertwined. In *B/ordering Space*, Henk van Houtum, Olivier Kramsch, and Wolfgang Zierhofer propose that borders connote "control of a bounded sphere of connectivity [that] constitutes a reality of (affective) orientation [and] power."[27] In the border space, there are constant tensions and a definitive division between those individuals inside the space of power and those outside who want in. The border space, because of these two realities, is subjected to extremes of order and chaos. These extremes make us aware of "how the concept of 'place' as a social construction can evoke [an individual's] deviant identity as a form of resistance to dominate norms."[28] The film encourages thinking about how "the organization of space not only reflects power, but produces power," as Michel Foucault notes in *Discipline and Punish*.[29]

BOUCHAREB'S GLOCAL BORDER SPACE

Bouchareb's films generally show that local communities never remain untouched by the forces of networks and systems beyond their control. His cinematic oeuvre reflects recent scholarship on how local and global networks and systems influence individuals' identities. The plot development in *Two Men in Town* exemplifies how, according to Houtum and colleagues, "local id/entities have become informed by globalizing economic, political, cultural and technological developments" that are subjected to "the various spatial b/*orderings* involved in identity-construction."[30] In *Two Men in Town*, the binary tensions between inside the border and outside it, the foreign and the domestic, as well as social order and disorder, determine the outcome of characters' choices, particularly Garnett's, as he seeks to stay on his moral path after being released from prison. In keeping with Bouchareb's global perspectives, all audiences, no matter their continent, region, or language, are likely to understand the universalisms explored in *Two Men in Town*. The cineaste weaves a network of connections that allows characters to interact using universal human responses easily recognized by viewers: anger at injustice, perseverance against stacked odds, and love across ethnic differences. Although ending in brutal violence, reminiscent of the classic Spaghetti Westerns of the 1960s, the juxtaposition of conflicting elements makes it a film about the quotidian tensions emanating from glocal migrations across the border space, ethnicity, linguistic barriers, and rights to the land. Bouchareb's preference for shooting his film in Cinemascope, the wide-angle lens of choice for most desert Westerns, further pays homage to the classics of the past, emphasizing familiar tropes of lone cowboys, vigilante gunmen and mercenaries, isolated out in the open, vast expanse of arid space.

As an outsider himself to the US border landscapes of his film, Bouchareb has no allegiances and, thus, is able to explore the possibility of other non-normative narratives, or stories that have not yet been told. With respect to *Two Men in Town*, these narratives redefine the expected Anglo-European storylines of Westerns and crime dramas to make what Mireille Rosello calls the "could be" centers seem possible.[31] These possible centers include African American Garnett's conversion to Islam in a state where barely 2 percent of the population is African American and less than 1 percent is Muslim.[32] Others include Garnett's white mother (Ellen Burstyn), who remains nameless and whom he resembles very little. Also incongruous with what is expected are the protagonist's friendship with his white, middle-aged parole officer, Emily Smith, as well as his romantic relationship with a Hispanic bank teller, Teresa (Dolores Heredia), with whom he speaks in Spanish most of the time. Despite their novelty, these narratives spark our imagination because on the surface they seem unlikely, but become plausible in an era where diverse encounters can and do take place at the most micro levels of society.

Appadurai's various scapes of disjuncture weave themselves into the fabric of Bouchareb's film, playing out in different ways. Disjunctive relationships fuel tensions in the realms of identity and cultural politics for all the characters portrayed, thus drawing audiences' attention to the fact that individuals today are often not construed within the structures of positive cosmopolitanism forged through linkages and affiliations. Bouchareb's protagonists are caught in the world-in-motion where they are not defined by allegiance to nations, communities, or ethnic origins. They are left alone, cut off in solitude, and marginalized on economic, social, and political fronts. Glocal subjects for the filmmaker are producers and consumers as well as victims of the interconnections in which they are implicated. Such subjecthood is always influenced by mobility and, ultimately, determines the positive and negative outcomes of identity formation; of moving forward, or staying stuck with nowhere to go, consumed by the present socioeconomic and political forces from which the individual cannot extrapolate her/himself. This is Garnett's predicament. Although an imam tells him on the day of his release that "redemption is always possible," emphasizing that "he has done his time" and, therefore, paid his dues to society, freedom is elusive once Garnett leaves the penitentiary. The ex-convict exits one prison only to enter others: that of the desert town and the confines of his *mektoub*, as well as the constant haunting of his past crime. Moving forward is impossible. From his first steps out of prison, Garnett is fated to remain in a circle of rage and violence, condemned by the destiny that has been written for him.

MIGRATION, MOBILITY, AND DELOCALIZATION IN BOUCHAREB'S WORLD-IN-MOTION

I will now analyze the extent to which mobility (or lack thereof) and landscapes of disjunctures dictate the outcomes for Bouchareb's protagonists. The film entreats us to think about how Appadurai's *scapes* determine individual subjects' ability to move (or not) in glocal, multiethnic, and linguistic socioeconomic environments. Lack of mobility increases Garnett's rage and violent reactions to being confined within the town. The film compels us, thus, to consider to what extent subjects who are marginalized from family ties (Appiah's "kith and kind") and unable to enjoy free circulation suffer in their isolation, ultimately failing to become something other than what seems to have been already written for them. For Garnett, redemption is impossible despite his education, his linguistic ability (in Arabic and Spanish), and remaking his identity as a devout, practicing Muslim. He is unable to extract himself from the surrounding violence and unable to make positive connections in order to realize his potential. Philosophically, he cannot "deterritorialize" and follow "lines of flight" to new becomings.[33]

Although seemingly constructed on a cosmopolitan platform that puts into conversation multiple ethnic and linguistic registers depicting the diversity of the US, Bouchareb's film also warns us that many societal realities in our millennial era negatively influence individuals' power over their own lives. White hegemony, unequal rates of incarceration between whites and people of color, and the plethora of injustices committed against minorities every day impede their becoming and access to power in society.

Despite the barriers his protagonists face, as a delocalized filmmaker Bouchareb is able to explore themes of connection and decentering that are only possible because of a world-in-motion. Delocalization with respect to language and place from his own national narratives (French and Algerian) has allowed the filmmaker to extend his narrative networks across the globe. These encourage transnational audiences to think about mobility (voluntary or not, realized or not), financial stress, pan-terrorism, climate change, and an array of other universal themes. As a filmmaker who exemplifies the category of cinéma-monde as it has been theorized, Bouchareb decenters himself from his own roots and origins in order to make films with plots that resonate everywhere. In many of his films (particularly *Little Senegal* and *London River*), migration plays an important role in the denouement of the story. Scripts detailing the lives of people on the move reflect our current century of failed nations and insecure populations (at home and abroad) who have been forced to leave one land for another.

Two Men in Town features primarily an American cast rooted in Hispanic culture in a desert space that is isolated, yet crossed by migrant subjects seeking the American dream. Undocumented Hispanic laborers crossing into the US intersect with African American Garnett's own local narrative of marginalization, and persecution would be particularly recognizable to American audiences in the current climate of police repression and harsh border control. The story of an educated African American condemned by white power and police brutality is entwined with those of people moving from the impoverished south to the north of the American continent. Making visible these mobile peoples encourages audiences to "actively contemplate ... porous borders and migratory circulations" often erroneously touted as a positive aspect of globalization.[34] Bouchareb utilizes the familiar US–Mexican borderland Western narrative to underscore the importance of thinking about globalization and transnational exchange. Although porous, as often seen in classic Westerns such as Nate Watt's 1937 *Borderland*, this particular border space has always been associated with lawlessness, violent exchange, exploitation, and death. Due to its past history, the US–Mexico borderland Western is the perfect trope through which to consider transnational and domestic travel and the challenges to free circulation in the twenty-first century. *Two Men in Town* requires us to think about who has, and who does not have, the right to enjoy "deterritorialization."[35] As the film demonstrates, global transnational movement, and whether or not it is entered into through free will, is determined by geographical position and wealth.[36] Certainly, twenty-first-century migration flows indicate that patterns of circulation are usually hindered, dangerous, and, more often than not, mandated by economic and/or political necessity. Terence's lucrative smuggling business, which includes trafficking migrant labor across the border, signifies what Ursula Heise explains is the defining force of global consumption, where migrants must "follow the flows of capital experience." Their "choices . . . are dictated to by the needs of First World markets."[37] *Two Men in Town* suggests that migratory flows are usually south to north.

Race and gender also influence the individual's ability to access new spaces in *Two Men in Town*. Like Teresa and Garnett's mother, parole officer Emily Smith is relegated to the peripheries of the overtly dominant male space of the town under Sheriff Agati's rule. Smith is often seen alone, gazing out across the vast expanse of the desert from the porch of her small house. A transplant from Chicago who listens to Edith Piaf singing in French while cleaning her gun and drinking a bottle of wine, Emily Smith is as unique and non-stereotypical as Garnett is when he steps out of prison as a convert to Islam fluent in Arabic. Their uniqueness, or rather isolation from others, is often evoked through wide-angled scenes where they seem swallowed up by the desert. Most of these marginalized characters, whether they are women or men of color, fit into Appadurai's "landscape of persons who constitute the shifting world in which we live," but who are unable to "affect the politics" of their environments.[38] Garnett, Emily, Teresa, and Hispanic migrants are all precluded from subverting the politics and policing of Sheriff Agati's town devoid of justice, or escaping Terence's illegal dealings and brutality.

GEOGRAPHIES OF ISOLATION IN THE ETHNOSCAPE: THE DESERT AS EMPTY LAND

The ethnoscape is defined by Appadurai as a space of "human motion" where people "deal with the realities of having to move or the fantasies of wanting to move."[39] This quality is one of the most notable in Bouchareb's film. In stark contrast to *London River*, which examines an urban cosmopolitan space in the UK with all its contemporary racial tensions and the challenges of a dense city environment,[40] *Two Men in Town* is set in the expanse of the sparsely populated US desert Southwest. Bouchareb's American desert falls into the trope of "the myth of the empty land, involving both gender and racial dispossession."[41] The film's ethnoscape is defined by movement, or lack of it, as it affects the relationships between characters. Appadurai defines the ethnoscape as a space where "there are no relatively stable communities and networks of kinship, friendship, work and leisure . . . residence, and other filial forms."[42] Those who cannot move or do not want to—Garnett, Terence, and Agati—must operate in a common sphere that is shaped by both lawlessness and too much law. Garnett, as an ex-convict, is mandated by his parole to stay in the county, and in the eyes of the law, he remains a deviant. Agati, as a powerful warden who has free rein over the town's space, continues to deal the hands of law as he sees fit. Terence exerts the power of lawlessness through multiple connections on both sides of the border, which facilitates his avoidance of Agati and his ability to harass Garnett.

Bouchareb makes a point of defining his bordering ethnoscape as one of isolation managed by white men who make their own laws and systems of order and justice. Sheriff Agati's rule of law affords him the power to harass Garnett in town as he seeks to force him back to jail for a crime for which he has already paid his dues. In the name of maintaining order and some semblance of justice, the open expanse of the unruly, boundless space outside the town's limits gives the lawman free rein to pardon (or not) illegal Hispanic migrants caught crossing the US–Mexican border. Agati's interpretation of laws and justice becomes increasingly schizophrenic. Confronting a camp of white vigilantes patrolling the border who "wear no badges," the sheriff screams: "You have no right to arrest illegal immigrants. The law is the law . . . You can't break the law to enforce the law." Agati's disregard for his own laws in this scene stands in stark contrast to the rules he devises to restrict Garnett's movement.

The binary good-bad rules in the film's ethnoscape are dictated by Agati and the Mexican-American Terence, who is a violent drug dealer and people trafficker. Both these men's spheres dominate and entrap Garnett as they cut through the "virgin space"[43] of the desert, each struggling to conquer it with his power. Caught within the power plays, Garnett can be neither lawful nor unlawful because he has been stripped of all ability to take charge of his life and follow his own path (in a sense, deterritorialize and then reterritorialize an identity that is of his own making). He is impeded by Agati from being able to enjoy his American dream to "live in peace," have a family, and possess a modest home; and he is pressured by Terence to "come back and work" with the gang in order to "finish what he started" when they were running drugs and trafficking people across the border.

A cosmopolitan African American man, well dressed in a suit and tie, sporting a goatee beard and glasses, Garnett is an intellectual. He is seen reading *Fortress of the Muslim: Invocations from the Qur'an and Sunnah* by Sa'id Bin Ali Bin Wahf Al-Qahtani, which contains prayers and "words of remembrance" from the hadiths of the Sunnah.[44] Garnett's physique is reminiscent of Malcolm X as leader of the Nation of Islam, or Black Panther

Stokely Carmichael, stoic and passionate. The modicum of free movement he does enjoy is on a used motorcycle he has been able to buy from his minimum-wage job as a cattle worker on a ranch. Although Garnett feels free as he rides through the desert space, circulating seemingly unencumbered, in reality he is watched constantly by Agati's police force and by Terence and his men. Both wait for the former convict to stumble into their traps.

Bouchareb's Belgian-US-Algerian-French production is exemplary of global films that appeal to multiply diverse audiences. The filmmaker remarks in an interview that Whitaker's portrayal of Garnett is meant to orient Algerian audiences to protagonists with whom they can identify in the context of America's racialized history:

> This aspect interests Algerians: an African American, who plays the role of a man who has converted to Islam in prison and who, not without difficulties, tries to reinsert himself in society. Americans are not that foreign for Algerians. We remember the Black Panther movement, of which certain figures took refuge in Algeria. Someone like Forest Whitaker, who has already played the role of Africans, does not seem so far-fetched.[45]

The desert ethnoscape of *Two Men in Town*, despite its vast expanse encompassing a variety of people and degrees of power, provides freedom only for some. Wide-angled camera shots reduce the powerless (Garnett, Emily, and Teresa) to the size of dolls as they gaze out into the open expanse of the arid land. In scenes like the one pictured in Figure 12.1, protagonists are always on the peripheries. Even inanimate objects (the motorcycle, for example) displace them in order to take center stage.

Figure 12.1 *Two Men in Town*, Garnett (Forest Whitaker) facing the desert

IDEOSCAPES AND MEDIASCAPES: ISLAM, LAW, AND JUSTICE

Appadurai suggests that mediascapes and ideoscapes are

> closely related landscapes of images. These images involve many complicated inflections, depending on their mode ... their hardware ... their audiences ... and the interests of those who own and control them. Mediascapes ... tend to be image-centered, narrative-based accounts of strips of reality, and what they offer to those who experience them is a series of elements ... out of which scripts can be formed of imagined lives, their own as well as those of others living in other places.[46]

Throughout *Two Men in Town*, Bouchareb juxtaposes disparate ideologies. The filmmaker explores white Puritan American ideals pertaining to the American dream, law/lawlessness, and who has the right to circulate and be an individual in the landscape. These are contrasted to what is perceived as foreign, encroaching ideoscapes such as Garnett's Islam. Although born and raised in the desert town, when Garnett emerges from prison as an ex-convict and a devout Muslim, he is considered an outsider, incongruent as a deviant trying to infiltrate Agati's white-bread America. His belief system disrupts this very recognizable, American Southwestern space, destabilizing what Cross and Hernández Hernández define as the "'we-ness' [that stresses] the similarities or shared attributes around which group members coalesce."[47] As a post-9/11 film, Bouchareb's interjection of messages that focus on Islam as a peaceful religion demonstrates the wider ethos of contemporary Maghrebi filmmakers who constantly deal with "the relentless process of neoliberal globalization, the geopolitics of neo-imperialism, the rise of a civilization discourse in which 'Islam' is positioned in opposition to the 'West.'"[48]

Bouchareb's choice to challenge recognizable stereotypes and prejudices that exist in the US, and more singularly, in the desert space of the film, was calculated, as he notes in an interview:

> I didn't see the point in just remaking a film that was well-made for its time. So, I wrote a new story that deals with the subject matter of immigration and how Islam is seen in the United States and I decided my character would be played by an Afro-American. All these elements were of great interest to me.[49]

In several scenes in the film, Garnett prays, holding onto his faith as the only means to find calm in his local world of constant motion and escalating tensions. For him, Islam represents the hope for a clear path forward, which

Figure 12.2 *Two Men in Town*, Garnett (Forest Whitaker) and Agati (Harvey Keitel) in the town diner

enables him to achieve what was lost in his past. The adoption of his new faith only further cultivates Agati's ire, as demonstrated in one pivotal scene in the film. The sheriff cannot accept the fact that Garnett can be anything other than a deviant. In the scene pictured in Figure 12.2, as the former convict sits reading *Fortress of the Muslim* while calmly eating his dinner in the local diner, Agati shows up, takes a seat beside him, and tauntingly remarks: "You're a cultured guy now . . . Shari'a law? Jesus didn't do it for you? So what do we call you now?" When Garnett protests that he has "just chosen another way of life, that's all," Agati does not believe him, saying: "Hmmm, so what's your next caper?" Islam as sinister, foreign, and terror-oriented can only be for the sheriff a "caper" that masks ulterior motives.

Garnett will be forever under Agati's rule, denied his version of the American dream that he describes as to "live in peace, have a little family, a little house, a little lawn, little lawnmower, wife, kids, neighbors." The ex-convict's dream, according to Agati, is only "a fairy tale." Antagonistic scenes like this one, focusing on religious faith and ideals of being-in-the-world as an individual making his way in peace and spirituality, resonate in many of Bouchareb's films. In *Two Men in Town*, the filmmaker places Garnett in what Cross and Hernández Hernández describe as a quandary: "Once a person is identified as a deviant . . . his own self-conception must increasingly center on his acceptance or repudiation of the role allocation."[50] In order to find and establish his identity, Garnett's sense of self must be tied to "location, material form, [and] meaningfulness." These are essential to defining his place in the community.[51] Despite the former prisoner's efforts to integrate and lead a peaceful life, Agati puts up barricades at every turn.

Garnett's Islam is multifaceted and nuanced. As we have seen, he is not reading the Qur'an but rather *Fortress of the Muslim*, featuring "invocations from the Qur'an and Sunnah" that pertain to moral codes prescribed for the individual's daily life. The author, Sa'id Bin Ali Bin Wahf Al-Qahtani, stresses that this minimalist publication is an abridgment of an earlier work. The small, pocket-sized book is meant to be "portable," containing only "words of remembrance" from the Hadith.[52] Thus, Garnett departs from the foundational Qur'an in order to move out to the margins, exploring the Sunnah, which was "used in *tafsīr* (Qur'ānic exegesis) to supplement the meaning of the text and in *fiqh* (Islamic jurisprudence) as the basis of legal rulings not discussed in the Qur'ān."[53] The Sunnah, as described here, offers codes for moral conduct in existence since pre-Islamic times:

> The term became associated more specifically with the actions and sayings of the Prophet Muhammad. Inspired by God to act wisely and in accordance with his will, Muhammad provided an example that complements God's revelation as expressed in the Qur'an. His actions and sayings became a model for Muslim conduct as well as a primary source of Islamic law.[54]

As in *London River*, for example, Bouchareb's *Two Men in Town* reiterates Mireille Rosello's affirmation that "just as places are filmed in a way that refuses to adopt contemporary frames of reference, Islam, and religion in general, are presented from the very first scenes from a very specific point of view."[55] This viewpoint represents "Islam as a difference that does not make a difference . . . because it refuses to fall into the trap of having to choose between accusation and justification"[56] or the stereotypical categories construed for it by the West. For Garnett, Islam is an essential component in establishing his right to be in the world as a redeemed individual, exercising his "plenitude of existence"[57] in a defined community. *Fortress of the Muslim* is Garnett's moral guidebook, and its tenets, as stated in one key passage, resonate throughout the film: "Guide me to the best of characters for none can guide to it other than You, and deliver me from the worst of characters for none can deliver me from it other than You."[58]

Drawing constantly on the moral codes outlined in *Fortress of the Muslim*, Garnett constructs an alternative view of Islam as it is projected to Western audiences. What Agati defines as foreign and deviant, Garnett assumes as a humanist moral code that is essential to his post-convict identity. Striving to live by the Sunnah, Garnett searches to establish in the hegemonic white Anglo space of Agati's policing an alternate way of living a life of peace and justice that draws on ancient established laws of moral conduct and order. The American dream is juxtaposed with what the Sunnah was created for: to offer to Muslims "a formal, rigorous, and text-based framework for Muslim jurisprudence and legal practice."[59]

FINANCESCAPES: HUMAN FLOWS AND FINANCIAL TRANSFERS IN THE GLOCAL DESERT

Appadurai affirms that

> the current geographical mobility of capital is unique in its own history and unmatched by other political projects or interests ... a significant number of observers agree that the scale, penetration, and velocity of global capital have all ... in the last few decades of this century [become stressed].[60]

Relations of disjuncture pertaining to financescapes are, in the global context, complex and daunting. They are "now a more mysterious, rapid, and difficult landscape to follow than ever before, as currency markets, national stock exchanges and commodity speculations move megamonies through national turnstiles."[61] Global economic power flows tend to influence local communities at the levels of politics, justice, equality, and equity. This globalized capital power, for example, plays out in the film in Terence's running across the border of undocumented pregnant Hispanic women for his "anchor baby business" and migrant laborers to fuel his lucrative ventures. His success depends on constant violence and the flow of transnational capital over the border that disrupts the US desert town as his dealings subvert domestic laws.

Glocal money, capital flows, and work (and lack of it) all contribute to Garnett's compromised ability to reformulate his identity outside prison. Upon his release, one of the stipulations for his rehabilitation is to find work. At the local unemployment office, the employment officer immediately tells him: "You have a criminal record. That doesn't leave us with too many options." She follows this pronouncement with "They need help on a ranch on the border; minimum wage, no benefits." Garnett agrees to take the menial job, feeling that working as a local ranch hand will help lead him to redemption. Although meager, his earnings allow him for a time to set things right in his life, stabilize his lodgings, and open an account at the local bank where he meets his romantic interest, Teresa. Working with the cows, "out in the open air," where he is able to pray as a Muslim on his lunch hour in the desert as his coworkers (mainly Hispanic laborers) look on with curiosity, again highlights the discordant glocal elements that come together in Bouchareb's cinematic tableau. Nevertheless, Garnett's independent wage-earning stage is brief, terminated when Agati manages to convince the ranch owner to fire him. Additionally, the peaceful and ordered life of the cattle ranch on the border is subsumed by the chaotic and violent territory controlled on both sides of the border by Terence, who constantly harasses Garnett to come back to work for him, reminding him that he owes his amazing "business" to his once lawless friend:

> The anchor baby business is booming, the fucking wetbacks pay me seven Gs so the little ones can be born on this side then shazam, the whole beano family gets to come over and stay . . . we throw in a free car seat, a free gift for Mamacita . . . God damn, I love being in America . . . I owe it all to you, you could have ratted us out, but you didn't . . . you stood by your family . . . You need to come back to us, you aren't made for cleaning shit . . . Let me send you to a safe place in Mexico.

Garnett protests, replying: "You don't owe me anything, I have a new path, a new life . . . I have Allah." Whereupon Terence remarks: "What is Allah going to do for you? . . . You know that sheriff is going to try to send you back to prison, is that what you want?" The tensions between Terence's and Agati's separate laws pertaining to forcing human movement, curtailing or fostering mobility, and consumption of capital, goods, and markets in the glocal arena, reveal that "one of the prominent effects of glocalization is [that the] human condition [is] suspended between two universes," one with power and the other devoid of it. Each of these spheres has its own "distinct set of norms and rules."[62]

Two Men in Town exposes financescapes as driven by "the neoliberal alliance between capitalism and the state apparatus: all numbers of smooth flows have been territorialized and institutionalized through regimes."[63] Garnett's precarious financial reality entraps him in situations from which he cannot free himself. He is kept from earning wages legitimately and refuses to enter into illegal dealings with Terence because not only will this jeopardize his parole, but it also morally goes against his newly adopted code of Muslim conduct.

Agati's and Terence's regimes control spaces of work and money making in the film. In Garnett's case, his access to work on the ranch, approved by the state, is now impeded by Agati's local rule of law, and also the illegal dealings of Terence's sphere, driven by "networks and flows across national borders."[64] Both these regimes present insurmountable hurdles and impossibilities for the parolee. Therefore, Garnett becomes a victim of what Appadurai notes is a primary factor of disjunctive financescapes: "predatory mobility," wherein the individual has no recourse against the socioeconomic forces that dictate his or her ability to move within the system.[65] Garnett can neither move in the approved capital flow of the US, nor engage with the illegal dealings across the border. He remains fixed in immobility. This hard, cold fact is revealed in a scene where parole officer Emily Smith confronts Agati after Garnett's termination on the ranch:

Emily: Why are you wrecking everything that Garnett is trying to do? Why did you get him fired? He's broken no laws, none. You're not letting your paranoia run away with you, Sheriff, are you?
Agati: Whoa, back the truck up, we're not in Kansas anymore, Toto, you understand me? Maybe you haven't noticed, but I don't just come into work, twiddle my thumbs, and wait for something bad to happen.
Emily: The state granted him parole.
Agati: The state did, I didn't.
Emily: Well, that's not your prerogative. It's my job to make those eighteen years count for something.
Agati: Eighteen years? My deputy is still dead. You set [Garnett] up at the border where he grew up, running drugs and shooting at cops.

Agati and Emily's conversation marks the definitive framework of Garnett's *mektoub*. Deadlocked in a confrontation that pits justice against injustice, order against disorder, and the possibility of redemption against the impossibility of changing the former inmate's destiny, Bouchareb's world-in-motion remains chaotic. Garnett's ability to access his idealized space of the white-picket-fenced American dream is an illusion.

After Terence attacks Garnett's love interest, Teresa, in his effort to convince the ex-convict to come back to a life of crime, the parolee decides to take matters into his own hands. Stalking the drug dealer from a mountain hideout overlooking his desert operation, Garnett waits for his prey, which he captures by running his motorcycle into Terence's car. Hauling the thug out of his vehicle, Garnett savagely beats him into unconsciousness. He then picks up a rock and mercilessly bashes Terence's head in, killing him. Garnett walks to a nearby creek to wash himself, as we previously saw him do before praying. Cleaning himself of the crime, though, is impossible, as he has abandoned his faith. He is lost in the chaotic sociocultural and political disjunctures of the desert space. The film ends where it began, in a *mektoub* that has been written and cannot be altered.

On a universal level, Bouchareb's film shows us that in our contemporary world-in-motion, the local and the global are intertwined, providing means of movement for some and imprisonment for others. Individuals are impeded by infractions of justice, obligations to others, and systems of law and order that are not grounded in traditional, local structures nor in cosmopolitan nation-states. In the twenty-first century, the tides of disjunctures that influence the socioeconomic, cultural, and political landscapes of our being-in-the-world are constantly washing ashore as we seek to navigate life in the vast oceans, or in the case of *Two Men in Town*, deserts, of the everyday.

NOTES

1. Arjun Appadurai, "Grassroots Globalization and the Research Imagination," *Public Culture* 12, no. 1 (2000): 5.
2. Ibid., 5.
3. Ibid., 6.
4. Arjun Appadurai, *Modernity at Large: Cultural Dimensions of Globalization* (Minneapolis: Minnesota University Press, 1996), 27.
5. Appadurai, "Grassroots Globalization and the Research Imagination," 5 (emphasis added).
6. Appadurai, *Modernity at Large*, 3.
7. As explained in Martin Heidegger, *Being and Time*, trans. John Macquarrie and Edward Robinson (New York: Harper, 1962), as well as in the phenomenological philosophy and writings of Maurice Merleau-Ponty and Jean-Paul Sartre.
8. Mark Meyers, "Liminality and the Problem of Being-in-the-World: Reflections on Sartre and Merleau-Ponty," *Sartre Studies International* 14, no. 1 (2008): 79.
9. Kwame Anthony Appiah, *Cosmopolitanism: Ethics in a World of Strangers* (New York: W. W. Norton, 2006), xv.
10. Appadurai, *Modernity at Large*, 33.
11. Appadurai, "Grassroots Globalization and the Research Imagination," 5.
12. Appadurai, *Modernity at Large*, 33.
13. Ibid., 35.
14. The list of films that could be defined as exemplifying cinéma-monde is extensive. In my area of expertise, many films from North and West Africa released in the 2000s fit the criteria of cinéma-monde films. See my *New African Cinema* (New Brunswick, NJ: Rutgers University Press, 2017).
15. See Chapter 2 of this volume.
16. Florence Martin, "*Cinéma-Monde*: De-orbiting Maghrebi Cinema," *Contemporary French Civilization* 41, no. 3–4 (2016): 463.
17. Dayna Oscherwitz, "Looking beyond Afropolitanism: Globalization, Francophonie and the Work of Abderrahmane Sissako," in *Cinéma-Monde: Decentred Perspectives on Global Filmmaking*, ed. Michael Gott and Thibaut Schilt (Edinburgh: Edinburgh University Press, 2018): 106.
18. See Martin, "*Cinéma-Monde*"; Bill Marshall, "*Cinéma-Monde?* Towards a Concept of Francophone Cinema," *Francosphères* 1, no. 1 (2012): 35–51.
19. See Chapter 7 of this volume.
20. Bouchareb's film is a remake of the Franco-Italian *Deux hommes dans la ville/Two Men in Town* (José Giovanni, 1973), starring Alain Delon (also the producer) and Jean Gabin.
21. I have accessed this film through several streaming services and none of the versions include subtitles in any language for scenes taking place in Spanish. Commenting on the languages that he had to learn, Whitaker notes: "I studied Arabic extensively with an imam so I can do the entire prayer of Islam . . . in fact, Rachid didn't put most of it in the movie, but in some scenes I would be speaking five minutes of Arabic. I also had to brush up on my Spanish to play this part. Lots of different challenges." Stephen Dalton, "Forest Whitaker Talks about Learning Arabic and Playing an Islamic Convert in *Two Men in Town*," *The National*, 12 February 2014, https://www.thenational.ae/arts-culture/forest-whitaker-talks-about-learning-arabic-and-playing-an-islamic-convert-in-two-men-in-town-1.319806.
22. Also a trope in *Little Senegal* and *London River*, in which characters find themselves in foreign spaces, cut off from family, kith, and kin, where they must navigate hurdles and challenges construed along the lines of nationality, skin color, language, place of origin, and so on.

23. John C. Cross and Alfonso Hernández Hernández, "Place, Identity, and Deviance: A Community-Based Approach to Understanding the Relationship between Deviance and Place," *Deviant Behavior* 32, no. 6 (2011): 508.
24. "Mektoub," CNRTL website, accessed 27 March 2020, http://www.cnrtl.fr/definition/mektoub.
25. Victor Roudometof, "The Glocal and Global Studies," *Globalizations* 12, no. 5 (2015): 776.
26. Appadurai, *Modernity at Large*.
27. Henk van Houtum, Olivier Kramsch, and Wolfgang Zierhofer, ed., *B/ordering Space* (Aldershot: Ashgate, 2005), 3.
28. Cross and Hernández Hernández, "Place, Identity, and Deviance," 504.
29. Michel Foucault, *Discipline and Punish: The Birth of the Prison*, trans. Alan Sheridan (New York: Vintage, 1979): 143–4, cited in Cross and Hernández Hernández, "Place, Identity, and Deviance," 506–7.
30. Houtum et al., ed., *B/ordering Space*, 1 (original emphasis).
31. See Chapter 7 of this volume.
32. "Health Indicator Report of New Mexico Population—Race/Ethnicity," New Mexico's Indicator-Based Information System, 31 January 2019, https://ibis.health.state.nm.us/indicator/view/NMPopDemoRacEth.NM.html; "Religious Landscape Study: Adults in New Mexico," Pew Research Center, accessed 27 March 2020, https://www.pewforum.org/religious-landscape-study/state/new-mexico.
33. Here I'm drawing on Gilles Deleuze and Félix Guattari's concepts as explored in their seminal work *Capitalisme et schizophrénie, vol. 2: Mille plateaux* (Paris: Minuit, 1980).
34. Oscherwitz, "Looking beyond Afropolitanism," 87.
35. Here I refer to another celebrated concept proposed by Deleuze and Guattari in *Mille plateaux*. In the 1990s, "deterritorialization" was used to positively describe the postcolonial potential of the openness of subjecthood for characters in novels written by authors from emerging nations.
36. In the francophone literary context, see recent works by Maryse Condé, Louis-Philippe Dalembert, Fatou Diome, and Faoud Laroui. These works, as well as many African films, paint dire pictures of the impossibility of free movement in a globalized world.
37. Ursula K. Heise, "Deterritorialization and Eco-Cosmopolitanism," in *Literature and Globalization: A Reader*, ed. Liam Connell and Nicky Marsh (Abingdon: Routledge, 2011): 159.
38. Appadurai, *Modernity at Large*, 33.
39. Ibid., 34.
40. Carolina Sanchez-Palencia, "Cosmopolitan (Dis)encounters: The Local and the Global in Anthony Minghella's *Breaking and Entering* and Rachid Bouchareb's *London River*," *Cultura, Lenguaje y Representación / Culture, Language and Representation* 11 (2013): 113.
41. Anne McClintock, *Imperial Leather: Race, Gender, and Sexuality in the Colonial Contest* (New York: Routledge, 1995), 30.
42. Appadurai, *Modernity at Large*, 33–4.
43. McClintock, *Imperial Leather*, 32.
44. Sa'id Bin Ali Bin Wahf Al-Qahtani, *Fortress of the Muslim: Invocations from the Qur'an and Sunnah* (Algiers: Dar Beni Mezghana, 2018). There are multiple editions of this book published in various countries in the Arab world.
45. Bouchareb is referring to Whitaker's portrayal of Idi Amin in *The Last King of Scotland* (2006), among others. Whitaker would later portray Desmond Tutu in *The Forgiven* (2017). For the article in French, see Renaud de Rochebrune, "Rachid Bouchareb: 'L'Amerique est une terre d'Islam,'" *Jeune Afrique*, 20 May 2014, https://www.jeuneafrique.com/133341/culture/rachid-bouchareb-l-am-rique-est-une-terre-d-islam.

46. Appadurai, *Modernity at Large*, 35.
47. Cross and Hernández Hernández, "Place, Identity, and Deviance," 508.
48. Asef Bayat and Linda Herrera, "Introduction: Being Young and Muslim in Neoliberal Times," in *Being Young and Muslim: New Cultural Politics in the Global South and North*, ed. Linda Herrera and Asef Bayat (New York: Oxford University Press, 2010): 3.
49. Dalton, "Forest Whitaker Talks about Learning Arabic."
50. Cross and Hernández Hernández, "Place, Identity, and Deviance," 509.
51. Ibid., 510.
52. Al-Qahtani, *Fortress of the Muslim*. On the first page the author notes: "This book is an abridgment of my earlier work entitled *Adh-Dhikr wad-Du'a wal-'Ilaj bir-Ruqyah mina'-Kitab was-Sunnah*. In order to make it small and easily portable, I have chosen only the section on words of remembrance for this abridgment."
53. Asma Afsaruddin, "Sunnah," *Encyclopaedia Britannica*, accessed 30 March 2020, https://www.britannica.com/topic/Sunnah.
54. "Sunnah," Oxford Islamic Studies Online, accessed 30 March 2020, http://www.oxfordislamicstudies.com/article/opr/t243/e332.
55. See Chapter 7 of this volume.
56. Ibid.
57. Meyers, "Liminality and the Problem of Being-in-the-World," 84.
58. Al-Qahtani, *Fortress of the Muslim*, 22.
59. "Sunnah," Oxford Islamic Studies Online.
60. Appadurai, "Grassroots Globalization and the Research Imagination," 16.
61. Appadurai, *Modernity at Large*, 35.
62. Roudometof, "The Glocal and Global Studies," 778.
63. Keith Woodward and John Paul Jones II, "On the Border with Deleuze and Guattari," in Houtum et al., ed., *B/ordering Space*, 240.
64. Ibid., 240.
65. Appadurai, "Grassroots Globalization and the Research Imagination," 16.

Appendix: Filmography of Rachid Bouchareb

Compiled by Gemma King

Title	Year	Production countries	Languages
Le Flic de Belleville/ Belleville Cop	2018	France	Chinese, English, French, Spanish
A Belleville police officer (Omar Sy) travels to the US and teams up with a Miami detective (Luis Guzmán) to help investigate his friend's murder.			
Louisette	2018	France	French
Documentary (25 minutes) featuring Louisette Ighilahriz, a former FLN militant who fought for Algeria's independence and was tortured by the French army.			
La Route d'Istanbul/ Road to Istanbul	2016	Belgium, France	French
A Belgian woman (Astrid Whetnall) discovers her daughter has run away to join Islamic State and travels to the Syrian border in an attempt to bring her back.			
Champions de France/ France's Champions	2015–16	France	French
Documentary mini-series of forty-five 2-minute episodes about French national sporting champions of diverse cultural origins.			
Frères d'armes/ Brothers in Arms	2014–15	France	French
Documentary mini-series of fifty 2-minute episodes exploring the soldiers from French-controlled overseas territories and other international origins who fought for France during World Wars I and II. Released on the 100th anniversary of the beginning of World War I and the seventieth anniversary of the Normandy landings.			
La Voie de l'ennemi/ Two Men in Town	2014	Algeria, Belgium, France, USA	Arabic, English, Spanish
A New Mexico parole officer (Brenda Blethyn) forms an unlikely friendship with an African American Muslim ex-prisoner (Forest Whittaker) despite the disapproval of the local sheriff (Harvey Keitel). An adaptation of José Giovanni's 1973 Franco-Italian film *Deux hommes dans la ville/ Two Men in Town* transplanted to a US–Mexico border context.			
Just Like a Woman	2012	France, UK, USA	English
Two women—a white American (Sienna Miller) and a naturalized Arab American (Golshifteh Farahani)—escape their oppressive lives in Chicago and drive to Santa Fe to compete in a belly dancing competition.			

(Continued)

Title	Year	Production countries	Languages
Hors la loi/Outside the Law	2010	Algeria, Belgium, France, Italy, Tunisia	Arabic, French
In the 1950s three brothers and their mother lose their home in Algeria and migrate to France, where one brother (Roschdy Zem) enlists to fight in the Indochina War and the two others (Jamel Debbouze and Sami Bouajila) join a branch of the FLN (Algerian National Liberation Front) based in their outer-Paris shantytown.			
Oscars	2010	France, USA	French
Documentary short (2 minutes) about switching from limousines to hybrid cars at the US Academy Awards. Part of a collection of thirty short films by different directors entitled *Télégrammes visuels: les cinéastes s'engagent pour l'environnement/Visual Telegrams: Filmmakers Stand Up for the Environment*.			
Exhibitions	2009	Algeria, France	French
Documentary short (8 minutes) about "human zoos" consisting of exhibitions of colonized peoples that were held in France and other European countries from the early nineteenth century up until World War II. It is one of ten films that make up the collection *Afrique vue par.../Africa as Seen by...*			
Houme/Espoir	2009	France	French
Short film (2 minutes) set during the Algerian War of Independence that was released as part of the collection *Vivre Ensemble: 10 cinéastes contre le racisme ordinaire/Coexist: 10 Filmmakers against Everyday Racism*.			
London River	2009	Algeria, France, UK	Arabic, English, French, Mandinka
In the wake of the 2005 London terrorist attacks, a woman from Guernsey (Brenda Blethyn) and a Malian man (Sotigui Kouyaté) unite in a shared search for their missing children.			
Indigènes/Days of Glory	2006	Algeria, Belgium, France, Morocco	Arabic, French
Three Algerian *tirailleurs* (colonial infantrymen enlisted to the French Army, Sami Bouajila, Jamel Debbouze, and Roschdy Zem) and one Moroccan *goumier* (Moroccan soldier enlisted to auxiliary units of the French Army, Samy Naceri) are sent to fight in France in World War II.			
L'Ami y'a bon/The Colonial Friend	2004	Algeria, France, Germany	French
Animated short about the Senegalese *tirailleurs* drafted to fight in the blitzkrieg invasion of France by Nazi Germany during World War II. Included on the DVD of *Days of Glory*, released two years later.			
Le Vilain Petit Poussin/The Ugly Chick	2003	France	N/A
Documentary short exposing the poultry industry through a focus on one chick.			
Little Senegal	2001	Algeria, France, Germany	Arabic, English, French, Wolof
A Senegalese man (Sotigui Kouyaté) leaves his job as a guide in the Maison des esclaves at Gorée and travels to the US to retrace the steps of his enslaved ancestors, finding a distant relative (Sharon Hope) in New York City.			
L'Honneur de ma famille/My Family's Honor	1998	France	Arabic, French
Made-for-television film in which two Roubaix women—one white (Karole Rocher) and one of Maghrebi descent (Seloua Hamse)—secretly work in a nightclub over the Belgian border and dream of traveling to Goa.			

Title	Year	Production countries	Languages
Poussières de vie/ Dust of Life	1995	Algeria, Belgium, France, Germany, Hong Kong	French, Vietnamese
Following the 1975 fall of Saigon during the Vietnam War, the son of a black American soldier and a South Vietnamese woman (Daniel Guyant) attempts to escape a re-education camp in North Vietnam.			
Des Années déchirées/ Torn Years	1993	Algeria, France	French
Made-for-television film about the struggles of two former FLN fighters in the face of a changing Algerian society.			
Déposez armes/ Lay Down Arms	1992	France, Tunisia	French
Rarely screened made-for-television film set in Tunisia.			
Cheb	1991	Algeria, France	French
A young Algerian man raised in France (Mourad Bounaas) is deported to Algeria and faced with living in a country he does not know.			
Bâton Rouge/ Baton Rouge	1985	France	English, French
Three young men from the outskirts of Paris—two of Maghrebi origin (Hammou Graïa and Pierre-Loup Rajot) and one majority-ethnic (Jacques Penot)—concoct a scam that grants them passage to the US, where they make their way to Baton Rouge.			
Peut-être la mer/ Perhaps the Sea	1983	France	French
Short film about two French-born children of Algerian descent who find themselves stranded in Le Havre while trying to reach Algeria.			
Le Banc *	1978		
La Chute	1977		
La Pièce	1976		

* No further details about Bouchareb's first three short films have been found.

Index

3B Productions, 8, 9–10, 38n27, 38n29

accented cinema, 13, 14, 205
Adi, Yasmina, 194n21
African Americans, 29, 33, 34–5, 36, 44, 49, 53, 88, 102, 104, 105, 106, 110, 111, 114, 115, 136, 170, 171, 172, 176, 220, 222, 224–5
Aftab, Kaleem, 132
Agamben, Giorgio, 156–7
airports, 44, 50, 52, 56
Al-Qahtani, Sa'id Bin Ali Bin Wahf: *Fortress of the Muslim*, 224–5, 227–8
Algeria
  colonization, 5, 125
  FIS (Front Islamique du Salut), 66
  FLN (National Liberation Front), 82, 109, 110, 125–6, 181, 186, 188, 189, 192, 193n2
  Family Law Code, 66
  feminism, 66, 68, 69–70, 72
  International Film Festival of Algiers (1–9 December 2018), 105
  Islamism, 30, 66, 67
  MNA (National Algerian Movement), 109, 125–6
  Pan African Festival (1969), 111
  pieds-noirs, 1, 123, 182
  Sétif massacre (1945), 117, 124–5, 127, 128, 181, 182, 183
  and Vietnam compared, 120
Algerian War of Independence, 1, 3, 82, 97n27, 100, 108, 109, 117–18, 119, 125, 128, 181, 182, 192
Allouache, Merzak: *Salut Cousin! / Hi Cousin!* 83
American culture, 2, 6, 45, 100–1, 102, 103–4, 115
American dream, 45, 102–3, 121, 136, 187, 222, 224, 226, 227, 228
American Indians, 111, 210–11
Ami y'a bon, L' / The Colonial Friend, 6, 113, 151
Anderson, Benedict, 115n10, 153

Anh, Duyên: *La Colline de Fanta / Fanta Hill*, 29, 151, 163
Appadurai, Arjun, 215, 216, 217, 219, 221, 223–4, 226, 229, 230
Appiah, Kwame, 215, 216, 221
Arabic, 57, 140
"Arabs": representation of, 118–28, 140
archetypes, 2, 121, 137, 186, 189
archipelagos, 25–6, 27–32, 36
Audé, Françoise, 173, 175
Augé, Marc, 48
Austin, James, 43

Badache, Raphaël, 173
Bakhtin, Mikhail, 84
Balibar, Étienne, 84
Bancel, Nicolas, 184
banlieue films, 12, 43–4, 45–6, 135, 136, 141
Barlet, Olivier, 124, 126, 195n56
Barnes, Leslie, 13
Basinger, Jeanine, 87
Bâton Rouge / Baton Rouge, 12, 28, 121, 210
 dialogue, 39n40
 funding, 8
 rencontres (encounters), 33
 as a road movie, 107, 212n8
 themes, 6, 30, 41, 42–3, 44–52, 58–9, 60–1, 64, 83, 101–3, 104, 135–6
Beaucarne, Christophe, 204
Bedjaoui, Ahmed, 210
Bendjedid, President Chadli, 66
Berghahn, Daniela, 42
"beur" cinema, 12, 42, 44, 82
"beurs," 1, 65–6, 87, 119, 122
 "Marche des beurs" (1983), 37n17, 111
 see also Maghrebi-French people
Beverly Hills Cop series, 93, 105
Bigot, Jean, 8, 19n3

Black Panthers, 111, 224–5
Blancan, Bernard, 109, 117
Blanchard, Pascal, 9, 116n25, 184
Blethyn, Brenda, 11, 12, 36, 54, 92, 132, 218
borders, 56–8, 60, 137, 229–30
 and citizenship, 53
 definition, 51
 and identity, 54
 mobile, 52–8
 and order, 219
 porous, 222
 road movies, 42, 49, 51–2
 Westerns, 92
 see also boundaries
Bouajila, Sami, 9, 11, 12, 109, 117, 123, 125, 181, 188, 191
Bouchareb, Rachid
 background, 1–2, 13, 100
 César award, 3
 creative process, 27
 early career, 3–12
 as a global French filmmaker, 12–16
 influences, 26, 82–3, 101, 102, 106, 107–10, 114–15, 120–1
 Oscar nominations, 3, 115, 117, 194n21
 vision, 28
Boudraa, Chafia, 11, 74, 199, 209
Boukhrief, Nicolas: *Made in France*, 144n5
boundaries, 13, 42, 49, 52, 57, 171–2, 210–11; *see also* borders
Brakni, Rachida, 9, 72
Bréhat, Jean, 8, 10
Breton, Émile, 171–2
bridges, 47–8, 50–1, 55, 142, 143, 146n26, 174, 198
Broe, Dennis, 186
Brothers in Arms see *Frères d'armes / Brothers in Arms*

buddy films, 93, 95, 105–6, 198
Butler, Judith, 133, 147n34

Cadé, Michel, 141
Cannes Film Festival, 3, 10, 15, 29, 91, 117, 118, 125, 127, 182, 185, 187, 194n21
Carter, Matthew, 90
cartography *see* maps and mapping
casting, 10–11, 14, 35, 136–7, 191, 199, 202, 218
Champions de France / France's Champions, 9
Chang, Justin, 203
Chapier, Henri, 91
Charef, Mehdi, 82, 101
  Le Thé au harem d'Archimède / Tea in the Harem, 43
Cheb, 8, 28
  Cannes Film Festival premier, 91
  as a road movie, 107
  themes, 6, 13, 30, 64, 65–70, 79, 87, 101, 103, 113, 169
  as a war film, 87, 88
  Western iconography in, 90–2
Chicago, 75, 78, 198, 209
Chirac, Bernadette, 117, 182
Chirac, President Jacques, 117, 182, 183, 184
Christianity, 133, 137, 140, 141, 142, 159
Cimino, Michael: *The Deer Hunter*, 89, 120
cinéma-monde, 2, 15, 25, 32, 34, 41, 42, 60, 167, 168, 169, 217; *see also* transnational cinema
Cinemascope, 92, 220
Clair, René, 168
Cohan, Steven, 76
Collinson, Gary, 146n30
Colonial Friend, The see *Ami y'a bon, L' / The Colonial Friend*

colonization, 5, 117, 125, 184, 192, 211
  and decolonization, 36, 82, 128, 188–9
confinement, 89, 154–5, 158, 159
  cinema of, 162–3
Conley, Tom, 58
Connelly, Thomas J., 162
Cooper, Nicola, 182
Coppola, Francis Ford
  Apocalypse Now, 125, 127, 185
  Godfather, The, 82, 107, 108–9, 120, 190
cosmopolitanism, 40–1, 216, 221, 222, 223, 224
Craven, Alice Mikal, 189
crime fiction, 185–6, 188
Croix, La (newspaper), 120, 122, 123
Cross, John, 218, 226
cultural mixings, 2, 4–6, 9, 10, 13, 26, 27, 28, 29, 34, 51, 54, 71, 74–5, 78, 103, 104, 105–6, 112, 119, 141–2, 198, 203, 205, 211, 220; *see also* ethnic diversity; miscegenation
Cyprus, 56, 58

Davies Hayon, Kaya, 208
Davis, Andy: *The Fugitive*, 86
Days of Glory see *Indigènes / Days of Glory*
de Palma, Brian
  Scarface, 190
  The Untouchables, 109–10
Debbouze, Jamel, 7, 9, 12, 86, 117, 121, 122, 123, 125, 181, 188, 191
Deleuze, Gilles, 115n4, 233n33, 233n35
dialogue, 13, 15, 35, 94, 122–3, 166, 167, 168, 178, 187, 200–1, 206, 208
diasporas, 34, 83, 136, 151, 164n2
disjunctures, 216–17, 219, 221–3, 229–31
Dixon, Wheeler Winston, 131

Donadey, Anne, 64, 109–10, 165n20, 189, 190, 195n41
Doueiri, Ziad: *L'Insulte / The Insult*, 10
Douin, Jean-Luc, 121
Doussot, Marion, 211n2
Dridi, Karim, 9, 101, 145n17
Dumont, Bruno, 10
Dust of Life see *Poussières de vie / Dust of Life*
Duvivier, Julien, 168

Eberwein, Robert, 87
Eleftheriotis, Dimitris, 42, 50
Elsaesser, Thomas, 95
Emerson, Caryl, 84, 85
encounters *see rencontres*
Enemy Way see *Voie de l'ennemi, La / Two Men in Town*
English language, 110, 143, 166, 170, 171, 176, 178, 217, 218
epics, 107, 165n20, 165n23, 190
ethnic diversity, 29, 71
ethnoscapes (Appadurai), 223–5, 226
Exhibitions (short documentary film), 116n25
Express, L' (newspaper), 123
Ezra, Elizabeth, 14, 25, 34, 41

Fanon, Frantz, 188–9
Farahani, Golshifteh, 74, 112, 113, 198, 213n25
Farhadi, Asghar, 15
Faucon, Philippe
  Dans la vie / Two Ladies, 145n17, 146n29
  La Désintégration / The Disintegration, 147n37
feminism, 65, 72, 112
  Algeria, 66, 68, 69–70, 72
  belly dancing and, 76, 77
  post-colonial feminist films *see Just Like a Woman*

Ferroukhi, Ismaël: *Le Grand Voyage / The Grand Voyage*, 60
financescapes (Appadurai), 216, 229, 230
Firpo, Christina Elizabeth, 159
Flic de Belleville, Le / Belleville Cop, 6, 28, 121
  as a buddy cop film, 93–5
  dialogue, 13, 85–6, 94
  themes, 169
  transnationality of, 10, 12, 14, 101, 105
forgetfulness (Ricoeur), 152, 153, 157, 164
Foucault, Michel, 219
France
  anti-colonialism, 119, 126
  armed forces, 29, 35–6
  *banlieue*s, 100–1
  CNC (Centre national du cinéma et de l'image animée), 8, 15, 21n32, 169
  colonialism, 3, 5, 59, 82, 100, 117, 119, 122, 125, 127, 128, 136, 159, 169, 178, 184
  double peine (double punishment) law, 30, 87
  film industry, 2, 7–8
  identities, 101, 103, 183–4; *see also* Frenchness
  immigration, 1, 100, 183–4; *see also* "*beurs*"; Maghrebi-French people
  Institut français, 15
  post-colonialism, 34, 40, 136, 184
  racism, 37n17, 191
  slavery, 136
  Superior Council of the Audiovisual (Conseil supérieur de l'audiovisuel), 127
  youth riots (2005), 184
  see also Cannes Film Festival; Paris

France Télévisions, 127
France's Champions see *Champions de France / France's Champions*
franco-zones, 168
francophone cinema, 13, 25
francospheres, 15, 40, 60, 61n4, 167–9, 177
French language, 2, 6, 10, 54, 142, 143, 169, 171
   International Organization of La Francophonie, 184
French New Wave cinema, 85
Frenchness, 4, 120, 122, 135, 136
Frères d'armes / Brothers in Arms, 9
funding, 2, 8, 12, 14, 15–16, 95, 169, 191

Gamal, Samia, 205
gangster movies, 107, 126, 185–6;
Gatlif, Tony: *Exils / Exiles*, 60
gender
   and disempowerment, 65–70, 223
   and epic genre, 165n20
   and friendship, 70–8, 112–13
   male subjectivities of, 197–8
   and oppression, 171
   stereotypes of, 64, 69, 70, 71, 72, 76, 77, 79, 190, 199, 200–1, 202, 205, 206, 208–9, 210, 211
   see also women
genres, 82–96, 199
   and double-voicing, 84–5
   Hollywood's influence on, 95–6
   see also buddy films; gangster movies; road movies; war films; Westerns
Gesbert, Bernard, 29
Giovanni, José: *Deux hommes dans la ville*, 91, 92–3
Gledhill, Christine, 97n16
Glissant, Édouard, 25, 103, 105

globalization, 18
   and depiction of terrorism, 131–44
   and identity, 220, 229
   and motion, 222
   and movement, 41, 215–16, 223
   neoliberal, 105–6, 226
glocal, 219, 220–1
Godard, Jean-Luc, 85
Gorée Island (Senegal), 53–4, 113, 136, 171, 172, 176, 177, 178
Gott, Michael, 32, 34, 168, 169, 217
Graziano, Manlio, 51
griots (storytellers), 137, 170
Gross, Larry, 93
Gruson, Luc, 122
Guardian, The (newspaper), 132
Guattari, Félix, 115n4, 233n33, 233n35
Guédiguian, Robert, 11
Guerdjou, Bourlem: *Vivre au paradis / Living in Paradise*, 9
Guernsey, 54, 141, 178
Guichard, Louis, 170
Guzmán, Luis, 10, 11, 12, 92, 93, 105, 219

Halle, Randall, 15, 50–1
Hannoum, Abdelmajid, 165n7
Harbi, Mohammed, 127
Hargreaves, Alec G., 6–7, 28, 101, 191, 213n25
Hark, Ina Rae, 76
Hayward, Susan, 186–7
Heise, Ursula, 223
Hernández, Alfonso Hernández, 218, 226, 227
heroes, 120, 121, 187, 188
Higbee, Will, 7, 43, 45, 143, 208
Hjort, Mette, 32, 34
Holden, Stephen, 132
Hollywood, 14, 74, 75, 83, 85, 89, 90, 95, 131, 168, 197, 206

INDEX 243

Honneur de ma famille, L' / My Family's Honor, 6, 11, 28
   gender/cultural differences, 64–5, 70–3, 79, 209
Hors la loi / Outside the Law, 3, 6, 7, 11, 13, 14, 15, 28, 86, 120, 124–5
   archetypes, 121, 186, 189
   Cannes Film Festival, 29, 118, 125, 127, 182, 185, 194n21
   criticisms, 110, 117–18, 126–7, 128, 181, 182–3, 184, 185, 186, 189, 190, 192
   dialogue, 187
   as a gangster film, 107–9, 185–92
   names of characters, 212n6
   politicization of, 187, 192–3
   themes, 29, 36, 56, 64, 82, 128, 169, 181, 187, 188, 191
   title, 188
   trailers, 187–8
human rights, 6, 31, 66, 111

identity, 100, 103
   and belonging, 164, 227, 229
   and borders, 54
   double culture, 4, 40
   and labeling, 218
   national, 183
   see also Frenchness
ideoscapes (Appadurai), 216, 226
immigration, 26, 28, 83, 85, 100, 110, 122, 123, 124
   France, 1, 100, 183–4
   United States, 30, 111–12, 113
Indigènes / Days of Glory, 3, 6, 13, 14, 28, 35–6, 36n1, 64, 86
   Arab identity, 121
   archetypes, 121
   Cannes Film Festival, 29, 117, 187
   casting, 11–12

   criticism, 126
   dialogue, 122–3
   ending, 163–4
   French identity, 122
   impact, 117
   political significance, 182
   reaction to, 181–2
   themes, 29, 82, 106, 107, 119–20, 122–3, 128, 169
   trailers, 187
interzones (Halle), 50–1
intimiste films, 17, 64, 78, 79, 204, 211, 213n17, 213n19
Islam, 34–5, 60, 134, 139, 140, 141, 142, 218, 220, 224, 226–8;
   see also mosques; Muslims
Islamophobia, 1, 110, 111, 140
Islamism, 30, 34, 66, 67
islands, 62n44; *see also* Cyprus; Gorée Island; Guernsey
Istanbul, 58, 60

Jarmakani, Amira, 205, 207, 209
Jeffries, Stuart, 132
Johnston, Cristina, 25
Just Like a Woman, 6, 11, 13, 28, 64, 85, 86, 101, 107
   belly dancing, 74, 75, 76–7, 78, 112, 201, 205–9
   camera work, 199, 201, 204, 206, 208, 209
   casting, 202
   dialogue, 200–1, 206, 208
   as a feminized buddy/road movie, 198–205, 210–11
   intimiste nature of, 204–5, 211
   lesbian subtext, 203, 209
   as a postcolonial feminist film, 197–8, 209–10, 211
   script, 212n2
   themes, 14, 30, 73–8, 79, 112–13, 169, 203, 204

Kaganski, Serge, 114, 173
Kandiyoti, Deniz, 209
Kealhofer-Kemp, Leslie, 70–1, 204, 209
Kechiche, Abdellatif, 82
    L'Esquive / Games of Love and Chance, 146n24
    La Graine et le mulet / Couscous, 208
Keitel, Harvey, 92, 110, 202, 218
Khadra, Yasmina, 13, 218
Khouri, Callie, 213n25
King, Martin Luther, 111
Koran see *Qur'an*
Kouyaté, Sotigui, 11, 36, 54, 114, 137, 169, 170, 173
Kramsch, Olivier, 219
Kubrick, Stanley
    Full Metal Jacket, 87–8
    Paths of Glory, 106

Laclau, Ernesto, 96n8
Laderman, David, 42, 46, 91, 199
landscape, 49, 57, 90, 91, 92, 107, 111, 112, 138, 142, 153, 199, 201, 204, 211, 217, 218, 220, 223
language
    contact zones, 168
    and culture, 142
    multilingualism, 10, 11–12, 86, 94, 137, 167, 178
    translanguaging, 20n23
    unanchored, 169
    see also Arabic; English language; French language; Wolof language
Lanzoni, Rémi Fournier, 135
Laxe, Oliver, 15
Lazreg, Marnia, 69
Lemaire, Sandrine, 184
Lethal Weapon series, 93, 94, 105

Letort, Delphine, 34, 54, 136, 171, 172
Levine, Alison J. Murray, 43
Libération (newspaper), 120, 126
Libiot, Éric, 195n50
Little Senegal, 6, 11, 28, 30, 86, 104, 166–78
    casting, 136–7
    as cinéma-monde, 177
    cultural references, 114
    as decentered cinema, 176–8
    dialogue, 35, 166, 178
    financing, 176
    geographical focal point of, 176
    intimiste nature of, 213n19
    rencontres, 33
    tree symbolism, 167, 170, 172–5, 176
    themes, 27, 33–5, 52–4, 59–60, 113–14, 136–7, 169–76, 176–7, 178, 232n22
Lockard, Joe, 188–9
Loeb, Édouard, 187
London bombings (2005), 132
London River, 6, 36n1, 178
    archetypes, 137
    casting, 11, 36, 92, 132, 137
    criticism, 132
    cultural references, 114
    global nature of, 143
    intimiste nature of, 213n19
    language, 11, 12, 13
    religion, 139–42, 143
    themes, 26, 31, 36, 54–5, 59, 60, 134, 137–9, 169, 232n22
    tree symbolism, 139, 140, 173
Lorelle, Olivier, 33, 35–6, 197, 218
Luca, Lionnel, 181–2

McDonald, Christopher, 202
McGonagle, Joseph, 71
Madsen, Michael, 202

Maghrebi-French people, 1, 3–4, 5, 6–7, 8, 9, 12, 19n6, 26, 28, 30, 37n17, 45, 100, 103, 106
   and gender, 71–2
   as stereotypes, 70–1, 73
   as war heroes, 120, 121, 187
   see also "beurs"
Maira, Sunaina, 76
Malcolm X, 111, 224–5
Mann, Michael: *Heat*, 109
maps and mapping, 2, 4, 16, 41, 50, 58–61, 160
Marshall, Bill, 25, 42, 168, 217–18
Martigny, Vincent, 183
Martin, Elaine, 147n35
Martin, Florence, 15, 217
Martin, Thomas, 184
Maslin, Janet, 212n15
Mazierska, Ewa, 212n4, 212n13
mediascapes (Appadurai), 216, 226
memory, 151, 152, 155, 156, 159–60, 161, 162–3
   event of, 183
   memento mori, 18, 152, 153, 154, 159, 160, 163
   moment of, 183
   see also forgetfulness (Ricoeur)
Méranger, Thierry, 186, 191
Merlin, Muriel, 20n19
Mielusel, Ramona, 204
migration, 222; *see also* immigration
Miller, Sienna, 74, 77, 112, 198
miscegenation, 104–5, 159
mobile movies *see* road movies
mobile vision, 50
mobility, 54, 56, 58, 60, 136, 199, 216, 221–3, 230; *see also* migration; movement; road movies
Moe, Angela, 76
Monde, Le (newspaper), 120, 121, 130n32, 185

Morson, Gary Saul, 84, 85
mosques, 34–5, 39n34
mothers: agency of, 209–10
motion, 215; *see also* mobility; movement
movement, 53, 170, 176–7; *see also* mobility; motion
multiculturalism, 60, 142
Mulvey, Laura, 206
Murphy, David, 25
Muslims, 224, 226–8, 229, 230; *see also* Islam; mosques
My Family's Honor see Honneur de ma famille, L' / *My Family's Honor*
MyFrenchFilmFestival.com, 21n32

Naceri, Samy, 11–12, 117, 123, 191
Naficy, Hamid, 13, 14, 21n29, 21n37, 145n15, 213n25
names of characters, 77, 212n6
national cinema, 8, 12, 95, 134–5; *see also* transnational cinema
nationalism, 91, 114, 153, 155
Neale, Stephen, 87
New Mexico, 91, 110, 199, 200, 201, 212n16, 215
New Wave cinema *see* French New Wave cinema
New York: World Trade Center, 131, 132, 174
New York Times, The, 132
Nicholson, Amy, 203
Noiriel, Gérard, 127
Nouvel Observateur, Le (newspaper), 121, 122

Oscherwitz, Dayna, 217
O'Shaughnessy, Martin, 199
otherness, 45, 70–1, 103–4, 112–13, 114, 119, 147n35

Outside the Law see *Hors la loi / Outside the Law*
outsiders, 35, 49, 52, 115, 188, 191, 218, 220, 226

Pacini, Giulia, 173
Paris
   Argenteuil, 37n
   Belleville, 93, 94
   Bobigny, 3
   Nanterre, 88, 126, 181, 184, 186, 189
   Orly airport, 44, 50
   terrorist attacks (2015), 144n5
   youth riots (2005), 184
patriarchy, 210, 211
Peckinpah, Sam: *The Wild Bunch*, 82
Perhaps the Sea see *Peut-être la mer / Perhaps the Sea*
Péron, Didier, 126, 186
Peut-être la mer / Perhaps the Sea, 3–7, 12
Pontecorvo, Gillo: *La Bataille d'Alger / The Battle of Algiers*, 107, 110, 147n37
Positif (magazine), 173
Potier, Marc, 122
Poussières de vie / Dust of Life, 3, 6, 10, 13, 85, 101, 151–64
   cultural mixings, 29
   ending, 163
   as a *memento mori*, 18, 152, 153
   as a prisoner of war film, 88–90
   themes, 28, 31, 104, 114, 136, 151, 154–7, 169
   title, 152
Pratt, Mary Louise, 167–8
pre-production process (Bouchareb), 25, 26–7, 31–6
Première (magazine), 120
prisoner of war (POW) films *see Poussières de vie / Dust of Life*
Pulvard, Audrey, 9

Qur'an, 228

racism, 19n6, 34, 35, 37n7, 78, 105, 110, 111, 114, 121, 184, 191; *see also* Islamophobia; stereotypes: racial
Rahal, Malika, 185
Rascaroli, Laura, 212n4, 212n13
religion, 139–42, 143; *see also* Christianity; Islam
religious symbols, 159, 163
rencontres (encounters), 27, 32–6
Renoir, Jean, 168
Ricoeur, Paul, 152, 153, 157, 164
road movies, 41, 107, 112, 198, 205, 210
   and borders, 42, 49, 51–2, 60
   definition of, 44
   European, 200, 212n4
   gender in, 44, 76, 204
   and home, 50
   and road events, 44, 49
   and Westerns, 91
Rochebrune, Renaud de, 189–90
Rosello, Mireille, 101, 182, 183, 218, 220, 228
Route d'Istanbul, La / Road to Istanbul, 6, 28
   themes, 26, 31, 55–8, 59, 147n32, 169
Rowden, Terry, 14, 34, 41

Said, Edward, 147n35
Salhi, Zahia Smail, 66, 68
Sarkozy, President Nicolas, 128, 182, 183–4, 185
Schilt, Thibaut, 32, 34, 168, 169, 198, 199
Scorsese, Martin, 86, 120
Scott, Ridley: *Thelma and Louise*, 76, 112, 199, 200, 202, 203–4, 205, 210, 213n25
Séguret, Olivier, 120

Senegal, 176; *see also* Gorée Island
Serreau, Coline: *Chaos*, 72
Shaheen, Jack, 74
Shohat, Ella, 90
slave trade, 33, 52, 146n21, 166, 170, 173, 183; *see also* Gorée Island
slavery, 33, 59, 136, 158, 166, 171, 172, 173, 175, 176, 178, 183, 188–9
Sotinel, Thomas, 120
Spielberg, Steven, 86
  Saving Private Ryan, 106, 119–20
Springer, Paul J., 88, 89
Stam, Robert, 90
stereotypes, 143, 226
  cultural, 43, 129n7, 146n24
  gendered, 64, 69, 70, 71, 72, 76, 77, 79, 190, 199, 200–1, 202, 205, 206, 208–9, 210, 211
  racial, 56, 73, 74–5, 77–8, 119, 200–1, 211
Stone, Oliver: *Platoon*, 125
Stora, Benjamin, 119, 120, 126, 127, 130n32, 185, 189–90
Stratton, David, 173
Sundance, 106
Sy, Omar, 10, 12, 93, 94, 105
Syria, 26, 31, 41, 55, 56, 57, 58

taboos, 124, 128, 132, 159
Tadrart Films, 20n19
Tarantino, Quentin, 85
Tarr, Carrie, 37n16, 44, 64, 69, 71, 72, 73
technoscapes (Appadurai), 216
Télérama (magazine), 130n36, 170
television: films made for, 9, 14, 204–5, 207, 209
terrorism, 1–2, 6, 11, 22n44, 54, 56, 131–2, 134–7, 139, 142–4
  counterterrorism, 195n43
Tessalit Productions, 8–9, 9–10
Third Cinema, 147n35

Thomas, Dominic, 13
Thompson, David, 131
Touma, Joëlle, 211n2
Tournées Film Festival, 21n32
tracking shots, 90, 161, 199; *see also* traveling shots
transnational cinema, 14–15, 16–17, 28, 30, 31, 32, 34, 41–2, 52, 54, 95, 99, 101, 143; *see also* cinéma-monde
transport, 46, 55, 177, 200
travel, 60, 177
traveling shots, 49
  borders, 52–3, 54, 55, 56
  mobile perspectives, 42–6
  mobile vision, 46–8
tree symbolism, 139, 167, 170, 173–5, 176
Truffaut, François, 85
Turkey, 55, 56, 58, 147n32; *see also* Istanbul
Two Men in Town see *Voie de l'ennemi, La / Two Men in Town*

unemployment, 6, 30, 43, 74, 75, 83, 102, 112, 202, 229
UniFrance Films, 21n32
United States, 99–100, 167–8
  African travelers, 53
  Arab Muslims, 74, 85
  borders, 92, 111, 219, 220–1, 222–3, 224, 229–30, 231
  colonization, 211
  immigration, 30, 111–12, 113, 224, 226
  Islam, 34–5, 226–7
  Muslims, 220, 221, 226
  nationalism, 114, 155
  New France, 61
  see also American culture; American dream; Chicago; Hollywood; New Mexico; New York; Westerns

universalism, 83–4, 220
Urry, John, 48

van Houtum, Henk, 219, 220
Variety (publication), 173
Vietnam
  children, 153
  human rights, 31
  re-education camps, 28, 152–3, 156, 158–9
Vincendeau, Ginette, 208
violence, 82, 109–10, 135, 141, 186, 218–19
  against children, 158, 159
  and globalization, 139
  and memory, 83
  political, 126, 188–9, 189–90
  and racism, 34, 35, 103
  religious, 141–2
  against women, 66, 68, 70, 78, 90, 200–1, 201–2
  youth, 184
Voie de l'ennemi, La / Two Men in Town, 10, 11, 12, 13, 28, 104, 215–31
  as an American tragedy, 110–12
  camera work, 225
  casting, 218, 222, 225, 226
  as cinéma-monde, 217–20
  Cinemascope format, 220
  cultural mixings, 220
  deterritorialization, 222–3
  disjuncture, 217, 221
  ethnoscape, 223–5
  fatalism, 219

financescapes, 229, 230
gender, 223
glocal border space, 220–1, 229–31
ideologies, 226
location, 212n16, 215
mobility, 221–3
narratives, 220
pre-production, 36
script, 217–18
themes, 30, 169, 218–19, 220, 231
as a Western, 91–3, 111

Walker, Janet, 90
war films, 87–8, 106, 119, 125, 197
Westerns, 90–3, 111
Whitaker, Forest, 12, 91, 110, 218, 222–3, 225
Wolof language, 166, 170, 171
women
  Arab, 64–5, 74, 77, 78–9, 190
  as audiences, 205
  as protagonists, 197–8, 205
  violence against, 66, 68, 70, 78, 90, 200–1, 201–2
  see also feminism; mothers
Wood, Jason, 44
Wright, Lawrence, 131

Young, Charles, 89

Zem, Roschdy, 9, 11, 12, 53, 70, 74, 117, 121, 125, 181, 188, 191, 199, 202, 209, 212n6
Zierhofer, Wolfgang, 219
Zwick, Edward: *Glory*, 106

EU representative:
Easy Access System Europe
Mustamäe tee 50, 10621 Tallinn, Estonia
Gpsr.requests@easproject.com

www.ingramcontent.com/pod-product-compliance
Lightning Source LLC
Chambersburg PA
CBHW051608230426
43668CB00013B/2034